HANDSWORTH COLLEGE

T25396

KU-573-227

Dawson
£16·99
11/02
KC.
941·07

# Revolutionary B

WITHDRAWN

MANCHESTER
UNIVERSITY PRESS

# Revolutionary Britannia?

## Reflections on the threat of revolution in Britain 1789–1848

Edward Royle

MANCHESTER UNIVERSITY PRESS
Manchester and New York

distributed exclusively in the USA by St. Martin's Press

Copyright © Edward Royle 2000

The right of Edward Royle to be identified as the author of this work has been asserted by him in accordance with the Copyright, Designs and Patents Act 1988.

*Published by* Manchester University Press
Oxford Road, Manchester M13 9NR, UK
*and* Room 400, 175 Fifth Avenue, New York, NY 10010, USA
http://www.manchesteruniversitypress.co.uk

*Distributed exclusively in the USA by*
St. Martin's Press, Inc., 175 Fifth Avenue, New York,
NY 10010, USA

*Distributed exclusively in Canada by*
UBC Press, University of British Columbia, 2029 West Mall,
Vancouver, BC, Canada V6T 1Z2

*British Library Cataloguing-in-Publication Data*
A catalogue record for this book is available from the British Library

*Library of Congress Cataloging-in-Publication Data applied for*


ISBN 0 7190 4802 8 *hardback*
    0 7190 4803 6 *paperback*

First published 2000

09 08 07 06 05 04 03 02 01 00    10 9 8 7 6 5 4 3 2 1

| City College LRS Site | Order No. |
|---|---|
| Acc. T25396 | |
| Class 941.07 | |

Typeset in Palatino with Frutiger
by Servis Filmsetting Ltd, Manchester, UK
Printed in Great Britain
by Biddles Ltd, Guildford and King's Lynn

# Contents

## Contents

# Acknowledgements

A wide-ranging work of this kind could not have been written without the previous research of dozens of other scholars whose hours of painstaking labour in the archives, especially in the voluminous files at the Public Record Office, have been put into the public domain in the monographs and articles cited in the notes. I have merely added my own research and interpretation but could not have proceeded without their help, which I gratefully acknowledge. Wherever possible I have checked the references for lengthy quotations found in such secondary works and have cited the original references as well as the secondary locations. I wish to acknowledge the Crown Copyright of records in the Public Record Office, and the following for permission to quote from manuscripts in their care: the British Library Board (London Corresponding Society, Place Papers and Letter Book of the Convention); the County Archivist, Tyne and Wear Archives (Joseph Cowen Papers); the County Archivist, West Yorkshire Archives Service, Wakefield (Elland Clerical Society records); the Trustees of the Rt Hon. Olive, Countess Fitzwilliam's Chattels Settlement and the Head of Leisure Services, Sheffield City Council (Wentworth Woodhouse Muniments, Sheffield Archives); the Fitzwilliam (Milton) Estates and the County Archivist, Northamptonshire CRO (Fitzwilliam Papers); Lord Halifax and the Director of the Borthwick Institute, York (Hickleton Papers); the International Institute of Social History, Amsterdam (Harney Papers); the Trustees of the National Library of Scotland (Melville Papers); Lord Sidmouth and the County Archivist, Devon CRO (Sidmouth Papers); and the Principal Archivist, Manchester Local Studies Unit, Manchester Central Library (J. B. Smith Papers).

## Acknowledgements

While every reasonable effort has been made to attribute quotations and trace holders of copyright, if any infringement of copyright has taken place, I apologise and ask anyone claiming copyright to write to me. I should also like to record my thanks to the staff at the above archive offices and at the city libraries in Leeds, Manchester and York, the British Newspaper Library at Colindale, and the University Library, York.

Edward Royle
University of York

# Abbreviations

| | |
|---|---|
| BIHR | Borthwick Institute of Historical Research, University of York |
| BL, Add. MSS | British Library, Additional Manuscripts |
| BPU | Birmingham Political Union |
| CRO | County Record Office |
| FO | Foreign Office papers |
| HO | Home Office papers |
| LCS | London Corresponding Society |
| LWMA | London Working Men's Association |
| NCA | National Charter Association |
| NUWC | National Union of the Working Classes |
| *OED* | *The Oxford English Dictionary*, second edition (Oxford, Clarendon Press, 1989) |
| PC | Privy Council papers |
| *PMG* | *Poor Man's Guardian* |
| PP | Parliamentary Papers |
| PRO | Public Record Office, Kew |
| TS | Treasury Solicitor's papers |
| WWM | Wentworth Woodhouse Muniments |

CITY COLLEGE
LEARNING RESOURCE CENTRE

# Introduction

The detachment of Britain from the mainstream of political development on the continent of Europe has a long history. In the age of revolutions between 1789 and 1848, in Britain there was no revolution – at least, not in the sense that the word had acquired by the early nineteenth century. The concept preferred by contemporaries was 'reform' or even 'amendment', comfortable words suggesting minor and sensible adjustments to changed times, however radical the changes might actually be.[1] Even before 1850 there was a confidence among contemporaries that Britain (or England) was somehow different from Europe. Revolutions were how 'foreigners' conducted their political affairs. In Britain things were managed better.

This complacency became deep-rooted in historical writing because the reason that Britain (meaning England) was different was due to the earlier revolution of 1688 and the Whig constitution derived from it. Successful negotiation through the difficulties of 1831–32, and the sensible extension to the franchise enacted in 1832, simply confirmed a confidence in the stability of the British political system which could be accepted by politicians and historians of all parties. Britain was self-consciously different and, by implication, superior.

Yet it was not always so. In the eighteenth century Britain was seen as a revolutionary state with an 'ungovernable people'.[2] The English and Scots had defeated their king in battle and executed him in 1649. They had deposed another king in 1688 and their kith and kin in the American colonies had dispensed with the services of a third in 1776, establishing the first modern republic in the western world. These events were alive in recent memory in 1789 when the absolutist monarchy collapsed in France. There was nothing to suggest then that

1

Britain would be immune from the French contagion which swept across Europe, destroying old political systems in its path.

The aim of this book is to invite the reader to take this perspective seriously and to suspend that hindsight by which we know Britain to have been different. Two interesting questions follow. What is the evidence for the contemporary belief that Britain came near to revolution? How did Britain avoid revolution? When the French historian, Elie Halévy, raised the second of these questions in 1913 he was unusual in seeing a potential for revolution in Britain as something needing prevention.[3] Most British historians of the earlier twentieth century thought there was little to explain away. They attributed unrest to economic conditions – high prices and unemployment: when conditions improved, the causes of discontent went away. Only troublemakers, an untypical and unpatriotic minority, sought to turn such economic unrest into revolutionary protest. The mainstream of the British radical tradition was peaceful and non-revolutionary. In *The French Revolution in English History* (1918), P. A. Brown identified the importance of what he called 'The survival of the Revolutionary Tradition in Politics', but then marginalised it as follows:

> The strain of violence which runs through the constitutional agitation of the Chartists can be traced backwards for a considerable period. Some traces of Physical Force can be found at the time of the Revolution. But, though inflammatory speeches and even plans of violence can be found to match the evidence of this kind at a later date, they were not characteristic of the English school between 1790 and 1800. The fire-eating orators, Henry Hunt, before the Reform Bill, O'Connor and others between 1830 and 1850, were not in the old tradition of English political reformers. Its truer heirs were Place and Lovett, leaders who differed in most points except the belief that full political education was the only road to reform.[4]

He was followed in this interpretation by generations of scholars who, like him, read William Lovett's *Chartism* (1840) and *Life and Struggles* (1876), and delved into the riches of the Francis Place Papers in the library of the British Museum. This influential collection of manuscripts, press cuttings and commentaries shaped the way much radical and labour history was interpreted throughout much of the twentieth century, establishing Place's own approach to political action as the norm from which others misguidedly deviated.

However, the most recent biographers of Hunt and O'Connor, though they would agree that their subjects did indeed offer a different way from 'the old tradition', have identified them not as revolutionaries but as occupying a position mid-way between Place and the violent revolutionaries, advocating peaceful, mass action to force political change on reluctant governments and pushing to the margins of history both the extreme revolutionaries and people such as Place and Lovett.[5]

Brown's work, undertaken before the First World War, in which he was killed, was written contemporaneously with *The Chartist Movement* (1918) by Mark Hovell, who was another wasted victim of the war. In this book Hovell saw Chartism as primarily the product of 'hunger politics'. The masses, incapable of political action, were responding to economic and social grievances. The political dimension, if it existed at all, was supplied by a minority of what Disraeli called 'trading agitators'.[6] This view also shaped the work of sympathetic liberals like J. L. and B. Hammond, whose *The Skilled Labourer, 1760–1832* (1919), remains a moving tribute to the victims of early industrial society. In turn, their work influenced F. O. Darvall in his important study of Luddism published in 1934. His conclusion was well-reasoned and became orthodoxy:

> There was no cause, and no banner, for the discontented and disorderly manufacturing population in Regency England. Each of the disorderly districts had its own cause, and its own banners. It was for particular limited objects – their old conditions – and not for the general causes of the time, repeal of the Orders in Council, peace or parliamentary reform, that the riotous mobs in 1812 were willing to fight. Until some general cause should arise with a powerful enough appeal to rally all these different elements in the nation's life, and to make them forget their particular selfish objects, there was, despite all the discontent and the restlessness of the workers, and despite the weakness of the forces of order, no serious danger of revolution.[7]

This approach to popular movements as manifestations of economic discontent has sometimes degenerated into a crudely economic interpretation of history in which hunger is made to explain everything. When the economic historian, W. W. Rostow, in 1948 constructed a 'social tension chart' out of stages in the trade cycle and the price of bread, he appeared to offer the unwary an instant explanation for most upsurges of discontent and agitation between 1790 and 1850. Students who have not read the original remain unaware of Rostow's opening caveat: 'It is perhaps unnecessary to emphasise the essentially approximate and *descriptive* nature of these calculations', and instead they take them to be *explanations*. Rostow's theory provides no more than

> a useful summary of a considerable body of evidence, and the results conform fairly well to qualitative political and social data. Intervals of 'high social tension' bred known symptoms of unrest, which, in many cases, expressed themselves in important legislation or in the activities of the Luddites, the Chartists, and other groups.[8]

A different form of economic argument, equally simplistic when misapplied, is Marx's 'historical materialism' – that is, the view that historical development takes the form of class struggle which is generated by and in reaction to underlying economic structures.[9]

Both forms of economic determinism were challenged in 1963 by Edward Thompson's *The Making of the English Working Class* which, rejecting the cruder forms of historical materialism, took the insights of the younger Marx to develop a genuinely dialectical view of the relationship between economic and cultural causes, between structural influences and the free human agency of active participants in history – the view that men make their own history. Thompson's book put politics back into the picture and invited the reader to see them not as an alternative to economics but as their complement. This called for a rethinking of the nature of popular politics and of the relationship between the alleged minority of political troublemakers and the majority of supposedly unreasoning hungry protesters.[10] Though Thompson did not abandon the 'England is different' thesis, he detected a different English tradition, drawing on the seventeenth century and the idea of the liberties of 'the freeborn Englishman', which was capable of sustaining revolutionary activity.[11]

One of the first scholarly examinations of popular radicalism in the 1790s was G. S. Veitch's *The Genesis of Parliamentary Reform*, first published in 1913. He argued persuasively that

> [Pitt's] policy of repression was supported by the majority of the nation, and supported so emphatically as to render it unnecessary. It was as if a nation of self-appointed policemen had turned

out in force to keep guard over a handful of suspected pickpockets. Both Pitt and the nation were, in fact, over-anxious. Their fears were wasted, and they spent much rhetorical and legislative powder upon foemen who had neither the desire nor the strength to fight. But it is both just and easy to make excuses for the man, as for the nation, that erred in an hour of conflict when mankind was struggling with one of the darkest problems in its history, and when, in the words of Grattan, it seemed as if the fortunes of the world were in the scale, and the intellectual order in danger of kicking the beam.[12]

This interpretation remained current until challenged by Thompson in 1963, but in 1977 it was upheld by Malcolm Thomis and Peter Holt in *Threats of Revolution in Britain, 1789–1848*. Like Veitch they examined carefully the Home Office, Treasury Solicitor's and other files, concluding that the anxiety of the authorities was understandable but misplaced. The threats of revolution, and actual risings, were real enough, but they were the work of a small and untypical minority whose plans and exploits were exaggerated by magistrates' spies whose evidence was by its very nature highly suspect. Thomis had earlier (1970) also supported the older view of Darvall, that Luddism was an industrial movement of protest in defence of an older way of life, literally reactionary though none the less bitter and violent for that.[13]

The debate since 1963 has been shaped largely by Thompson's book and reactions to it. Thompson responded in a lengthy Postscript to the 1968 paperback edition of his work. In reviewing his critics, he was right to observe that a key controversy concerned his 'suggestion that there is a continuous underground tradition, linking the Jacobins of the 1790s to the movements of 1816–1820', with its implication that Luddism was in part a political movement and within this tradition.[14] He was also right to avow 'that I was too reticent about this underground', for even in 1968, subsequent research had shown – and has continued to show – evidence for the existence and importance of this tradition. This present book draws on such research and these interpretations. Not all agree with one another or with all that Thompson wrote, but the general drift of the argument has moved in his direction. Roger Wells has probably gone furthest in his claims, but he has been supported by the findings of Ann Hone and Iorwerth Prothero on London, and Marianne Elliott on the Irish dimension to British radical protest.[15] Further light on the nature of radicalism, which adds to the plausibility of Thompson's account, has been shed by Albert Goodwin's work on the popular societies of the 1790s and Iain McCalman's study of the Spenceans from the 1790s to the 1820s.[16] Even a considered sceptic like John Dinwiddy came to accept that a Lancashire spy with the improbably apt name of Bent could be believed on occasions,[17] and most scholars would now settle for the measured conclusion of H. T. Dickinson that, 'it is no longer possible to accept that the Luddite disturbances of 1811–12, any more than the naval mutinies of 1797 or the Black Lamp agitation of 1801–2, were solely and simply the product of economic distress and sought only the amelioration of material conditions.'[18] This political reinterpretation of economic protest has also been applied to Chartism, principally by Dorothy Thompson and a stream of younger scholars influenced by the work of both Thompsons.[19]

If it is now widely accepted that politics should be reinstated within the protest movements of early industrial Britain, there is still little agreement about their nature and extent. In his survey of Chartism (1971), J. T. Ward continued to emphasise the social and economic dimension to Chartist unrest,[20] while Dorothy Thompson, who maintains the centrality of the political dimension, stresses the constitutional nature of those politics. From their very different perspectives neither historian has regarded the revolutionary threat as serious in the 1840s. If they are correct, then had this always been so? If it had, why was this? And if it had not, then what had changed and why, between the 1790s and the 1840s?

All history is a matter of interpretation: it is what historians believe the past to mean. This is not to say that historians can invent the past, but the ambiguities of the evidence and the language in which the evidence is expressed will always lead to disputed conclusions. I have therefore inserted into the argument throughout the book extracts from primary sources to give a sense of what the evidence is and I ask the reader to assume that those responsible for policy at the Home Office were not stupid and that the evidence presented to them was neither wholly fabricated nor distorted beyond credibility. This enables me to put positively in Chapters 1–3 the argument for the existence of serious incidents of revolutionary activity at various critical points in the history of Britain between 1790 and 1850, leaving Chapter 4 for some thoughts on why, after all, there was no revolution.

Introduction

To keep the work within limits, I have had to make some arbitrary decisions about subject matter, so I shall not examine every 'disturbance' in the period. Some riots have by general consent been interpreted as concerned mainly with the price of food, or seats at the theatre, or the way the army and navy got their recruits. The history of these events and their cultural implications has been well told elsewhere.[21] If they can also be shown to have a political dimension which was potentially revolutionary, that would strengthen my point. Neither am I concerned with the history of all attempts at radical political reform. Again, that has been the subject of many books.[22] Though constructed as a narrative, Chapters 1–3 will refer only to a selection of those events which were widely believed, or were alleged at the time, to constitute a real threat to the established political order.

One of the most important developments in recent historical writing has been a growing awareness of the language used to describe events.[23] Far from words having a prescribed meaning, they assume shifting identities to fit the contexts within which they are used. Words such as 'Jacobin', 'patriot', 'revolutionary' and 'constitutional', employed in contemporary propaganda, embodied values and ideologies that constituted an important element in *shaping* the events they purported to *describe*. They were used to manipulate events. For example, those opponents of revolution who applied the word Jacobin to British reformers were seeking to identify them with a certain style of French politics associated with extremism and violence, a charge denied by many so-called Jacobins but which came to be widely believed. The word revolution in its conservative sense meant a return to the former proper state of affairs, so that the restoration of Charles II in 1660, no less than the replacement of James II by William and Mary in 1688, could be described as a revolution.[24] Radicals seeking to defend and restore the ancient constitution could identify with this conservative use of the word to emphasise their British credentials at the same time as conservatives could use the radical meaning associated with the French experience after 1789 to assert the alien nature of the reformers. In an age when 'the right to bear arms' was regarded by some as 'constitutional', and the demand for a radical but peaceful reform of existing institutions could be seen as 'revolutionary', no contemporary usage can be taken at face value and there are many surprises awaiting the unwary.

Virtuous words were claimed by each side and denied to the

other. Conservatives and radicals alike identified themselves as patriots, lovers of their country, and defenders of the true constitutional liberties of the people. The concept of 'the people' was itself a matter of fierce debate, depending on the political angle being argued. They were the electors – the political nation; or they were those who sought to become electors by virtue of their similarity to those who were; or they were those who were excluded from the political nation.[25] Language was thus used to organise how different parties wished their 'reality' to be represented, to include and to exclude, to praise and condemn, according to the political object of the speaker or writer. However, in stressing the importance of language in historical interpretation, I do not propose to adopt the extreme 'postmodernist' position of denying to the past any existence separate from the language in which it is expressed.[26]

A further difficulty with language comes with changing styles of delivery. Much of the period studied in this book falls within what is conventionally regarded as the age of romanticism, when melodramatic forms were current on the platform as well as in the pulpit and on the stage. The problem, as summed up by G. Kitson Clark in 1955, is,

> the relation of what is mere literary form to what is a not unreasonable appreciation of the real situation. On the one hand many orators are using language in which appeals to dread alternatives, just vengeance, or liberty or death, are almost a literary convention, but on the other hand the misery of sections of the working class in England and the peasantry in Ireland was so great and the obduracy with which redress seemed to be refused was so impregnable that without that stimulus men might understandably come to believe that violence was the ordinary resort.[27]

In other words, the language of revolutionary oratory may have been empty rhetoric conditioned by the dramatic conventions of the day and understood for what it was by both speaker and audience; or it may have expressed in the rhetoric of the day a reality of revolutionary anger which was heard by the audience as a call to action. It was sometimes hard for magistrates' spies to tell the difference. Sometimes one wonders if the speakers or audiences themselves knew. It is very hard for the historian to unravel the layers of possible meaning within the words of the historical evidence.

In Chapters 1–3, I recognise that contrasting categories of historical explanation – economic or political, peaceful or violent, constitutional or revolutionary – do not exist in the 'reality' of the past but merely as representations of different arguments in the past. While acknowledging these problems of the status and meaning of language, I have chosen to interpret the language of revolution in the light of the context within which the evidence is found. My conclusion is that much of the revolutionary rhetoric should be taken as both expressing and creating a situation in which violent action was intended to accomplish – or was perceived as aiming to accomplish – political changes which more peaceful means had failed to achieve. For an event to be discussed as revolutionary, therefore, I have taken it as sufficient that some significant group chose to regard it as revolutionary, whatever that might mean. In Chapter 4, I then consider in further detail the implications of this ambiguity of language for the nature of revolutionary movements and the opposition to them.

If it can be established in Chapters 1–3 that these threats of revolution, rebellions, uprising or 'ebullitions' – to use a contemporary term, with all its significant medical connotations – were serious, then the question posed in Chapter 4 becomes historically far more interesting than if there had been little to explain: that is, why did revolution not take place? In 1969, George Rudé's answer for the early 1830s was that 'nobody of importance wanted one' and, with reference to 1848, the question was 'hardly worth asking'.[28] Nevertheless, since Ian Christie's 1984 Ford lectures the question has continued to be asked with increasing frequency, particularly of the period 1790–1820.[29]

When mildly accused by one reviewer of ignoring 'the flag-saluting, foreigner-hating, peer-respecting side of the plebeian mind', Edward Thompson accepted the criticism as fair.[30] Since then there has been a resurgence of interest in the nature and strength of popular conservatism. The credibility of its ideology was restored in 1977 by H. T. Dickinson, *Liberty and Property*, followed by A. D. Harvey, *Britain in the Early Nineteenth Century* (1978), Jonathan Clark's general survey of the 'long' eighteenth century, *English Society, 1688–1832* (1985), and a series of studies on the development of the British 'nation' in relation to its Protestant identity, notably Linda Colley's *Britons* (1992).[31] The cumulative effect of this new interest in conservatism has been to make the case for the revolutionary threat far more plausible, for the conservatives' success lay in their opposition to something worth opposing.

The reality of revolutionary contagion in Europe in 1789 and 1848 was brought home once more by events in central Europe in 1989 when apparently strong if not stable political regimes crumbled over-night before the forces of popular revolution. With this experience of revolution in our own time we can more easily shake the kaleidoscope of history to seek different and more diverse patterns in the past than might be suggested by the assumption that stability was the norm, against which men and women strove to create forces for change. Maybe in Europe for the generation or two after 1789, revolution should be seen as the norm and what has to be explained is the stabil-ity created in the larger of two smallish islands off the northern coast of France.

The conclusion offered by Christie was that the strength of the British state and society prevented the *desire* for revolution; mine is that this strength undermined any realistic *hope* of successful revolu-tion. The equilibrium about which the British people felt so compla-cent by 1850 was a delicate balance, achieved with difficulty over the two generations since 1789. During this period forces operating on one side of the fulcrum pressed hard for radical political change and were prepared on occasion to use force to achieve it, while on the other side equal force was applied to resist them. The result was a compro-mise. That there was no revolution should therefore be seen not as a negative consequence of the superiority of the British system and natural good sense of the British people over their continental neigh-bours, but as the positive achievement of a governing class willing to concede in detail while maintaining the essentials of power by all the means at its disposal: legal, political, economic, ideological and – in the last resort – military.

### Notes

1   D. Beales, 'The idea of reform in British politics, 1829–1850', in T. C. W. Blanning and P. Wende (eds), *Reform in Great Britain and Germany, 1750–1850*, Proceedings of the British Academy, 100 (Oxford, Oxford University Press, 1999), pp. 159–74.
2   J. Brewer and J. Styles, *An Ungovernable People: The English and their law in the seventeenth and eighteenth centuries* (London, Hutchinson, 1983).

# Introduction

3   E. Halévy, *England in 1815* [1913], translated by E. I. Watkin and D. A. Barker, (London, Benn, 1961), pp. 424–8.

4   P. A. Brown, *The French Revolution in English History* (London, Crosby, Lockwood and Son, 1918), pp. ix, 206.

5   J. C. Belchem, *'Orator' Hunt: Henry Hunt and English Working-Class Radicalism* (Oxford, Clarendon Press, 1985); J. Epstein, *The Lion of Freedom: Feargus O'Connor and the Chartist Movement, 1832–1842* (London, Croom Helm, 1982).

6   *Hansard's Parliamentary Debates*, House of Commons, 12 July 1839, col. 247.

7   F. O. Darvall, *Popular Disturbances and Public Order in Regency England, being an account of the Luddite and other disorders in England during the years 1811–1817 and of the attitude and activity of the authorities* (London, Oxford University Press, 1934), pp. 317–18.

8   W. W. Rostow, *British Economy of the Nineteenth Century* (Oxford, Clarendon Press, 1948), pp. 123–4; my italics in the first quotation.

9   See, for example, J. Kuczinski, *The Rise of the Working Class*, translated by C. T. A. Ray (London, Weidenfeld & Nicolson, 1967), pp. 140–60.

10  E. P. Thompson, *The Making of the English Working Class* (London, Gollancz, 1963). In later notes the Penguin Books edition (Harmondsworth, 1968) has been used.

11  D. Eastwood, 'E. P. Thompson, Britain, and the French Revolution', *History Workshop Journal*, 390 (Spring 1995), pp. 79–88.

12  G. S. Veitch, *The Genesis of Parliamentary Reform* (London, Constable, 1913), p. 342.

13  M. I. Thomis and P. Holt, *Threats of Revolution, 1789–1848* (London, Macmillan, 1977); M. Thomis, *The Luddites: Machine-breaking in Regency England* (Newton Abbot, David & Charles, 1970).

14  Thompson, *The Making*, p. 923. He was not the first to advance this view: see A. W. Smith, 'Irish rebels and English radicals, 1798–1820', *Past & Present*, 7 (April 1955), pp. 78–85.

15  R. Wells, *Insurrection: The British Experience, 1795–1803* (Gloucester, Sutton, 1986); J. A. Hone, *For the Cause of Truth: Radicalism in London, 1796–1821* (Oxford, Oxford University Press, 1982); I. Prothero, *Artisans and Politics in Early Nineteenth-Century London: John Gast and his Times* (Folkestone, Dawson, 1979), republished (London, Methuen, 1981); M. Elliott, *Partners in Revolution. The United Irishmen and France* (London and New Haven, Yale University Press, 1982).

16  A. Goodwin, *The Friends of Liberty: The English Democratic Movement in the Age of the French Revolution* (London, Hutchinson, 1979); I. McCalman, *Radical Underworld: Prophets, Revolutionaries and Pornographers in London, 1795–1840* (Cambridge, Cambridge University Press, 1988).

17  J. R. Dinwiddy, 'Luddism and politics in the northern counties', *Social History*, 4:1 (January 1979), pp. 33–63, reprinted in *Radicalism and Reform in Britain, 1780–1850* (London, Hambledon Press, 1992), pp. 371–401. Subsequent page references are to the latter.

18  H. T. Dickinson, *British Radicalism and the French Revolution, 1789–1815* (Oxford, Blackwell, 1985), p. 61.

19  D. Thompson, *The Chartists* (London, Temple Smith, 1984); D. J. V. Jones, *Chartism and the Chartists* (London, Allen Lane, 1975); D. Thompson and J. Epstein (eds), *The Chartist Experience* (London, Macmillan, 1982).

20  J. T. Ward, *Chartism* (London, Batsford, 1971).
21  See J. Stevenson, *Popular Disturbances in England, 1700–1870* (London, Longman, 1979) and later editions; K. J. Logue, *Popular Disturbances in Scotland, 1780–1815* (Edinburgh, John Donald, 1979); J. Bohstedt, *Riots and Community Politics in England and Wales, 1790–1810* (Cambridge, MA, Harvard University Press, 1983).
22  D. G. Wright, *Popular Radicalism: The Working-class Experience, 1780–1880* (London, Longman, 1988); C. Behagg, *Labour and Reform: Working-class Movements, 1815–1915* (London, Hodder & Stoughton, 1991); J. Belchem, *Popular Radicalism in Nineteenth-Century Britain* (Basingstoke, Macmillan, 1996); R. McWilliam, *Popular Politics in Nineteenth-Century England* (London, Routledge, 1998).
23  J. Vernon, *Politics and the People: A Study in English Political Culture, c. 1815–1867* (Cambridge, Cambridge University Press, 1993), pp. 295–330; J. Epstein, *Radical Expression: Political Language, Ritual, and Symbol in England, 1790–1850* (New York and Oxford, Oxford University Press, 1994), pp. 3–28; J. Vernon (ed.), *Re-reading the Constitution: New Narratives in the Political History of England's Long Nineteenth Century* (Cambridge, Cambridge University Press, 1996), pp. 1–122.
24  See the discussion of 'Revolution' in R. Williams, *Keywords* [1976], reissued (London, Fontana Press, 1983); also *The Oxford English Dictionary*, second edition, (Oxford, Clarendon Press, 1989) (hereafter *OED*).
25  J. Fulcher, 'The English people and their constitution after Waterloo: parliamentary reform, 1815–1817', pp. 66–70, 75–6 in Vernon, *Re-reading the Constitution*, pp. 52–82.
26  For the debate on 'postmodernism', see the exchanges in the journal *Social History*, 17–21 (1992–96) and for a subsequent review of the issues which approximates to my own position, see R. Price, 'Postmodernism as theory and history' in J. Belchem and N. Kirk (eds), *Languages of Labour* (Aldershot, Ashgate, 1997), pp. 11–43.
27  G. Kitson Clark, 'The romantic element, 1830 to 1850', in J. H. Plumb (ed.), *Studies in Social History* (London, Longman, 1955), pp. 234–5.
28  G. Rudé, 'Why was there no revolution in England in 1830 or 1848?', in M. Kossok (ed.), *Studien über die Revolution* (Berlin, 1969), reprinted in H. J. Kaye (ed.), *The Face of the Crowd* (Atlantic Highlands, Humanities Press International, 1988), pp. 148–63: the quotations are on pp. 160–1.
29  I. R. Christie, *Stress and Stability in Late-Eighteenth Century Britain* (Oxford, Oxford University Press, 1984).
30  G. Best, 'The Making of the English Working Class', p. 278, *Historical Journal* 8:2 (1965), pp. 271–81; E. P. Thompson, *The Making*, pp. 916–17.
31  H. T. Dickinson, *Liberty and Property: Political Ideology in Eighteenth-century Britain* (London, Weidenfeld & Nicholson, 1977), paperback edition (London, Methuen, 1979); A. D. Harvey, *Britain in the Early Nineteenth Century* (London, Batsford, 1978); J. C. D. Clark, *English Society, 1688–1832* (Cambridge, Cambridge University Press, 1985); L. Colley, *Britons. Forging the Nation, 1707–1837* (London and New Haven, Yale University Press, 1992).

# Sedition and treason, 1792–1820

CITY COLLEGE
LEARNING RESOURCE CENTRE

## The impact of the revolution in France

When news reached Britain of the political crisis in France in the summer of 1789, it was generally welcomed. The French king had supported the American republicans in their successful war against the British Crown and anything which might weaken his position was morally and diplomatically desirable. Whigs, Dissenters and parliamentary reformers in Britain interpreted the demands of the Third Estate – and subsequently of the National Assembly – as reasonable, embodying the constitutional aspirations enshrined in the Glorious Revolution of 1688. Edmund Burke was untypical in discerning as early as March 1790, in the debate on Fox's motion to repeal the Test and Corporation Acts, the dangers of abstract reasoning and the demand for natural rights common to both English Dissenters and French revolutionaries.[1] This argument he developed at length and published in November 1790 as *Reflections on the Revolution in France and on the proceedings in certain societies in London relative to that event.* The 'certain societies' included the London Revolution Society, a Whig dining club set up to commemorate the 1688 Revolution, at which Dr Richard Price, a leading Dissenter, had spoken in November 1789 in praise of the French Revolution which in his view had pointed the way forward for the incomplete revolution of 1688. Burke's publication was a manifesto of conservatism that was to grow in relevance and influence as reports from France appeared to fulfil his predictions and betray the optimism of the reformers.

Reactions to the French Revolution were not static, and over the next few years perceptions were continually revised as fears and hopes at home reflected the changing scene in France with its increasingly extreme impulse to innovation in church and state, leading from modest constitutional reform in 1789 to the flight and arrest of the king in June 1791 and the imposition of a new constitution in September. Worse was to follow: the declaration of war against Austria in April 1792; growing lawlessness in Paris which culminated in the September massacres; the trial of the king in December and his execution in January 1793 followed in February by war between France and Britain; the systematic use of Terror as an instrument of state during the period of Jacobin rule from June 1793 to the fall of Robespierre in July 1794; the abandonment of Christianity; and the increasing military threat to France's neighbours. These events explain the attitude of the government, that all reform was a revolutionary threat, as well as the willingness of extreme reformers to believe that the world really could be made anew. As Lafayette said and Thomas Paine quoted approvingly: 'For a nation to be free, it is sufficient that she wills it.'[2]

In the first phase of reaction to the revolution, the lines of dispute, as drawn up by Burke, lay between Church and Dissent, arising out of the defeat of Fox's motion to give equal citizenship to religious Dissenters in Britain. This was a right already conceded in France on the eve of the revolution and helps explain the Francophile outlook of English Dissenters. Their defeat in March was the first signal for Church and King celebrations, and in Manchester the original Church and King Club was formed as a dining club in jubilation at the defeat of Fox's motion. The reformers responded in October with the Manchester Constitutional Society. Though set up on the initiative of Thomas Walker, an Anglican Whig merchant, many of its members were leading Dissenters and this, and similar societies that were formed elsewhere over the next few months, were usually associated with Dissent. In Norwich, for example, the Revolution Society, which like its namesake in London grew out of the 1688 centenary, was identified with the elite of Rational Dissent in the city. These men, and their counterparts in Birmingham, Derby, Nottingham, Bristol and many other provincial towns and cities, were often leading intellectuals in their communities, the philosophers of the English Enlightenment. In their reform societies they identified themselves with France where liberties denied to British reformers were being conceded. On the second anniversary of the fall of the Bastille in July 1791, Church and King mobs attacked their homes and chapels in Nottingham, Manchester and Birmingham where the rioting directed against Joseph Priestley was especially ferocious.[3]

Thereafter, the terms of the debate began to change as the revolution in France grew more extreme. In March 1791, Paine published the first part of his *Rights of Man*, a scornful attack on Burke's defence of the British constitution. At the same time, as in France, the social base of the reform movement in Britain expanded beyond the elite to include lesser merchants, shopkeepers and even artisans. In London, the Society for Constitutional Information (founded 1780) became more radical and encouraged the formation of similar societies in the provinces to agitate for parliamentary reform. In Sheffield, the local Society for Constitutional Information recruited its members from among small masters and artisans; and in January 1792 the London Corresponding Society (LCS) began to meet, with Thomas Hardy, a Scottish shoemaker, as secretary.

The avowed aim of these and other popular societies remained the reform of Parliament but they identified themselves (and were identified by the government) with French ideas and the extremist views expressed in the second part to Paine's *Rights of Man*, published in February 1792. This work went beyond the programme of the moderate reformers to call for a sweeping reconstruction of the British constitution and a redistribution of wealth through taxation. Paine now replaced Dissent as the principal object of attack by Church and King loyalists. A Royal Proclamation was issued in May against seditious writings, and proceedings were begun against Paine. Loyalist forces were rallied by the Association for the Preservation of Liberty and Property against Republicans and Levellers, organised in November by John Reeves. As Louis XVI was brought to trial in December so too was Paine, on a charge of seditious libel. Tried in his absence – for by this time he was in France, ironically arguing in the Convention for the life of the king – Paine was found guilty. Whatever their intentions, reformers who now identified themselves with Paine could be deemed seditious by association and, once war had broken out with France, those who praised France could even be represented as traitors. Looking back from the year 1795, the *Annual Register* rewrote the history of 1791 in the most alarmist terms which tell us more about attitudes in 1795 than 1791:

> The publication of Mr. Burke's sentiments on the French revolution, and the subsequent answer to [*sic*] Mr. Paine, in his celebrated performance, styled the Rights of Man, were the first signals to the ministerial and popular parties in this country, to

engage in that violent and acrimonious contest, which is not yet terminated. These two famous performances revived, as it were, the royal and republican parties that had divided this nation in the last century, and that had lain dormant since the Revolution in 1688. They now returned to the charge with a rage and animosity equal to that which characterized our ancestors during the civil wars in the reign of King Charles the First; and it remained a long time in suspense, whether this renewed contest would not be attended with the same calamities: so eager were the partizans of the respected tenets contained in those performances, to assert them with unbounded vehemence.[4]

## Plots, real or imagined, 1793–95

A growing suspicion of French intentions and the growing presence of French exiles in London in the autumn of 1792 created the first insurrection scare later that year. At the end of November extra troops were brought into London and defences at the Tower and Bank of England were strengthened. After a lengthy cabinet meeting on 1 December a new Royal Proclamation was issued and the militias were called out in ten counties – a measure warranted only by threat of invasion or insurrection. The Foxites were sceptical and claimed that the idea of a plot was a government device to consolidate its own power and suppress the liberties of the British people. News of what the government feared was leaked to the press just before Christmas: there had been a serious threat of insurrection which had successfully been prevented by prompt government action. The propertied and political classes were left to imagine what had so narrowly been avoided: the Gordon Riots in London in 1780 were still fresh in their memories, and the September massacres in Paris had come too close for comfort.

On what were these fears based? There is very little on the public record, but the Home Office files show that through much of November and into December alarmist reports were being received of Frenchmen armed with daggers on the road from Harwich to London, of quantities of muskets in private hands in the capital, of potentially dangerous unrest in Newcastle-under-Lyme and an actual disturbance in Dundee where a liberty tree was planted. Two reports from a French royalist emigré, Dubois de Longchamp, were particularly worrying. As the Prime Minister himself later admitted, the evidence for a French plot was only hearsay, yet the reports were sufficiently convincing for the government to take swift action. So, the historian is left with inconclusive evidence of an insurrection that did not happen. What we can say is that the government did not invent the evidence or the apparent seriousness of the situation. If it over reacted, it did so on reasonable grounds.[5]

One serious feature of the situation continued to alarm the government: the connection between the plotting and arming of a small minority, inspired and possibly aided by the French, and openly seditious pro-French talk in the popular debating societies. So the government was understandably nervous when, on 11–13 December, in the midst of this scare, the Scottish Friends of the People, organised by a young pro-French lawyer called Thomas Muir, summoned a Convention in Edinburgh with some 160 delegates from 80 societies in 35 towns. The word Convention was associated not only with the over-throw of James VII and II in 1689 but more immediately with the French constitution of 1792, an identification which was evident in the language used by the delegates.[6] The government immediately began proceedings for sedition against some of the leading members of the Friends of the People, and Thomas Muir was pursued on a charge of high treason. He was subsequently tried in August on the lesser charge of sedition but was still sentenced to fourteen years' transportation to Botany Bay.[7] Thomas Palmer, an outspoken reformer and Unitarian minister from Dundee, received seven years the following month. The Convention was briefly reconvened in April 1793, then met again in November, attended by delegates from the LCS amid the outrage caused by the savage sentences passed on Muir and Palmer. The government's response was to close down the Convention and to arrest its secretary, William Skirving, and the two English delegates, Joseph Gerrald and Maurice Margarot. They met the same fate as Muir.

The deteriorating international situation and continued evidence of seditious activity at home prompted the government to act next against reformers in England. At a meeting called by the LCS at Chalk Farm in London on 14 April 1794, a further Convention was demanded and language adopted that filled the government with alarm.[8] A month later, on 12 May, leading reformers – fourteen members of the LCS including Thomas Hardy and John Thelwall, and six members of the Society for Constitutional Information, including

John Horne Tooke, were arrested. The government was convinced that treasonable activity was rife, and a Secret Committee of the House of Commons produced the evidence for it in a lengthy report, sufficient to persuade Parliament to suspend *Habeas Corpus* on 23 May. A second report in June and further events in Scotland confirmed the government's resolve. However, when the treason trials came to court in October, Hardy, Horne Tooke and Thelwall were all acquitted and the cases against the others were dropped.[9]

The evidence for a revolutionary threat during these years was published in the early summer of 1794 in the two *Reports of the Committee of Secrecy*. Much of what they revealed was already public knowledge and hardly treasonable, but other information made available to the committee in private, including what historians can now read in unpublished files in the Public Record Office (PRO), shows clearly why the government believed it had cause for concern. The adversarial situation in Parliament and at the various trials was not such as to encourage an impartial review of the evidence. Government and prosecuting counsels needed to make their case, whether they believed it as much as they said or not. Conversely, the beleaguered Whig opposition in Parliament and defendants aiming to avoid transportation had an interest in stressing the harmless and constitutional nature of their ideas, organisations and literature. So what should the historian make of the view that there was a serious threat of revolution in the early years of the revolutionary wars with France?

Seditious language was frequently reported and did undoubtedly occur. Whether arising from loose talk or calculating rhetoric, this was dubiously legal and in the prevailing international situation alarming to the government. But such talk was hardly treasonable, which is why the treason trials of 1794 failed to secure any convictions. Seditious and potentially subversive words were, however, turned into deeds in Scotland in 1794, as the second *Report of the Committee of Secrecy* set out in chilling detail for the benefit of the House of Commons in June 1794. The aim of the prosecution was to implicate the LCS in these events north of the border. They failed, but the Scottish threat was no false alarm.

Following the break-up of the Convention in Edinburgh, a Committee of Union had been formed, of which Robert Watt was a leading member. On 5 March 1794, a secret Committee of Ways and Means was appointed with the ostensible object of meeting secretary

Skirving's debts but actually with a deeper purpose. The Home Secretary, Henry Dundas, sent a series of letters to the Prime Minister in which he gave an account of what he had discovered. The Sheriff's officers had obtained a warrant to search Watt's house for embezzled bankrupt stock. There they found twelve pike heads and two battle-axes. A further search of two blacksmiths' premises produced more spears and axes. One of the men arrested now

> confessed, that these weapons were the first of a very large number and quantity, actually ordered to be made, and intended to be privately dispersed among the members of the various societies throughout Scotland, styling themselves Friends of the People, and who appear to be at present employed in taking measures for calling together another British Convention of delegates to be held in England. An order has been given from one town alone in Scotland, for a large quantity of weapons of the nature described; no less a number than 4,000 has been mentioned, and more are intended to be distributed in Edinburgh. Emissaries appear also to have been dispatched, within this fortnight or three weeks past, to the manufacturing towns in the west of Scotland, for the purpose of sounding the inclinations of such of the inhabitants there who are known to be members of these societies; and there is reason to believe, from information received from various different quarters, that these persons have by no means been unsuccessful.[10]

Paisley was said to have been ready for rebellion, and there were reports of night-time assemblies for practising the use of arms. The men behind this conspiracy were 'the principal and most active members of the British Convention'.

These letters were laid before the Committee of Secrecy, which was also told that Watt had been in correspondence with the London Corresponding Society. Indeed, at the trial of Hardy the prosecution suggested a connection between these events in Edinburgh, evidence of arming in London and the manufacture of arms in Sheffield. The plan, it was claimed, was to start a rising in London, Edinburgh and Dublin to replace Parliament with the Convention. The rising in Edinburgh was to begin with a fire in the Excise Office. This would draw off the troops from the castle and the conspirators would then attack the troops, seize the castle, and take over the banks and other public buildings; the judges and magistrates would be arrested, farmers would be ordered to bring their grain to market, gentlemen would be confined to within three miles of their homes, and the king would be required to dismiss his ministers and dissolve Parliament. Much of the evidence for this plot came from government spies. The only hard evidence was the dozen pikes found in Watt's house but this was enough to convict him and he was executed on 15 October. His co-conspirator and treasurer of the Committee of Ways and Means, David Downie, was pardoned and the London jury clearly did not believe the prosecution's attempt to implicate Thomas Hardy in Watt's plot.[11]

How seriously should this plot be taken? Evidently, if there really were plans for a rising not only in Scotland but also involving London and Dublin, this would indeed have been serious. On the other hand, Watt was a former government spy and he may have been acting as an *agent provocateur*, in which case the plot could have amounted to very little.[12] The government's case at the trials in both Scotland and London was that the aim of those behind the Convention was not to demand a reform of Parliament but to overturn the Constitution and replace Parliament with a popularly elected Convention. The government could not afford to ignore this possibility, given the deteriorating situation at home and abroad in 1794.

If there was little direct evidence against leaders of the LCS, others in that organisation were certainly acting suspiciously. John Philip Francklow, a tailor and an assistant secretary of the LCS in 1793, together with John Williamson, a shoemaker, formed an association in Lambeth for LCS members to learn the use of arms following the trial and transportation of Maurice Margarot.[13] Members of the LCS were widely believed to be implicated in almost any subversive activity detected in the capital. In 1795, for example, riots occasioned by recruitment to the militia were thought by the London magistrates to be 'the result of a deliberate system originating with the corresponding societies for the purpose of overthrowing the government'.[14] Taken together with Watt's plans in Scotland, there seemed a real possibility that the government's intelligence network had exposed the tip of a dangerous iceberg of subversive activity rather than simply the ill-considered posturing of a few hotheads, however much the defence and the Whig opposition might seek to present it in this light.[15]

The most dangerous aspects of the alleged conspiracy were its

Irish and French connections. In Scotland these went back to at least December 1792 when Thomas Muir had been in secret contact with the Committee of Public Safety in Paris and delegates from the United Irishmen had attended the Scottish Convention. In April 1793, while in Belfast attempting to evade arrest, Muir was made an honorary member of the United Irishmen, and in November of that year an avowedly republican society of United Scotsmen was formed in Glasgow on the Irish model.[16] In Ireland, the French Revolution had reinforced the desire of Irish patriots to make the Parliament granted in 1782 truly representative of the Irish people, both Protestant and Catholic, independent of Britain; and it was this alliance of confessions which had led to the formation in Belfast in October 1791 of the Society of United Irishmen, led by a Protestant, Theobald Wolfe Tone. Adopting the language and sentiments of Paine's *Rights of Man*, the United Irishmen demanded full religious and political rights.

Their expectation of gaining either by constitutional means was disappointed and their demands came to look more sinister once war had broken out in 1793. Lord Edward Fitzgerald, a leader of the United Irishmen and cousin to Charles James Fox, had corresponded with Paine in 1792 about possible French support for a revolution in Ireland, but when the French sent an agent to Ireland in May 1793 he was not impressed by the state of preparedness among the Irish. The extent to which reformers in Britain and Ireland might become implicated in French attempts at subversion emerged the following year when the Reverend William Jackson, an Irish-born clergyman and a member of the Anglo-Irish community in Paris, was sent over to England by the French government to ascertain how much support there might be for a French invasion. He found very little, but the mission had already been penetrated by government spies and when Jackson went on from England to Ireland to meet with the leaders of the United Irishmen he was accompanied by a spy and *agent provocateur*, John Cockayne. Jackson was arrested on 28 April 1794 and committed suicide in the dock when he was brought to trial for high treason a year later.[17]

The significance of Jackson's mission lies not so much in its existence – at a time of war, both sides were anxious for accurate information about the enemy – as in its conclusion that there was little support in England for a French invasion. Wolfe Tone in 1796 thought this true also of Scotland.[18] While both Irish and Scots looked to France to assist their efforts, the French expected the domestic revolutionaries to lay for themselves the foundations for a successful invasion. So to break this vicious circle of inaction as each waited for the other, the temptation was for the United men, and especially their representatives in Paris, to exaggerate their state of readiness at home in order to encourage a French invasion. Both the French and British knew that the weakest link in Britain's defences was always going to be Ireland, and the British were fortunate when an initial invasion fleet of thirty-five ships and nearly 15,000 troops commanded by General Lazare Hoche was dispersed by bad weather off Bantry Bay in December 1796. The first French force actually to reach shore landed at Fishguard in Wales in February 1797, precipitating a run on the Bank of England and the suspension of cash payments.

The exposure of Jackson's mission gave the government grounds for suppressing the United Irishmen in May 1794. Up to this point they had been a very Whiggish body, hoping for another 'Glorious Revolution' with the French playing the part of the Dutch in 1688 but not staying to become king. Thereafter the growth of extremist factions within the society made it more radical as the political situation in Ireland deteriorated following the dismissal of the new Whig Lord Lieutenant, the fourth Earl Fitzwilliam, in March 1795, after only a few weeks in office. This ended all hope of legitimate reform. Wolfe Tone left for America and then headed for France to seek French aid. At the same time what had been a Presbyterian-led organisation uniting reformers of both confessions increasingly became an expression of Catholic constitutional aspirations. This polarisation of attitudes in Ireland was furthered in 1795 by the rise of Protestant Orange loyalism. By 1796 the transformation of the United Irishmen was complete.[19]

The situation in Britain also deteriorated in 1795 as bread prices rose in the first subsistence crisis of the war. Opposition to the war and Pitt's government was fuelled by economic hardship. Membership of the LCS recovered from the set-backs of the previous year and reached new heights – perhaps as many as ten thousand. Public meetings in London were addressed by John Thelwall, the largest being in Copenhagen Fields on 26 October when 100,000 to 150,000 people were said to be present. A hostile crowd greeted George III on his way to open Parliament on 29 October and one of his coach windows was broken by a stone (or bullet) thought to have been fired from an air gun. A few weeks earlier the government had been informed of a 'pop-gun plot' to shoot a poisoned dart at the king from an air gun disguised as a walking stick, but this idea was fabricated by a spy.[20] In response to this alleged evidence of practical republicanism, a Royal Proclamation was issued and two Acts rushed through Parliament: the Treasonable Practices Bill, to make it easier to convict publishers of treasonable and seditious writings even if no treasonable or seditious act had occurred; and the Seditious Meetings Bill, to prevent mass meetings such as those being convened by the LCS and addressed by Thelwall. These measures, and an improvement in the economic situation, then subdued the mass popular movement for reform.

## United Irish, English and Scotsmen, 1795–1803

The ending of the French Convention and the beginning of the Directory in October 1795 marked a watershed between the most revolutionary phase of the French Revolution and the subsequent wars of nationalist expansion. While this strengthened anti-French feeling among all but a minority of extremists in Britain, the drain on British resources made Pitt's policy highly unpopular and threatened to destabilise the Ministry.[21] At the same time the repression of the reform societies in 1795, their consequent decline, and the collapse of open and constitutional reform movements, induced a sense of desperation which reinforced the arguments of the most subversive. Whatever the real nature of the threat before 1795, it was greatly increased thereafter.

CITY COLLEGE
LEARNING RESOURCE CENTRE

The crisis in the spring of 1797 which followed the Fishguard landing was made worse by mutiny in the navy. This began at Spithead in April with a demand for more pay and the removal of unpopular officers, but then spread to the Nore where the mutineers blockaded the Thames; some ships in the fleet at Plymouth was also affected. A combination of concessions to the men and punishment for the leaders brought the mutinies to an end by June. Then in October, as Austria made peace with France, Bonaparte assembled his army of invasion within sight of the English coast. It remained there until May 1798 when he turned instead to Egypt.

Meanwhile, the United Irishmen were threatening internal subversion. Wolfe Tone reached Paris in February 1796 intending to establish a United Irish mission to work with the French for an invasion of Ireland, but after Hoche's unsuccessful attempt in December 1796, events in Ireland itself pushed the Irish into premature rebellion. Relations between the government and the Protestant community on the one hand, and the Catholics on the other, deteriorated rapidly as members of the Protestant Orange Order, formed in 1795, joined the yeomanry to attack the Catholic 'Defenders'. The latter were members of an illegal terrorist organisation formed to defend Catholics in their struggle for civil rights and agrarian justice. A working alliance established in 1795–96 between the mainly urban United Irishmen and the mainly rural and more popular Defenders brought together political and economic grievances in a revolutionary drive against the Protestant ascendancy. The brutal suppression of Catholics in Ulster by the British army and the forces of Orangeism drove Catholics south and across into Britain where some of their number formed local units of United Britons or joined the LCS. Links between Irish exiles in Paris and Britain with subversive forces in Ireland were maintained by a Catholic priest, James Coigly (or O'Coigly), who was arrested together with Arthur O'Connor of the United Irishmen, John Binns of the London Corresponding Society and two others as they prepared to cross from Kent to France in 1798. Coigly was carrying an incriminating Address from the 'Secret Committee of England' assuring support for a French invasion to maintain 'the sacred flame of liberty'. He was tried in May and executed on 12 June 1798.

The French invasion, which had been expected in April, did not arrive. On 23 May the Dublin leadership of the United Irishmen gave the order to rise. Ulster failed to do so but Catholic Defender insurgents held their own against the British army and militia in the southeast, enjoying initial victories at Wexford and elsewhere before suffering a major defeat at Vinegar Hill on 21 June. It was another month before ruthless repression finally broke the rebels. When the French finally landed their expeditions in August, September and October 1798, they were too late.[22]

The response of the British government to this year of conspiracy, mutiny, rebellion and threatened invasion was to arrest leaders and break up popular societies, driving the extremists still further under ground. Following Coigly's arrest, between 18 and 22 April virtually all the leading members of the United Irishmen in Britain and the LCS, including its entire general committee, were arrested and, *Habeas Corpus* having been suspended again on 21 April, most were kept in prison until 1801. Further arrests in March and April 1799 culminated in July in 'An Act for the more effectual Suppression of Societies established for Seditious and Treasonable Purposes, and for better preventing Treasonable and Seditious Practices', namely the United Scotsmen, United Irishmen, United Britons, LCS and all other societies which corresponded, took secret oaths, kept no list of members, or which had branches capable of independent action.[23]

The prisoners held without trial were released when the *Habeas Corpus* Suspension Act lapsed in March 1801. They then resumed their activities. A coup was planned in London, but the arrest of its alleged leader, Colonel Despard of the United Irishmen, in November 1802 and his execution the following spring put an end to the attempt. In Ireland, Robert Emmet's badly co-ordinated and pre-mature rising in July 1803 was easily suppressed. His failure to per-suade others to join him before a French invasion force was ready, was a mark of the success of the British government's policy of repression in 1798.

The mutinies, invasions and armed uprisings which filled these years between 1795 and 1803 would suggest that revolution was not merely possible but likely. However, in view of the limited success enjoyed by the insurrections, the extent of this threat has been much debated. Although the government's sense of crisis was understand-able, it could be argued that the extremists were lent credibility only by the repressive nature of the government's reaction. The isolation of the violent fringe would have rendered them powerless had the sup-pression of legitimate forms of opposition not driven some reformers to take desperate measures to preserve what they regarded as 'liberty'. Only perhaps in Ireland is it conceded that a large section of the people was disaffected and, in sentiment at least, willing to see the overthrow of British government. The realisation that measures had to be taken both to control Ireland and to make timely but neutered concessions to Catholics brought Pitt to introduce the one major con-stitutional reform of this period – the Act of Union with Ireland, which came into force at the beginning of 1801.

## The seriousness of the threat

Even more so than in the early 1790s, an estimate of how serious the situation was in Britain itself depends on the weight given to the government's sources of information.[24] If they are credible, then the situation was indeed serious. The word 'spy' is often used in a derogatory sense. It implies a casual, amateur, individualistic and probably unreliable person. Undoubtedly some of the government's informers were spies in this sense. But to call them 'intelligence agents' is to imply organisation, professionalism, co-ordination and reliability, and there was much of this too in the 1790s. Though local magistrates might be prone to alarmism, some of it induced by the activities of the government's own agents operating unknown to those responsible locally for the maintenance of law and order, at the centre ministers were not wholly 'duped and deluded by their spies', as Sheridan suggested in 1795.[25]

The government had several sources of information. The Home Office, with its permanent under-secretaries, Evan Nepean and John King, sometimes employed its own special agents, the most prominent of whom was James Walsh. Another channel of information flowed through the seven London police offices, created in 1792 on the model of Bow Street, each of which had a stipendiary magistrate attached. Bow Street was the most important of these offices because here the police function of the court was undefined by legislation and finance came from unitemised expenditure in the civil list. A small secret service had been based on Bow Street since the 1780s and during the 1790s the second magistrate, Richard Ford, was the key figure co-ordinating a domestic secret service. This was a development of the local and informal system – which still continued – whereby information was gathered throughout the country by magistrates who had their own favourite informers. Government special agents received a regular salary. These individuals were thus spared the temptation to invent evidence in order to earn their pay and their information was usually more reliable. The information so gathered was co-ordinated by the Aliens Office at the Home Office, originally created by the Aliens Act of 1793 to keep an eye on French refugees, but from 1794 when William Wickham became superintendent it was used to oversee all the government's intelligence-gathering activities.[26]

Though some of this information was doubtless suspect or

exaggerated, much was of a high quality and the government relied upon it in the formulation of policy. By its very nature such information was sensitive and its sources could continue to be effective only so long as they remained unacknowledged. Some of the government's best sources of information, George Lynam, William Metcalfe, John Groves – all prominent members of the London Corresponding Society – became useless once their work had been made public. So the interpretation put upon events by the Secrecy Committees of the House of Commons in 1794 and 1799 looks more extreme than the evidence presented appears to warrant, not because the evidence was lacking but because it could not be acknowledged. Unpublished reports in the Home Office papers show that the Secrecy Committees did indeed know more than they admitted which was still less than ministers themselves knew. Of twenty-two bundles of evidence submitted by the government to the Committee of Secrecy in 1799, only five were read out. There was more than enough evidence to justify the legislation and arrests by which the radical movement was suppressed.[27]

Irish and French agents, for example, almost certainly did attempt to exploit the naval mutinies in 1797. Given the importance of the navy to British defences it would have been remarkable had the French not sought to do so. Though the mutinies were undoubtedly provoked by and supported largely for economic reasons, political forces were also at work, not least because some 15,000 of the 114,000 sailors in the navy in 1797 were Irish, the result of pressing convicts into the navy including many United Irishmen and Defenders. Another source of potential support for political discontent came from the quota system, introduced in 1796, which enlisted into the fleet reluctant young men not from seafaring backgrounds, such as urban artisans who were likely to have taken part in the popular political societies. Unlike the Irish, the object of their mutiny was not revolution but an end to the war and the reform of Parliament. Whether they were fighting the French, the Dutch or their own commanders, they did so in the name of English liberty.[28]

Active groups of reformers existed in both Portsmouth and the Medway towns, where missions had been undertaken respectively by John Binns and John Gale Jones of the LCS early in 1796.[29] Aaron Graham, one of the London stipendiary magistrates, was sent to Portsmouth after the outbreak of mutiny to investigate the extent of the rumoured political connection. He was unable to find any firm evidence of radical involvement from the shore, but it was true that Valentine Joyce, the leader of the mutiny, was a radical, that radicals in the port were active, and that pamphlets were sent to the ships. At their subsequent trials, political views and statements in favour of peace were attributed to some crew members.[30] Both John Bone, the LCS secretary, and Robert Watson of the LCS were in Portsmouth during the mutinies, supposedly to form popular societies, but Bone claimed at a meeting of the LCS on 25 May that Watson had gone to Portsmouth to foment mutiny on his own initiative and not as a representative of the LCS; Watson counter-claimed that Bone had undertaken unsanctioned treasonable activities. We now know from Watson's subsequent activities in United Irish circles and with Colonel Despard that he *was* a revolutionary.[31]

Following his mission to Spithead, Graham and another stipendiary magistrate, Daniel Williams, were next sent to interview prisoners from the Nore mutiny. Again, they found it difficult to gather hard evidence but they strongly suspected connections between the popular societies and leaders of the mutiny. This would not have been enough to secure a conviction in a civil court so the charge against Richard Parker and the other leaders was switched from treason, which would have been tried at the Assizes, to mutiny which was easier to prove before a court martial.[32]

The involvement of the corresponding societies in the mutinies, especially in an official capacity, must remain open to doubt, although individual radicals in the fleets and on shore probably did play some part in turning economic discontents into a demand for peace. The involvement of the United Irishmen can be asserted with more confidence. Though they did not know of the mutinies before they happened, they did then attempt to exploit them. There were, for example, cells of United Irishmen both in the fleet and in Portsmouth, and Dublin sent a special envoy to work with United Irishmen in England to prolong the mutiny at the Nore. Though some Irish sailors responded to this intervention, the English generally did not and even when they favoured peace they did not support an instruction issued by the United Irishmen for the mutineers to take their ships over to the French. A plan to divide the fleet, with only some ships going over to the French, was recognition that the extremists would not be able to sway every crew. In the end, as the mutinies collapsed, only a few of the extremists fled to France; others, including Richard Parker, were hanged.[33]

This Irish dimension to anti-war and, to a lesser extent, pro-French feeling was deeply worrying to ministers, particularly when evidence began to emerge during 1798 of a wider conspiracy to bring down the ministry, end the war and liberate Ireland. The background to this conspiracy was the dispersal of United Irish forces from Ulster in 1797 and the reinforcement of Irish communities in Britain with discontented refugees. Central to the scheme was James Coigly, and a section of the United Irish leadership including Arthur O'Connor. Coigly was born in Armagh in 1761 and, after ordination in 1785, went to Paris for his theological training. After the revolution he fled back to Ireland where he probably became involved with the Defenders at a time when agrarian, sectarian and political tensions were increasingly leading to violence in Armagh. These disturbances reached a peak in 1795 following the recall of Earl Fitzwilliam, and Coigly's parents were among the many victims of the Orange mob. All the while Coigly himself was being drawn more deeply into radical politics across the line dividing sympathetic pastoral care from radical activism. Following the failure of the Bantry Bay expedition in December 1796, he associated with the United Irish extremists led by Fitzgerald, O'Connor and Samuel Neilson, who were determined to plot an independent Irish rising to encourage the French to undertake a fresh invasion. By 1797 he was important enough to be reported on by one of the government's agents who was a member of the United Irishmen and in June of that year he joined those of his fellow Irish who, fearing arrest and the Orange mob, took the boat to England. Here he became a link between Dublin, Paris and the Irish communities in Britain. He travelled in the English Midlands, established contact with Manchester where the corresponding society had converted into a republican organisation known as the United Englishmen, and formed links also with the United Scotsmen. He then went to London where he met Irish republicans such as Valentine Lawless and Colonel Edward Marcus Despard, and also John and Benjamin Binns, leading members of the extreme faction within the LCS. At a meeting in London of delegates from both England and Scotland, 'the chief revolutionary committee of England' drew up a manifesto in support of a French invasion and Coigly conveyed this to Paris before returning to Dublin by way of London. He then returned to London to mature the plot before setting out with Arthur O'Connor, John Binns, John Allen and Jeremiah Leary for France. But the government was aware of their plans and as they sat at breakfast in the King's Head, Margate on 28 February 1798, they were arrested.[34]

Told in this way, it would seem that Coigly was at the heart of a serious plot with considerable support amongst the Irish community in Britain which could well have achieved its objective of persuading the French government to make a further invasion attempt. Yet, at the subsequent trial, only Coigly was found guilty, and that only on the evidence of the Address found in his pocket. No serious evidence of conspiracy was produced against the others despite all that the government's agents had been observing and reporting of their activities – Leary had wisely disposed of directly incriminating evidence down the privy at the King's Head. In his autobiography, Francis Place recalled how he had attended some of the London meetings at which Coigly was present but thought little of the conspiracy: 'A more absurd and ridiculous project never entered the heads of men out of Bedlam.'[35] He thought that the Committee of Secrecy which reported in 1799 grossly exaggerated the scale and extent of support for the revolutionary committee. Their *Report* alleged that for at least the past two years the real object of the LCS had been to form a republic with French assistance. John Ashley, a member of the committee in 1794 and secretary of the LCS in 1795–96, 'was now acting as their agent at Paris, and had recently given them hopes of the succour of a French army'. Meetings had been held in London 'to contrive the means of procuring arms, to enable them to co-operate with a French force, in case of an invasion'. One of these meeting places was a cellar in Furnival's Inn, which

> gradually became the resort of all those who were engaged the most deeply in the conspiracy. It was particularly attended by Arthur O'Connor and O'Coigly, previous to their attempt to go over to France; and by the persons chiefly instrumental in carrying on correspondence with the Irish conspirators; and secret consultations were repeatedly held there, with a view to projects, which were thought too dangerous and desperate to be brought forward in any of the larger societies. Among these plans, was that of effecting a general insurrection, at the same moment, in the metropolis and throughout the country, and of

directing it to the object of seizing or assassinating the king, the royal family, and many of the members of both Houses of parliament.[36]

Though mass political assassination seems unlikely, the men at the Home Office were better informed than Francis Place, and they checked their information carefully. Having first been alerted by a Catholic priest from Stonyhurst in Lancashire that there were 20,000 United Englishmen in Manchester, the Home Secretary (the Duke of Portland) asked a leading Manchester magistrate, Thomas Butterworth Bayley, to check this claim. He was able to persuade a leading member of the local corresponding society, Robert Gray, to turn paid informer. Gray confirmed that the United Irishmen had indeed infiltrated the Manchester Corresponding Society and he was the source for the information provided to the committee that a society of United Englishmen had been established in Manchester before 1797.

At the beginning of that year it consisted of about 50 divisions and had grown to about 80 during 1798. Since each division contained between 15 and 36 members, this put their total numbers in the Manchester area at between 1,200 and 2,880 – about a tenth of what had originally been reported. These United Englishmen had attempted, unsuccessfully, to win over the troops but they had established 'an extensive district' around Manchester, managed by 'a very zealous and active committee' which 'frequently sent delegates to various parts of Yorkshire, Derbyshire, Nottinghamshire, and Cheshire' and also corresponded with 'the most distant parts of England as well as to Edinburgh and Glasgow'. There was a second central society in Liverpool which was in correspondence with other parts of England, and with Scotland and Ireland. At the same time attempts were made in Scotland to form a society of United Scotsmen on the same plan, the intention being 'to separate Scotland as well as Ireland from England, and to found, on the ruins of the established government, three distinct republics of England, Scotland, and Ireland'.[37]

Eleven United Englishmen were arrested, including one of the leaders, James Dixon, who stated that in fact only twenty-five divisions had been set up, thus reducing the total numbers involved in the Manchester area to under a thousand, but he did attest to the secret communications network. So, although the size and readiness of the organisation would appear to have been exaggerated by Coigly, the London committee and Robert Gray, it was true that support for the United Irishmen was being organised in Britain.[38]

Why then was this evidence not used at the trial of Coigly and the others? Edward Thompson, who was one of the first historians to take this mass of secret government evidence seriously, plausibly argued that it was not in the government's interest to reveal all that it knew but only sufficient to serve its purpose.[39] Informing was not a popular trade and informers preferred the anonymity of a written or verbal report to the public exposure of an appearance in the witness box; and a good spy would be useless once he had been produced in court.

One of the key agents was Samuel Turner, a lawyer, a United Irishman and member of the Ulster Revolutionary Committee. It was he who supplied the information leading to the arrests at Margate, and when he fled to join the community of Irish exiles in Hamburg he continued to supply information on activities there. Using the alias of 'Richardson' or 'Mr R' (Lord Edward Fitzgerald's wife was called Pamela, as was the heroine in Samuel Richardson's 1740 novel, *Pamela*), he supplied the British government with information for eight years and his cover was never broken. If he had given evidence against O'Connor he could not have done this.

Similarly successful was James Powell, assistant secretary to the LCS, who began working for the government in 1795. He was probably the source of the information supplied in April 1798 which implicated some members of the LCS in the United English/Irish plot which brought about the arrest of the leaders of the corresponding society. Powell was included among those arrested: it would have looked suspicious for him not to have been as he was a noted extremist. 'Powell was honest, but silly,' thought Francis Place, totally taken in by the spy as he helped him escape – to Hamburg! He was still working for the government when he returned in 1802 and the nature of his true work was never exposed. In correspondence he was 'Mr P'. A third spy whose name was not revealed even to the Committee of Secrecy, was George Orr who fled to England before the Irish rebellion and then proceeded to Hamburg where he reported on and followed Napper Tandy, founder of the United Irishmen in Dublin, and another leader of the extremists.[40]

With information such as could be gained from men like these, the government had good reason to believe that a widespread and potentially dangerous plot existed, involving not only Ireland and France, but Britain itself, and Pitt's fury at not being able to convict Arthur O'Connor provoked him into a foolish duel with the Foxite MP and Irishman, George Tierney. The government suspected that the Foxite opposition was not so innocent of the conspiracy as they liked to pretend. Suspicion had already been aroused during the Spithead mutiny when Samuel Whitbread, a Foxite MP, was reported attending a pre-arranged meeting in Purfleet with a leader of the mutiny. How far the Foxites were prepared to go in their anxiety to bring about the fall of Pitt's administration, end the war and secure English liberties is unclear. Fox was, after all, Lord Edward Fitzgerald's cousin and Arthur O'Connor had been noticeably active in Whig circles in London at the same time as he was conspiring with Coigly. Sir Francis Burdett's friendship with O'Connor was especially suspicious. The Foxites gave evidence of O'Connor's good character at his trial, when the government already knew him to be a traitor.

How much the Foxite Whigs knew or were prepared to take advantage of can only be surmised, and the evidence is only circumstantial. The Foxites were certainly in a difficult position after 1795 and genuinely seem to have feared that Pitt was a threat to constitutional liberty.[41] The Foxite secession from the House of Commons in November 1797 coincided with Grattan's secession from the Irish Parliament and appeared to be co-ordinated. Lord Lansdowne thought that 'secession means rebellion, or it is nonsense' and William Wilberforce thought of the Foxites that 'a conviction of their weakness alone prevents their taking up the sword against the government'. What did Fox know when he wrote in March 1798 that 'no good can ever be done now, but by ways in which I will never take a share, and for which I am as unfit, as I am indisposed to them'? Why was Lady Holland concerned lest Holland House be thought 'a *foyer* for Jacobinism'? Is it just coincidence that the papers of the leader of the Whigs, the fifth Duke of Bedford, were destroyed after his death in 1802 and that Lord Holland destroyed Lord Stanhope's political correspondence relating to this time? Nothing can be proved, but if the Foxites were aware of the plans of the United Irishmen and were contemplating exploiting the political instability which might follow an invasion to save English 'liberty' from Pittite repression, the Margate trials were enough to warn them off. The exposure of Coigly silenced them as effectively as the suspension of *Habeas Corpus* enabled the government to silence Binns and others, against whom it was now unnecessary to bring evidence to secure their imprisonment.[42]

The fall of Pitt in 1801, occasioned by the refusal of the King to contemplate repealing anti-Catholic legislation after the Act of Union, brought about the political conditions in which the prisoners could be released, among them Colonel Despard. His subsequent activities need to be placed in the context of this earlier attempt to rouse Britain to support an Irish rising, though the fact that Britain was at peace with France between March 1802 and May 1803 removed both the war-weariness and the immediate threat of a French invasion which had made the situation during 1797–98 so dangerous. After 1798, the revolutionary organisation built up by the United Irishmen and their British supporters was severely weakened but the United Irishmen still maintained an Executive Directory linked to both France and London where the Irish community had been augmented by a fresh influx of refugees following the defeat of the 1798 rising. The extent to which an underground revolutionary organisation was maintained has been documented from the Home Office papers by Marianne Elliott: William Duckett in Hamburg had contacts with the French government; Patrick Finney organised the Irish in London where a National Committee had been formed by early 1801; in Lancashire and Cheshire, former United Britons were ready to resume their activities and when one of the most prominent local leaders, William Cheetham, was released from gaol in 1801 he continued where he had left off. The government set up a new Committee of Secrecy, suspended *Habeas Corpus* again and arrested thirty radicals whom they had good reason to suspect of treasonable activity. Though Napoleon had little time for republican conspirators, his government encouraged them as a useful adjunct to his greater aim of defeating Britain.

The Peace of Amiens only temporarily interrupted this strategy. The release of prisoners when the *Habeas Corpus* Suspension Act again expired fuelled preparations for a new conspiracy and magistrates' spies reported increased activity and organisation in the industrial districts of both Lancashire and the West Riding. Although the Lord Lieutenant of the West Riding, Earl Fitzwilliam, was sceptical and despite good reasons not to believe everything reported by Thomas Hirst, whom the government had provided as a spy, other and more reliable sources of information, such as that provided by Charles Bent, a Manchester tailor employed as a spy by Colonel Ralph Fletcher of Bolton, show Fitzwilliam to have been too complacent.[43]

Irish activity quickened during the summer and autumn of 1802 in the hope that a French invasion would follow the expected breakdown of the peace. So the arrest of Colonel Despard at the Oakley Arms in Lambeth in November 1802 can be seen as a pre-emptive strike by the government in circumstances where Despard's committee were winning some support among the Guards and was possibly in a position to begin a rising in London that would then have been taken up in the industrial north. Had the full plan been allowed to mature until 1803, when Napoleon's invasion army was again assembled and Ireland was ready to rebel, the danger to British security could have been considerable. By acting to stop Despard in November 1802, the government did not have to admit publicly the extent of subversion in the country, but it lost the opportunity of bringing the most dangerous leaders to trial without putting valuable informers in the witness box and thus ending their usefulness. The alternative of suspending *Habeas Corpus* as in 1797 was not available because Addington's government needed the support of the Foxites to resist opposition demands for a renewal of the war. So, the 'Despard conspiracy' was presented and prosecuted in isolation from the main events of which it formed but a small part.[44]

## Luddism

Magistrates and ministers alike feared that republicanism and subversion might get mixed up with economic grievances. The decision in 1799 to make combinations of workmen illegal had placed societies organised for economic purposes in the same illegal category as political societies. 'The republicans are drinking Mr Pitt's health,' reported one spy, concerned about a union of industrial and political discontents.[45] Some historians have dismissed this fear as groundless, and the nature of the relationship between political protest and economic discontent is not easy to establish. But governments in the decades after the French Revolution continued to feel anxious that the troublesome minority of revolutionaries might achieve a following by appearing to offer solutions to the grievances of the lower classes in times of economic hardship. It was no coincidence that the political

CITY COLLEGE
LEARNING RESOURCE CENTRE

crisis of 1795 came in a year of record bread prices, supplying a ready audience for Thelwall's inflammatory speeches. Similarly, one of the most disturbing things about the turn of events during 1801–2 was the possible connection between revolutionary politics and industrial unrest in the West Riding and Lancashire.[46] Local magistrates such as Colonel Ralph Fletcher of Bolton and Joseph Radcliffe of Huddersfield grew alarmed at what their spies were telling them and even Fitzwilliam, the phlegmatic Lord Lieutenant, asked for reinforcements of regular troops – just in case.[47] Bread prices in 1801 were twice what they had been in 1797 and remnants of the United Irish were reported still active.

A major source of discontent in the north of England was the introduction of new machinery into the textile industries to help manufacturers meet the rising demand for cloth and to reduce their reliance on organised groups of skilled workers. In the cotton industry, where the factory system was well-established for spinning, the main industrial disputes were over hours and conditions of work for the (mainly) child and female labour force, while for the predominantly male handloom weavers the question was one of wages, as manufacturers ignored apprenticeship, recruited new workers (including many Irish) and attempted to drive down wages to factory levels. The failure of Rose's Bill, which would have introduced some regulation of handloom weavers' wages, led to a major strike in Lancashire and Cheshire in 1808 when, according to a local magistrate, Blackburn was 'in a state approaching to that of a general insurrection in consequence of a dispute betwixt the weavers and their employers on the subject of wages'.[48] The small gains made at this time were wiped out by the next depression in 1811.[49]

In the Yorkshire woollen industry, where the factory system was still in its infancy, the master clothiers passed resolutions in 1806 urging Parliament to protect the domestic system by enacting that no individual or firm should own more than 5 looms or 160 spindles or employ children other than those who had served a seven-year apprenticeship.[50] The response of Parliament was to do nothing until 1814 when the apprenticeship clause of the Statute of Artificers (1563) was repealed. Apprenticeship was also a cause of a strike by all 80 croppers at Benjamin Gott's woollen mill in Leeds in 1802 when Gott attempted to circumvent the apprenticeship regulation by indenturing boys over the age of 14. His real aim was to break the croppers' union, for the croppers controlled the last stage in the production of woollen cloth and so could regulate the output of the whole trade. On this occasion 80 croppers were able to force one of the biggest capitalists in the industry to back down.[51]

The position of the croppers was being undermined by the introduction of new machinery, invented in 1787, to both raise and shear the nap on woven and fulled cloth enabling a man and a boy to do in a day what a skilled cropper had formerly done in a week. Textile workers in the east Midlands stocking industry were similarly under pressure at the beginning of the nineteenth century, as employers resorted to using large numbers of apprentices and wide knitting frames in an effort to increase output and cut costs. Although many of the problems arising from changing methods of production had been developing for most of the previous century, they reached crisis point in 1811 as high bread prices coincided with a collapse in markets.[52]

The reason for the recession lay in international relations and economic warfare with Napoleonic France. In 1807, Orders in Council were issued which required all neutral shipping trading with France to call first at a British port and pay duty. This led to a deterioration of relations with the United States, a collapse in British exports to the United States and war between the two countries in 1812. The loss of the American market coming on top of the exclusion of Britain from French controlled ports left unwanted goods piling up in warehouses. Employers retrenched by cutting wages and laying off labour. At the same time the price of bread climbed to a peak three times that of before the war.

Against this background a new and intense phase of machine-breaking began, starting in Nottinghamshire in the spring of 1811. Rioting and frame-breaking were widespread over the winter of 1811–12, presenting a severe threat to law and order as the anonymous 'General Ludd' made his appearance in threatening letters. One newspaper correspondent from Nottingham wrote that, 'The insurrectional state to which this country has been reduced for the last month has no parallel in history, since the troubled days of Charles the First', echoing language used by the *Annual Register* back in 1795 of the impact of the French Revolution.[53]

The movement and the name of 'Luddism' spread to the West Riding where shearing frames were just beginning to take hold in the smaller communities of the Colne and Calder valleys to the south and west of Leeds. In February 1812 machines were smashed in a finishing shop less than a mile from Milnsbridge House, home of the vigilant magistrate Joseph Radcliffe. Other attacks followed in the district and threatening letters were received by prominent mill-owners and magistrates. The laws were tightened against Luddism: machine breaking was made a capital offence in February 1812 as was the taking of unlawful oaths in May. Two mill-owners were singled out by the Luddites: William Horsfall, who had installed some of the new machines in his mill at Marsden and who was an outspoken member of the 'Committee for Suppressing Outrages' formed in Huddersfield; and William Cartwright, who was also fitting new shearing frames at his Rawfolds mill in the Spen valley between Bradford and Dewsbury. On 11 April 1812 about 150 Luddites attacked Rawfolds mill. They were repulsed by an armed guard and two of their number were killed. A week later an attempt was made on Cartwright's life and on 28 April Horsfall was murdered as he rode home to Marsden: he had promised to ride up to his saddle girths in Luddite blood and they had extracted their revenge.[54]

This murder intensified the efforts of the authorities to find out who was responsible but, unlike the 1790s, in this period the magistrates were remarkably deficient in secret intelligence. They picked up rumours but found hard evidence difficult to obtain despite rewards of £2,000 being offered for the apprehension of the guilty. Arrests were finally made for the murder. The government was anxious to hold an exemplary trial before the winter and so pressed ahead with inadequate evidence. As a consequence 'clemency' was granted to some of those arrested because little evidence had been gathered against them, but George Mellor, William Thorpe and Thomas Smith were all convicted of murder on the evidence of their accomplice, Benjamin Walker, and they were hanged at York on 8 January 1813. Eight days later fourteen more were hanged for their part in the attack on Rawfolds mill and other property.[55]

The third scene of Luddite activity was the Manchester area, culminating in an arson attack on a cotton steam loom factory at Westhoughton on 28 March 1812, but here the unrest took an apparently different form from that in the east Midlands and Yorkshire. In the Midlands, acts of violence against property were sustained over several years, the last great outburst being an attack on John

Heathcote's lace factory at Loughborough in June 1816. In the West Riding the violence was more intense but also more short-lived, lasting less than a year. In Lancashire there is more evidence of political activity, spilling over into violence: more evidence, partly because political organisations, however clandestine, were as in the 1790s easier for spies to penetrate than oath-bound Luddite gangs; and partly because of Ralph Fletcher's industrious spy, John Bent.[56] But when Joseph Nadin, deputy constable for Manchester, arrested thirty-eight workers for administering an illegal oath at a meeting in a Manchester public house, their subsequent prosecution on the evidence of the thirty-ninth person present failed to secure a single guilty verdict thanks to the vigorous defence conducted by the Whig lawyer, Henry Brougham.[57]

Most historians have dismissed Luddism as a serious revolutionary threat, while admitting that it constituted a grave challenge to civil peace, private property and even life itself. Violence is in itself no more a proof of a revolutionary conspiracy than its absence demonstrates the lack of such a conspiracy. What can be shown, however, is that there were allegations and rumours and some circumstantial connections between the economic violence of Luddism and men who wished to change (and if not change, then of necessity overthrow) the political system.

The grievances that spilled over into Luddism were first expressed politically in petitions to Parliament for the enforcement of protective legislation, not only the wages clause of the Statute of Artificers (repealed in 1813) and the apprenticeship clause (repealed in 1814), but also the law prohibiting the use of gig-mills which were incorporated into the new shearing frames (repealed in 1809). It was the refusal of Parliament to listen to these petitions that fuelled the anger of Luddism. The 'Friends of Liberty' meeting on Steeton Moor near Keighley in April 1801 had rejected the idea of petitioning Parliament for redress of grievances, asking whether they should continue to submit to 'a Majority of mercenary Hirelings, Government pimps – Corn dealers – Place men – Pensioners – Parasites, &c, and yourselves Starving for Bread? – No, let them exist not one Day longer, we are the Sovereignty'.[58] It is hard to know how representative this group was in 1801, but by 1811 events had done a great deal to reinforce their sentiment.

In Nottinghamshire, there was even a suspicion that Gravener

Henson, leader of the Framework Knitters' Union which petitioned Parliament in vain, might be General Ludd; it is more probable that some of his frustrated followers, particularly those from the depressed country areas around Nottingham, resorted to violence as a response to parliamentary inaction.[59] In Yorkshire, George Mellor and other Luddites in York Castle awaiting trial joined a petition for parliamentary reform, but that does not provide a reason for their being Luddites. But many of those associated with the Luddites were also reformers. Foremost among these in Yorkshire was John Baines of Halifax, a hatter and a republican of twenty-three years' standing, who was tried at York for administering a Luddite oath to John McDonald, a police spy, a couple of days before that became a capital offence, earning him seven years transportation instead of a hanging.[60]

A threatening letter sent by the Yorkshire Luddites to a Huddersfield factory master in 1812 shows something of their thinking. It began with the usual threats against machinery but then expanded in politics. However unrealistic this section of their letter was, it indicates the relationship between the failure of the petitioning movement and Luddism and also the ease with which industrial grievances could spill over into political hatreds.

> The immediate cause of us beginning when we did was that Rascally Letter of the Prince Regent to Lords Grey and Grenville which left us no hope of a chance for the better, by his falling in with that damned set of Rogues Perceval & Co to whom we attribute all the miseries of our Country but we hope for assistance from the French Emperor in shaking off the Rottenest, wickedest and most Tyrannical Government that ever existed, then down comes the Hanover Tyrants and all our tyrants from the greatest to the smallest, and we will be governed by a just Republic, and may the Almighty hasten those happy times is the wish and prayer of Millions in this Land, but we wont only pray but we will fight, the Red Coats shall know when the proper times come, we will never lay down our arms till the House of Commons passes the act to put down all the machinery hurtful to the Commonality and repeal that to the Frame Breakers but we Petition no more, that wont do, fighting must.[61]

With this perspective in mind, we can now review the evidence about Luddism and politics in Lancashire and Cheshire, much of which comes from the spy John Bent. Malcolm Thomis sees him as 'wild and imaginative' and his employer, Ralph Fletcher, as revealing an 'unbelievable naïveté'.[62] John Dinwiddy, on the other hand, thought him prone to exaggerate those matters about which he did not have direct knowledge but possibly 'giving fairly accurate accounts of proceedings in Manchester about which his employer might be suspected of having other intelligence'.[63] The extent of this Luddite activity became clear when General Maitland, in charge of the troops enforcing law and order in Lancashire and Cheshire, decided to apply the provisions of the Illegal Oaths Act which offered immunity to those who admitted their guilt. Hundreds rushed to take advantage of the indemnity in July and August 1812 – over eight hundred came forward in the last week in August in Stockport and Hyde alone.[64] This suggests widespread illegal organisation in Lancashire in the summer of 1812, coinciding with a spate of attacks on factories. Clandestine violence and open petitioning were taking place side by side, with some of the same people participating in both. Some of the thirty-eight alleged oath takers arrested by Nadin, tried and acquitted, who claimed they were innocent parliamentary reformers, later came forward under the indemnity to be 'untwisted' of their illegal oaths. This on its own would not make their illegal behaviour revolutionary in a political sense and much of the evidence suggests the oath was not overtly political.

However, some of the evidence points to a political oath calling for 'a general reform and general change'. Weaver informant, Humphrey Yarwood, came to understand that 'something further than the destruction of steam looms or machinery was intended', and Thomas Wood of Mottram was told when he took the oath 'that there was to be a revolution, and that all who were not for it, would be killed; and those who were for it, were to take the oath'.[65] If these statements are then put in the context of the evidence for United Irish activity in the area a decade earlier, Lancashire Luddism may appear not quite so purely economic after all. The same argument can be applied to Yorkshire. Although most of those convicted of machine breaking were workers in the woollen industry, mainly croppers, oath taking was more widespread, extending eastwards to Leeds and south to Sheffield.[66] In Barnsley, a weaver later gave information that 'The Luddites have in view ultimately to overturn the System of Government, by Revolutionising the Country.'[67]

However, this did not amount to the national network of revolutionary conspiracy that Bent imagined it to be. And, despite the lingering possibility in Luddite and other minds of links with the United Irish and the renewed possibility of a French invasion in 1812, Dublin Castle was not alarmed in the way it had been in the later 1790s.[68] If there were to be a threat of revolution on the Irish model in 1812, it was more likely to take the form feared by Sir Francis Wood, Vice-Lieutenant for the West Riding, who thought that the general lawlessness and collecting of weapons that was spreading in Yorkshire in the summer of 1812 could lead from robbery to assassination (which it did) and then 'end as the same Course of Outrage ended in Ireland, in open Rebellion against the Government of the Country; – The Similarity of our present State to that of Ireland strikes every one who witnessed the Transactions of 1797 and 1798 in that Country'.[69] This was perceptive. The assumption that there is a dividing line, however thin, between economic and political activity, is a rationalisation that lies in the historian's rather than the contemporary's mind. The hungry and desperate worker whose livelihood was at risk did not pause to categorise his motives or clarify his objectives, and what had begun as economic protest and direct action of an industrial nature could easily drift towards political subversion given the right conditions. Had the industrial counties presented the same face in 1801–2, with a French invasion imminent and Ireland preparing to rise, unrest on the scale experienced in 1812 might indeed have posed a serious revolutionary threat.

### The post-war crisis, 1817

The immediate post-war years, 1815–21, proved as difficult as any during wartime itself, as unemployment and high bread prices coincided with renewed political discontent. Lord Sidmouth feared, 'We must expect a trying winter, and it will be fortunate if the Military establishment which was pronounced to be too large for the constitution of the country shall be sufficient to preserve its internal tranquillity.'[70] In 1817 the price of wheat rose to heights previously unknown except in the crisis years of 1800–1 and 1812–13. Though this undermined the relevance of the Corn Law of 1815, which protected domestic agriculture from foreign imports when the price was below 80 shillings a quarter, this protectionism became a symbol for reformers of the way in which the old order represented in Parliament always looked after its own. During the wars, the armed forces of Britain had been increased to 400,000 men (with as many again in the reserves) compared with about 60,000 in 1791.[71] As the military establishment was reduced to peace-time levels, thousands of men trained in the use of arms were discharged on to the labour market. At the same time, sectors of the economy that had expanded to meet war-time demand – in the production of uniforms, munitions and ships – now had surplus capacity. Added to this came the strains of technological redundancy. The number of shearing frames in Yorkshire had increased in the past decade from under a hundred to over fourteen hundred, and in October 1817, 3,625 croppers (of whom only 860 were in full employment) petitioned Parliament for help.[72] In Lancashire, the number of handloom weavers continued to rise while their wages continued to fall.[73]

At the same time the ending of the war re-invigorated the demand for parliamentary reform which had been kept alive by campaigners such as Major Cartwright, political organisers like Francis Place in Westminster, and a minority of Whig politicians such as Sir Francis Burdett. During the war, to demand reform implied a lack of patriotism and Cartwright, Place and Burdett had each at some point been suspected of seditious activity, but all three and their like had wisely avoided direct involvement with the extremist and illegal revolutionary fringe. The same was true of William Cobbett who was probably the most popular journalist of the reform movement. He had been imprisoned for two years in 1809 for a seditious libel on 'the borders of high treason' in his *Political Register* in which he had condemned the use of German mercenary troops to flog mutinous militiamen.[74] After the war he issued the *Register* in a cheap edition at twopence a week, in which he denounced Luddism and advocated political reform as the means to redress grievances. He was widely read, his paper reaching an initial circulation of 40,000, stimulating a legitimate and popular movement for political reform in London and across the troubled industrial areas of the Midlands and the north. Popular societies sprang up as in the early 1790s, often called Union Societies, or Hampden clubs after the style of the London Hampden Club established by Major Cartwright, but appealing to a lower social class. There were twenty-one such societies in Lancashire alone at the beginning of 1817.

Other influences were also at work, but it is hard to tell how wide-spread or influential they were. Chief among them were the followers of Thomas Spence, whose natural environment was the clubs and taverns of London which the loyalist pamphleteer, William Hamilton Reid, had recognised as hotbeds of subversive republicanism in the 1790s, and where Despard had found support.[75] Spence was a revolutionary land reformer who had sold his tracts in London and inspired a band of dedicated followers during the lean years of the reform movement after 1799. These followers regrouped after Spence's death in 1814 under the leadership of Thomas Evans, one-time secretary of the London Corresponding Society in its revolutionary phase after 1797, whose house had been a base for United English planning in 1798. On release from prison in 1801, Evans had resumed his revolutionary activities until the exposure of Despard's plot had brought him greater discretion. Thereafter he was to be found with other old 'Jacobins' in the 'free-and-easy' atmosphere of London tavern life. Their historian, Iain McCalman, has constructed a list of some of their number in 1811–12: they included several former United Englishmen and Irishmen, arrested during 1798–99 and plotters with Despard in 1802.[76] Around 1810–11 they were joined by Maurice Margarot, returned from Australia, and Arthur Thistlewood who visited Paris with Evans's son in 1814 where they met up with John Ashley, formerly of the LCS, and other members of the Anglo-Irish community of revolutionary exiles.[77]

Leading members of Evans's Society of Spencean Philanthropists at the end of the war included Arthur Thistlewood, 'Dr' James Watson and Thomas Preston. Thistlewood was the illegitimate son of a Lincolnshire farmer. He had been a lieutenant in the Yorkshire militia and then gambled himself into debt in London where Place suspected him of being a paid informer. Watson was a surgeon–apothecary from Cheshire whose businesses repeatedly failed in London, as did his marriage, and who eked out a marginal existence. Preston was a master shoemaker similarly fallen on hard times, and also with a failed marriage.[78] These men might be compared to that political 'low life' identified by Robert Darnton in Paris before the 1789 Revolution.[79] Well-fitted to be their leader after 1814, Thomas Evans is described by McCalman as 'a marginal, restless artisan, an incorrigible revolutionary, a tavern *bon vivant* and balladeer, a radical black-mailer and smut-pedlar; yet at the same time, an ambitious, conscientious father, an aspiring self-improver, a moderate Westminster activist, a *philosophe-manqué* and . . . a fervent millenar-ian.'[80]

The concept of millenarianism is important for understanding the revolutionary outlook of this group. Since the French Revolution, the prospect of a new world and a new beginning had given rise to a number of millenarian sects. Some of them, like that attached to Richard Brothers in 1795, had political implications; others, like the followers of Joanna Southcott, were apolitical, though this cannot be said of all Joanna's successor prophets. Speakers fired with biblical language and apocalyptic visions filled pulpits and inspired crowds, especially in London. From the 1790s to at least the 1830s, radical mil-lenarianism could pose a real threat because it inspired a brand of fanaticism which did not respond to the rationalities governing normal political behaviour, such as the calculation of likely success and the deterrent effect of punishment. One such preacher was the ex-Methodist tailor, Robert Wedderburn, a discharged black sailor who may have been present at the Nore in 1797. By 1818 he was a leading Spencean and his Hopkins Street chapel, where he moved after break-ing with Thomas Evans in April 1819, was a centre for revolutionary plotting.[81]

By 1816 the Spenceans were divided into two groups. The main-stream, followers of Evans, adhered to Spence's revolutionary plan for the redistribution of the land but did not espouse revolutionary methods. The minority, among whom Thistlewood and 'Dr' Watson and his son (also James) were the leading figures, were more in the Watt or Despard tradition, looking to create a revolutionary spark which would fire the country.[82] Their hope in 1816 was to achieve this in alliance with the most popular radical speaker of his day, Henry Hunt. Hunt hoped to exploit the Spencean connection with tavern radicalism to extend his own political base in his competition for support with Cobbett and other radical leaders.[83] So when Preston invited leading reformers, including Hunt, Cobbett and Burdett, to address a meeting to be held on Spa Fields in north London on 15 November 1816, Hunt alone accepted but on conditions which enabled him to keep control of the meeting. Nothing daunted, Thistlewood and the younger Watson decided to mount an attack on the Tower of London on the morning before Hunt's next Spa Fields meeting on 2 December. Despite the efforts of Thistlewood's associate, John Castle, to persuade Hunt to become involved, he refused. This was wise, for Castle was a government agent who later gave evidence against the conspirators. Thistlewood and young Watson led a crowd of about five thousand through London, raiding gun shops on the way to the Tower. Rioting went on all day, but little was achieved other than the arrest of most of the leaders. Remarkably they were released on bail, as if the government wanted to give them the opportunity for further revolutionary activity (monitored by Castle) in order to justify the kind of repression of free speech which would not otherwise be acceptable in peacetime.[84] They did not have to wait long. On 28 January the events of 1795 were repeated. A projectile, supposedly a bullet, broke a window in the Prince Regent's coach on his way to open Parliament. Then, on 8 February, Thistlewood and his co-conspirators were arrested and committed to the Tower on a charge of high treason. On 4 March *Habeas Corpus* was suspended. The Seditious Meetings Act of 1795 was revived on 14 March and it was made a treasonable offence to attempt to persuade soldiers and sailors to break their oaths. Magistrates were reminded to suppress all blasphemous and seditious literature.

The severity of this reaction has to be put in the wider context, not only of the riot in London, but also of its effect in the rest of the country, especially in the industrial Midlands and north where Luddites disturbances were of very recent memory. Fitzwilliam felt that the public temper at a riotous public meeting in Sheffield was 'the offspring of a Revolutionary spirit', though this worried him less than if it had been the product of distress. Nevertheless it was enough for him to vote with the government for the repressive legislation.[85] One of the men who had come from the north to London for the second Spa Fields meeting was Joseph Mitchell, a journeyman printer from Liverpool who since 1816 had been operating as a radical missionary in Lancashire. He reported back to a meeting at Middleton near Manchester in December, which nominated him and William Benbow, a local shoemaker, as delegates to visit the distressed areas of Lancashire and Yorkshire. At a further meeting of Lancashire reform societies on 1 January 1817, Samuel Bamford, a young weaver, was chosen to represent Middleton at a national gathering of reformers at the London Hampden Club. Bamford's recollections of events over the next two years provide a graphic insight into the twilight world of conspiracy which linked London and the northern industrial communities. His autobiography, however, is not an untainted source. It was written in a didactic spirit in the late 1830s and early 1840s as a warning to Chartists not to indulge in violence and to beware of spies, and it carefully represented the author as an innocent and rather naive participant in events which he did not fully understand.[86]

In London he was met by Benbow, who was already in the capital 'agitating the labouring classes at their trades' meetings and clubhouses'.[87] He also met Mitchell, with whom he looked up a friend in the Foot Guards. They just happened to have with them copies of Cobbett's *Register* and Hone's *Political Litany* (1817), which they read out to the troops and gave them to read – an act shortly to be made illegal. Mitchell and Benbow also introduced Bamford to the Spenceans, including the elder Watson and Thomas Preston; he later recalled that 'Mitchell and Benbow had cultivated a rather close acquaintance with these men'. On his return to Lancashire, Benbow began organising a march of weavers to London to petition the Prince Regent, the so-called 'Blanketeers'. None of this was illegal, but Bamford was right to observe that it was on the illegal side of what Cobbett, Hunt, Cartwright and the other legitimate popular reformers were advocating: the whole idea, he thought, 'was one of the bad schemes which accompanied us from London, and was the result of the intercourse of some of the deputies with the leaders of the London operatives – the Watsons, Prestons, and Hoopers'.[88]

The Blanketeers gathered in the rain, about five thousand strong, on St Peter's Field, Manchester, on 10 March. The Riot Act was read and two of the leaders were arrested before no more than six or seven hundred set out for London, only to be turned back before they got as far as the county boundary. It is likely that this march was intended to be a mass demonstration to gain support along the route and so put pressure on the government in London, rather than the gathering of a revolutionary army to overawe the capital, but it is also true that the men were desperate and angry, powerless rather than passive in their suffering. The day after the St Peter's Field meeting a stranger called on Bamford and his friends with a plan to march on Manchester, divert the military, raid the garrison for arms, fire the houses of marked individuals and release the prisoners; they would make 'a Moscow of Manchester'. Bamford wisely (in retrospect) ignored the man; he was probably an *agent provocateur*. Others were not so careful and a group of delegates who gathered at Ardwick Bridge to hear news of risings elsewhere was informed on and arrested at the end of March.[89]

The suspension of *Habeas Corpus* enabled the government to terrorise suspects and scatter any incipient cells of revolution. Bamford has left a graphic account of what this could mean:

> Personal liberty not being now secure from one hour to another, many of the leading reformers were induced to quit their homes, and seek concealment where they could obtain it. Those who could muster a few pounds, or who had friends to give them a frugal welcome, or who had trades with which they could travel, disappeared like swallows at the close of summer, no one knew whither.[90]

Twenty-three prominent radicals were arrested; others, including Cobbett, fled. Mitchell ominously 'moved in a sphere of his own, the extent of which no man knew except himself'.[91] In London in April he met up with Charles Pendrill, first arrested in 1798 and a veteran of the Despard conspiracy, who was about to flee to Philadelphia. Pendrill introduced Mitchell to his friend, William Oliver, and on 23 April, Mitchell and Oliver set out on a provincial tour which culminated in a delegate meeting in Wakefield at which a rising was planned for 26 May 'to cause a finishing blow to be levelled at the boroughmongers'.[92] Mitchell was arrested on 4 May, leaving Oliver as the only London representative available to take part. Unknown to Bamford, and indeed to Mitchell himself, the latter's movements were not at all secret – Oliver was reporting everything to the Home Secretary. Oliver's method of working is illustrated in the following sworn deposition:

> about 11 or 12 Weeks ago, invited Walker the Painter to Dinner: found at his Lodgings two strangers, Mitchell & Oliver – after dinner Walker intimated that those two friends of his had expressed a desire to have conversation with you – W & I went to meet them, we four then went 2 Miles out of town, & went into a publick House at Mirfield – the two strangers stated themselves advocates of Parl[iamen]t[ar]y Reform, but Oliver signified that as the H of Cs *notified* [inserted above (probably not inclined)] to listen to Pet[ition]s on that subject, O said Force must be used – that he had instructions from his friends in London to come into this country to sound the minds of the

People on that subject, and that he should appoint meetings to mature the Plan and then communicate to his friends in London. He signified that the physical Force was in the Hands of the People, & that his friends in London were confident of success, if things were properly organized according to his wish; on that account he shd visit the different manufacturing towns, & he should appoint meetings to determine how to act.[93]

But, as Edward Thompson argued, this does not mean that Oliver fabricated or caused the whole provincial conspiracy single-handed. Although he reported it to be 'a weak and impractical scheme',[94] the delegates and their plans for a rising were real enough. Those who brought Bamford news of the Wakefield meeting were the veteran Paineite, Thomas Bacon from Pentrich, and William Turner from nearby South Wingfield.[95] What is true, is that Oliver, as the London delegate, now took charge. The date for the rising was switched to 9 June, and the government was ready. Ministers did not need the additional information about the collection of weapons which informers sent to the Home Office.[96]

Whatever the rumours and allegations of widespread plotting, the actual rising took place in only two places, both of them former centres of Luddite violence. The danger may possibly have seemed greatest in the West Riding, but here the authorities accidentally made a pre-emptive strike when a local magistrate arrested ten delegates at Thornhill Lees, not knowing that Oliver had arranged the meeting. This provoked fewer than a hundred cloth workers from the Holme Valley, including desperate croppers led by George Taylor, said to be a veteran of the Rawfolds attack, to march on Huddersfield on the night of 8 June. A sworn deposition relating to the planning of this insurrection gives some sense of the atmosphere of the times, and also of links back to Luddism:

Riley has sometimes talked to me about their plans he said that the rising was to be in the Night time, and to be general through the Kingdom wherever they had formed a Union all Communication was to be stopped, the Coaches were to be stopped, the Magistrates were to be seized and kept as Hostages until there was a regulation at London – Riley frequently said to me – 'you see Buckley that Petitioning is of no use we are like to do something else.' Riley told me that Veevors had laid down a plan for seising the Military in Huddersfield and that there was

a list of the Quarters where the Soldiers were billeted at, that
they were to divide into Parties and go and surprize them before
they were aware – he said men like me that had been Soldiers
must March off to Sheffield the first day after the great Heads
were secured – I asked what was to become of the Families of
Men like me? and he said that such as him who stopt at home,
would take care of them and that they should not want – he has
an old Halbert which he said had been used in Ludding time
and I might have it if I would join them. I recollect that when
Riley brought me the Lead and Bullet Moulds, he said that he
wanted the Lead casted into Bullets and that somebody would
want them at the time Rising if I did not, and that they would
be ready – he said it would begin the Monday following and
that he wished it was over – he said that altho' he himself did
not know the use of Arms, yet he would do what he could to
assist it.[97]

On the night of Sunday, 8 June, they rose and were dispersed by the
yeomanry just short of the town on the bridge over the River Colne at
Folly Hall.[98]

The next night, a similar rising took place in the vicinity of
Pentrich in Derbyshire to the west of Nottingham. About 400 men
armed with guns and pikes set out from the villages around Pentrich
to march on Nottingham where they expected to be joined by other
bands of revolutionaries, including 16,000 from Nottingham itself.
They would then attack the barracks and seize the town before taking
boats down the Trent to Newark, with the eventual aim of reaching
London where the forces promised by Oliver would overthrow the
government. Their 'captain' was Jeremiah Brandreth, a framework
knitter from Sutton in Ashfield, though the actual planning was probably the work of Thomas Bacon who, with a warrant already out for
his arrest, did not take part in the rising itself. The armed band got as
far as Giltbrook, about thirteen miles from the start of the march and
still eight miles short of Nottingham. Here, those who had not already
thought better of this midnight outing in the rain fled at the sight of
soldiers on horseback. Over eighty arrests were made during the next
few weeks and as a result of the trials in October, three men, including
Brandreth, were hanged; eleven, including Bacon, changed their pleas
to guilty and were transported for life and three others for fourteen
years; and six were gaoled. The prosecution centred its case, as with

Despard's conspiracy, on the actual rising for which the evidence was easy to present, and not the extensive plot behind the rising centred on Bacon. To have exposed this would have meant putting Oliver in the witness box. Already the treason trials against Thistlewood, Watson, Hooper and Preston had foundered because the jury would not convict on an informer's evidence; and the exposure of Oliver by the *Leeds Mercury* on 14 June had resulted in the acquittal of those arrested after the Folly Hall rising. By abandoning the idea of prosecuting Bacon first and trying Brandreth instead, there was no problem in securing guilty verdicts and exemplary punishments.[99]

The Folly Hall and Pentrich risings can be regarded as the last flickers of Luddism in its desperate, violent and political phase. While awaiting transportation for life, George Weightman told the gaol chaplain of a conversation with Brandreth about the latter's part in a Luddite attack at Basford; many years later, Weightman himself was recalled as 'a young man whose face would be familiar to the Luddites of the West Riding' at delegate meetings at the St Crispin Inn, Halifax, the old haunt of John Baines.[100] Machine-breaking could sit alongside the Jacobin politics of Baines and Bacon; armed attacks on mills and masters could grow into revolutionary plots, assisted by – but not necessarily originating with – agents employed by local magistrates and the government.

### From Peterloo to Cato Street and Bonnymuir

The Thistlewood group was encouraged rather than intimidated by the collapse of the case against them following their attempt to seize the Tower of London in December 1816. They discussed plans for another rising in the capital, to take place in October 1817, and in February 1818 plotted to assassinate the Home Secretary, Lord Sidmouth, and other members of the government.[101] Finally in May, when Thistlewood challenged Sidmouth to a duel, the authorities thankfully put him in gaol for a year. The rest of the group, led by the Watsons, modified their tactics and continued their mission more openly in association with Henry Hunt. They made considerable progress, particularly in Lancashire.

On his release in May 1819, Thistlewood resumed his conspiratorial approach along with Preston, William Davidson and other associates who frequented Robert Wedderburn's Hopkins Street chapel.[102] They hoped to exploit a meeting in Smithfield chaired by Hunt on 14 July 1819 to commemorate the thirtieth anniversary of the fall of the Bastille but, as in 1816, Hunt was able to retain control and thwart the revolutionaries. He was determined to divert the energies of the reform movement away from conspiracy towards an open policy of platform agitation, based on the strategy of the mass meeting.[103] The government, however, did not see the clear distinction between the two. Any assembly calculated to strike terror 'in minds of ordinary firmness' was unlawful, which meant in effect that local magistrates could declare unlawful any public meeting which they felt to be a threat; and they could order any such meeting to disperse by reading the Riot Act. Since one aim of Hunt's strategy of the mass platform was to demonstrate force of numbers, potentially striking terror in the minds of ordinary citizens, Hunt's constitutionalism was therefore at best on the margins of legality.

Furthermore, on 30 July a Proclamation had been issued against seditious meetings, which included meetings to coerce Parliament. For this reason the magistrates banned a proposed meeting in support of parliamentary reform planned for 9 August 1819 at St Peter's Field, Manchester, at which Hunt was to be the main speaker. When he moved the meeting to the following week, the magistrates ordered his arrest at the start of the meeting, sending in the troops to effect this. What followed, as the Manchester and Salford Yeomanry lashed out with their swords, contrary to military discipline, killing eleven people and injuring hundreds, has entered the folk history of radical protest and was quickly dubbed the 'Peterloo' massacre.[104]

Hunt's strategy was confrontational but not revolutionary. However, the meeting was held against a background of social tensions which were potentially revolutionary. Joseph Johnson of the Manchester Patriotic Union Society had written to Hunt on 3 July 1819, inviting him in very ambivalent language to come to Manchester to address the meeting:

> Trade here is not worth following. Everything here is almost at a stand still, nothing but ruin and starvation stare one in the face. The state of this district is truly dreadful, and I believe nothing but the greatest exertions can prevent an insurrection. Oh, that you in London were prepared for it!

Though Johnson did not know it, James Norris, the Manchester stipendiary magistrate, had written to Lord Sidmouth on 30 June with an almost identical assessment of the situation.[105] Most ominous were reports of armed drilling on the moors at night and the military-style discipline shown by those who attended the mass meetings.

The real danger came after news of the massacre spread, first to the Lancashire and Cheshire communities represented at the meeting and then, within a couple of days, to the rest of the country. Fear and anger, coming on top of economic hardship and thwarted political demands, produced a revolutionary cocktail and it is a measure of Hunt's stature that he was able to restrain the crowds who treated him as a hero while he was on bail awaiting trial for seditious conspiracy. Even so, there is evidence of further arming at public meetings which the magistrates dared not disrupt in open confrontation with the crowd. In their defence, those accused of bearing such weapons claimed that they were carried for self-protection, and not for illegal aggression. Peterloo turned out to be a disaster for the authorities as the radicals now seized the moral high ground. John Gale Jones later recalled his reaction to the news:

> From that fatal day when the sword was drawn and war declared against the people of England, by the bloody and unavenged massacre of the defenceless men, women and children of Manchester, I was one of those, who made up their mind that all further praying and petitioning ought to be at an end, that the *time for Reform was past and the hour of Revolution come*.[106]

At one meeting held near Burnley in November to protest at Peterloo and to advocate parliamentary reform, the crowd marched to music in an orderly fashion, carrying sticks and banners. But when someone – in panic or mischief-making – raised the cry that the soldiers were coming, 'many persons' produced pike-heads from up their coat sleeves, which they tied to their sticks ready to repulse their attackers.[107] Elsewhere events could not be presented in so innocent a light and the government took new powers by the so-called Six Acts on 1 January 1820 to ban meetings of more than fifty people, suppress or tax out of their market blasphemous and sedition publications, and prohibit unauthorised military training.

There were three main theatres of action during the winter of 1819–20: London, the textile districts in the north of England, and the

Glasgow area of western Scotland. Of the three, events in London were, despite appearances, the least threatening. Here, Thistlewood continued with his plots to overthrow the government by some bold revolutionary *putsch*, following which popular risings would occur elsewhere. The tone was set at Wedderburn's chapel. According to one informer at a meeting in October:

> Principal Speaker was Wedderburn, who dwelt chiefly on the late Affair at Manchester; that the bloody Revolution had begun in blood there, & must now end in blood – that the Prince Regent had lost the Confidence of & affection of his People, but being supported by the army & surrounded by his vile Ministers, nothing short of the People taking arms in their own defence, could bring about a Reform & prevent the same bloody scenes taking place at the next Smithfield Meeting, as had taken place at Manchester, for his own Part old as he was, he was learning his exercise as a Soldier & could be on[e] if he fell in the cause, for he would rather die like Cashman, if he could but have the satisfaction of plunging a Dagger in the heart of a Tyrant. That the next meeting, on 1 Nov would be such a General Meeting throughout the Country as well as London that then only was the time *'therefore all come armed or its of no use and be sure you bring plenty of Ammunition with you'*.[108]

Even discounting Wedderburn's pulpit rhetoric, this message created a mood of heightened expectation on both sides, but on 1 November only forty armed men gathered in London and so the revolution was postponed until 15 November and this was later deferred until 24 November. The revolutionaries were committed to their course but were unable to muster sufficient numbers to turn words into deeds. Preparations were then made for a rising in reaction to the Prince Regent's speech from the throne announcing repression, beginning with simultaneous meetings in London, Scotland, the north and the Midlands on 13 December. Thistlewood's numbers in London, however, were too small and when this failed he turned to an alternative plan to assassinate the ministers at a cabinet dinner. This would be followed immediately by a number of simultaneous attacks on key targets throughout London.

Several dates were fixed and postponed. Matters were finally brought to a head by a spy and *agent provocateur*, George Edwards, leading to the arrest of the group in Cato Street on 23 February 1820 as they prepared to set out on their mission to destroy the cabinet. One of their number turned King's evidence so the government did not have to use Edwards as a witness and risk the jury again refusing to convict. Thistlewood, Davidson and three others were found guilty and executed in May; five others changed their pleas to guilty and were transported. What had become an increasingly marginal activity, involving neither the mainstream radicals who followed Hunt nor the orthodox Spenceans who followed Thomas Evans, finally appeared to have been put to rest.[109]

What did stir the people of the capital was not republican revolution, but the cause of Caroline whom George IV and his ministers wished to exclude from her position as Queen. The riotous demonstrations that accompanied the attempt to carry a Bill of Pains and Penalties through Parliament brought to the capital scenes which in Manchester or Glasgow would have been called revolutionary – and which in Paris would probably have *been* revolutionary. There was some repetition of these events the following August at Caroline's funeral and there the matter ended – with a few broken windows – but the ministry survived. And yet, of all the anti-government demonstrations of this period, this was the only one to be supported by a section of the propertied classes and indeed leadership from the Whig opposition, daring to do in the name of royalty what it may have wished to do (but dared not) in the name of peace in 1797. The disturbances were greater than any London had seen since the Gordon Riots of 1780. Thistlewood had missed his opportunity, but he was dead and other key radical leaders were safely in gaol.[110]

Thistlewood's belief in the possibility of simultaneous meetings was not wholly misplaced. Lord Sidmouth was aware in early March that 'an expectation prevailed among the disaffected in the northern parts of the Kingdom that an important blow would be struck in London, previous to the expiration of the month of February'.[111] But Lancashire was weakened by divisions between the Huntite majority and the conspiratorial minority followed by the arrest of key figures on 22 December, and only Yorkshire and Scotland actually rose in the early spring of 1820. One link between these places was James Brayshaw of Leeds, a Paineite republican and Freethinking Christian, who proposed a motion (which was carried) in favour of arming at a meeting in Leeds to protest at the Six Acts in December 1819. He later blamed the attempted rising in Yorkshire on James Mann, another

CITY COLLEGE LEARNING RESOURCE CENTRE

Leeds radical and supporter of Hunt who had been one of those arrested at Thornhill Lees in 1817.[112] Brayshaw was also active in the west of Scotland, having visited the area in 1819 to spread radical union societies such as those formed in the Manchester area in 1818. He was there again in March 1820, visiting Strathaven, Paisley and Parkhead where he stayed with James Wilson, an old radical and noted extremist whose involvement with the reform movement went back to the Friends of the People in 1792. It was here that Brayshaw probably helped draft an Address which was pasted up in Glasgow on 1 April to signal the start of the Scottish insurrection.

The background to this series of alarming and violent events was widespread depression and hardship among the weavers of Lanarkshire, Renfrewshire, Dunbartonshire, Stirlingshire and Ayrshire, but this was politicised through the union societies and led to organised protest meetings following Peterloo. Paisley was particularly disturbed and there was serious rioting between 11 and 18 September, with gun shops looted and property attacked. Mass meetings continued throughout the autumn, amid rumours of arming and preparations for a rising. As a precaution, the yeomanry paraded in Glasgow on 13 December, Thistlewood's first date for simultaneous meetings. Three hundred armed men who had marched into Kilsyth on their way to Glasgow disbanded and went home on learning that Glasgow was quiet. Charles Hope, Lord President of the Court of Session, wrote to Lord Melville on 17 December that, 'the people are rife for rebellion as ever, and only in sullen and sultry silence waiting for a more convenient opportunity'.[113] The unrest appears to have been co-ordinated by a shadowy Committee for Organising a Provisional Government comprising twenty-eight men, one of whom, John King, may have been a spy. On 22 February, the night before the Cato Street arrests, this entire committee was arrested. The effect was to spur on a determined minority. Historians are divided over whether or not the events which followed were encouraged by spies who, like Edwards in London, were officially or otherwise determined to flush the conspirators out by leading them to their own destruction.[114]

On the night of 1 April, the Address prepared by Wilson, Brayshaw and others was pasted up on the streets across the industrial districts of western Scotland so that on the morning of Sunday, 2 April crowds of weavers, spinners and other workers could read the call for a general strike and threats of armed resistance. The army, yeomanry and police were put on the ready and prayers were offered for deliverance from civil war. The strike was remarkably solid in the Glasgow area, through a combination of persuasion and intimidation, but it lasted less than a week. The threatened uprising was less coherent and lasted scarcely longer.

On the night of 4/5 April a small contingent of thirty-five men, led by John Baird and Andrew Hardie, set out to collect weapons from striking workers at the Carron ironworks. They were caught by the cavalry on the moor near Bonnybridge, where they stood their ground and fought, but the 'Battle of Bonnymuir' was an unequal contest. Eighteen prisoners, some of them wounded, were taken, including Baird and Hardie. The following night there was to have been an attack on Glasgow, but only James Wilson's contingent of about twenty-five armed men from Strathaven rose and they melted away when they realised that no one else was marching on Glasgow. Further arrests followed, and weapons and ammunition were seized as the authorities sought to dismantle the disillusioned and defeated remnants of the revolutionary movement, but still sporadic unrest continued into the summer. In all, eighty-eight people were charged, of whom all but thirty fled or went into hiding. They were outlawed. Of the remainder, two were acquitted and twenty-four were sentenced to death. The death penalty, however, was carried out only in the cases of Wilson, Baird and Hardie. The others were transported. In 1835, a young Scot called Peter Mackenzie wrote a book in which he claimed that the spy, Alexander Richmond, was behind the events of 1820. Richmond sued for libel and lost. Though the evidence was by no means certain, the government then granted an absolute pardon to those it had outlawed and exiled in 1820. Historians still differ over how large a part was played in the rising by spies, but the persistent unrest and numbers of weapons subsequently recovered would suggest that, if spies and *agents provocateurs* were involved, they did no more than bring into the open a genuine and widespread conspiracy to levy war against the King.[115]

Coincidences of date suggests that the Scottish insurrection was not conceived in isolation from events in England. Indeed the *Leeds Mercury* believed that the fall of Huddersfield was to have been the signal for a simultaneous rising 'throughout all the manufacturing districts in the Kingdom, extending even to Scotland'.[116] On the night before the Address was placarded in Scotland, the men of

57

Huddersfield, whose Luddism had been at the heart of similar unrest in 1812 and who had also responded in 1817, were rumoured to be ready once more to answer the call. Contingents from the Calder and Spen Valleys were to assemble at the old Luddite meeting place where the River Colne joined the Calder and then march on Huddersfield. The magistrates sat up all night in the principal hotel overlooking the market place, surrounded by infantry and cavalry. When a beacon on Castle Hill outside the town gave the signal, only about two hundred insurgents had gathered, so they quickly abandoned their attempt, agreeing to reconvene on 11 April at Grange Moor where an earlier generation of rebels had gathered in 1801.[117] The Grange Moor plan, conceived in Barnsley, was betrayed to the magistrates and when the Barnsley contingent of about three hundred arrived on Grange Moor, instead of a force of some three thousand like-minded men from Huddersfield, Leeds, Wakefield and Sheffield, the moor was deserted. The insurgents ran for their lives, even before a detachment of yeomanry and dragoons arrived from Huddersfield.[118] In Sheffield, John Blackwell's simultaneous attempt to storm the barracks and seize weapons came to nothing when his followers decided to postpone the event. Blackwell was arrested next day. In all, twenty men were charged with high treason and others with lesser offences. Those found guilty were transported.[119]

## Conclusion

There seems little doubt that revolutionary conspiracies did exist in Britain at various times in the thirty years following the revolution in France. More contentious is the interpretation given to these events: their scale and significance. Where outbursts occurred, these were generally small, involving a few hundred men at most, usually poorly armed and badly led. The nature of the government's reaction, however, suggests a greater threat to public order than actually materialised. Were they just being cautious? Did their sources of information mislead them? Did the government's over-reaction cause them to drive legitimate reformers into the arms of the subversive minority, thus strengthening the latter and giving them credibility? Or were ministers rather better informed than sceptical historians have sometimes liked to think?

Much of the evidence is circumstantial. The individual historian must use judgement to interpret the evidence offered by reports from spies or statements given by witnesses in court who had turned King's evidence to save their own skins – two of the principal sources for what was going on. Taken as a series of isolated incidents, the case for a sustained revolutionary impulse is not strong, but it is easier to accept the general drift of the evidence, however weak, suspect and implausible some of it might be, than to believe that all we are examining in these years is no more than a series of coincidences.

The continuities are striking but not surprising. With a limited number of obvious meeting places to choose from, their frequent use might be expected. The same could be said of people. If the source of unrest lay in prevailing industrial conditions, then the same areas and the same sorts of people might be expected to respond in similar ways at similar points in the economic cycle, and the same individual names might emerge from a limited pool of local leadership. Does all this amount to anything more sinister than the obvious?

Edward Thompson set the terms of the historical debate in *The Making of the English Working Class*, beginning his argument in chapter 14, 'An Army of Redressers', with the assertion that 'Between Despard and Brandreth there stretches the illegal tradition. It is a tradition which will never be rescued from its obscurity.'[120] The memory of such a tradition was recorded in the late nineteenth-century journalism of Frank Peel's *The Risings of the Luddites, Chartists and Plug-Drawers* (1880), which contained family and community memories and values handed down not only from the 1790s to the 1820s but beyond to Chartism. This tradition linking Despard to Brandreth was described by Thompson as an 'underground' tradition, implying perhaps the deliberate and concealed tunnelling of the miner or mole.[121] My preference is for the less precise 'underworld' used by McCalman: an environment in which all kinds of subversive cultures could knock against one another and thrive, generating from time to time surges of rebellious energy which drew upon ideas and personalities nurtured in the warmth of village ale houses, city taverns and artisan workshops.

The story of the whole makes greater sense than the sum of the parts. When John Blackwell led his attack on the local militia armoury in Sheffield on 14 April 1812 he might have been expressing his anger at the price of bread that year, though if so he would have done better to attack a bakery. Certainly, he was to be found leading a food riot demanding 'Bread or Blood' on 3 December 1816, the day that news of the Spa Fields riot would have reached Sheffield. But the suspicion that Blackwell was not just a food rioter is increased when we then find him attempting to attack the barracks in Sheffield on 11 April 1820, the day appointed for the Grange Moor rising.[122] Perhaps he was just an eccentric troublemaker, but if so he was not the only one. The arrest of William Wolstenholme on 29 May 1817, a delegate at a secret meeting conspiring to join the insurrection on 10 June, might seem melodramatic had he not earlier boasted of being 'a Despard's man' and been a member of a secret revolutionary committee in Sheffield broken up by the authorities in November 1802.[123] Among incriminating papers found in Yorkshire in 1802 was a declaration of aims also found when Despard was arrested in London the same year, though this may be no coincidence since both took their wording from the United Britons' declaration reported to the House of Commons in 1801.[124] But what are we to make of three Luddite 'twisters in' of 1812, Craven Cookson, Stephen Kitchenman and William Thompson of Barnsley, turning up on Grange Moor in 1820?[125] The 'Jacobins' of 1792 might well have been peaceful parliamentary reformers, but John Baines's later connection with the Luddites suggests that either he had become more radical and incautious with age, the reverse of the usual trajectory, or the divisions between what made a man a reformer or a revolutionary, a politician or an economic protester, were neither hard nor fast. The same point can be made about Thomas Bacon of Pentrich and James Wilson of Strathaven. If these men were prepared to resort to violence in one context, were they far from it in another? Apparently random stitches of evidence may in this way be knitted with a little imagination into a garment of some substance, a revolutionary underworld feeding sporadic outbursts and an ever-present threat demanding sustained vigilance from magistrates and ministers.

### Notes

1   See the debate on Fox's motion to repeal the Test and Corporation Acts, *Cobbett's Parliamentary History*, House of Commons, 2 March 1790, cols. 432–3.
2   T. Paine, *Rights of Man*, part 2 [1792], chapter 5, second paragraph. Repeatedly quoted in the early nineteenth century, the full quotation reads, 'For a nation

to love liberty, it is sufficient that she knows it; and to be free, it is sufficient that she wills it': see the running title caption for the *Chartist Circular* (28 September 1839–2 July 1842).

3  Goodwin, *Friends of Liberty*, pp. 138–58.

4  *Annual Register* (1794), History of Europe, p. 266.

5  C. Emsley, 'The London "Insurrection" of December 1792: Fact, Fiction, or Fantasy?', *Journal of British Studies*, 17:2 (Spring 1978), pp. 66–86.

6  For the history of the concept of the Convention in this period, see T M. Parssinen, 'Association, convention and anti-parliament in British radical politics, 1771–1848', *English Historical Review*, 88:3 (July 1973), pp. 504–33.

7  For Muir's subsequent escape and remarkable adventures, which confirm that he was a revolutionary then if not before, see P. B. Ellis and S. Mac a' Ghobhainn, *The Scottish Insurrection of 1820* (London, Gollancz, 1970), re-issued (London, Pluto, 1989), pp. 67–9, 79–81, 84.

8  M. Thale (ed.), *Selections from the papers of the London Corresponding Society, 1792–1799* (Cambridge, Cambridge University Press, 1983) (hereafter *LCS*), pp. 135–41 (Report from spy Groves, 14 April 1794; spy Gosling's 'Information', 11, 15 April 1794; Report from spy Taylor, 15 April 1794).

9  A. Wharam, *The Treason Trials, 1794* (Leicester, Leicester University Press, 1992).

10  'Second Report from the Committee of Secrecy of the House of Commons respecting seditious practices', *Cobbett's Parliamentary History*, House of Commons, 6 June 1794, cols. 696–8. See also Goodwin, *Friends of Liberty*, pp. 334–7.

11  *Trial of Thomas Hardy for High Treason*, pp. 62–3 in J. Bell, *Bell's Reports of the State Trials for High Treason* (London, Bell, 1794); Wharam, *Treason Trials*, pp. 95–100; H. W. Meikle, *Scotland and the French Revolution* (Edinburgh, Maclehose, 1912), reprinted (New York, Augustus Kelley, 1969), pp. 150–3.

12  C. Emsley, 'The home office and its sources of information and investigation, 1791–1801', p. 551 in *English Historical Review*, 94:3 (July 1979), pp. 532–61.

13  Thale (ed.), *LCS*, p. 83 (LCS General Committee, 19 September 1793); p. 91 (note on government paraphrase of report from spy Lynam, 5 November 1793); p. 131 (note on summary of Report from spy Nodder, 7 April 1794); pp. 155–7 and 165–8 (spy Gosling's 'Information', 9 and 16–17 May 1794).

14  Quoted in Stevenson, *Popular Disturbances*, pp. 168–9.

15  See the debates on the *Habeas Corpus* Suspension Bill, *Cobbett's Parliamentary History* (1794), House of Commons, 15–17 May 1794, cols. 497–573; on Sheridan's motion for the repeal of the *Habeas Corpus* Suspension Act, ibid. (1795), House of Commons, 5 January 1795, cols. 1062–1130; and on the continuation of the *Habeas Corpus* Suspension Act, ibid., House of Commons, 15–28 January 1795, cols. 1144–93.

16  Ellis and Mac a' Ghobhainn, *Scottish Insurrection*, pp. 58–9, 63, 72.

17  Goodwin, *Friends of Liberty*, pp. 322–4; Elliott, *Partners in Revolution*, pp. 62–7.

18  Berresford and Mac a' Ghobhainn, *Scottish Insurrection*, pp. 72–3.

19  The most complete treatment of Ireland is provided by Elliott, *Partners in Revolution*; see also her 'French Subversion in Britain in the French Revolution' in C Jones (ed.), *Britain and Revolutionary France: Conflict, Subversion and Propaganda*, Exeter Studies in History No. 5 (Exeter, University

of Exeter, 1983), pp. 40–52; and 'Ireland and the French Revolution' in H. T. Dickinson (ed.), *Britain and the French Revolution, 1789–1815* (London, Macmillan, 1989), pp. 83–101. Also, M. Duffy, 'War, revolution and the crisis of the British empire' in M. Philp (ed.), *The French Revolution and British Popular Politics* (Cambridge, Cambridge University Press, 1991), pp. 118–45.

20  Emsley, 'The home office', pp. 551–2.

21  For general background and the difficulties of the ministries during these years, see C Emsley, *British Society and the French Wars, 1793–1815* (London, Macmillan, 1979), pp. 41–98.

22  Goodwin, *Friends of Liberty*, pp. 428–38; Wells, *Insurrection*, pp. 64–130.

23  39 Geo III, cap. 79.

24  This subject is discussed in B. Porter, *Plots and Paranoia: A History of Political Espionage in Britain, 1790–1988* (London, Unwin Hyman, 1989), pp. 24–40; and Hone, *Cause of Truth*, pp. 65–82.

25  Sheridan's speech in the debate on his motion for repeal of the *Habeas Corpus* Suspension Act, *Cobbett's Parliamentary History*, House of Commons, 5 January 1795, col. 1068; see also his speech on the *Habeas Corpus* Suspension Bill, *Cobbett's Parliamentary History*, House of Commons, 17 May 1794, col. 544.

26  Hone, *Cause of Truth*, pp. 65–82; Emsley, 'The home office', pp. 532–65.

27  Hone, *Cause of Truth*, p. 51.

28  The most thorough investigation of the naval mutinies is in Wells, *Insurrection*, pp. 79–109; see also Goodwin, *Friends of Liberty*, pp. 407–11 and Elliott, *Partners in Revolution*, pp. 134–44.

29  Thale (ed.), *LCS*, pp. 341–9 (Reports from spy Powell, 5, 12, 22 February 1796).

30  Wells, *Insurrection*, pp. 92–8.

31  Thale (ed.), *LCS*, pp. 396–8 (Minutes of General Committee, 25 May 1797); Goodwin, *Friends of Liberty*, p. 437; Elliott, *Partners in Revolution*, pp. 141–2.

32  Wells, *Insurrection*, pp. 93–5.

33  Wells, *Insurrection*, pp. 102–4.

34  D. Keogh (ed.), *A Patriot Priest. The Life of Father James Coigly, 1761–1798* (Cork, Cork University Press, 1998); Wells, *Insurrection*, pp. 121–8; Elliott, *Partners in Revolution*, pp. 174–83.

35  F. Place, *The Autobiography of Francis Place*, ed. M. Thale (Cambridge, Cambridge University Press, 1972), p. 178.

36  'Report of the Committee of Secrecy of the House of Commons relative to the Proceedings of different Persons and Societies in Great Britain and Ireland Ingaged in a Treasonable Conspiracy', *Cobbett's Parliamentary History*, House of Commons, 15 March 1799, col. 600.

37  'Report of the Committee of Secrecy', *Cobbett's Parliamentary History*, cols. 602–4.

38  Goodwin, *Friends of Liberty*, pp. 438–42; Wells, *Insurrection*, pp. 124–5.

39  Thompson, *The Making*, p. 636.

40  Hone, *Cause of Truth*, pp. 61–3; Thale (ed.), *LCS*, p. 426 (Deposition from spy [Powell?], *c.* 15 April 1798); Place, *Autobiography*, p. 180.

41  F. O'Gorman, *The Whig Party and the French Revolution* (London, Macmillan, 1967), p. 235.

42  Hone, *Cause of Truth*, pp. 42–7 and for Burdett's later association with Despard, see pp. 113–14. The quotations are as given by Hone.

43  M. Elliott,'The "Despard Conspiracy" reconsidered', *Past & Present*, 75 (May 1977), pp. 46–61; Wells, *Insurrection*, pp. 232–37.
44  Wells, *Insurrection*, pp. 237–52; Elliott, *Partners in Revolution*, pp. 285–97; Smith, 'Irish Rebels', pp. 81–3.
45  PRO, PC 1/44A, fo 161, 'R. F.' to Privy Council, 8 August 1799, as quoted in J. Foster, *Class Struggle and the Industrial Revolution* (London, Weidenfeld & Nicholson, 1974), p. 38.
46  Wells, *Insurrection*, pp. 226–37.
47  E. A. Smith, *Whig Principles and Party Politics. Earl Fitzwilliam and the Whig Party, 1748–1833* (Manchester, Manchester University Press, 1975), p. 246.
48  T. D. Whitaker to Lord Sidmouth, 17 September 1808, as quoted in Stevenson, *Popular Disturbances*, p. 231.
49  Dinwiddy, *Radicalism and Reform*, p. 375.
50  PP (1806) 268, *Minutes of Evidence taken before the Committee appointed to consider the State of Woollen Manufacture in England*, pp. 448–9 (6 June 1806).
51  R. Reid, *Land of Lost Content: The Luddite Revolt, 1812* (London, Heinemann, 1986), pp. 46–7.
52  Reid, *Land of Lost Content*, pp. 41–5; Thomis, *Luddites*, pp. 47–65.
53  *Leeds Mercury*, 26 December 1811, as quoted in Reid, *Land of Lost Content*, p. 60.
54  In addition to Reid, Thomis and Dinwiddy, cited above, the most influential and controversial study of Luddism comes in Thompson, *The Making*, pp. 569–659. Useful local studies of Yorkshire Luddism are J. A. Hargreaves, '"A Metropolis of Discontent": Popular Protest in Huddersfield, *c.* 1780–1850', pp. 195–204, in E. A. H. Haigh (ed.), *Huddersfield. A Most Handsome Town: Aspects of the History and Culture of a West Yorkshire Town* (Huddersfield, Kirklees Cultural Services, 1992), pp. 189–220; and A. Brooke and L. Kipling, *Liberty or Death. Radicals, Republicans and Luddites, 1793–1823* (Honley, Workers History Publications, 1993). The enthusiasm of the latter can be offset by the scepticism of B. Bailey, *The Luddite Rebellion* (Stroud, Sutton Publishing, 1998).
55  *Proceedings under the Special Commission at York* (Leeds, Baines, 1813), pp. 70–1.
56  Possibly the same person as, or related to, the Charles Bent employed in 1802. For John Bent, a buyer and seller of waste cotton, see PRO, HO 40/1(8), fos 40–5, Statement of Humphrey Yarwood, 22 June 1812.
57  Dinwiddy, *Radicalism and Reform*, pp. 382–6; Reid, *Land of Lost Content*, p. 201.
58  Sheffield Archives, Wentworth Woodhouse Muniments [hereafter WWM], F45a/12, Copy of Resolutions of the Friends of Liberty, 10 April 1801, for a meeting on Steeton Moor on 20 April 1801, sent to Earl Fitzwilliam by J. R. Busfield, 14 April 1801.
59  R. A. Church and S. D. Chapman, 'Gravener Henson and the Making of the English Working Class', pp. 137–45 in E. L. Jones and G. E. Mingay (eds), *Land, Labour and Population in the Industrial Revolution* (London, Arnold, 1967), pp. 131–61.
60  Reid, *Land of Lost Content*, pp. 211–12, 252–5.
61  PRO, HO 40/1(7), fo 18, copy of a letter sent to Mr Smith, a Huddersfield master, 1812.
62  Thomis, *Luddites*, p. 91.
63  Dinwiddy, *Radicalism and Reform*, pp. 378–9.

64  Dinwiddy, *Radicalism and Reform*, p. 386.
65  PRO, HO 42/123, Statements of J. Taylor and T. Whitehead, 7 May 1812, HO 40/1(8), fos 40–5, Statement of H. Yarwood, 22 June 1812; and Deposition of Thomas Wood [August 1812] printed in F. Raynes, *An Appeal to the Public containing an account of service rendered during the disturbances in the north of England in the year 1812* (London, John Richardson and Baldwin, Cradock and Joy, 1817), p. 92, all as quoted in Dinwiddy, *Radicalism and Reform*, pp. 388–9.
66  Dinwiddy, *Radicalism and Reform*, pp. 392–3.
67  WWM, F46/122, Deposition of Thomas Broughton, 26 August 1812.
68  Elliott, *Partners in Revolution*, p. 362.
69  PRO, HO 40/1, fo 224, F. L. Wood to Earl Fitzwilliam, 17 June 1812.
70  Lord Sidmouth to Lord Sheffield, 1 November 1817, as quoted in Stevenson, *Popular Disturbances*, p. 207.
71  Emsley, *British Society*, pp. 11–12, 133.
72  Reid, *Land of Lost Content*, p. 275.
73  D. Bythell, *The Handloom Weavers. A Study in the English Cotton Industry During the Industrial Revolution* (Cambridge, Cambridge University Press, 1969), pp. 99–104; G. Timmins, *The Last Shift: The Decline of Handloom Weaving in Nineteenth-century Lancashire* (Manchester, Manchester University Press, 1993), p. 28.
74  Hone, *Cause of Truth*, p. 197.
75  W. H. Reid, *The Rise and Dissolution of the Infidel Societies in this Metropolis* (London, Hatchard, 1800) was a tract by an ex-radical turned loyalist.
76  McCalman, *Radical Underworld*, pp. 19–20.
77  McCalman, *Radical Underworld*, pp. 7–25.
78  McCalman, *Radical Underworld*, p. 49.
79  R. Darnton, 'High Enlightenment and the low life of literature in pre-revolutionary France', *Past & Present*, 51 (May 1971), pp. 81–115.
80  McCalman, *Radical Underworld*, p. 49; see also Hone, *Cause of Truth*, pp. 223–37.
81  McCalman, *Radical Underworld*, pp. 50–72, 124–39; D. Worrall, *Radical Culture: Discourse, Resistance and Surveillance, 1790–1820* (Hemel Hempstead, Harvester Wheatsheaf, 1992), pp. 165–200. For millenarianism in general, see J. F. C. Harrison, *The Second Coming: Popular Millenarianism, 1780–1850* (London, Routledge & Kegan Paul, 1979) and C. Garrett, *Respectable Folly: Millenarians and the French Revolution in France and England* (Baltimore, Johns Hopkins University Press, 1975).
82  T. M. Parssinen, 'The Revolutionary Party in London, 1816–20', *Bulletin of the Institute of Historical Research*, 45:111 (May 1972), pp. 266–82.
83  For Hunt's relationship with the Spenceans, see Belchem, *'Orator' Hunt*, pp. 54–70.
84  Belchem, *'Orator' Hunt*, pp. 58–70; Hone, *Cause of Truth*, pp. 263–6.
85  Smith, *Whig Principles*, pp. 334, 336; Hone, *Cause of Truth*, p. 265.
86  S .Bamford, *Passages in the Life of a Radical* [1844], ed. W. H. Chaloner (London, Cass, 1967), chapters 2–7, 12–13, and 26. See also Thompson, *The Making*, pp. 713–26.
87  Bamford, *Passages*, p. 15.
88  Bamford, *Passages*, p. 31.
89  Thompson, *The Making*, pp. 714–15.

90  Bamford, *Passages*, p. 42.
91  Bamford, *Passages*, p. 44.
92  Bamford, *Passages*, p. 156.
93  WWM, F45/177, Deposition of John Dickinson, linen draper of Dewsbury, sworn before J. P. Heywood, 16 June 1817.
94  Thompson, *The Making*, p. 717, following Cobbett's Petition to the House of Commons and the Deposition he obtained from William Stevens in America, both printed in *Cobbett's Weekly Political Register*, 33:18 (16 May 1818), cols. 539–64.
95  Bamford, *Passages*, pp. 155–8.
96  The fullest account of the Pentrich rising is J. Stevens, *England's Last Revolution: Pentrich, 1817* (Buxton, Moorland Publishing Co., 1977).
97  WWM, F45/189–91, Information and Examination of John Buckley, sworn before Benjamin Haigh Allen, 18 July 1817.
98  Hargreaves, 'Metropolis of Discontent', p. 205.
99  Stevens, *England's Last Revolution*, pp. 11–108; and map on pp. 26–7.
100  Stevens, *England's Last Revolution*, p. 103; F. Peel, *The Risings of the Luddites, Chartists and Plug-Drawers*, 4th edition [text of 3rd edition of 1895, with a new introduction by Edward Thompson] (London, Cass, 1968), p. 285.
101  Prothero, *Artisans and Politics*, pp. 91–2.
102  McCalman, *Radical Underworld*, pp. 132–3.
103  Belchem, *'Orator' Hunt*, p. 57.
104  The best account is D Read, *Peterloo: The 'Massacre' and its Background* (Manchester, Manchester University Press, 1958).
105  The text of both letters is given in J. Macdonnell (ed.), *Reports of State Trials, new series vol. 1, 1820–1823* (London, HMSO, 1888), Appendix B, cols. 1372–3.
106  Letter from John Gale Jones, *Republican*, 6:5 (28 June 1822), p. 138. Emphasis in original.
107  Trials of John Knowles, James Morris, George Dewhurst and others at Lancaster Assizes, 1820, in Macdonnell (ed), *State Trials*, cols. 497–608.
108  PRO, HO 42/197, fo 384, 11 October 1819, as quoted in Worrall, *Radical Culture*, p. 170. Emphasis in original. Cashman had been executed for his part in the Spa Fields riots in 1816.
109  Worrall, *Radical Culture*, pp. 178–200; Prothero, *Artisans*, pp. 116–31.
110  Prothero, *Artisans*, pp. 132–55; J. Stevenson, 'The Queen Caroline Affair' in J. Stevenson (ed.), *London in the Age of Reform* (Oxford, Blackwell, 1977), pp. 117–48. See also his *Popular Disturbances*, (London, Longman, 1979), pp. 199–203. For a summary of the significance of the affair, see R. McWilliam, *Popular Politics*, pp. 7–13.
111  Devon CRO, Sidmouth Papers, Sidmouth to B. Bloomfield, 3–4 March 1820, as quoted in Stevenson, *Popular Disturbances*, p. 198.
112  Belchem, *'Orator' Hunt*, pp. 130, 155; Thompson, *The Making*, p. 725.
113  National Library of Scotland, MS 10, Melville Papers, Charles Hope to Lord Melville, 17 December 1819, as quoted in Ellis and Mac a' Ghobhainn, *Scottish Insurrection*, p. 131.
114  Ellis and Mac a' Ghobhainn, *Scottish Insurrection*, pp. 34–5, 140–1. For a different reading of the evidence, see Thomis and Holt, *Threats of Revolution*, pp. 62–84.

115 Ellis and Mac a'Ghobhainn argue persuasively from a range of primary sources but their lack of detailed footnotes makes it hard to check their interpretation which is imaginative and highly emotive; Thomis and Holt (*Threats of Revolution*, p. 79) are hightly critical, commenting that circumstantial evidence offers 'some slight support to the view advanced at the time and later that the Scottish rebels, like their English predecessors of 1817, were the victims of *agents provocateurs*', but adding, 'The documentary evidence does not support this view; nor do the known facts support the latest extravagant version of the *provocateur* thesis, that the rebels were Scottish nationalists who were led into a trap by the machinations of the Westminster government and its agents.'

116 *Leeds Mercury*, 8 April 1820

117 *Leeds Mercury*, 8 April 1820; *Manchester Observer*, 8 April 1820, drawing on *Leeds Intelligencer* account; Brooke and Kipling, *Liberty or Death*, pp. 75–90; Thompson, *The Making*, p. 776; Hargreaves, 'Metropolis of Discontent', p. 206; Peel, *Risings of the Luddites*, pp. 307–8.

118 *Leeds Mercury*, 15 April 1820; *Manchester Observer*, 15 April 1820; Thompson, *The Making*, pp. 776–7; Hargreaves, 'Metropolis of Discontent', p. 206; Peel, *Risings of the Luddites*, pp. 308–12; F. J. Kaijage, 'Working-class Radicalism in Barnsley, 1816–1820', pp. 122–3 in S. Pollard and C. Holmes (eds), *Essays in the Economic and Social History of South Yorkshire* (Sheffield, South Yorkshire County Council, 1976), pp. 118–34.

119 F. K. Donnelly and J. L. Baxter, 'Sheffield and the English Revolutionary Tradition', pp. 108–9, in Pollard and Holmes (eds), *Essays*, pp. 90–117.

120 Thompson, *The Making*, p. 515.

121 Thompson, *The Making*, p. 923; see also A. W. Smith, 'Irish Rebels', pp. 78–85.

122 Donnelly and Baxter, 'Sheffield', pp. 99, 107

123 Donnelly and Baxter, 'Sheffield', pp. 100–10.

124 J. R. Dinwiddy, 'The "Black Lamp" in Yorkshire, 1801–1802', *Past & Present*, 64 (August 1974), pp. 119–20.

125 Dinwiddy, *Radicalism and Reform*, p. 393. Peel was to claim that it was Cookson and Kitchen[man] who betrayed the Grange Moor rising in 1820: *The Risings of the Luddites*, pp. 311–12.

# Revolution or reform, 1830–32

CITY COLLEGE
LEARNING RESOURCE CENTRE

Between 1830 and 1832 Britain underwent major constitutional change during a period of economic hardship, with unrest in both agricultural and industrial areas. At the same time, a new series of revolutions on the Continent reminded politicians of the impermanence of political regimes, as the Restoration settlement of 1814–15 was torn up first in Paris and then in Brussels. The July 1830 revolution in Paris was a clear warning of what might happen when an intransigent and reactionary government was faced with a strengthened opposition party, supported by popular pressure on the streets fuelled by economic discontents.

In Britain, where the Duke of Wellington's Tory ministry had been weakened by the secession of the ultra-Tories after Catholic Emancipation, George IV died on 26 June. The change of monarch necessitated a general election, in the middle of which came news of the revolution in France on 29 July. A month later, the first threshing machine was destroyed in what was to become known as the 'Swing' riots. The Duke refused to contemplate reform, leading the Whigs to compel his resignation on 16 November and to introduce their reform proposals, thus precipitating a political crisis which was not resolved until June 1832. By this time, not only had large parts of the south and east of England been engulfed by riots, but Merthyr Tydfil, in south Wales, had fallen to an insurrection which lasted three days; Bristol had suffered major destruction of property; Nottingham castle had been burnt down; middle-class political unions had prepared to form their own National Guard, and working-class political unions had again talked of arming and revolution. During May 1832 there had seemed a genuine possibility that, had Wellington played a Polignac and formed a ministry to serve a reactionary king, then William IV might have suffered the fate of Charles X and the last of the Bourbons would have been followed by the last of the Hanoverians.

## The Reform Bill crisis

There was a variety of possible approaches to constitutional change in Britain between 1790 and 1850. At one extreme, revolutionaries demanded a complete renewal of the constitution; at the other were those who wanted Parliament merely to be reformed so that certain specific social and economic measures could be carried to remedy the grievances of the people; and in the middle were those who wished to maintain the existing framework of the constitution but with a franchise widened to recognise the political rights of all (males) who paid taxes. The most common position was based on a combination of the second and third positions, extending parliamentary representation as a right but linking it to the need to remedy specific grievances. On two occasions, however, a fundamental change was made to the constitution, and in each case the reason was Ireland.

The first was the 1801 Act of Union between Britain and Ireland, carried as a result of government policy and not by popular demand. The second was the 1829 Catholic Relief Act (usually called Catholic Emancipation) which admitted Catholics to the Union Parliament at Westminster and finally broke the link between Protestantism and the British state. This latter was not achieved without a struggle and resulted from the re-organisation of Irish popular politics in the 1820s by Daniel O'Connell. Although he abandoned the methods of the United Irishmen, his Catholic Association of 1823 was nevertheless revolutionary in intent. Its combination of a formidable, nation-wide organisation and the support given to it by a peasantry notorious for their propensity to civil disorder and rural terrorism, led the government to ban the Association by name in 1825. By the simple device of renaming it the New Catholic Association, O'Connell continued.

Matters were brought to a head in 1828, when he was elected to Westminster at a by-election in County Clare. The Duke of Wellington's government gave way and carried the Catholic Relief Act, using all the 'corrupt' devices known to unreformed ministers to force their will on a reluctant House of Commons. Robert Peel later explained his change of approach: whereas formerly he had 'much doubted whether the removal of the disabilities complained of would restore tranquillity to Ireland', in 1828 there were 'circumstances which the time is not yet come to disclose, which convinced me there would be more danger in continuing to resist these claims than in yielding to them'.[1] By this he appears to have meant that he had information of a real threat of major disorder in Ireland if the government continued to resist. Two conclusions were apparent from O'Connell's success. One, reached by outraged Tory Protestants, was that the House of Commons needed reforming to make it more representative of British Protestant opinion. The other, reached by parliamentary reformers, was that a peaceful, organised mass movement, backed by the unspoken threat of force by numbers, could compel a hostile Parliament to concede fundamental constitutional change. O'Connell went on to inspire the formation of the Birmingham Political Union (BPU) at the end of 1829 and to be associated with the beginning of the movement for the People's Charter in 1837.[2]

O'Connell's peaceful revolution not only destroyed the remnants of the Protestant Constitution: it split the Tory party which had formed the core of administrations since the French Revolution, it made reform an election issue, and it gave the Whigs the chance to take the initiative and introduce reform. The years 1830–32 therefore provided a unusual opportunity for change. The movement for reform in the country was, for once, campaigning *for* the implementation of government policy, not against it.

Earl Grey's first Whig ministry, which introduced the first Reform Bill in March 1831, was a minority government supported by disillusioned Tories. Although the terms of the Bill fell far short of the universal manhood suffrage demanded by the extremists, its proposals for the abolition of many rotten and nomination boroughs, and transfer of seats to new boroughs as well as subdivided counties, went further than many of the propertied classes had expected. The Bill passed its second reading by only one vote. Amid mounting tension in the country, Grey asked the King to dissolve Parliament and call a General Election. This was most unusual, but not without precedent – the King had prematurely ended parliaments in 1784, 1806 and 1807 – but for ministers to take the initiative and go to the country seeking support on a single issue – in effect a plebiscite – was revolutionary. Grey received the support he sought and was now able to confront the two unelected parts of the legislature, the Lords and the King, with the will of 'the people'. So long as the government remained in control of the situation, the revolution from above was likely to proceed peacefully; but, in relying on public support to rally wavering supporters and put pressure on the Lords and King to acquiesce, Grey knew he was riding the back of a tiger.

Twice his opponents threatened to push him off. In October 1831, the House of Lords rejected the Reform Bill by 41 votes; and in May 1832 the King refused Grey's request to create a Whig majority in the House of Lords and so the government resigned. The King then called on the Duke of Wellington to form an administration. In the event, Wellington failed to form an administration and instead persuaded opponents of the Bill in the Lords to abstain. Parliament was thus peacefully reformed. The property base of the House of Commons was extended without altering the overall balance of power or yielding anything of substance to those who wanted fundamental constitutional change. The Whig version of history, whereby revolutions were to be directed peacefully by themselves from above, was confirmed; only, they no longer spoke of revolution but simply of Reform.

## Political unions and urban riots

The Whig view of the Constitution was aristocratic. That is, it identified the Lords as occupying the sensible middle ground between the dangers of democracy (the Commons) and autocracy (the King). Whig aristocrats were the safest and surest means of providing enlightened government for the benefit of all. But from the later eighteenth century an alternative view was growing which identified the middle ground as that existing between the old landed and political classes represented in Parliament on the one hand, and the propertyless majority on the other.[3] This new middle 'class' was quite narrowly defined although it claimed to lead and speak for the whole 'people'. It was urban and drew on the commercial and manufacturing classes whom David Ricardo (1772–1823), the political economist, identified as those deriving their incomes from profits in his threefold division of society into rent, profit and wages – landlords, capitalists and workers – but it did not necessarily include lesser middle men such as shopkeepers and small employing artisans whose politics were often 'working class'.

This political – and, to a lesser extent, economic – middle can be called a middle class provided this phrase is not confused with the *bourgeoisie* of later Marxist theory. It thought of itself in economic terms as leading the industrious classes: that is, all who worked and added to the country's wealth as opposed to the idle rich, whose rentals were the first charge on their profits (which excused low wages), and whose political places and pensions were funded by the taxes paid by the honest and industrious. Occupying the moral high ground between aristocratic vice and vulgar licence, this middle class led the popular demand for reform of the political system in 1830–32. Though some who spoke with the more democratic voice of the people did not share the middle class's image of itself, only when the 1832 Reform Act had drawn a line through the reformers, including the 'middle class' among those directly represented in Parliament and excluding the rest, did democratic leaders finally create a separate political movement among those with little or no property, and appropriate to themselves the phrase 'working classes' now that the 'middle classes' had joined the exploiting rich. Though it is easy with such language still in the process of formation to slip into the parallel socialist language which has since dominated the writings of historians, it is important to remember that in the early nineteenth century this language of class was primarily political, employed for propagandist purposes to persuade reformers to support a moderate 'middle class' or extremist 'working class' stance, irrespective of actual economic class.

The first political unions were middle-class affairs, set up in the major and largely unrepresented urban centres of Britain to demand an extension of the franchise and separate representation for urban interests. Political unions in Birmingham, Leeds, Manchester, Newcastle upon Tyne and London took the lead in articulating public opinion through the local press and mass meetings to put pressure on the government to persist with its programme of reform. Their image and strategy demanded they speak on behalf of the whole outraged community. In Birmingham, where the first union was founded in December 1829, it was a 'Political Union for the Protection of Public Rights' – a 'General Political Union between the Lower and the Middle Classes of the People'.[4] In London, the National Political Union was not 'a Union of the Working Classes, nor of the Middle Classes, nor of any other Class, but of all Reformers, of the masses and of the millions. The *National Political Union*, is essentially a Union of the People.'[5]

This degree of co-operation across such a wide political and social spectrum proved hard to maintain and, during 1831, rival democratic unions were formed in some cities, notably the National Union of the Working Classes (NUWC) in London, which explicitly rejected the middle class view of itself and reform. As Philip Brown pointed out, these democratic unions were able to draw on a tradition of political thought and organisation reaching back to the French Revolution and, as then, they presented the greatest potential threat of revolution in that their demands went beyond anything Whig ministers were prepared to contemplate.[6] But to judge by their ambiguous language and actions, the middle-class unions could also be seen as a threat in 1831–32.

The reaction to the impending defeat of the first Reform Bill in March 1831 was a sign of what was to come. The *Annual Register* voiced the concerns of the conservative classes and captured the mood of impending revolution:

> Everywhere, the political unions boasted of the numbers whom they could bring into the field. The chairman of that of Birmingham openly declared, that they could supply two armies, each of them as numerous and brave as that which had conquered at Waterloo, if the king and his ministers should require them in the contest with the boroughmongers – under which appellation were comprehended all who differed from them in opinion.

The paper went on to ask, with some rhetorical sarcasm, 'In what ways were the armies to support ministers against an anticipated vote of the House of Commons?' and then answered itself in language drawing on the Cromwellian nightmare of the seventeenth century to which conservatives usually appealed in such circumstances. In fact, as the *Register* admitted, the real reason for the talk of armies was to force opponents into making a concession to reform.[7]

By going to the country to increase his majority in the House of Commons, Grey defused the situation.

The reality of the violence became apparent in October, when Grey's Second Bill was rejected by the House of Lords. Even though the leaders of the political unions drew back from carrying out their threats, the popular mood was less easily contained. The Lords had rejected the Bill by 41 votes and it was quickly noticed that 21 bishops had voted against the measure and only 2 for it. The bishops had, in effect, determined the fate of the Bill. The anger of the mobs was turned against known opponents of Reform, especially bishops.

Demonstrations were held in London during which the windows of the houses of prominent opponents of the Bill were broken, and the Dukes of Cumberland and Wellington, and the Marquis of Londonderry were assaulted in the street. In Derby, the mob released prisoners from the gaol and had to be quelled by the army after two days of disturbances. While the cavalry was in Derby, in Nottingham another mob broke into the Castle, home of the Duke of Newcastle, and burnt it to the ground. In the House of Commons, Sir Charles Wetherall, Recorder of Bristol, used these incidents to mount a Tory attack on Lord John Russell and the government. Wetherall's arrival in Bristol on 29 October then became the signal for a worse outbreak of rioting. The Mansion House (including its wine cellar) was sacked and the troops failed to contain the mob who rioted unrestrained for three days: the Mansion House, Excise Office, Customs House, 4 toll houses and 3 prisons were destroyed, along with the Bishop's palace and 42 houses and warehouses. Parts of Queen's Square were reduced to ruins. The casualty list was greater than at Peterloo.

The exact number is unknown but a conservative estimate was 12 people killed and nearly 100 injured, although the latter figure could have been up to 400; 180 individuals were committed for their part in the riot and 50 were charged with the capital offences of rioting and burning, of whom 5 were eventually executed. It was the worst urban disorder since the Gordon Riots of 1780.[8]

This extensive rioting did not constitute a revolution but it was the sort of behaviour out of which revolutions could be made. More ominous was what was happening in Birmingham. Peace, law and order were the watchwords of the Political Union but there was a growing movement in the wake of the Bristol riots for the formation of a French-style National Guard to secure property, which would in effect be a private army of citizens under the control not of the magistrates but the Political Union. Although no one was to be armed by the Union there was nothing to prevent individuals from arming themselves in self-defence. The Duke of Wellington was convinced that this was a proposal for an armed association comparable to that of the United Irishmen, and the government persuaded Thomas Attwood to drop the plan.[9] At the same time a Royal Proclamation was issued against political unions adopting a military-style organisation.[10] Whether this proposal was ever seriously intended has been questioned by Attwood's biographer. The unions needed the Whig ministers as much as the ministers needed the unions in their struggle to carry their Bill. So long as Grey remained in charge at Westminster, peace, law and order were secure.[11]

When Grey's government resigned in May 1832, therefore, the resolve of the political unions was tested as they sought to imply revolution without actually precipitating it. There was widespread talk of withholding taxes, and normally law-abiding newspapers screamed in fury. The *Dispatch* declaimed:

> '*Reform or Revolution*' is the cry of every man who deserves the name of Englishman. The idea of twenty-four millions of free men submitting to a denial of their undoubted rights by less than two hundred beings called Peers, is utterly out of the question. The only wonder is, that the people have so long submitted to the delay of their new Magna Charta. The time has at length arrived when Englishmen are called upon to act – to show their strength – to teach these insolent and ignorant aristocrats that with all their boasted wealth and empty titles, they are but dust in the balance, compared with the mighty energies against which they have dared to array themselves.[12]

The paper was of course, referring only to Tory peers, not to Whigs, and in higher Whig circles Lord Milton, heir to Earl Fitzwilliam, actually began withholding his taxes, later justifying his action with typical Whig logic: '*Illegal* it may have been . . . *unconstitutional* I do not think it was, for it is consistent with the spirit of the constitution that the subject should refuse his taxes when the government acts in such a manner as to forfeit its claim to obedience.'[13]

When men of property could claim that their understanding of the constitution was above the law, and that there was a constitutional right to bear arms in self defence, then revolution might indeed be near at hand.

This is what Francis Place thought. The fear which he appears to have shared with many in the political unions was that if the Duke of Wellington were given a free hand, he would use troops to suppress the reform movement. Under these circumstances liberty would need to be defended as in 1642 and 1688. As a lesser evil to the financial panic and economic ruin which this would bring, Place and his co-conspirators devised a plan of economic action to prevent the Duke forming a government, and on 12 May the London Political Union issued its celebrated placard, 'TO STOP THE DUKE GO FOR GOLD'. Despite Place's recollection that the intention was to avoid revolution, he must have known that a financial crisis would not only affect the propertied classes but also, by causing widespread economic dislocation and unemployment, threaten further civil unrest. This has led some historians to conclude that the reformers were playing a dangerous game of bluff. If so, it appeared to work, for three days later Wellington advised the King to send for Lord Grey and the crisis was soon over.

We shall never be sure whether Place and the others would actually have been prepared to precipitate a financial crisis but it is clear from the way in which Place represented the episode that he regarded the alternative as worse. On Sunday 20 May Place sat down to review the events of the past few days and record his assessment of them:

> The impending mischief has passed over us, thanks to the inlightened [sic] state to which large masses of the people have attained; thanks indeed to their foresight, the steady conduct of their leaders and the unlimited confidence the people felt in themselves, and that which they placed in the men who came forward in the common cause. But for these demonstrations a revolution would have commenced, which would have been the act of the whole people to a greater extent than any which had ever before been accomplished. Now, relieved from all present apprehension, the Sunday was indeed a day of repose, of solid gratulation, and satisfaction to the people generally, in every rank and station.

Place attributed this state of affairs to the 'middle class' who had steered a moderate and sensible course between the extremes of aristocratic reaction and popular licence.[14] He was aware that the latter still remained a threat, as he continued:

> Here let us hope the turmoil will end. We were within a moment of general rebellion, and had it been possible for the Duke of Wellington to have formed an administration, the King and the people would have been at issue, it would have been soon decided, but the mischief to property, especially to the great Landowners and the Fundholders – and personally to immense

CITY COLLEGE LEARNING RESOURCE CENTRE

numbers would have been terrible indeed. . . . Happily the general demonstration of resistance compelled the Duke to withdraw and made it necessary for the king to recal [*sic*] Earl Grey to office, with the assurance of means to carry the Reform Bills unimpaired and unmutilated in their principal clauses. The bold honest discreet men who took the lead during the eleven days from the 7th to the 18th of the month have saved the country.[15]

Whereas Place was always ready to regard the revolutionary threats of others as foolish or empty, he did not see his own involvement in this light. Thus May 1832 was for him the moment when revolution was avoided only by timely concession. Many historians from all points of the political spectrum have come to a similar judgement. Edward Thompson, who was not a historian to trust Francis Place's judgement, wrote: 'In the autumn of 1831 and in the 'days of May' Britain was within an ace of a revolution which, once commenced, might well . . . have prefigured, in its rapid radicalization, the revolutions of 1848 and the Paris Commune.'[16] His reason for this belief lay in the activities of the popular political unions which were gaining ground in 1831 and were prepared to support the middle-class effort, if at all, only as a first step towards a real reform.

So far as the government's perceptions were concerned, the most immediate threat came in London, from the NUWC, founded in April 1831 by radicals schooled in the literature of Paine, Spence, and socialists such as William Thompson and Robert Owen. Some of their speakers, like John Gale Jones, were veterans of the 1790s; others, like William Benbow, had emerged as extreme radicals after 1815. At the heart of their organisation were the publishers and editors of the 'blasphemous and seditious press' which, in response to the reform agitation, had revived in open defiance of the restrictive stamp legislation which had suppressed them at the end of 1819. The most influential of these men was Henry Hetherington whose *Poor Man's Guardian* led the way in the 'war of the unstamped'. These extreme radicals met at various places in London but were identified with the Rotunda, a lecture theatre in Blackfriars where people like Robert Taylor ('the Devil's Chaplain'), Richard Carlile, and John Gale Jones performed for the benefit of their radical audiences, and police informers were sent with their notebooks to gather evidence for possible prosecutions and to keep a watchful eye and ear on what was happening there.

Very early in the crisis, two of the leaders were disposed of when Carlile was sentenced to two years for sedition in January 1831 and Taylor received a similar sentence for blasphemy in July.[17]

Place knew these people well, and appreciated the danger they posed not only to civil order and property but also to his own view of how a successful and peaceful revolution should be conducted. To begin with he did not think much of the organisation of the NUWC, but by late October, he had to admit that

> The influence of the union had become extensive, and was increasing, it was felt, acknowledged and acted upon in many places, especially in the large manufacturing towns, in Bristol and in the southern and south western parts of England.
>
> The resolutions passed at the weekly meetings of the Union in London, and the speeches made at these meetings being regularly published in the *Poor Man's Guardian* induced large numbers of the working people in the country to attribute an importance to the union it did not possess.

With this growth of provincial organisations came a dangerously exaggerated notion of their own strength and their capacity for conducting a serious revolution by physical force:

> The leaders of all these unions, with but a few exceptions had suceeded [sic] in persuading themselves that the time was coming when the whole of the working men would be ready to rise en masse and take the management of their own affairs, i.e. the management of the affairs of the nation into their own hands . . .
>
> There were, at this time, several delegates from Manchester, and some from other places in London. Most of these came to me and I conversed with them. So thoroughly satisfied were these men that in a very few months 'the people would rise and do themselves justice', that when I expressed my doubts, they became irritated, and on being pushed to extremities, they threw aside all disguise and declared their conviction that within a few months there would be a simultaneous rising of the whole working population, and then the proud tyrants who oppressed them and kept them out of their just rights would be taught a lesson, such a lesson as none before had ever been taught. They admitted it was probable that large numbers of their fellows would be slain in the contest which might, and probably would take place. A great many they said might perhaps be *'murdered'*,

but numbers would prevail and then ample revenge would be taken. They talked of the men they would lose as a matter of very small importance, a trifling sacrifice to obtain a great good, they said it would be of no importance to the great body, they would not be missed, and might as well be killed in so righteous a cause, as linger on in a life of privation and misery. I should be convinced by the circumstances which would take place that what they said was true. I need only wait until a commencement was made the result of which was certain.[18]

This was dangerous talk if the men of Manchester and elsewhere really believed it and were then prepared to act on their belief.

The popular or 'low' unions peaked in the late autumn of 1831 at the time of the Nottingham, Bristol and other riots when the middle-class political unions were planning their National Guard. The London leaders proposed a meeting in White Conduit Fields on 7 November to coincide with simultaneous mass meetings across the country. Those attending were advised to take pointed staves with them – for self defence: the memory of Peterloo ran deep, or was a ready excuse. A manual was published on street fighting, entitled *Defensive Instructions for the People. Containing the New and Improved Combination of Arms called Foot Lancers; Miscellaneous Instructions on the subject of Small Arms and Ammunition, Street and House Fighting, and Field Fortification*, by Colonel Francis Macerone. Although this cost five shillings, the *Poor Man's Guardian* obligingly printed extracts in a special number in April 1832.[19] It gave instructions on the use of staves against cavalry.

The White Conduit Fields meeting was postponed, however, after the Home Secretary had threatened to prosecute the organisers, and on 9 November the committee of the NUWC meeting at Benbow's house rejected a motion from one of the Rotunda leaders, George Petrie, to drill the people in military fashion. Nevertheless, police spies continued to inform the Home Office of extreme plans to arm the people and it was this knowledge, taken with the Birmingham plans, which led the government to recall Parliament early on 6 December and to issue the Royal Proclamation against the political unions.

Even so, the 'low' unions were not as easily brought into line as the middle-class unions. In Manchester a series of mass meetings was held between 28 November and 22 January in defiance of the

Proclamation, at which, it was alleged, there was a concerted plan 'to disturb the public peace, and by seditious and inflammatory speeches and otherwise to excite the subjects of our lord the King to insurrection and insubordination, and to subvert and overturn lawful and settled institutions of the realm'. The jury at the subsequent sedition trials disagreed, but did find the leaders guilty on a lesser charge of 'having riotously and tumultuously assembled together to disturb the public peace'.[20] The jury was probably right. There was much heated talk, and the placard summoning a meeting on 26 December had called for a National Convention, for which Benbow repeatedly pressed at meetings of the NUWC, but by December the worst appeared to be over. The peak of independent popular protest had come in the autumn when the middle-class unions held back in the face of popular violence, allowing the government to suppress illegality and proceed with moderate reform. By May 1832, when Place and others were willing to talk of revolution, popular support had been brought firmly into line behind the strategy of the middle class. The protests of the *Poor Man's Guardian* or Henry Hunt about the folly of supporting a Bill which did not give truly radical reform went largely unheeded until too late. The different nature of the two revolutionary peaks, and their failure to synchronise, considerable reduced the threat of these years. The undirected violence of October 1831 was alarming but largely negative; the potential for violence in May 1832 was real but never tested.

## The Welsh rising, 1831

English concerns with the prospect of revolution in October 1831 and May 1832 should not obscure the fact that one major insurrection did occur, far more serious than the Bristol riots. Yet it resulted in no state trials for treason and of the twenty-eight people charged, most were only for riot. Five capital sentences were passed but only one man, Richard Lewis (*alias* Dic Penderyn) was hanged. In the raw, half-formed society of the Welsh valleys, Merthyr Tydfil was the largest town in Wales, with a population of about 27,000, a quarter of whom were iron workers. It was here that riot passed into insurrection during the summer of 1831.

The industrial workers of South Wales had a long history of

violent protest, partly generated by conditions in the valleys and partly responding to the wider British movement for revolutionary change. During the winter of 1816–17, a paper found in the Tredegar ironworks urged

> The Poor Workmen of Tredegar to prepare Yourselves with Musquets Pistols, Pikes, Spears and all kinds of Weapons to join the Nattion and put down like torrent all Kings, Regents, Tyrants, of all description and banish out of the Country, every Traitor to this Common Cause and to Bewry famine and distress in the same grave [sic].[21]

More specific was a paper found near Penydarren, dated 20 December 1816:

> everyone are required as soon as the news arrives of our preparing to take up arms to enforce these just demands, that all will hold themselves in readiness and Procure arms or some other weapons for either defence or annoyance as circumstances may require and to accomplish this you are recommended to observe that the Soldiers are every night dispersed about the Public Houses and in a defensive state so that when the time comes it would be an easy matter to take them and their officers firearms at a stroke and seize their arms, Horses and all, without any bloodshed: and you ought also to take every one of your Masters Prisoners as well.

The grievances were low wages and bad trade. The latter, together with high taxes, was blamed on the government. Thus economic conditions prompted political protest,

> so join hand and heart to overthrow tyranny and oppression and be a people at once free and happy therefore shout out with one voice down with all tyrants and oppressors and woe be to all that will take their parts [sic].[22]

So the mood which created the insurgencies at Spa Fields, Folly Hall and Pentrich had its counterpart in South Wales.

In the great south Wales strike of 1816, the most resolute resistance was shown in the east of the region, in Brecknockshire and Monmouthshire, and it was here that a particularly violent movement known as the 'Scotch Cattle' developed among ironworkers and colliers during the next few years. Though there were many subdivisions of workmen, the main social cleavage ran between a small middle class and a much larger working class distinguished by language and religion as well as manual labour. The Scotch Cattle was an illegal organisation which operated in a similar manner to the Luddites, beginning with threatening letters to intimidate employers, blacklegs and strike-breakers, and following up with damage to the property of those who were judged to have offended. The men's purpose was industrial, obtaining by terror what they lacked the industrial strength to achieve.[23]

Though few direct links can be suggested between the industrial violence associated with the Scotch Cattle and the reform movement of the early 1830s, the violent background of the Scotch Cattle helps explain the turbulent politics of the valleys throughout the 1830s. Following the defeat of the first Reform Bill in March 1831 there was rioting in several parts of Wales, notably in Carmarthen where there was sporadic unrest throughout May with a resurgence of violence in October,[24] but it was in Merthyr that the most alarming events occurred. Here on 9 and 10 May 1831, a pro-reform mob attacked the courtroom and then forced the release of prisoners. This gave the rioters confidence to go further. They took over a Reform meeting on 30 May in order to voice their local, mainly economic grievances, and then, amid increasing violence, shops were attacked in an attempt to secure the return of goods seized in settlement of debts. On Thursday 2 June the Riot Act was read and ignored. By midnight Merthyr was in the hands of the mob. The following morning an attempt at negotiation failed and the mob attacked the troops. In the gunfire that followed, at least sixteen rioters were killed. They dispersed to arm themselves and on 4 June managed to ambush and disarm a detachment of the Swansea Cavalry on its way to reinforce the troops in Merthyr. Violence continued in the town and surrounding area for several more days and it was not until 6 June, after 450 soldiers with fixed bayonets near Dowlais had cut off a supporting crowd advancing from Monmouthshire, that the military finally gained the upper hand in Merthyr itself.

The nature of this Merthyr rising has been much disputed. Many of its ritualistic features were reminiscent of the Scotch Cattle, although the main area for Scotch Cattle activity was further east in Monmouthshire. Economic and employment issues were clearly important in the rioters' demands and the local liberal press naturally stressed these aspects of the affair, but two of the rising's most recent historians were agreed that economics and industrial relations were not the whole story. According to David Jones

> The Merthyr massacre was a unique popular disturbance, one which indicated the changing nature of society. Plunged into the economic and political turmoil of the 1790s and the post-war depression, the 'lower orders' of Merthyr Tydfil emerged during the reform crisis with a new awareness of themselves as a body or 'class' oppressed alike by employers, magistrates, and legislators.[25]

Less circumspectly, Gwyn Williams declared, 'from the beginning it was an *insurrection* designed to effect *Reform* and overthrow a social order'.[26] The symbol adopted by the leaders was the red flag of Reform, so the Tory press may not have been too fanciful in seeing the riots as the work of 'revolutionary forgemen, Jacobin moulders, democratic colliers, and demagogue furnace-men'.[27] Political preachers fanned the flames of rebellion no less than union organisers.

The idea of using an industrial strike to promote radical political reform was being advocated in London at this time by William Benbow and there was some support for this approach in Merthyr. Magistrates were therefore alarmed when, in August, the colliers' union spread across the Valleys, apparently in association with political clubs and protected by a secret oath. The employers responded with a lock out, supported by the magistrates who denied poor relief to union men and their families. The struggle was bitter and the climax of the workers' desperation coincided with the Bristol riots and preparations for simultaneous reform meetings on 7 November. 'This place is in a dreadful state', wrote one informant. 'The moment the news arrived of the disturbance at Bristol, the Union Clubs all met, what happened I know not. All is quiet but everyone is apprehensive. Thousands are out of employment and starving. The men know all that passes and are evidently plotting. They talk of revolution.'[28]

But despite the fears of the magistrates, nothing happened. Torrential rain and tight military precautions saw to that. Even more so than Bristol, Merthyr in 1831 demonstrated what could develop when economic and political grievances came together to overwhelm the inadequate local forces of law and order. It also demonstrated that, whatever the popular leaders might think and say, effective economic and political power ultimately lay not with the people, but with their employers and the military.

**Rural unrest**

Urban riots were worrying to local property owners but most were usually containable and the Home Office overall seems to have taken a relaxed attitude to all but the most alarming reports received from magistrates. Industrial unrest was a problem for the manufacturing classes and the occasional urban disturbance was as much to be expected as rioting at election time. If the severity of the government's reaction is a measure of the seriousness with which unrest was regarded, then things were very different in the countryside. Poaching and incendiarism were endemic. Where the image was of a paternalistic and deferential society, the reality was often an oppressed and resentful class of labourers, ill-paid, underemployed, and unable to escape the controlled environment of rural life for the anonymity and freedom of the town. Occasional outbursts drew attention to the unease beneath the calm. One such had swept through the Cambridgeshire Fens in 1816. No one has claimed that these riots were overtly political. Their long-term causes were enclosure, deteriorating conditions of labour and abject poverty; their immediate causes were the high price of bread and unemployment inflated by the return of militiamen from the war. The target was often the property of particular individuals – farmers and clergymen – whose conduct had been offensive to the popular sense of 'justice'. Rioting was widespread through the early summer of 1816, but centred on Ely and Littleport where troops opened fire to disperse the crowd. At the subsequent Special Assizes at Ely, twenty-four men were sentenced to death, of whom five were hanged, nine were transported and ten were sentenced to a year in gaol.[29]

This was a foretaste of the rural riots associated with the name of 'Captain Swing' in 1830–31. These latter riots were far more extensive, reaching through southern England from Kent as far as Dorset, and up the eastern side of England to Lincolnshire. The worse affected counties were Kent, Berkshire, Sussex, Hampshire, Wiltshire and Dorset in the south and Essex, Suffolk and Norfolk in the east. Cambridgeshire, which had been at the centre of the 1816 riots, was less affected and Littleport and Ely were quiet. The principal counties of industrial unrest – Nottinghamshire, Derbyshire, Lancashire, Cheshire and Yorkshire – were little involved. The main reasons for the outbreaks were as in 1816, but the situation was made worse by the introduction of threshing machines which threatened a major source of winter employment for agricultural workers. The outbreaks took the form of machine-breaking and arson, followed by wage riots and robbery.[30] As with Luddism, threatening letters were an important device to put preliminary pressure on farmers to get rid of their hated machines:

> this is to inform you what you have to undergo Gentelmen if providing you Don't pull down your messhines and rise the poor mens wages the maried men give tow and six pence a day a day the singel tow shilings. or we will burn down your barns and you in them this is the last notis [sic].[31]

Clerical magistrates were also objects of popular hatred. The following more literate letter, with its concluding echo of the prayer of general confession in the Book of Common Prayer, may include a pun rather than a spelling mistake:

> Your name is down amongst the Black hearts in the Black Book and this is to advise you and the like of you, who are Parson Justasses, to make your wills.
> Ye have been the Blackguard Enemies of the People on all occasions, Ye have not yet done as ye ought.[32]

Retribution, tempered with 'mercy', was swift. Hobsbawm and Rudé have calculated that 1,976 prisoners were tried by 94 courts in 34 counties. Of 252 death sentences, all but 19 were commuted; of 505 who were sentenced to transportation, 24 were reprieved; 644 were imprisoned; 7 were fined, 1 was whipped and 800 were acquitted or bound over to keep the peace. The totals indicate the extent and severity of the riots, but did this amount to a serious threat of revolution?

In one sense it did, in that in peasant societies throughout Europe, risings in the countryside were recognised as having the potential to destabilise the whole of society, and the role of the *jacquerie* in 1789 was not easily forgotten. But in the English case there is little evidence of direct involvement by rioters in political activities. The Royal Commission on the Poor Laws in 1834 found that in most instances the causes of the riots were economic: 300 cases being attributed to low wages and unemployment compared with 110 blamed on agitators and beer shops.[33] The latter figure is high, due more to beer shops than agitators. Out of 1,475 incidents counted by Hobsbawm and Rudé, only twenty-three were classified as 'political' and only an additional three were for 'sedition'. The only counties with more than two incidents under these headings were Cumberland, with three political cases and Lancashire with five. Neither of these was a 'Swing' county.[34] This is not to deny that there were small groups of radicals in villages who would have liked to turn the riots to political effect, and there is some evidence of urban radicals attempting to capitalise on the rural unrest.

The election campaigns of 1830, 1831 and 1832 took politics to almost every market town, if not every parish, in the country. One of the most celebrated cases was at Blandford in October 1831 where the Dorset county by-election resulted in a narrow victory for the Tory candidate, Lord Ashley, whereupon a mob attacked several houses, including the property of two lawyers who had acted for Ashley, and were prevented from burning down the parsonage only by the arrival of troops. Here local grievances and score-settling merged with anger at the failure of the reformers to carry the seat. Rural artisans, and urban artisans 'on tramp' were able to spread the political message sufficiently far to cause the magistrates some anxiety lest the grievances of the labourers should become infected with politics. Cobbett's reform lecture tour of Kent and Sussex in October 1830 was, therefore, viewed with suspicion, as were the Rotunda radicals when they took up the agricultural riots in their London lectures. Carlile issued an 'Address to the Insurgent Labourers', for which he was prosecuted for sedition and sentenced to two years in gaol; and Taylor wrote and produced a play called *Swing: Who are the Incendiaries?* which indirectly led to his prosecution for blasphemy.[35] Though the majority of the Rotunda audiences would have been from London, James Thomas Cooper, a Swing leader in Fordingbridge, Hampshire, cannot have been alone in attending the Rotunda when he was in London.[36] Also, radical literature was widely available in towns and villages. One report from Sussex claimed that the agricultural labourers were 'ripe for anything'.

> Moreover, they are all politicians. In one field 30 or 40 are set to work breaking stones; and in the midst of them on a heap of flints at meal times, one of the most learned of their number, may be seen reading aloud the *Morning Herald*, and expounding the clauses of the Reform Bill, in which they take a great interest, to his fellow workmen.[37]

In Dorchester, a hand bill was stuck around the town at the end of October 1831, denouncing those who had voted against the Reform Bill in the Lords and listing government pensioners.[38] 'I am very confident, that ever since the Reform Bill was first talked of in this neighbourhood, it has produced a great deal of disorder and immoral state of the population', claimed B. S. Escott of Somerset in 1837.[39]

The growth of labourers' friendly societies and chapels in the years after Swing confirms the capacity of rural workers to organise themselves, and the fact that one such group of labourers in Tolpuddle in Dorset could form a branch of the London-based Grand National Consolidated Trades Union in 1834 suggests that the interchange of ideas between town and country was not so improbable as the usual emphasis on the isolation of the rural worker might suggest. Even so, the culture and mentality of agricultural labourers were such as to make some forms of communication difficult. Arson and other acts of immediate response to grievances were the usual manifestation of discontent, whatever dark discussions might also go on in low beer shops beyond the reach of parson and licensing justices.

Remarkably, this rural culture flared into outright revolt once more in the later 1830s. As with Swing, the affair started in Kent, though this time it did not spread beyond three villages: Boughton, Dunkirk and Hernhill, situated between Faversham and Canterbury. The area had already seen Swing riots in 1830 and anti-Poor Law riots in 1835 but in 1838 an added ingredient was millenarianism. The Messiah was John Tom or Thoms, *alias* Sir William Courtenay, who on 20 May 1838 led his small group of between thirty-six and forty-eight disciples through the villages of north Kent as far west as Sittingbourne, before being confronted on 31 May in Bossenden Wood near Dunkirk by a detachment of the 150 men of the 45th Infantry sent to hunt them down. One soldier, a special constable and nine rioters were killed, including Courtenay. The latter had previously stood for East Kent in the general election of December 1832 and was a political demagogue with a radical appeal. But to the rioters, two-thirds of whom were labourers, he was the Messiah come to bring the Jubilee when all oppression would end and debts be cancelled.[40] One of those killed, was Edward Wraight, a sixty-year-old yeoman farmer who could both read and write; his son, of the same name, was taken prisoner. In answer to the question whether she 'really had believed that Thoms was our Saviour', the son's wife replied:

Oh yes sir, certain sure I did believe him; and good warrant I thought I had. William Wills, you see, sir, came one day to our cottage, and we had some ale; and, says he, 'Have you heard the great news, and what's going to happen?' – 'No,' says we, 'William Wills; what be it?' And he said, the great Day of Judgment was close at hand, and that our Saviour had come back again; and that we must all follow him. And he showed us in the Bible, in the *Revelations*, that he should come upon a white horse, and go forth and conquer; and sure enough, sir, the day after, as we were coming in our cart from market, we met the groom leading Sir William's white horse; and he told us that all the country would be up, for the great jubilee was to come, and we must be with 'em. And so, sir, you see, next day poor Edward certainly did go to join 'em, little thinking what was to happen. And the day after, as they were all passing by the house, I looked out, and Muster Foad was just at the tail of them. And I said, 'Do you, Muster Foad, believe he is our blessed Saviour?' – 'Oh, yes', he says, 'Mrs Wraight, for certain sure he is, and I'll follow him to the world's end.'

Asked whether his death had not convinced her that Courtenay was an imposter, she went on:

Not at once, sir; for we was told he would surely rise again; and, for certain, after poor Edward was taken prisoner, me and a neighbour sat up the whole of that blessed night reading the Bible, and believing the world was to be destroyed on the morrow.

Asked whether this was also the belief of her neighbours, she replied:

I can't say for all, sir, but many of them did. There was Mrs.—— opposite, who asked him to a tea-party; and she said afterwards to me, 'You may be sure he isn't one of us; he isn't like to us. To hear him talk, and see him, it's not at all like talking to a man. He sings the beautifullest hymns, and talks the finest words that ever you heard.'

CITY COLLEGE LEARNING RESOURCE CENTRE

Courtenay had also administered the sacrament and anointed his followers to make them invulnerable.[41]

The interviewer, Frederick Liardet, who was a barrister and supporter of the Central Society of Education, found this a 'strange infatuation', but it was strange only to an educated, urban member of the middle class. To the peasantry of Kent, this cultural reaction to socio-economic deprivation was perfectly natural. It also defied the logic of

contemporary Chartists who saw the rising only as a response to the
new Poor Law, just as it continues to defy the logic of historians accustomed to secular revolutions which are economic or political in inspiration. The contrast should be made between this account of a
meeting in a Kent cottage and the deposition quoted earlier about the
meeting near Huddersfield before the Folly Hall rising of 1817.[42]
Culturally the two accounts were a world apart, and yet they
amounted to the same thing: not a riot but a revolution, in which old
forms of oppression were to be swept away. Courtenay was not far
from the teachings of Spence which encouraged the revolutionary
party in London from Spa Fields to Cato Street. As Liardet himself
realised:

> Although the late disturbance was undoubtedly of a religious
> character, it must not be supposed that it was altogether uncon-
> nected with views of another nature. Thoms, taking advantage
> of the occasional distress of some of his auditors, did not fail to
> represent it as owing to the enormous masses of wealth accumu-
> lated by the few to the disadvantage of the many. In his
> addresses, he often hinted at a more equable distribution of
> property; and declared that, when he was put into possession of
> the power God intended to give him, no man should have less
> than fifty acres of land.[43]

Courtenay himself seems to have participated in this belief.

## Conclusion

The uprising in Kent in 1838 gives an insight into the potential for revolutionary disturbances in Britain in the 1830s. At a time of rapid population increase, agricultural depression and deep cyclical industrial
recessions, when industrialisation was transforming the social frameworks of communities on the coal fields of Britain, there was much
inherent instability which on occasions spilled over from sporadic
rioting into actual insurgency. The army was kept on the alert. At
Bossenden Wood as many men were killed as at Peterloo; more at
Bristol and Merthyr Tydfil. There was clearly a revolutionary situation in 1830–32: one which in France would have led to revolution.
Reports suggest there were some people throughout the country who
would have taken Britain down the same path.

Lord Camden, Lord Lieutenant of Kent, believed the incendiaries were 'those who wish Revolution in England, in order to create confusion & that in London, the main directors reside'.[44] Tricolour flags, symbol of the new French regime, were paraded in Henry Hunt's Preston, and an ex-metropolitan policeman was charged in Battle, Sussex, with wearing a cap with tricoloured ribbons and saying 'if they were minded, there would be a revolution here'.[45] The red flag flew in Merthyr. But in the end, revolution did not happen; or, rather, the constitutional revolution was contained within constitutional bounds by the middle-class political unions and the Whigs. The crisis of May 1832 was resolved peacefully, and the leaders of popular radicalism who had provided the reality of the threat of physical force felt betrayed by the Reform Act that followed. Out of this sense of betrayal, the Chartist movement was born.

## Notes

1   Speech on the Reform Bill in 1832, quoted in *Annual Register* (1832), History of Europe, p. 39.
2   M. Brock, *The Great Reform Act* (London, Hutchinson, 1973), pp. 57–8.
3   D. Wahrman, *Imagining the Middle Class: The Political Representation of Class in Britain, c. 1780–1840* (Cambridge, Cambridge University Press, 1995).
4   Brock, *Great Reform Act*, pp. 59–60.
5   Handbill reproduced from the Place Papers, in D. J. Rowe, (ed.), *London Radicalism, 1830–1843* (London, London Record Society, 1970), p. 63.
6   Brown, *French Revolution*, pp. 193–7.
7   *Annual Register* (1831), History of Europe, p. 80.
8   *Annual Register* (1831), History of Europe, pp. 280–1; Chronicle, pp. 161–3, 171–8.
9   Wellington to Aberdeen, 22 November 1831, printed in A. R. Wellesley (ed.), *Despatches, Correspondence, and Memoranda of Field Marshall Arthur Duke of Wellington, K.G.*, continuation series, 8 vols (London, Murray, 1867–80), vol. 8, pp. 74–6.
10  *Annual Register* (1832), Chronicle, pp. 186–7.
11  D. J. Moss, *Thomas Attwood: The Biography of a Radical* (Montreal, McGill-Queen's University Press, 1990), pp. 205–9.
12  Quoted in *PMG*, 1:49 (19 May 1832), p. 398.
13  Northampton CRO, Fitzwilliam Papers, F(M) 732, Letter Book, Lord Milton to Denis O'Bryen, 29 November 1832, quoted in D. J. Gratton, 'Paternalism, Politics and Estate management: the fifth Earl Fitzwilliam (1786–1857)', Ph.D. thesis, University of Sheffield, 1999.
14  This view was echoed in Whig histories: see J. R. M. Butler, *The Passing of the Great Reform Bill* (London, Longmans, Green & Co., 1914), p. 137.

15  BL, Add MSS 27795, fos 26–9, Place Papers, Sunday, 20 May 1832, as printed in Rowe, *London Radicalism*, pp. 94–5.

16  Thompson, *The Making*, pp. 898–9.

17  J. H. Wiener, *Radicalism and Freethought in Nineteenth-Century Britain: The Life of Richard Carlile* (Westport, Greenwood, 1983), pp. 164–90.

18  BL, Add MSS 27791, fos. 333–5, Place Papers [October 1831], as printed in Rowe, *London Radicalism*, pp. 51–3.

19  *PMG*, 1:44, supplementary no (11 April 1832), pp. 345–52.

20  *Annual Register* (1832), Chronicle, pp. 38–9.

21  PRO, HO 40/5/5, fo 22, paper sent by Edward Thomas Fitzgerald, Capt. 25th Foot to Lord Sidmouth, from Abergavenny, 22 December 1816.

22  PRO, HO 42/158, fo 304, Copy of a Paper Found near Penydarren on Monday 27 January 1817. This is reprinted in D. V. J. Jones, *Before Rebecca* (London, Allen Lane, 1973), pp. 231–3.

23  Jones, *Before Rebecca*, pp. 86–113.

24  Jones, *Before Rebecca*, pp. 117–32.

25  Jones, *Before Rebecca*, p. 158.

26  G. A. Williams, *The Merthyr Rising* (London, Croom Helm, 1978), p. 224.

27  Quoted in Jones, *Before Rebecca*, p. 133.

28  Quoted in Williams, *Merthyr Rising*, p. 219.

29  A. J. Peacock, *Bread or Blood: A Study of the Agrarian Riots in East Anglia in 1816* (London, Gollancz, 1965).

30  E. J. Hobsbawm and G. Rudé, *Captain Swing* (London, Lawrence and Wishart, 1969), Appendix 1, pp. 262–3.

31  PRO, HO 52/10 (Sussex), fo 412, letter from Fulking near Hove, sent to Home Office 12 November 1830. There is a facsimile in Hobsbawm and Rudé, *Captain Swing*, p. 175.

32  PRO, HO 52/7 (Hampshire), fo 231. There is a facsimile in Hobsbawm and Rudé, *Captain Swing*, p. 177.

33  Hobsbawm and Rudé, *Captain Swing*, pp. 57–9.

34  Hobsbawm and Rudé, *Captain Swing*, Appendix 1, pp. 262–3.

35  Wiener, *Radicalism and Freethought*, pp. 165–6, 174–7.

36  R. Wells, 'Rural Rebels in Southern England in the 1830s', p. 135 in C. Emsley and J. Walvin (eds), *Artisans, Peasants and Proletarians, 1760–1860* (London, Croom Helm, 1985), pp. 124–65.

37  'State of the Rural Population', *Brighton Gazette*, 31 May 1832.

38  Mary Frampton's *Journal*, 6 November 1831, quoted in E. A. Smith, *Reform or Revolution? A diary of Reform in England, 1830–2* (Stroud, Sutton, 1992), pp. 105–6.

39  PP (1837) 464, 30, *Report from the Select Committee of the House of Lords appointed to inquire into the State of Agriculture in England and Wales*, June 1837, Q 4956.

40  B. Reay, *The Last Rising of the Agricultural Labourers: Rural Life and Protest in Nineteenth-century England* (Oxford, Clarendon Press, 1990).

41  F. Liardet, 'State of the Peasantry in the County of Kent', p. 90–1, *Central Society of Education Papers* 3 (London, Taylor and Walton, 1839), pp. 87–139.

42  See above, pp. 49–50.

43  Liardet, 'State of the Peasantry', p. 133.

44   PRO, HO 52/8 (Kent), fos 248–50, Camden to the Home Office, 12 November 1830.
45   G. Rudé, 'English Rural and Urban Disturbances 1830–1831', pp. 96–7, *Past & Present*, 37 (July 1967), pp. 87–102.

3

# Chartism,
# 1837–48

## The first Chartist crisis, 1839–40

The Chartist movement began as a peaceful pressure group, organised in London by some of the more moderate leaders of the London trade unions, former members of the NUWC and supporters of the unstamped press. In June 1836 a group of these men set up the London Working Men's Association (LWMA) to advance the cause of democratic radicalism by the peaceful means of education, moral improvement and reasoned pressure for further political change. Their approach showed the unmistakable influence of Francis Place and they had the support of several Radical Members of Parliament, including Daniel O'Connell. Their secretary, William Lovett, who was a former co-operative socialist and trade union official, was a model of rational moderation. It was this group that drew up the political programme for radical change expressed in the six points of Universal Suffrage, No Property Qualifications, Annual Parliaments, Equal Representation, Payment of Members and Vote by Ballot. Though the individual points of this programme had been around for at least two generations, taken together they summed up what was needed to make the Reform Act of 1832 effective for working men. Not only did all men need the vote, thus asserting individual political rights as opposed to the idea of the representation of interests, but to make that effective it would have to be possible for anyone to be elected, irrespective of property or income, it would be necessary for every vote to count equally with every other vote, the right to vote must be rescued from the threat of illegitimate pressure from employers or landlords, and those elected must be accountable.

2

There was no mention of women, or direct attack on the monarchy or the House of Lords. Nevertheless, this package of ideas would have revolutionised political life. As the Irish lawyer and one-time editor of the *Poor Man's Guardian*, James 'Bronterre' O'Brien, put it in 1837, 'Knaves will tell you, that it is because you have no property that you are unrepresented. I tell you, on the contrary, it is because you are unrepresented that you have no property.'[1] Thus the values of 1832 were reversed and that implicit challenge to property which had made Paine's *Rights of Man*, Part 2 so threatening, was again spelt out. Behind these radical political proposals lurked the threat of social revolution. But the methods chosen to achieve the end were strictly constitutional. A draft parliamentary Bill was drawn up which sought to implement the Six Points and also to rectify a number of administrative problems and anomalies created by the 1832 Reform Act.[2] Like the Reform Act, this was presented as a new Magna Carta: the People's Charter.

This constitutional approach was reinforced from Birmingham where former members of the Political Union were also disillusioned with the failure of the 1832 Reform Act to transform aristocratic politics to the extent they had hoped. So Thomas Attwood and others returned to the tactics of 1832, calling mass meetings in support of a National Petition for further change. In its bid for popular support, essential for the strategy of mass pressure to seem realistic, the BPU now declared for universal suffrage. The Charter was published on 8 May 1838, the National Petition on 14 May, and the two were merged at mass meetings in Glasgow on 21 May and Birmingham on 6 August. The strategy now was, as in earlier campaigns, to hold a series of mass meetings throughout the country to elect delegates to a Convention in London, the overt purpose of which was to oversee the presentation of the Petition to the House of Commons, but with the threat always implicit in the notion of a Convention that it might constitute an alternative and more legitimate version of the House of Commons.

Had the London Working Men's Association (LWMA) retained its dominant place in this campaign for radical reform, Chartism would never have become the movement that it did, but as the mass movement grew it was able to draw on other traditions, agitations and leaders with different ideas and approaches. In London, there were many radicals with roots in Paineite and Spencean radicalism who were unhappy with the moderation of the LWMA. Some of them, organised initially in the East London Democratic Association, reconstituted themselves in May 1838 as the London Democratic Association in opposition to the moderates. Their most outspoken leader, George Julian Harney, had three times been imprisoned in the war of the unstamped, and romantically regarded himself as playing Marat to O'Brien's Robespierre in a re-enactment of the French Revolution. He and others like him had to look outside London for election to the Convention.

Despite the enormous size of London as a centre of population and manufacturing, with long traditions of radical protest, early Chartism was not primarily a London movement: its origins as a mass movement lay in the provinces which had, with increasing frequency since the days of Luddism, taken the initiative in movements of popular protest. Chartism was a blend of political programme and economic discontents generated in the industrial Midlands and north of England, fused in the severe trade depression which began to affect Britain in late 1836 and which continued with intermissions until the summer of 1842.

The oldest industrial district of the north was around the mouth of the river Tyne, where the economy had been stimulated by the demand for sea-borne coal for London. There was a long tradition here of turbulent industrial relations, among the colliers who dug the coal and the keelmen who conveyed it from the shore to waiting ships. In 1792 and again in 1819, major strikes had occurred which governments had feared might lead to revolution. In the later 1830s, this region was again to the forefront of what was known as 'physical force' Chartism, in contrast to the 'moral force' of the LWMA. The engine which drove the physical force approach was partly economic, with a severe depression at the rather outdated iron works at Winlaton where idle hands could be turned to the manufacture of pikes; and ideological, with the production of an uncompromising newspaper, the *Northern Liberator*. This was started by an American, Augustus Hardin Beaumont, who seems to have believed his own language of revolutionary violence. In November 1837 he called for 'five hundred thousand democrats in arms' and in January 1838 he sold his paper and went on a lecture tour to raise a force of five hundred to fight for the rebels in Canada, a task which his premature death prevented him from realising.

Beaumont's successors at the *Northern Liberator* were Robert Blakey, a subtle logician (who was to become Professor of Logic and Metaphysics at Queen's College, Belfast, in 1849) and Thomas Doubleday, a romantic poet and secretary of the Northern Political Union. Although initially more discreet, advocating arming only in self defence, in January 1839 this amounted to advice on how to make cartridges and barricades and information about the ready availability of hand grenades. Thomas Ainge Devyr, an Irish journalist (and son of a United Irishman) working on the paper, many years later recalled shells being manufactured in the rooms above the *Liberator* offices in Newcastle. Harney was unsurprisingly elected to the Convention as a delegate for Newcastle, along with another extremist, 'Dr' John Taylor of Ayr. The *Liberator* was finally silenced in 1840 by a crippling fine on Blakey for publishing a paper on the 'National Right of Resistance to Constituted Authorities'.[3]

In spite of the revolutionary voices and activities on Tyneside during the early years of Chartism, other forces minimised the potential danger. The economy of the area was generally buoyant, the Winlaton iron workers being untypical. The major industry, coal mining, was effectively unionised and conflict could be institutionalised within industrial relations; and the new Poor Law, which was to cause problems elsewhere, was introduced with less confrontation and greater discretion in the north-east. The *Northern Liberator* had an extensive circulation beyond Tyneside and sought to bring national and international perspectives to bear, but it was not entirely successful. Although Newcastle was to remain a centre of republican thought, and supported international revolution in the 1850s through the efforts of Joseph Cowen junior, it did not rise in 1839 and was not thereafter a major centre of Chartist activity. Iron working districts were always of concern to the government, whether at Winlaton, Carron in Scotland, Low Moor outside Bradford, Sheffield, Birmingham, the Black Country, or the valleys of South Wales, for it was here that the manufacture of arms for illicit purposes might be expected and revolution might become a cottage industry for unemployed workers, but the market for such weapons was more often to be expected elsewhere.

The textile producing counties of the east Midlands, northwards from Leicestershire through Nottinghamshire and into Derbyshire, across to north-east Cheshire, south-east Lancashire, and over the Pennines into the West Riding of Yorkshire were those associated with the greatest history of turbulent radicalism. Here the recurring problems of the domestic outworkers, mainly weavers, reached a climax as their earning power fell and bread prices rose in the late 1830s. These familiar causes of unrest merged with others, some old, some new. Fresh immigration from Ireland brought renewed bitterness born of despair in the famine years; and in Bradford technological redundancy hit the wool combers of the worsted industry as hard as it had destroyed the croppers of the woollen industry earlier in the century.

The social forces which created the Chartist movement began in the factory districts of Lancashire, Cheshire and, especially, the West Riding in 1830 (rather than 1838), with the movement to secure the enforcement of protective legislation in cotton factories and its extension of protection to Yorkshire worsted mills and other sections of the textile workforce. The majority of workers in factories were women and children but large numbers of men were employed as handloom weavers, kept on to supply surplus capacity to meet the demand for output in an industry notoriously vulnerable to booms and slumps. Not only was their employment uncertain, but their rates of pay were fixed by the cost of producing a piece of cloth on a power loom, not the time taken to produce a piece by hand.

The campaign for shorter hours in the factories was presented in humanitarian language as one to protect women and children from exploitation, but it was also aimed at driving up factory costs to increase the income of domestic workers. The problems of the textile districts centred on families, in which women and children were exploited in order further to exploit fathers and husbands. Although some of the children employed in factories went on to other forms of employment, and did so increasingly in times of economic expansion, some were not so fortunate and the depression of 1837–42 caused much hardship. A tinder-box of discontent was created which, as in 1812, 1817 and 1819, could easily be lit by the sparks of revolutionary oratory and the dedicated plotting of men who saw no other way of achieving reform. In the small mill towns and face-to-face communities of the textile districts, Chartism straddled the boundary between constitutional protest and insurrection.

The latter was personified by two men, neither of them Chartists: Richard Oastler, son of a leader of the Methodist New Connexion in Leeds, who adopted the position of Tory Anglican paternalist squire in his post as steward for the Thornhill estate at Fixby, between

Huddersfield and Halifax; and Joseph Rayner Stephens, a former Wesleyan Methodist minister in Stalybridge, the son of the Wesleyan superintendent minister in Manchester in 1819 who had praised the magistrates for their actions at 'Peterloo'. Oastler led the campaign for factory reform, later also taking up leadership of West Riding opposition to the Poor Law Amendment Act of 1834; Stephens, expelled from the Wesleyan ministry for advocating the disestablishment of the Church of England, led the anti-Poor Law movement in Lancashire and Cheshire and was a prominent speaker on early Chartist platforms across the north of England. These campaigns were whipped up into mass movements of working people convinced by practical experience of the 'Whig betrayal' in 1832. This phrase referred not only to the fact that the 1832 Act did not deliver the promised change in politics, but also to the legislation which followed. This seemed to favour the interests of newly enfranchised urban and manufacturing elites, not 'the people'. The coercion of Ireland, the attack on trade unions, and the 1833 Factory Act which in part met the humanitarian issue without helping male adults, were all parts of this betrayal, but the measure which hurt most of all was the Poor Law Amendment Act of 1834, enforced in the factory districts in 1837 as the depression deepened.

The orchestrated violence which greeted the attempt to implement the Act showed the strength and ferocity of public feeling. By force of numbers, rate payers were intimidated and meetings disrupted, delaying and in some cases preventing the implementation of the Act. A great anti-Poor Law rally on Peep Green, midway between Leeds, Bradford, Halifax and Huddersfield at Whitsuntide 1837 was followed by a campaign of intimidation, led in Huddersfield by Oastler, which on 5 June prevent the newly-elected Poor Law Guardians from choosing a clerk and so setting about their business.[4] On 20 June, William IV died and in the consequent general election Oastler stood for Huddersfield. His narrow defeat caused a riot and a detachment of cavalry had to be called to restore order. The example spread and in October the Bradford Guardians wavered under public pressure and there were serious riots there in November. Two troops of cavalry were needed to enable the frightened Guardians of Huddersfield to elect a clerk in January 1838 and so to proceed with business.[5]

The success of the anti-Poor Law Movement in Huddersfield and

other northern towns demonstrated the power of the crowd to determine events when combined with a measure of support from
members of the local elite, whether Tories or radicals, opposed to centralisation and Whig reforming dogma. This experience was carried
over into northern Chartism, though at first some anti-Poor Law agitators considered Chartism a London plot to divide the people from
their Tory supporters. This suspicion was unfounded but it did have
that effect. While the popular movement flowed seamlessly from the
one to the other, the Chartists lost what support the upper classes had
given to their social protest. Oastler was an isolated figure, soon to be
imprisoned by his employer on a charge of debt. John Fielden, the
Todmorden factory master and MP for Oldham since 1832, was one of
the few factory movement and anti-Poor Law leaders to make the
transition to advocacy of Chartist democracy.

Oastler's principal Huddersfield supporter was Lawrence
Pitkethly, a prosperous draper who had achieved the vote in 1832.
Two days before the Poor Law Guardians met to elect their clerk,
Pitkethly addressed a mass meeting in the town on the subject of the
five leaders of the Glasgow cotton spinners' union who had just been
sentenced to transportation for their technical complicity in the death
of blacklegs during a prolonged and bitter strike in the west of
Scotland. His speech is worth considering at length, not only for the
language used, but also for the rhetorical devices employed and the
issues raised. According to the *Northern Star* report,

> Mr Pitkethley said . . . The resolution described tyranny, which
> was disgraceful to any civilised country and barbarity which
> ought not to be submitted to: it was clear that the Whigs were
> resolved to reduce the people to the lowest possible state of exis-
> tence. That this was one of their acts, and in perfect consonance
> with Starvation Law, the Rural Police Law, and the transporting
> of the Dorchester Labourers, and those five virtuous men, the
> coercing of the Irish and the Canadians, left it impossible for us
> to be astonished at any Act which they might perform, and
> exhorted the meeting to place no confidence in them whatever;
> but to unite, be firm, depend upon their own energies, or they
> must remain slaves.

Here Pitkethly was drawing up a general indictment of government
policy, ranging from the Poor Law and the Tolpuddle martyrs to Irish
coercion and the suppression of the Canadian rebels. This illustrates

the degree to which a crowd, presumably motivated by local social and economic grievances, could be led to think nationally and even internationally about political issues related to their own local situation. The report continued:

> He then read some extracts from speeches made at a meeting held at Newcastle-upon-Tyne last Wednesday, on the same subject; which showed that Sir Robert Peel had got his £100,000 from Cotton Spinners, that Brougham had provided Bastiles for them, that they were determined to fight with their tongues, but if that would not do they would use their arms; then one speaker said he would rather than see those men leave Britain's Isles he would lose his life, and added now is the time to plunge your swords into the Whig and Tory faction; those profit-mongers must be consumed in a universal conflagration; and asked if they would permit them to leave Britain's Isle, (and was answered no, no, by the meeting.) and if so sent, then war to the knife; and that another speaker at the same meeting said the time was arrived when the exhortation once given in the land of Judea should be followed in this country, he that hath no sword let him sell his garment and buy one. After stating that rather than see the men leave the country, he would throw a firebrand into the bastile, and see them perish in the flames; that he agreed to petition with reluctance, concluded by asking, what an awful condition they would be placed in if those men were transported, and that a rural police will be established to watch them in their walks, and assassins would be hired to butcher their fellow-creatures; that he objected to revolution but rather than submit to live a slave, he would die. He then moved a resolution pledging the meeting to obtain by every possible means the total omission of the sentence on their five unfortunate brethren of Glasgow.

CITY COLLEGE
LEARNING RESOURCE CENTRE

Pitkethly was here playing a clever game. By quoting from the report of another meeting, he could use seditious language by proxy and achieve his desired effect upon the crowd without serious risk of prosecution. And even in the original speeches, there was a delightful ambiguity in the contrast between 'tongues' and 'arms' which could have been exploited if necessary by a defence counsel in court. The report of Pitkethly's meeting ended: 'Mr P. said he had read those few extracts to show that the men in the north were not less determined than the men of Huddersfield, and concluded by reading the resolution.'[6] This was the well-worn device of using reports of meetings elsewhere to bolster the morale of local groups and convince them that they were but a small part of a much greater movement. In the spring and early summer of 1838, that greater movement became Chartism on a swelling tide of hunger and hatred.

The man who exploited this was Feargus O'Connor, a disaffected former O'Connellite MP and, more importantly, nephew of the United Irishman, Arthur O'Connor, who was still living in exile in Nemours. O'Connor united in his complex personality the aspirations of his revolutionary uncle with the popular journalistic style of Cobbett and the platform appeal and oratory of Henry Hunt. When both Cobbett and Hunt died in 1835, O'Connor stepped into their shoes. His initial political base was Marylebone, a huge urban parish on the north western edge of London, the size of a large provincial town. Here vestry politics were almost democratic. He then extended his influence to the north, where his legal expertise was employed in the anti-Poor Law struggle.[7] He was present at the great West Riding meeting at Whitsuntide 1837, and in November played a leading part in starting in Leeds a radical anti-Poor Law weekly stamped newspaper which was called, like Arthur O'Connor's Ulster paper of the 1790s, the *Northern Star*. This was a very English paper, however, drawing on the style of its publisher Joshua Hobson's own earlier unstamped *Voice of the West Riding* and Cobbett's *Political Register*.

O'Connor never edited this paper, but he wrote many leading articles and controlled its overall direction from behind the scenes. His forte was the platform and the Huntite role of patriotic radical gentleman demagogue. Like Hunt, he stood just on the legal side of illegality, though his passionate language could easily take his followers beyond that point and some later came to believe that he had exhorted them to go where he was not prepared to lead them.

Between the launching of Chartism in May 1838 and the presentation of the National Petition in June 1839, the Chartists concentrated on gathering signatures and electing their delegates to the National Convention. The latter assembled in London on 4 February 1839 and immediately the tensions within the movement became apparent. Aware that the show was being run by the moderates of the LWMA, with William Lovett elected secretary of the Convention, the London Democratic Association provided an alternative focus for more extreme views. One motion, proposed by William Rider of Leeds and seconded by Richard Marsden of Preston,

> Resolved that this meeting convey to the General Convention, their opinion that for the due discharge of the duties of the Convention it is essentially necessary that there be no delay, except what may be absolutely necessary, in the presentation of the National Petition, and we hold it to be the duty of the Convention, to impress upon people the necessity of an imme- diate preparation for ulterior measures.[8]

This last phrase encompassed a wide range of ideas, from traditional legal measures for putting pressure on electors, such as buying goods only from the shops of supporters, and the more unlikely abstinence from excisable goods (drink and tobacco) to wreck government finances; to William Benbow's 'General Strike' as propounded in 1832; to vague threats of arming and drilling such as the *Northern Liberator* was favouring at this time. Already the country was growing impatient. Rioting broke out among the flannel weavers of Llanidloes and Welshpool in the upper Severn Valley at the end of April. Other disturbances were reported in the West Country, the Potteries, Sheffield, Bolton and Newcastle.

The volatility of the situation became clear in early May when the Whig government, which had been remarkably tolerant of the Chartists so far, collapsed and the prospect loomed of a Tory govern- ment under Robert Peel, founder of the hated Metropolitan Police in 1829, and of the Irish police before that. Fearful of suppression by the London police, the Convention adjourned to Birmingham. Here the Chartists held nightly meetings in the Bull Ring, much to the alarm of the magistrates who had recently banned meetings there. On 5 July the Home Office sent sixty metropolitan police to restore order. However, they had the reverse effect, and their attempt to disperse the crowd led to a riot which was only ended when the dragoons were called in. This incident raised a number of issues about violence and constitutionality. There was the irony that the magistrates who sent for the police included members of the BPU, some of whom had been delegates to the Convention but had withdrawn over talk of ulterior measures. The government which sent the police was a Whig one, Peel having refused to form a minority administration. The legality of the Home Office employing metropolitan police outside the London police area was not universally accepted: indeed, in a subsequent report on the riots, Joseph Sturge dissented from the views of his middle-class colleagues on this point. For publishing the protest of the

Convention about the 'wanton, flagrant, and unjust outrage . . . made upon the people of Birmingham by a bloodthirsty and unconstitutional force from London, acting under authority of men who, when out of office sanctioned and took part in the meetings of the people', William Lovett and local BPU delegate, John Collins, were prosecuted and imprisoned for a year.[9] Thus two of the mildest and most unrevolutionary of Chartists were punished, leaving Chartists to consider who was constitutional and who was in subversion of the law.

The constitutional niceties of physical force were pondered by the moderate London periodical, the *Chartist*, in May 1839 when news broke of the first riots in Wales.[10]

> That Englishmen have a right, *in extreme cases*, to have recourse to physical force to free themselves from an unendurable tyranny, is a truth so important and so undisputed that it forms the very foundation of our system of government. It is not only admitted, but it is even asserted, reiterated, defended, and justified, by the most zealous of the Tory writers upon, the Constitution of the country.

Sir William Blackstone, the eighteenth-century jurist, was the authority being appealed to. In true Whig fashion, the argument for physical force could be justified, but only in the last resort:

> But although this is upon all sides admitted, it is also upon all sides agreed that this is a fearful remedy, which, like hazardous, extreme, and painful operations in surgery, is only to be brought into action in very extreme cases, when all ordinary courses of treatment have failed. Physical force is a thing not to be lightly had recourse to; it is the last remedy known to the Constitution.

The paper then went on to assess the likelihood of physical force being employed and the conditions which might lead to its use. The very possession of weapons, taken with loose talk about their use, could lead to the kind of outburst which governments since the 1790s had feared:

> We have said long ago that all this light and meaningless talk about physical force is calculated to produce isolated and unsupported ebullitions of men, who, having arms in their hands, and being taught that they should use them, do so upon the impulse of passion. They are fierce and destructive in proportion to their weakness.

This is an instructive caution against the assumption that, just because the likelihood of success was small, a revolutionary outburst was unlikely. The reverse was true but would be self-defeating:

> Brother Chartists, this must not – this shall not be. We are as you know, with you arm and heart; but a noble cause shall not be thus foully lost. We will not see you throw away your lives only that your blood may stiffen the bonds that bind your brethren.

However, this did not mean that in the right conditions physical force should not be appealed to. Those conditions, hoped for in 1794, 1798, 1802, 1812, 1817, 1819, and 1832, were that: 'Nothing but a simultaneous rising at the same hour all over the kingdom could give you a *chance* of success by arms – even that would give you but a slender chance, and that you cannot effect.' This realisation of the weakness and likely failure of the only physical force strategy likely to be effective was a sobering thought and restrained the hands of all but the most headstrong. However, this was not to say that Chartists should not arm and drill. Again, in an argument common since the 1790s and almost universal since Peterloo, the *Chartist* urged, 'Retain your arms then, for it is possible that you may have to use them in your own defence, with the law and the Constitution upon your side. But use them not until that time comes.' In the mean time there was only one course of action for Chartists: 'Pursue the course of *peaceful* agitation – press forward your great cause under the watchwords of "Peace, Law, Order". It may be delayed, but it must prevail. Continue these acts of buccaneering folly, *and you and your children are slaves for ever.'* This appeal was in May. On 12 July the House of Commons rejected the Petition. The Convention, which had returned to London two days earlier, had to consider what to do next. The members were divided, but half-heartedly called for a sacred month – that is a general strike. Support across the country was limited. On 6 August the strike was called off and the Convention prorogued. The problem was what to do next. The hopes and expectations of over a year had led to nothing and all ulterior measures had failed, except the last which was yet to be tried. Many in crushed bewilderment went back to their homes. Some Chartists, armed, angry, frustrated, and filled with heady words of Old Testament prophetic fire, were ready for revolution.

## The Monmouthshire and Yorkshire risings

In February 1839, John Frost, Newport draper and magistrate and Monmouthshire delegate to the Convention in London, reported twenty working men's associations in his area with a membership of 15,000 to 20,000. Throughout the spring of 1839, tension grew in south Wales as the Chartist movement expanded rapidly and began to appeal beyond its original artisan membership to workers in the coal fields and ironworks of the valleys north of Newport where it capitalised on industrial disputes between employers and workers over truck payments, low wages and harsh terms of employment. In March, Frost, who was on the 'physical force' wing of the Convention, was relieved of his commission of the peace. In the valleys of Scotch Cattle violence, magistrates grew nervous. As David Jones observed in his history of the Newport rising, 'the working class of Blaina and Ebbw Vale, of Clydach and Pontypool, and of Blackwood and Risca were not only "rebellious and easily roused", but were also past masters in the art of organization, intimidation, and violence.'[11] Jones estimates that at the height of Chartism over 25,000 people, a fifth of the population, were Chartists. On 19 April, Henry Vincent of the LWMA delivered a characteristically colourful speech in Newport which allegedly concluded with the words: 'When the time for resistance arrives, let your cry be 'To your tents, O Israel!' and then with one heart, one voice, and one blow perish the privileged orders! death to the aristocracy! up with the people, and the government they have established!'[12]

The Newport magistrates took alarm, and on 24 April issued a proclamation declaring all meetings and processions illegal. Vincent immediately challenged this with a parade and meeting. On 27 April, Frost published an open letter describing the magistrates' proclamation as 'a declaration of war against your rights as Citizens, against your liberty, against your property' and warned the magistrates and constables to 'beware how they act'.[13] With magistrates and employers restricting and victimising Chartists, and the latter in open defiance, battle lines were being drawn. An unfortunate clash of policies appeared to encourage this sense of conflict when the government issued a Royal Proclamation nationally on 3 May prohibiting military exercises, and then four days later the Home Secretary, Lord John Russell, wrote to Lord Lieutenants and magistrates offering to provide local associations with arms for the protection of property. Warrants were issued for the arrest of Vincent and three others on 7 May and riots greeted their return to Newport which resulted in several further arrests. Despite the efforts made by Frost at this time to calm popular passions, the situation in south Wales was slowly slipping out of control.

The heightened tension in Birmingham, fears that the Petition might be rejected, and organisation to collect subscriptions for the Chartist prisoners sustained and increased Chartist support in the valleys throughout the early summer of 1839, but by August the authorities believed the worst to be over. At the Monmouth Assizes on 2 August, Vincent was sentenced to a year in gaol and the others received lesser sentences. This attack on a popular leader helped con-solidate the Chartist belief that it would be necessary to take up arms in self-defence. As early as April, Frost had argued in speeches in Newport and Glasgow that if members of the Convention were taken prisoner, 'we are determined to lay hold upon some of the leading men in the country as hostages for the Convention' and this was now threatened locally. Others recalled how Vincent himself had observed in March that 'A few thousand armed men on the hills could success-fully defend them. Wales would make an excellent republic.'[14] In September, Chartists began manufacturing and hoarding pikes and muskets.

These plans for a rising were rooted in the particular circum-stances of life and tradition in the valleys, but they were not isolated from reactions elsewhere to the failure of the petitioning movement. The Convention, which had been reconvened on 26 August, finally dissolved itself on 14 September, and it was later claimed by William Ashton, a Barnsley Chartist, that Frost, Peter Bussey of Bradford and others had then fixed 3 November as the date for a simultaneous rising. There was talk in London of using the services of a Polish army officer, Major Beniowski, who had been involved in the Polish rising of 1831. Whether these details were accurate or not, there were over the next few weeks discussions about a projected rising in several dif-ferent parts of the country, including the West Riding. As Joseph Crabtree of Barnsley later recalled, 'I heard of the expected rise at Newport and that there was to be a rise elsewhere.'[15] Secret meetings and detailed planning continued in Monmouthshire throughout October, and contacts were maintained with the north of England where preparations were less advanced. As the date approached, the difficulties of co-ordinating a simultaneous rising became apparent. Peter Bussey in Yorkshire asked for a postponement, but it was too late to stop the movement towards revolution in Monmouthshire.

On Friday 1 November a meeting in Blackwood made final arrangements for the rising to begin on the night of Sunday, 3 November. The insurgents were divided into three groups. Those at Pontypool, commanded by William Jones, were to march on Newport from the north, while the rest, led from Blackwood by John Frost and Ebbw Vale by Zephaniah Williams, were to meet up outside Newport and attack the town from the west. This is roughly what happened, but torrential rain and slower progress than expected meant that the 7,000 armed Chartists from the valleys did not reach Newport until after dawn and the attack by Frost and Williams began before Jones was ready. The sixty or so troops garrisoned in the workhouse were alerted and a detachment of thirty-two moved into the town to guard the mayor's headquarters at the Westgate Hotel. The Chartists arrived at 9.20 in the morning. What happened next, and who fired first, is lost in the confusion. Each side naturally blamed the other at the subsequent trials. But the outcome was clear. After no more than twenty-five minutes of fierce fighting outside and inside the hotel, the battle was all over. There were deaths and injuries on both sides, but mainly on the Chartist side. The number of casualties is unknown – probably fifty or more seriously injured and at least twenty-four dead. 'What is definite', wrote the historian David Jones, 'is that on this morning in November 1839 the British authorities inflicted greater casualties on the civilian population than at any other time in the nineteenth and twentieth centuries.'[16]

Even so, the rising was not over, not even in the vicinity of Newport itself. William Jones's force of 2,000 men was still intact until news of the defeat caused them to disperse, and there were other contingents in the valleys ready to proceed the following night against towns on the Usk once Newport had fallen. The area had very few troops: perhaps three or four hundred at Brecon, and only thirty-six in each of Monmouth and Abergavenny. Although a troop of Hussars reached Newport from Bristol on 5 November, a letter dispatched that day by the Home Secretary to Thomas Phillips, mayor of Newport, scarcely conceals its mixture of panic and relief as it detailed the inability of the government to provide major reinforcements immediately:

I hasten to acknowledge the receipt of a letter which I have received from Mr Blewitt of yesterdays date written at your request reporting the attack made upon the Town of Newport by a large body of Chartists from the neighbouring Country & to inform you that I have lost no time in communicating with the military authorities, and an arrangement has been made for the immediate march of eight companies of the 45th Reg[imen]t from Winchester for the district in which the deplorable event has occurred, orders have been already dispatched for their march & They will probably arrive at Bristol on the 10th inst. & can of course if necessary cross over by steamer to Newport the same evening. Two Guns with a proportion of Gunners have also been ordered from Woolwich to Monmouth. They will proceed by the Railroad to Twyford from there by forced marches to Bristol – I regret much that there are no Troops stationed at any nearer points that would be available for this service but I think that the check which these Insurgents have received from the Firmness of the Inhabitants of Newport & the small body of Troops stationed in the Town, together with the active measures taken by the Magistrates will have induced their dispersion for the time & the presence of the large force which will arrive in the course of a few days be sufficient to maintain future Tranquillity.[17]

Gradually over the next few days the initiative was regained by the authorities and Chartist insurgents sank back into their communities: 125 men were arrested, two-thirds of whom were later discharged for want of evidence. Twenty-one, including Frost, Williams and Jones, were charged with high treason. Their cases came before a special commission convened on 10 December.

The two most recent historians of this event, David Jones and Ivor Wilks, both emphasised its insurrectionary nature. It was more than a riot, or a demonstration, or an attempt to rescue Vincent or other Chartist prisoners. It was a serious rising, involving careful planning and large numbers of people with a purpose as much political (however vague and unrealistic) as social and economic. This interpretation rests on an examination of the evidence gathered locally by magistrates at the committal hearings shortly after the event, which bears out the otherwise unsubstantiated 'confession' of Zephaniah Williams made on board his transportation ship to Australia. The later treason trials played down the extent of the rising: the defence for obvious reasons, and the prosecution because the government was reluctant to admit the scale of the challenge or the good fortune by which the damage had been limited. Had the Chartists had better military leadership they would have planned a simultaneous rising in south Wales, rather than leaving the other attacks until after success at Newport was reported. They would not have attempted a full frontal assault on the Westgate hotel, and they would not have fled and dispersed at the first set-back. This is not to argue that in the long run the Newport rising could have achieved anything, at least not without similar risings throughout the rest of Britain, but in the short-run matters could have been far worse for the authorities than they were.

Much of the explanation for the scale and ferocity of the Newport rising is found in the peculiar nature of the society and economy of the Welsh valleys at this time, but that cannot be the whole story. There are too many references to the wider movement for the broader Chartist context to be neglected. Newport was fought in isolation, but it was not planned in isolation from revolutionary schemes in other parts of Britain. In the dark days after the House of Commons had rejected the constitutional approach, the idea of a simultaneous rising throughout areas of Chartist strength appealed increasingly to a hardened and desperate minority of the leadership. These included John Taylor of Ayrshire, a romantic with a strong line in revolutionary rhetoric; William Burns, the Convention delegate for Dundee; William Ashton of Barnsley; and Peter Bussey of Bradford. The latter took a prominent part in organising the plot which centred on the West Riding. He was a former wool comber turned innkeeper who had risen to prominence in Bradford as leader of the local anti-Poor Law movement.

Evidence for what was happening in Bradford and elsewhere between the ending of the Convention in London on 14 September and the risings which occurred in January 1840 is thin and inconclusive, but a story can be stitched together from the fragments. There was clearly evidence of arming but the magistrates found it hard to penetrate the local sections into which the Chartist organisation was now divided, and strangers could not eavesdrop on conversations held in private houses. The magistrates eventually learnt enough through spies to abort the risings when they occurred, but they did not know enough in advance to prevent them. The historian has to rely in part on the stories told subsequently by William Ashton and William Lovett in their arguments with Feargus O'Connor over his alleged part in events.[18] Although polemical in nature, these accounts are sufficiently consistent with each other and the other fragments of evidence to enable the story to be told.[19]

Having agreed on 12 September that a rising should take place, Taylor remained in London while Bussey and Ashton returned to Yorkshire. A meeting attended by about forty delegates was called at Heckmondwike on 30 September, at which Halifax was represented by Thomas Kitchenman, a Grange Moor veteran from 1820.[20] There was nothing in the public business to suggest anything illegal, but a subsequent meeting referred back to an unreported resolution carried at this first meeting which was to be sent on to Robert Blakey at Newcastle. This appears to confirm Lovett's account which he got from one of the delegates, that the secret purpose of the Heckmondwike meeting was to allow Bussey and Ashton to communicate to the Yorkshire delegates the London resolution about a rising. According to Zephaniah Williams, messages were sent out to the north of England and Scotland as soon as the day was fixed in Wales. Frost, who was in Manchester on a lecture tour of Lancashire and Yorkshire, was suddenly called back to Wales some time after 10 October. Burns, who was in Manchester with Frost, took the message to Newcastle on his way back to Dundee. The messenger, probably Charles Jones who was wanted in connection with the Llanidloes riots at the end of April, then brought the news to Yorkshire. Feargus O'Connor was probably not at this stage privy to the plot, though he must have known what was generally being discussed, and he conveniently found business to attend to in Ireland.[21]

Bussey doubted O'Connor's commitment and was getting cold feet; so too was Ashton who hurriedly took the boat from Hull to visit his wife in France. Bussey feigned illness and sent a message back to Frost to say that Yorkshire would not be ready for another ten days. George White, an Irish wool comber and Chartist lecturer, was sent round the West Riding to call off the rising planned for 3 November. Charles Jones returned to Wales from Yorkshire by way of the steamer from Hull to London, where he was to alert Taylor before going back to Wales to warn Frost of the unreadiness of Yorkshire. Unfortunately Jones was shipwrecked and Taylor did not get the message until 29 October. He then hurried to Newcastle where he found Robert

CITY COLLEGE
LEARNING RESOURCE CENTRE

Peddie, an Edinburgh staymaker with a revolutionary temperament to match his own, inciting the Winlaton ironworkers to arms.[22] They waited for the news that Newport had fallen. By the time Jones got back to Wales it was too late to delay the rising.

The news of the defeat of the Welsh Chartists caused alarm in the West Riding. Bussey went into hiding and subsequently emigrated. Taylor's men in Newcastle stood down. But that did not mean that the danger of a rising in the north was now over. Indeed, determination to save Frost added urgency to their plans. Taylor and Peddie lectured across the four northern counties. Sheffield organised a mass meeting in Paradise Square on 11 November, and then elected a delegate to attend a meeting in Newcastle at which plans were made for a Convention in London on 19 December. The Yorkshire leaders chose three delegates at a meeting held on 10 December in Manchester and then returned to Dewsbury which they had selected as the starting point for the rising in the West Riding. After an interchange of messages between London and Dewsbury, the rising was fixed for 12 January. Lovett's account becomes confused at this point, but it was probably here that O'Connor was asked to lead the north. He later denied this and supported his editor's decision to use the *Northern Star* of 11 January to denounce such attempts at physical force.

The Yorkshire rising was a disaster. James Allen, an informer, told the authorities in Rotherham of the rising at eight o'clock on the evening of 11 January. A message reached Sheffield in time for the authorities to arrest the local leader, Samuel Holberry, at midnight. The revolution, due to begin at 2.00 a.m., was aborted and only about fifty men turned out. After a brief skirmish, they fled or were arrested. The Barnsley Chartists waited in vain for the news of Holberry's success in Sheffield, and then went sadly home. The Bradford rising similarly came to nothing, amid a rumour (spread by a spy, James Harrison) that the magistrates had been informed of the plans and, without a signal from Bradford, the men of Dewsbury also went home. Newcastle also waited on events which never happened. The rising turned out to be the kind of hopeless shambles that O'Connor had prophesied it would be, although the demoralising effect of the *Northern Star*'s condemnation should not be underestimated. Ashton later recalled with bitterness how this article in the *Star* 'struck dismay into tens of thousands; the whole affair was blown to atoms by that cursed paper'. But the real reason why the risings fizzled out was that in both south and west Yorkshire the authorities had eventually found local Chartists willing to inform on what was being planned.

However, Bradford was not yet finished, for on Saturday 25 January, Robert Peddie arrived in town to address a meeting in support of Frost. Here he met up with Harrison and William Brook, a revolutionary joiner who felt thwarted by the failure of 12 January, a sentiment shared by Peddie. Arrangements, orchestrated by Harrison, were made for a new rising on 26 January. Cannon were to be taken from the Low Moor iron works, the Green Market and centre of Bradford were to be seized, and the Bradford men would then march on Dewsbury. Peddie was appointed leader. The story of the confused happenings on the night of 26 January can be told by one of the participants, Emanuel Hutton, a wool comber sentenced to eighteen months' hard labour in Wakefield House of Correction following his trial at York for riot:

> I was called up at night and when I came down a gun was put in my hands. I don't know who gave it to me. I wish I had. If I had known it at York it would have been told. I went down stairs and saw a man who told me to follow him – I did so for about 200 yards and there I saw a lot of men who bade me go into the market place with them – one gave me a gun. I asked several questions – there seemed no one appointed to lead. We went into the market place and as soon as I saw the Constables I set off – but I was caught. I had been at the Meetings. I was a Chartist only by reading the Star newspaper. I had heard my neighbours talk of a rising – they had fixed many a day.[23]

Others did not live to tell their story. John Clayton, one of the Sheffield insurgents, died in Northallerton House of Correction, and the Sheffield leader, Samuel Holberry, died in York Castle.

The risings were real but futile in the opinion of many at the time and of historians since. They neither removed the government nor won the Charter, but they appeared to succeed in one of their aims – to rescue John Frost. Frost, Williams and Jones were found guilty before Christmas and received the death sentence for high treason on 13 January. On 1 February this was commuted to transportation for life. The petitions for a reprieve contained more signatures than the first Chartist Petition, rejected in July 1839, and they were generated in an atmosphere more angry and desperate than had prevailed in the summer. Though the commutation was actually owing to the recommendation of the Lord Chief Justice, its effect was to defuse what might otherwise have become a very dangerous situation.[24] A firmly effective but not savage sentencing policy in this and in the hundreds of lesser cases brought before the courts in the winter of 1839–40, avoided the danger of provocation and brought the first Chartist crisis to a sullen but peaceful end.

## The second Chartist crisis, 1842

The Chartist movement which imprisoned Chartists rejoined on their release from gaol during 1840 and 1841 was superficially the same as in 1838 and 1839 but in important respects was quite different. It still supported the strategy of a National Petition for the People's Charter, but the broad alliance of reforming movements and leaders which had come together in 1838 was now shattered. Some early leaders, like Oastler and Stephens, had never been Chartists as such. The same could be said of Thomas Attwood and the Birmingham Political Union contingent who had left the Convention over physical force and then imprisoned one of their own members, John Collins. Moderates, like Collins and William Lovett, now followed their own 'moral force' route away from the mainstream. They were joined by former extremists, such as Robert Lowery and Henry Vincent. Others, such as John Frost, were safely in Australia, while yet others, such as Bussey, were in voluntary exile in the United States. Mainstream Chartism was more closely than ever identified with Feargus O'Connor and the *Northern Star*. As such it was likely to be demagogic but peaceful, appealing to the moral force of peaceful mass support, constitutional methods and, if armed, then constitutionally armed. It was also better organised, with the National Charter Association (NCA) being formed in Manchester in July 1840. Henceforward Chartism was to be more like a modern mass political party, with a membership, a bureaucracy, and a certain amount of discipline. Meetings were more like party rallies and the annual Convention was a regulated party conference at which policy could be developed and dissidents expelled. If the lesson of 1839–40 had been the futility of physical force, that lesson had been learned.

The release of prisoners and a general election in 1841 stimulated a new and better-organised drive for a second National Petition. As in

1838–39, signatures were gathered against a background of gloomy economic conditions with increasing unemployment and rising bread prices. Again all hopes were pinned on the Charter to resolve these problems, though middle-class radicals offered the alternative of a repeal of the Corn Laws. Again, as in 1839, the National Convention met in London, and on 2 May again the House of Commons rejected the Petition although it claimed the support of 3,317,752 signatures compared with 'only' 1,280,000 in 1839. The coming summer was a troubled one, with widespread strikes and rioting on a scale greater than in 1839. The question which has troubled historians is how far was this activity connected with Chartism? Were the strikes political as well as economic?

Phrases to describe the events of the summer of 1842 have been loaded with meaning, both at the time and since: the 'Plug Plot' suggests conspiracy while 'General Strike' describes widespread industrial action with, following Benbow's pamphlet on the *Grand National Holiday* of 1832, perhaps also a political purpose. 'Riot' suggests localised and undirected violence, while to one contemporary in Accrington, the disturbances of August 1842 seemed 'more like a revolution than anything else'.[25] One can understand why. The strike came closer to the ideal of a simultaneous rising than any other disturbances in the period covered by this book, with the possible exception of the 'Swing' riots of 1830: within a space of a few weeks, fifteen English and Welsh counties were affected, as well as eight Scottish. London experienced disturbances at the same time as the major provincial industrial districts. Local forces for maintaining order were unable to cope and the deployment of troops was stretched by the geographical scale of the disturbances. In the balanced view of one historian

> the disturbances of 1842 were the most intense of any that occurred in Britain from the time of the French Revolution to the Chartist *détente* of 1848. They covered a wider geographical area than Luddism, embraced more trades than the Agricultural Labourers' Rising of 1830, and broke with more concentrated force than the Chartist unrest of 1839 and 1848.[26]

Initially both the Chartist leadership and the Home Secretary, Sir James Graham, believed that the strikes were an Anti-Corn Law League plot, consistent with the way middle-class reformers had used the threat of working-class violence to further their own ends in 1832. Superficially this was plausible. Most factories in the textile districts at the heart of the strike were working short-time anyway, and there would have been little to lose economically by a shut-down. John Bright of Rochdale did in fact suggest using lock-outs to provoke a challenge to the Corn Laws. The strikes began in the Manchester area following a 25 per cent cut in wages at Bayley's factory in Stalybridge – the Bayleys were supporters of the Anti-Corn Law League.[27] The manufacturers and the newspapers that supported them, however, thought the strikes a Chartist plot. The *Leeds Mercury* in the same report on 20 August referred to events as both 'The Holiday– Insurrection' and 'The Chartist Insurrection'.[28] Yet the Chartist leadership, meeting in Manchester in the middle of the strikes to commemorate Henry Hunt and the 'Peterloo' massacre on 16 August, appeared surprised by events which they then followed rather than led. The evidence is, as usual, contradictory, but what has become clear is that local Chartists were closely involved in the strikes, that there was some co-ordinated leadership, and that there was a groundswell of local Chartism which used its position within striking communities to turn industrial action into a strike for the Charter. Just as some Chartists leaders, such as O'Brien, argued that Corn Law repeal would not be to the workers' advantage unless guaranteed by the Charter, so Chartist strike leaders argued that good wages could only be guaranteed by a government elected under the Charter.

The strikes began in early July in the Staffordshire coalfield where the issues were wage cuts, a system of employment known as 'buildas' (work without pay) and the truck system but the resolutions setting out the demands of the south Staffordshire miners on 1 August were proposed by two Chartists, Joseph Linney and Arthur O'Neill.[29] This set the pattern. The Chartists did not create the grievances, or the economic depression which caused employers to demand wage reductions, but they did organise the workers' reaction and turned local strikes and an inclination to riot into a concerted challenge to the authority of employers, the forces of law and order and ultimately the government itself. And they did so all the more effectively because they were not outside agitators with an abstract political programme but members of their own local communities caught up in their own and their neighbours' grievances.

At the end of July, factory masters south-east of Manchester, in

Ashton, Stalybridge, Dukinfield and Hyde, announced a 25 per cent reduction in wages. On 26 July a large public meeting chaired by William Woodruffe, an Ashton Chartist delegate, resolved to stop work 'until we obtain a fair day's wage for a fair day's work'.[30] The two main speakers, William Aitken and Richard Pilling, were both Chartists. This was followed by a further meeting at Stalybridge on 29 July, also addressed by known Chartists. Both meetings were primarily about the wages issue but they also supported the Charter and called for arms to be raised to protect the working classes. Further meetings were held in Hyde and Dukinfield over the next few days with the same and similar speakers to the same effect. As a result most employers withdrew the cuts, but at Bayleys' factory there was some confusion. The employers claimed that Bayleys' offer was rejected and the workers struck work; the workers claimed they were locked out. On Sunday, 7 August a large meeting was held on Mottram Moor where the main speakers were, again, Chartists. Resolutions were carried in support of a strike for a fair day's wage and the Charter, and it was announced that there would be a general turn-out throughout Lancashire and Cheshire on the following morning.

The success of the turn-out in the Ashton–Stalybridge area, straddling the county boundary between Lancashire and Cheshire, points to something more than spontaneity in the strike. It had clearly been organised by that group of Chartist speakers who had led the preliminary meetings.[31] Their leader was Richard Pilling, a weaver from Ashton with a long history of active participation in Chartism, and radicalism before that. O'Connor, quoting a witness against Pilling at his trial at the Lancaster Assizes, subsequently referred to him as 'the father of the movement' and in 1848 Pilling himself boasted that he 'was the sole cause of the turn-out in Lancashire, the originator of the whole proceeding'.[32] But at Lancaster, Pilling had argued more politically, 'I say it is not *me* that is the father of this movement; but that house. Our addresses have been laid before that house, and they have not redressed our grievances; and from there, and from there alone, the cause comes.'[33]

Pilling was clearly unrepentant that this was a politically-inspired strike. On the afternoon of 8 August he led a party from Ashton to Oldham to spread the strike. Then on 9 August the strikers were ready to march on Manchester. Sir Charles Shaw, the commissioner of police in Manchester, wanted to keep them out, but Daniel

Maude, the stipendiary magistrate, who had ultimate authority, saw the women in the procession and the generally peaceful demeanour of 'the mob' and thought it better to allow their passage. Although troops did in fact block several streets, the strikers were allowed to hold a peaceful rally addressed by Pilling. Most of the factories turned out with little or no violence until the crowd reached Birley Mills in Oxford Street. Here a battle began which dragged on into the next day and was ended only by soldiers with fixed bayonets. The senior member of the Birley family, Hugh Hornby Birley, had commanded the yeomanry at Peterloo. By the Saturday 13 August, Birley's too was forced to close.

The turn-outs now spread northwards and eastwards to Rochdale and Bolton, then to Blackburn, Todmorden and over the Pennines to Halifax as the strike went into its second week. Everywhere the pattern was repeated. A party of strikers asked the workers to leave their employment; most did so readily. The factory was then immobilised by driving in the boiler plugs, releasing the water and extinguishing the fire, thus cutting off the motor power and bringing the whole works to a standstill. This prevented the workers from being coerced back to work. Very little damage was done; the plugs on the boilers of high pressure steam engines were not driven in, for fear of causing an explosion. There was little indiscriminate looting, excepting demands for bread. Where there were clashes with the police or troops, the principal weapons were stones. Intimidation came from superior numbers. Outright violence was the exception. In Preston, where a policeman had been killed in an election riot the year before, a stone-throwing crowd ran up against a small detachment of troops who opening fire, killing four rioters and seriously wounding several more. Beyond the Manchester area, there was a serious riot in the Potteries. As in south Staffordshire, the strike began in the north Staffordshire collieries in early July in protest at wage cuts. By mid July, colliers were roaming the coal field halting other pits and stopping their steam engines by driving in the boiler plugs. The shortage of coal then stopped the potteries, creating greater distress and unemployment. On 6 August three miners were arrested for begging. This provoked an attack on the town hall to release them. The local newspaper was in no doubt that, 'The perpetrators of these wanton outrages are believed to consist principally of the more disaffected turn-out colliers, instigated, there is but little doubt, by the

Chartists.'[34] The role of Chartists, as in Lancashire and Cheshire, was as organisers of meetings, providing leadership and oratory.

Thomas Cooper, the Leicester Chartist, addressed one such meeting on Sunday 14 August at Hanley. Next morning, he delivered an ambiguously worded address to a crowd of several thousands, after which a resolution was adopted in favour of the strike. The crowd then dispersed and turned into a mob, raking out the fires and removing the plugs at Shelton colliery, attacking the police station and releasing the prisoners, looting the pawnbrokers' shops, and destroying the poor law records and the court room – all symbols of the oppression of the poor. They then went on to other towns in the Potteries. In Longton they attacked the town hall, the police station and the parish office, and fired the house of the rector, Dr Vale, who was a poor law guardian. Cooper addressed another meeting that night, urging (by his own account) 'Peace, Law and Order!', but the crowd did not disperse and held sway all night. Cooper fled to Macclesfield on his way to Manchester. Next day, troops confronted the rioters in Burslem but were able to reassert control only by firing into the crowd. At least three rioters were killed and several injured. Gradually order was restored in all Five Towns.[35]

As the movement spilled over the Pennines from Lancashire into Yorkshire, the *Leeds Mercury*, the paper read by most Whig mill-owners, reported events in terrifying detail. Despite the obvious bias in the reporting, it conveys a sense of the power and terror of the plug-drawing mob:

> The concourse of people, which has been computed at not less than from 15,000 to 20,000, came from the neighbourhood of Bradford, Hebden Bridge, Todmorden, and there were some women who had even walked from Oldham, and appeared quite hearty in their novel undertaking. There were at least 5,000 from Hebden Bridge, and they entered the town singing the hundredth psalm, the women forming the middle portion of the procession. On the arrival of the procession from the neighbourhood of Bradford, at about eleven o'clock, the riot act was read by George Pollock, Esq., and it was read again on the arrival of the Todmorden men.
>
> The mob, some of them ferocious looking, directed their malice first at the mill of Messrs. Jon. Akroyd and Son, the Shade mill, at Haley Hill.

The number of men and women who marched up to Mr. Akroyd's mill could not be less than 10,000, covering, as they did, the whole line of road from the North Bridge to Haley Hill. They arrived at this mill shortly after twelve, and the work-people being at dinner, the turn-outs were saved the trouble of clearing the premises, but two of their number demanded an interview with Mr. Akroyd, at which they insisted that the plugs should be drawn out of the boilers. Mr. Akroyd, thinking probably that opposition would be unavailing, not only agreed to this *modest* request, but also permitted one of his workmen to assist the deputation in their labour of mischief. The mob outside, however, would not rest satisfied until they had full confirmation that the work had been done effectually, and in a few minutes afterwards a deputation of six presented themselves to see that all was *right*. Having all doubts removed respecting the plugging of the boilers, they then not only requested, but insisted, that the reservoir should be let off. On this point they were met on the part of Mr. Akroyd with a decided negative, which only tended to increase the eagerness of the turn-outs, to effect their object. In order to prevent so disastrous a calamity, (for, by turning off the reservoir, which is merely supplied by rain and other smaller reservoirs, the works would have been stopped for several weeks) a present of a £5 note was tendered to the men to induce them to go quietly about their business. This temptation not having the desired effect, the military were hastily sent for, and in a few minutes they were at the scene of action, and arrived just at the moment to prevent incalculable mischief; . . .

The soldiers secured six young men near to Mr. Akroyd's mill, for riotous conduct, – apparently about the ages of from 18 to 23, – and they were taken from Mr. Akroyd's grounds to the Magistrates' office, under an escort of about a dozen foot soldiers, with loaded muskets.

On their way through the streets an attempt was made to rescue them, and stones were frequently thrown at the soldiers, one or two of whom, it is said, but we cannot vouch for the fact, in a moment of excitement, fired upon the people, wounding one young man in the legs.

Another man, in the course of the afternoon, was taken into custody and placed in the prison, for breach of the peace – thus making seven in all; and no doubt numbers more might have been taken up, but for the leniency of the military and the special constables.[36]

Akroyd had been one of the first manufacturers in the area to reduce wages.

The magistrates decided next day it would be best to move the prisoners to Wakefield. The railway had not yet reached Halifax, and so the prisoners had to be transported by coach with a military escort down the steep hill at Salterhebble to the station at Elland in the Calder Valley. The crowd decided to ambush the coach and release the prisoners. They failed to do so, but were able to take their revenge on the returning troops as they made their way slowly up the hill back to Halifax.

> But, on a sudden a cry was raised that the soldiers were advancing, and as suddenly the apparent calm was succeeded by an overwhelming tempest, for, in a moment as it were, a shower of large stones were hurled from all parts of the eminence among the soldiers, who then came up at full gallop, and on to the heads of the devoted and innocent passengers, who thus suffered severely from the accidental circumstances of being compelled, though only for a few moments, to be apparently under the protection of the soldiery. With such direct aim were these missiles hurled, that scarcely a soldier escaped unhurt – some of them received severe cuts – three of them were fairly felled from their horses, the animals setting off and leaving their late riders to the mercy of the mob. . . . Of course there was a scene of very great confusion; an express was sent to Halifax for the infantry, and the gallant Hussars, after charging with ball, returned, headed by Mr Briggs, to the rescue of their companions, which they effected. During the affray, Mr Briggs received a wound on the arm from a stone, which disabled him, and he went home: the soldiers had previously received orders to fire, and these orders were carried into effect, we are afraid with a fatal result, but of this we cannot speak with certainty; the soldiers' horses were retaken at Elland.[37]

The final irony was that one of the passengers wounded on the coach was a reporter for the *Northern Star*.

The above account illustrates both the methods by which the strikers proceeded, with a very orderly negotiation over stopping Akroyd's mill and a quite proper rejection of his bribe while he played for time; and the suddenness with which violence could flare up, demonstrating the vulnerability of both sides but ultimately the superiority of the force available to magistrates like the gallant William Briggs.

Despite such occurrences, most of the strike was conducted with an ominous restraint, indicating a more sophisticated approach than would have been expected of a mere hunger riot. Back in Manchester, the extent of this organisation was apparent and it was this aspect of the strike that worried the Home Secretary most.

The form that central leadership of the strikes took was the Great Delegate Conference meeting in Manchester under the chairmanship of Alexander Hutchinson, an Owenite Socialist and Chartist who was secretary of the Manchester smiths and a member of the National Charter Association (NCA) executive. On 11 August at a meeting in the Carpenters' Hall, a delegate conference of mechanics, engineers, millwrights, moulders and smiths met to agree a common pro- gramme of action. The following morning a delegate conference of the mill trades met at the Sherwood Inn to do the same. Both confer- ences carried almost identical motions in favour of the Charter.[38] The two conferences then made arrangements for the Great Delegate Conference at the Sherwood Inn on Monday, 15 August. This was adjourned to the Carpenters' Hall to better accommodate the 143 del- egates who attended. The following day, 16 August, 141 delegates representing eighty-five trades met in the largest hall available in Manchester, the Owenite Hall of Science – the Carpenters' Hall had already been booked by the Chartists. Here the trades delegates voted by a large majority to cease work until the Charter became the law of the land.[39] As the conference was coming to the end of its busi- ness for the day, the hall was surrounded by police and troops and the chief constable ordered the meeting to disperse. When Hutchinson refused on the grounds that the meeting was legal, the magistrates were sent for to pronounce it illegal. The delegates then complied, but defiantly issued a placard announcing the resolution of the meeting:

> that the delegates in public meeting assembled, do recommend to the various constituencies we represent, to adopt all legal means to carry into effect the People's Charter; and further we recommend that delegates be sent through the whole country to endeavour to obtain the co-operation of the middle and working classes in carrying out the resolution of ceasing labour until the Charter becomes the law of the land.[40]

Their ranks thinned by arrests and hurried departures out of Manchester, a rump of delegates reconvened the following day at the Sherwood Inn where they formed a central committee and urged the formation of local committees to direct the strike.

Meanwhile, the NCA executive had arranged to meet in Manchester on 16 August to commemorate Peterloo, with O'Connor unveiling a statue of Henry Hunt at James Scholefield's chapel in Ancoats. A placard had been issued on 1 August, announcing a procession from Stevenson Square to the Ancoats chapel, and then back to the Carpenters' Hall for a tea party and ball. Scholefield called off the procession on the morning of 16 August and in the evening, instead of attending the ball, O'Connor stayed behind at the chapel 'with other Chartists, engaged in considering what measures were best to be adopted in the present crisis'.[41] He was probably considering the reversal of Chartist policy towards the strike which emerged at the NCA executive conference the following day. Hitherto, O'Connor had agreed with William Hill, editor of the *Northern Star*, that the strike was probably an Anti-Corn Law League plot or a trap designed to discredit the Chartists, but on 17 August he supported Peter Murray McDouall's ringing endorsement of the strikes:

> That whilst the Chartist body did not originate the present cessation from labour, this conference of delegates from various parts of England, express their deep sympathy with their constituents, the working men now on strike, and that we strongly approve the extension and continuance of their present struggle till the People's Charter becomes legislative enactment, and decide forthwith to issue an address to that effect, and pledge ourselves, on our return to our respective localities, to give proper direction to the people's efforts.[42]

Only six delegates votes against this resolution, including Hill and, remarkably, the 'Marat' of the revolution, George Julian Harney.[43]

This resolution and two addresses that accompanied it committed Chartism to the strikes.[44] This fact was used against O'Connor and other leaders when they were brought before the Lancaster Assizes in April 1843 on a charge of seditious conspiracy. Although the strikes were to continue well into September, hunger, the arrest of leaders and a tightening of control by the police and military were already beginning to turn the tide against the workers. By October, around

1500 arrests had been made: about half were tried before magistrates' courts and half before special commissions held in Carlisle, York, Chester, Lancaster, Liverpool and Stafford. Fifty-nine of those arrested, including O'Connor and the rest of the Chartist leadership, were reserved for the Assizes at Lancaster. In the end, these were the lucky ones for, despite being found guilty, a fault in the indictment meant they were never called up for sentence.

In this interpretation of events, the strikes of 1842 were more than industrial actions, and the riots were not spontaneous outbursts of popular anger or anguish – though doubtless they were for some participants. There was a seditious conspiracy in that local Chartist leaders provided organisation and co-ordination and directed the strikes to a political end. The degree of co-ordination and organisation with its controlled use of violence seemed a real threat to the authorities. The government was particularly alarmed at the prospect of the strikes spreading to London where a large open-air meeting was held on 16 August on Stepney Green. It was addressed by a speaker from Ashton, and passed a resolution in favour of the Charter. Further meetings followed on Clerkenwell Green, Bethnal Green, Lincoln's Inn Fields and other open spaces throughout the city. The Duke of Wellington pressed for the Grenadier Guards, who had just been sent to Manchester, to be brought back to the capital. Further meetings on Kennington Common and Paddington Green on 22 August were dispersed by large numbers of police supported by troops.

The danger passed but it had seemed real enough while it lasted. Although in retrospect one can see that the authorities could hold out longer than the strikers, so that a strike until the Charter was enacted was simply not realistic, the threat to public order in the summer of 1842 was considerable. Yet, the very act of striking for the Charter was a constitutional one. It was not revolutionary in the conspiratorial sense of the United Irishmen or the Thistlewood group. The paradox of the Holiday–Insurrection of 1842, as the *Leeds Mercury* pointed out in its editorial for 20 August, was that the cause of their success was also the reason for their failure:

> Their entire want of cohesion, their going without weapons, and their abstinence from all but one act of violence at each mill, enable them often to *elude* the soldiery and the police, and to get into towns and into mills unawares: they also prevent the masters from having any great apparent interest in resisting them

and further, they blind the workmen to the real danger of this lawless movement. But that same want of cohesion, that want of any tangible and visible form of insurrection, render their operations as evanescent as they were surprising.

However, 'if the turn-outs were to change their character, and to form a rebel army, no sooner would they be thus brought to a head than they would be utterly demolished'. for 'the masters who submit quietly to the driving in of a boiler plug, would act in a very different manner if their property was threatened with serious and extensive mischief'. There may have been an air of complacency here, or the editor was trying to allay the fears of his readers, but he was right to note in the events of the summer of 1842 the unusually peaceful nature of the 'insurrection'. The Chartists had learned how to turn an 'ebullition' into an organised mass protest. That made it more, not less, of a challenge to the established order and an important development in the character of working-class politics.

## The third Chartist crisis, 1848

As the economic depression lifted and bread prices fell after 1842, mass Chartist support declined and the constitutional mainstream prevailed, but with the downturn in the European economy in 1847, revolution returned to Europe and with it the possibility of renewed violence in Britain and Ireland. The revolutionary upheavals of 'the springtime of the peoples' which swept the continent in the wake of the fall of the French monarchy in February 1848 seemed to promise as never before the realisation of the dream that, 'For a nation to love liberty, it is sufficient that she knows it; and to be free, it is sufficient that she wills it.' As the world was to rediscover again in 1989, the impossible could sometimes happen; immovable regimes could collapse before the power of the people; even constitutional revolution might be possible.

Chartism had already begun to revive before the news from France gave new heart to the movement. At the general election in 1847, Feargus O'Connor had been elected to the House of Commons for Nottingham and fear that his victory would be challenged reinvigorated the NCA in his support. As one old Chartist later recalled, perhaps with some exaggeration for the entertainment of his readers:

In this year flour was very dear, reaching the price of 5s. per stone, whilst trade was also very bad. This was the time to make politicians, as the easiest way to get to an Englishman's brains is through his stomach. It was said by its enemies that Chartism was dead and buried and would never rise again, but they were doomed to disappointment. . . . We were only waiting for the time to come again.[45]

The NCA launched a new National Petition in favour of the Charter and arranged mass meetings to whip up support. This time, though, the centre of the movement was London where the *Northern Star* and NCA were now based. The first wave of rioting began in early March, but little of this was specifically 'Chartist'. On 6 March a demonstration in Trafalgar Square against a proposed rise in the income tax (hardly a cause of immediate concern to Chartists) was banned and resulted in rioting and a rush towards Buckingham Palace that caught the police by surprise. A few lamps and windows were broken on the way but it was three days before the metropolitan police were fully in control. Of the 127 rioters arrested, two-thirds were aged between 16 and 22.[46] Worse news was received from elsewhere in the country. In Glasgow, a crowd of several thousand unemployed, reported to be mainly Irish, complained about the quality of the food provided by the Relief Committee and resorted to looting local shops including gunsmiths. A barricade was erected and cries of 'Bread or Revolution' and '*Vive la République*' were heard. The Riot Act was read and troops were called out. Three people were killed as soldiers fired to clear the threatening crowds. The knowledge of recent events in Paris gave this occasion greater significance than it might otherwise have had.

On 8 and 9 March a similar though lesser riot took place in Edinburgh. In Manchester the unemployed rioted at the imposition of oakum picking by the poor law authorities, but they were dealt with by the police. On 17 March (St Patrick's Day) the Chartists held a demonstration on Kennington Common in south London, which was followed by some looting in Camberwell. The authorities nervously enrolled special constables. On the same day in Salford a Chartist meeting outside the town hall voted a congratulatory address to the French people and a Chartist–Irish Confederate alliance was cemented.[47] Again, nervous magistrates enrolled special constables. As the day for the presentation of the Petition drew near, there was heightened expectation on both sides throughout the country and, anticipating its rejection by the House of Commons, Chartists were reported to be arming and drilling on the moors as in 1839.[48] In the *Northern Star*, the editor, Harney, outdid even his usual revolutionary rhetoric as he proclaimed:

> The work goes bravely on. Germany is revolutionised from end to end. Princes are flying, thrones are perishing. Everywhere the oppressors of nations yield, or are overthrown. 'Reform or Revolution' is now the order of the day. How long, Men of Great Britain and Ireland, how long will you carry the damning stigma of being the only people in Europe who dare not will their freedom?
>
> Patience! the hour is nigh! From the hill-tops of Lancashire, from the voices of hundreds of thousands has ascended to Heaven the oath of union, and the rallying cry of conflict. Englishmen and Irishmen have sworn to have THE CHARTER AND REPEAL, or VIVE LA REPUBLIQUE![49]

The Chartist Convention met in London on 4 April and arranged to present the Petition on 10 April. The plan was to convene a large demonstration on Kennington Common, with parallel meetings elsewhere in the country (and, indeed elsewhere in London), after which the Petition would be taken in procession to the House of Commons. The very idea was intimidating and the government was concerned that London should not slide into revolution as had happened in Paris and Berlin. Accordingly, massive steps were taken to ensure that the meeting would not get out of hand. Initially the government would have banned the meeting, but then realised that this would be more likely to cause trouble than allowing it to proceed on a peaceful basis. But they banned the procession, closed the bridges across the Thames to confine the Chartists to the south of the river, and organised their own massive counter-demonstration of physical force throughout the capital: 85,000 special constables, many of them workmen enrolled to defend their own places of work and possibly to prevent them attending the meeting; 4,000 police, mainly on the bridges and in the vicinity of Parliament; and 8,000 troops in reserve. Estimates of Chartist numbers range from the official 15,000 to O'Connor's 'rather under than over 400,000'. The latest scholarly guess suggests somewhere around 150,000.[50]

Much of the mythology about the great Kennington Common

meeting on 10 April is based on hindsight. Within a few days, every-one knew that the meeting had dispersed as peacefully as the Chartists had always intended, that the Petition had been taken to the House of Commons in six cabs, and that the number of signatures was not the 5,706,000 claimed but 'only' an estimated 1,975,496. London could afford to relax and laugh at the Chartist 'fiasco'. This view needs revising in three respects: most people were not laughing at the time; the 'fiasco' effect was in part planned by the government to discredit Chartism; and from the point of view of revolutionary threat, the worst was still to come.

Most people were not laughing until it was all over. This is clear from diaries kept at the time by prominent figures. John Cam Hobhouse, one-time Radical but now deeply conservative and anti-Chartist Whig minister, recorded 10 April apprehensively:

> There was an appearance of the expectation of some strug-gle or disastrous event. When I got to the Indian Board I found some clerks rather annoyed at there being no arms nor any mil-itary force there. I cannot say I felt quite easy, separated as I was from my children, and recollecting that my door had been chalked, as also had Lord Grey's and Labouchere's. Lord J. Russell had a force of constables in his house.
>
> I sat down to office business, not expecting, but thinking it by no means improbable that I should hear discharges of mus-ketry or cannon from the other side of the river. Indeed, the slam-ming of doors made me start once or twice, and I looked at Westminster Bridge to see whether it was crowded. I heard cheers, and, going to the window, saw a boat with soldiers going under the bridge, and a crowd on the bridge, with men on horse-back waving hats; and shortly after the bridge was completely empty, and a few mounted police were guarding it. Shortly after, Mr. Plowden came into the room full of glee, and said, 'It is all over.' He had been to the Home Office and learned that Feargus O'Connor had just been with Sir George Grey to announce that the meeting had broken up, that the procession was abandoned, and that he was about to take the monster petition to the House of Commons in six cabs.
>
> I went to the House of Commons at half past four, and saw the petition in two great rolls on the floor of the outward lobby.[51]

Charles Greville, secretary to the Privy Council, noted on 9 April the extensive preparations being made for the following day, uncertain whether they were 'very sublime or very ridiculous'.[52] However, all doubt had been removed as to which when he wrote his next diary entry, at Newmarket races on 13 April:

> Monday passed off with surprising quiet, and it was considered a most satisfactory demonstration on the part of the Government, and the peaceable and loyal part of the community. Enormous preparations were made, and a host of military, police, and special constables were ready if wanted; every gentleman in London was sworn, and during a great part of the day, while the police were reposing, they did duty. The Chartist movement was contemptible; but everybody rejoices that the demonstration was made, for it has given a great and memorable lesson which will not be thrown away, either on the disaffected and mischievous, or the loyal and peaceful; and it will produce a vast effect in all foreign countries, and show how solid is the foundation on which we are resting. We have displayed a great resolution and a great strength, and given unmistakeable [sic] proofs, that if sedition and rebellion hold up their heads in this country, they will be instantly met with the most vigorous resistance, and be put down by the hand of authority, and by the zealous co-operation of all classes of the people. The whole of the Chartist movement was to the last degree contemptible from first to last.

CITY COLLEGE LEARNING RESOURCE CENTRE

Here he gives not only the typical reaction of those whose fears had not been realised, but also suggests that the build up on 10 April had been government policy, partly to overawe and discredit the Chartists once and for all, and partly to impress foreign governments which had shown themselves unable to cope with their own revolutionary crowds. There is a coincidence between the sentiments expressed in this diary entry and words used by the prime minister, Lord John Russell, writing to the Queen on the afternoon of 10 April: 'A quiet termination of the present ferment will greatly raise us in foreign countries.'[53]

One of the advantages of the defeat of Chartism was, in Greville's opinion, its effect on the Irish. Hobhouse too had the Irish on his mind and the major event in the House of Commons on 13 April was not the discrediting of the People's Charter but the debate on the bill 'for the more effectual repression of seditious and treasonable proceedings' in Ireland. This Treason–Felony Act was followed on 22 July by the suspension of *Habeas Corpus* in Ireland where the situation had deteriorated since 1847, partly as a result of nationalist anger over the famine and partly an outcome of the realignment in Irish politics that was accelerated by Daniel O'Connell's death in 1847. A group of romantic nationalists, including Charles Gavan Duffy, had started a paper, the *Nation*, in October 1842. They did not favour violence and were opposed to the Chartists. This moderation was carried over, even after the miseries of the famine had begun, by Duffy and William Smith O'Brien in a secession in early 1847 from O'Connell's Repeal Association, known as the Irish Confederation. A minority of Confederates, however, took up the cause of tenant right and in early 1848 two of this group, John Mitchel and Thomas Devin Reilly, set up their own paper, the *United Irishman* in rivalry to the *Nation*. The news from France then brought the two groups closer together again. O'Brien called for the formation of a National Guard, for which he was charged with sedition but acquitted when the jury was unable to agree a verdict. The Confederates also struck a working relationship with the Chartists in Britain. This had always been Feargus O'Connor's dream, but he had been thwarted while O'Connell lived.

The old fear of an Franco-Irish alliance in revolution revived. Russell was under no illusions about what the Irish might do. As he wrote to Lord Clarendon, the Lord Lieutenant, on 1 March 1848, 'The Irish are not the French but they have a knack of imitation.'[54] Indeed the very next day the Duke of Wellington, as Commander in Chief, sent a memorandum to his opposite in Dublin warning that 'the Irish Revolutionary or Repeal leaders had sent over to Paris persons to enquire respecting the mode of constructing the Barricades in the streets which have been used there and have been considered so formidable'.[55] The government acted swiftly. By the time Smith O'Brien (on bail for sedition) got to Paris with a congratulatory address at the end of March, Britain had already agreed with the French Provisional Government a pact of mutual non-interference in each other's internal affairs. If the Irish were to rise successfully they would have to rely on their own resources, which meant looking to the Irish in Britain to cause a diversion and in North America for military support.

By 1848 London, Manchester, Liverpool, Bradford, Glasgow and smaller British towns such as Barnsley and Ashton had considerable Irish minorities. In Bradford and Ashton, even in 1841, some 10 per cent of the population was Irish.[56] The threat of a Chartist–Confederate alliance was considerable. In Manchester just such an

alliance had been formed on St Patrick's Day, and in his letter to the
Queen on 10 April, Lord John Russell had noted amid his pleasure
over the London débâcle, 'At Manchester, however, the Chartists are
armed, and have bad designs.' In London, Confederate clubs had
been spreading since the autumn of 1847 and on 4 April 1848 they
came together with the Chartists at a meeting arranged by the
Fraternal Democrats. There was a separate Irish contingent at
Kennington Common on 10 April. Thereafter, some joint associations
were formed.[57] Thomas Frost later recalled, 'Communications passed
at this time between the plotters of revolution on both sides of St
George's Channel.'[58] In Glasgow, where pikes were being manufactured at Anderston, Thomas D'Arcy McGee tried to persuade the
Glasgow Irish to seize the Clyde steamers and sail for Ireland, presumably with weapons. As another Irish speaker informed his audience: 'prayer and petitions were the weapons of slaves and cowards;
arms were the weapons used by the free and the brave. They would
best help Ireland by keeping the army in Scotland'.[59] These were brave
words, but a proposed National Guard materialised only in
Aberdeen, Dundee and Edinburgh, and not on the scale of the 6,000
at Aberdeen that Ernest Jones later claimed. In Liverpool, ships from
North America were searched on entering British waters, and the
police in Dublin were instructed to arrest all returning Irish emigrants
and search them for treasonable papers.[60] In Bradford throughout
April and May there were reports of drilling and pikes being manufactured. Desperate, unemployed wool combers, many of them Irish,
attended meetings at which inflammatory language was used. One
informer reported, apparently without exaggeration, 'that there is
reason to apprehend that the Chartists here would rise if there should
be an outbreak in Ireland or anywhere in England'.[61]

The background to mounting unrest in the early summer of 1848
was the impending trial of John Mitchel under the new Treason–
Felony Act, following his arrest on 22 March for publishing seditious
articles in the *United Irishman*.[62] There was widespread fear of a rising
should he be convicted. In London, where the Chartist Convention
had been succeeded by a National Assembly on 1 May, a New Plan of
Organisation was agreed, similar to that employed by the United
Irishmen in the late 1790s, with a basic unit of ten men to a class and
ten classes to a ward. This structure was both flexible and opaque,
lending itself to conspiratorial organisations which in individual

localities easily merged with local Irish Confederate clubs. At the same time, regular outdoor meetings were held, particularly in East London. Chartism at this level was more active than ever. Mitchel was tried on 25 and 26 May and sentenced to death, later commuted to transportation for fourteen years. Meetings in his support were held on Clerkenwell Green during the trial, and on 28 May perhaps 10,000 to 12,000 people gathered on the Green. The following evening several thousand gathered again and hear a rousing speech from John Fussell in which he said 'If John Mitchell [*sic*] is sent to Spike island then it is quite evident that you may use spikes for the government. I have five sons and I would disown them if they were not ready to assassinate men who sent me out of the Country for such a crime as that of which John Mitchell is said to be guilty.'[63]

The crowd then marched towards Trafalgar Square. They were joined *en route* by another 3,000 who had been listening to speeches from Ernest Jones and other Chartist leaders on Stepney Green. They marched through the West End and then back east in a formidable display of strength. At its height the crowd was estimated to be between 50,000 and 60,000 strong. Although the main procession was peaceful, there was some marginal rioting and next morning the police banned all assemblages and processions in the capital. Meetings nevertheless continued: on Clerkenwell Green on 31 May where troops stood by as the police cleared the Green; and in Bonner's Fields on 4 June, where Ernest Jones was the main speaker. These and smaller, simultaneous meetings, often unannounced so no reporter could be present to collect evidence for a prosecution, were gradually wearing down the police and demoralising property owners in the vicinity of the meetings. On 4 June the police snapped and rioted against the crowd.[64] The tone of Charles Greville's diary was very different from that of 13 April. The mood of the people had changed for the worse and

> many who on 10th of April went out as special constables declare that they would not do so again if another manifestation required it. The speeches which are made at the different meetings are remarkable for the coarse language and savage spirit they display. It is quite new to hear any Englishman coolly recommend assassination and the other day a Police Superintendent was wounded in the leg by some sharp instrument. These are new and very bad symptoms, and it is impossible not to feel

alarm when we consider the vast amount of the population as compared with any repressive power we possess.[65]

Finally, warrants were issued for the arrest of the leading speakers, including Jones and Fussell.

The culmination of these meetings came on Whit Monday, 12 June, on Bonner's Fields. This was a re-run of 10 April but in far less auspicious circumstances. The government banned all meetings and called up over 5,000 troops and 4,000 police; only a few special constables re-enlisted, and they did the duties of the ordinary police who were on riot duty.[66] David Goodway has offered the conclusion that 'The Chartist leadership would probably have welcomed the Bonner's Fields demonstration developing into a rising.'[67] In fact the only member of the Chartist Executive left in London was Peter Murray McDouall. He sized up the situation, and called the meeting off. A heavy thunderstorm did the rest.

That evening, at the Albion beershop in Bethnal Green Road, McDouall sat down to plan an insurrection, but two days later called it off on the instructions of the Chartist Executive: spies had been detected. Nothing further happened until 10 July when the conspirators resumed their meetings, this time independently of the Chartist Executive, although the latter came to know of the plot. On 20 July a secret committee was formed to plan for the day of insurrection which was to be 16 August. Then, on 27 July news came that Smith O'Brien had attempted a rising in Ireland which had been a complete failure and the leaders had all been arrested. Neither this, nor a realistic (and justified) fear of spies, deterred the conspirators who were now in deadly earnest.[68]

The conspiracy was not just a London one, for events in London since April had been repeated elsewhere.[69] The main centres of concern to the authorities were Manchester, Liverpool and Bradford where the situation was especially dangerous. Bradford, which had grown rapidly over the past two decades and become the centre of the worsted trade, had been incorporated as a borough and acquired its own police force only in 1847. This numbered sixty-nine men, or one to every 1,343 inhabitants. With such an inadequate force, the mayor was powerless to stop Chartist activities. As one correspondent complained to the Home Office:

Nothing can induce him to put a stop to illegal meetings, drillings and secret armings of the tumultuous mob who even hold

CITY COLLEGE
LEARNING RESOURCE CENTRE

their meetings and perambulate the streets on the Sabbath day, marching in military style with their captains in red and green caps and divided into sections and companies, keeping the step with true military precision, carrying tricolour flags and others bearing abominable inscriptions such as 'more pigs and less parsons', 'down with the aristocracy', 'England free or a desert' etc., etc. A ferocious looking Blacksmith named the Wat Tyler of Bradford and who openly makes pikes and other deadly weapons for the Chartists is allowed to carry on his nefarious traffic without ever being molested. He is not going to shave his beard until the Charter becomes the law of the land. I enclose you a Bill that they force upon the shopkeepers to put in their windows – those who refuse are told they will not support them nor will they let others. I will give you one case that came under my own notice. They called upon a shopkeeper to beg something for to purchase Flags etc, and he refusing, on the market night they surrounded his shop and would not let a single customer enter; so that he was compelled to apologize and give them 5s and promise to become one of them.[70]

'Wat Tyler' was Isaac Jefferson, a huge man whose wrists were too thick for the police to handcuff. But they had to catch him first. The centre of his power was Adelaide Street off Manchester Road, an area densely packed with unemployed wool combers. This was an area the authorities entered at their peril. On 13 May, the police attempted to make an arrest during a military-style parade and had been beaten up by the inhabitants who successfully retrieved their leader. The reluctance of the mayor to intervene was understandable. Then, on 23 May, a mass meeting was addressed by Peter Murray McDouall who made a seditious speech with impunity. The Home Office decided that action would have to be taken. With such a large Irish population – half the Chartists were estimated to be Irish – the Mitchel verdict was clearly going to be very important and the magistrates were informed that the intention, as in Scotland, was to tie troops up to prevent them being sent to Ireland. On 27 May, extra troops arrived bringing their numbers up to 800, and 1,500 special constables were sworn in. On Sunday 28 May the magistrates finally decided to act and next morning they sent the police into Adelaide Street to arrest Jefferson and conduct a house-to-house search for arms. The police and specials had got as far as the corner of Manchester Road and Adelaide Street when the inhabitants surged out of the back streets, armed with whatever came to hand, and drove the police back to the court house. They then marched triumphantly through the streets singing Chartist songs. Troops were sent for. The police armed with cutlasses, 1,000 special constables, 200 infantry with fixed bayonets, and two troops of Dragoons then advanced and drove the mob back to their homes. Nineteen arrests were made but the leaders escaped. The Chartists subsided, down but not out. They resumed their meetings. Jefferson was finally arrested on 16 July but the mob rescued him. On 15 August the magistrates reported that pikes were still being manufactured, as the Chartists waited for news from Manchester of the general rising. When the signal came, they had at least 4,000 men ready to take the town. The history of the past few months makes this informer's estimate credible.[71]

In Liverpool, things were quiet until after Mitchel's conviction when the number of Irish clubs began to grow under the direction of a central Club Council. As with the New Plan of Organisation in London, this arrangement provided a highly co-ordinated, secret organisation from which an insurrection could easily spring. The intention, as elsewhere, was to detain troops in England. With an estimated quarter of the population Irish, Liverpool clearly presented a considerable problem for the authorities. The situation was made worse by reports from the United States where the Irish Republican Union had been formed to extend to Ireland the republican freedom enjoyed in the United States. This involved raising an Irish Brigade which would return home under the guise of disillusioned emigrants to fight the Irish cause.[72]

Mitchel's conviction hardened their determination to assist a rising in Ireland with arms, men and money, which would take place by way of Liverpool. More troops were sent to the city; more police were appointed to what was already the largest police force outside London; and there were gunboats in the Mersey. Unlike in Bradford, however, there was very little Chartist involvement. The unrest in Liverpool was an extension of the Irish problem. On 25 July, the day that *Habeas Corpus* was suspended in Ireland, a 1,000-signature petition from Liverpool asked for the Suspension Act to apply to their city also. Towards the end of July, with the corporation unable to pay for any more troops to be billeted, decisive action was taken by the police. The arrests which followed, the departure of the leader, Terence Bellew McManus, for Ireland to join the rebellion there, and then news of the failure of the Irish rising, enabled the magistrates to take control of what had been a potentially dangerous situation.[73]

In Manchester, the Irish adopted the club system as in Liverpool, and again the rhythm of protest followed the history of the Mitchel case, with a mass meeting in Stevenson Square planned for 31 May and a call for a one-day strike. The magistrates banned the meeting, and police and soldiers turned back contingents from Oldham and Ashton as they marched down the turnpikes to Manchester. There was some disturbance in the town but no serious rioting, and the police did not need to call on troops to restore order. On 6 June, Ernest Jones arrived to repeat the speech he had made in London on 4 June. Next morning he was arrested. On Whit Monday, 12 June, in common with other towns Manchester held a meeting to protest at Mitchel's sentence and in support of the Charter, but again there were no serious disturbances. The magistrates now began to arrest leaders throughout the country, but the more they arrested the more they drove the rest to desperation.

As in London, it was now that secret plotting for a rising began, and on 18 July a delegate meeting on Blackstone Edge, high in the Pennines between Halifax and Rochdale, resolved that the moral approach had failed and the time had come for physical force. The plan was for Lancashire to rise on 15 August, followed by Bradford the day after – the same day as the London rising. The government was made aware of all this through its informers. On the night of 14 August, seventy armed Chartists left Oldham for Manchester and at Ashton-under-Lyne the Chartists paraded with their arms just before midnight and one policeman was killed before the military could be called out. In Hyde, a mob began drawing the boiler plugs and the local constable was greeted with cries of, 'They're now all out, all over England, Ireland and Scotland, and before this time tomorrow night we'll either make it better or worse.'[74] The following evening, 15 August, 300 police simultaneously arrested the Chartist and Confederate leaders in Manchester. The rising was aborted so the signal was never sent to Bradford.[75] On the next night, the metropolitan police raided the taverns where the London rising was about to begin. The revolutionaries had been betrayed by a spy named Thomas Powell. The revolution was over and the gaols were filled.[76] On 14 September, Isaac Jefferson was found in his bed in a remote inn at Illingworth, near Halifax. At the York assizes he was sentenced to four months in gaol.[77] The danger was past.

## Conclusion

'The conspiracy of 1848', writes David Goodway, 'was the last of the revolutionary attempts which originated in the 1790s.'[78] The violence was less widespread than in 1842, and nothing so spectacular occurred as the Newport Rising of 1839, but as a conspiracy it was the most serious since 1817 or 1819, if not 1802. With its French and Irish dimensions – the latter more than the former – it was comparable to the revolutionary plotting of the 1790s, but this time the French were not interested and the Irish were too debilitated by famine to provide the lead that their compatriots in exile looked for. So the scale of the subversive activity, all of which came to nothing, could be erased from historical memory. Chartism in 1848 came to mean only the 'fiasco' of 10 April. The idea that working people in Victorian Britain could threaten revolution became inconceivable and dropped out of the historical reckoning. Only by recovering that contemporary fear, and the reality behind that fear, can the historian come to address the question of how political stability was created and why there was no revolution in Britain.

### Notes

1   *Bronterre's National Reformer*, 15 January 1837, extract reprinted in Cole, *British Working Class Movements* pp. 351–2.
2   See M. Taylor, 'The Six Points: Chartism and the Reform of Parliament', in O. Ashton, R. Fyson and S. Roberts (eds), *The Chartist Legacy* (Rendlesham, Merlin, 1999), pp. 1–23.
3   J. Hugman, 'A Small Drop of Ink': Tyneside Chartism and the *Northern Liberator*', in Ashton, Fyson and Roberts (eds), *Chartist Legacy*, pp. 24–47.
4   N. C. Edsall, *The Anti-Poor Law Movement, 1834–1844* (Manchester, Manchester University Press, 1971), pp. 94–6.
5   Edsall, *The Anti-Poor Law Movement*, pp. 100–15.
6   *Northern Star*, 27 January 1838.
7   J. A. Epstein, *The Lion of Freedom: Feargus O'Connor and the Chartist Movement, 1832–1842* (London, Croom Helm, 1982), pp. 7–59, 90–101.
8   BL, Add MSS. 34,245, Letter Book of the General Convention, 1839, letter from the London Democratic Association to William Lovett, secretary to the Convention.
9   *Northern Star*, 13 July 1839.
10   'The First Essay in Physical Force', *Chartist*, 12 May 1839.
11   D. J. V. Jones, *The Last Rising: The Newport Insurrection of 1839* (Oxford, Clarendon Press, 1985), p. 45.

# Revolutionary Britannia?

12  PRO, HO 40/45, Deposition of S. R. Jeffreys, 26 April 1839, as quoted in Jones, *Last Rising*, p. 71.

13  J. Frost, *A Letter to the Working Men's Association of Newport and Pillgwenlly* (Newport, Partridge, 1839), pp. 3–7, quoted in Jones, *Last Rising*, p. 76.

14  *Western Vindicator*, 6 April 1839, quoted in I. Wilks, *South Wales and the Rising of 1839: Class Struggle as Armed Struggle* (London, Croom Helm, 1984), p. 145, and Jones, *Last Rising*, p. 94.

15  PRO, HO 20/10, Report of Inspector of Prisons, W. J. Williams, on an interview with Joseph Crabtree, 23 December 1840, facsimile printed in *Bulletin of the Society for the Study of Labour History* no. 34 (Spring 1977), pp. 33–4.

16  Jones, *Last Rising*, p. 156.

17  PRO, HO 41/15, Lord Normanby to Thomas Phillips, Mayor of Newport, 5 November 1839.

18  Ashton's account is in a letter of 30 March 1845, reprinted in *Northern Star*, 3 May 1845; and Lovett's appears in his *Life and Struggles of William Lovett* (London, 1876, new edition, MacGibbon & Key, 1967), pp. 196–9.

19  See Wilks, *South Wales*, pp. 166–75; A. J. Peacock, *Bradford Chartism, 1838–1840* (York, St Anthony's Press, 1969), J. L. Baxter, 'Early Chartism and Labour Struggle in South Yorkshire, 1837–40' in Pollard and Holmes (eds), *Essays*, pp. 146–50. See also his 'Armed Resistance and Insurrection: the early Chartist experience', *Our History* 16 (July 1984).

20  Baxter, 'Armed Resistance', p. 22.

21  *Northern Star*, 3 May 1845.

22  S. Roberts, *Radical Politicians and Poets in Early Victorian Britain* (Lampeter, Edwin Mellen Press, 1993), pp. 60–1.

23  PRO, HO 20/10, Report of Inspector of Prisons, W. J. Williams, on an interview with Emanuel Hutton, 23 December 1840.

24  Thompson, *Chartists*, pp. 80–5.

25  PRO, HO 45/249, W. Hutchinson of Accrington to W. L. Mabberley, 17 August 1842.

26  F. C. Mather, 'The General Strike of 1842', p. 116 in J. Stevenson and R. Quinault (eds), *Popular Protest and Public Order* (London, George Allen & Unwin), 1974, pp. 115–40.

27  *The Trial of Feargus O'Connor and Fifty-Eight Others on a Charge of Sedition, Conspiracy, Tumult & Riot* [1843], reprinted (New York, Kelley, 1970), p. v; N. McCord, *The Anti-Corn Law League* 1958, second edition (London, Unwin, 1968), pp. 123–31.

28  *Leeds Mercury*, 20 August 1842.

29  G. J. Barnsby, *Chartism in the Black Country* (Wolverhampton, Integrated Publishing Services, n.d.), p. 26.

30  Placard entitled 'Behold the Reckoning Day is Nigh', as quoted in M. Jenkins, *The General Strike of 1842* (London, Lawrence & Wishart, 1980), p. 64.

31  Jenkins, *General Strike*, pp. 242–3.

32  *Northern Star*, 27 December 1845, 13 May 1848, quoted in Jenkins, *General Strike*, pp. 117, 119.

33  *Trial of Feargus O'Connor*, p. 249.

34  *Staffordshire Advertiser*, 13 August 1842, as quoted in R. Anderson, *The Potteries Martyrs* (Newcastle, Military Heritage Books, 1992), chapter 1 (no page).

35  T. Cooper, *The Life of Thomas Cooper* [1872], reprinted (Leicester, Leicester University Press, 1971), pp. 186–96.

36  *Leeds Mercury*, 20 August 1842.

37  *Leeds Mercury*, 20 August 1842.

38  See the documents reproduced in Jenkins, *General Strike*, pp. 263–4.

39  The voting was 58 for the Charter, 7 against, 19 delegated to follow the majority and 1 with no instruction: see Jenkins, *General Strike*, p. 154.

40  As quoted in Jenkins, *General Strike*, p. 267.

41  *Leeds Mercury*, 20 August 1842; *Trial of Feargus O'Connor*, pp. 107–8, 309–10.

42  Text in Jenkins, *General Strike*, p. 275.

43  A. R. Schoyen, *The Chartist Challenge* (London, Heinemann, 1958), pp. 115–16.

44  For the full texts, see Jenkins, *General Strike*, pp. 270–4.

45  B. Wilson, *Struggles of an Old Chartist* (1887), p. 206, reprinted in D. Vincent (ed.), *Testaments of Radicalism* (London, Europa, 1977), pp. 195–242; K. Tiller, 'Late Chartism. Halifax, 1847–58', pp. 314–16 in Epstein and Thompson (eds), *Chartist Experience*, pp. 311–44.

46  D. Goodway, *London Chartism* (Cambridge, Cambridge University Press, 1982), pp. 111–15.

47  P. A. Pickering, *Chartism and the Chartists in Manchester and Salford* (London, Macmillan, 1995), p. 176.

48  Thompson, *Chartists*, p. 313.

49  *Northern Star*, 25 March 1848.

50  Goodway, *London Chartism*, pp. 129–42.

51  J. C. Hobhouse, Baron Broughton, *Recollections of a Long Life*, edited by his daughter, Lady Dorchester, 6 vols (London, Murray, 1910–11), vol. 6, pp. 214–15, diary entry for 10 April 1848.

52  C. C. F. Greville, *The Greville Memoirs*, edited by H. Reeve, new edition, 8 vols (London, Longman, 1888), vol. 6, p. 168, journal entry for 13 April 1848.

53  A. C. Benson and Viscount Esher (eds), *The Letters of Queen Victoria*, 3 vols. (London, Murray, 1908), vol. 2, p. 169.

54  Bodleian Library, Oxford, Clarendon Papers, Box 43, Russell to Clarendon, 1 March 1848, as quoted in J Saville, *1848* (Cambridge, Cambridge University Press, 1987), p. 81.

55  PRO, HO 45/2368, Irish Disaffection, 1848, as quoted in Saville, *1848*, p. 81.

56  D. Thompson, *Outsiders* (London, Verso, 1993), pp. 106–7.

57  Goodway, *London Chartism*, pp. 64–7, 80–5.

58  T Frost, *Forty Years' Recollections* (London, Sampson Low, Searle, and Rivington, 1880), p. 148.

59  L. C. Wright, *Scottish Chartism* (Edinburgh, Oliver & Boyd, 1953), pp. 194–5.

60  J. Belchem, 'Britishness, the United Kingdom and the Revolutions of 1848', p. 147 in *Labour History Review* 64:2 (Summer 1999), pp. 143–58. For further detail, see his 'Liverpool in the Year of Revolution: The political and associational culture of the Irish immigrant community in 1848', pp. 80–97 in J. Belchem (ed.), *Popular Politics, Riot and Labour. Essays in Liverpool History, 1790–1940* ((Liverpool, Liverpool University Press, 1992), pp. 68–97; and 'Nationalism, Republicanism and Exile: Irish emigrants and the revolutions of 1848', *Past & Present*, 146 (February 1995), pp. 103–35.

61  D. G. Wright, *The Chartist Risings in Bradford* (Bradford, Bradford Libraries, 1977), pp. 37–50.

62  What follows draws on Goodway, *London Chartism*, pp. 79–96; and Saville, *1848*, pp. 130–65.

63  TS 11/389, fo 70, transcript from shorthand reporter, Henry James Potter, 29 May 1848.

64  Goodway, *London Chartism*, pp. 81–4.

65  Greville, *Memoirs*, vol. 6, p. 193, journal entry for 3 June 1848.

66  Goodway, *London Chartism*, pp. 142–5.

67  Goodway, *London Chartism*, p. 86.

68  Goodway, *London Chartism*, pp. 87–93 gives full details of the development of the plot.

69  For a large but peaceful meeting in Edinburgh, see Wright, *Scottish Chartism*, pp. 197–201.

70  As quoted in Wright, *Chartist Risings in Bradford*, p. 49 [source not given].

71  Wright, *Chartist Risings in Bradford*, pp. 37–58; Saville, *1848*, pp. 144–50.

72  PRO, FO 5/488, fo 269, cutting from *New York Herald*, 7 May 1848, enclosed in Arthur Barclay to Lord Palmerston, 25 March 1848; see also Belchem, 'Nationalism, Republicanism and Exile', pp. 114–16.

73  Saville, *1848*, pp. 151–6; Belchem, 'Liverpool in the Year of Revolution' pp. 80–97; and 'Nationalism, Republicanism and Exile', pp. 114–31.

74  PRO, HO 48/40, Deposition of Thomas Brown, as quoted in F C. Mather, *Public Order in the Age of the Chartists* (Manchester, Manchester University Press, 1959), pp. 24–5.

75  Pickering, *Chartism and the Chartists in Manchester*, pp. 176–7; Saville, *1848*, pp. 142–4; Wright, *Chartist Risings in Bradford*, pp. 57–8.

76  Goodway, *London Chartism*, pp. 93–4. For lists of prisoners, see R. G. Gammage, *History of the Chartist Movement, 1837–1854*, second edition [1894], reprinted (New York, Kelley, 1969), pp. 336–44.

77  Wright, *Chartist Risings in Bradford*, p. 58.

78  Goodway, *London Chartism*, p. 94.

# 4

# Why was there no revolution?

CITY COLLEGE
LEARNING RESOURCE CENTRE

The absence of revolution in Britain becomes a historical problem in the light of what happened elsewhere. In the age of revolutions, Britain was largely unaffected by the challenges that shook and in some cases over-threw governments on the continent of Europe and beyond. Yet much of the story of social conflict in Britain between 1789 and 1850 suggests that the potential for revolution existed, so why was Britain different?

A theoretical approach to revolution risks imposing an unrealistic expectation of what a 'true' revolution is and how it should come about. The historical process is more complicated and much depends on how contemporaries understood the many shades of meaning behind such words as revolution, revolt, rebellion, insurgency and uprising in rela-tion to the less serious challenge implied by the more widely used dis-turbance and riot. As was suggested in the Introduction, the word revolution is difficult and ambiguous, partly because of the way differ-ent parties used it in their propaganda, and partly because the word itself was acquiring a new meaning during the 1790s.[1]

There was a significant shift in the idea of revolution following developments in France after 1789. Before that, 'the Revolution' in British history referred to what had occurred in 1688: it was a correc-tive, conservative event, a turning of the wheel of fortune to right a wrong state of affairs. When Edmund Burke wrote his *Reflections on the Revolution in France* in 1790 he was using the word in this sense, only with irony since his argument was against those who thought that France was simply experiencing a corrective measure to the excesses of Bourbon absolutism, analogous to the events of 1688. His point was that France was *not* experiencing this kind of revolution.[2] The Foxite Whigs and, to begin with, the United Irishmen continued to be supporters of revolution in the old sense until events and new definitions overtook them. By the late 1790s, the Whigs had substituted Reform for Revolution, and the United Irishmen had espoused revolution in its modern sense of 'a complete overthrow of the established government in any country or state by those who were previously subject to it; a forcible substitution of a new ruler or form of government'.[3] This modern definition, which assumes the use of force of some kind, will be the usual sense in which the word is used in the rest of this chapter. As one liberal member of the German National Assembly in 1848 asserted, 'We all know: revolution is constitutional change taking place against the will of the ruling power whereas reform means change taking place with the assent of that power.'[4] This is an important distinction.

Revolutionary change granted by a government of its own free will is not a revolution. But there is ambiguity if a government implements revolutionary change as a result of pressure put upon it from outside the normal political process. That *might* be called a revolution. If so, then even within the modern usage of the word there are two concepts of revolution to consider: the revolution which overthrows existing institutions by direct force; and the revolution which forces existing institutions to change themselves. From the point of view of the government under pressure, insurgents pressing for change might properly be called revolutionaries even if the historian doubts whether they could ever have overturned the existing government by force. The threat of revolution might therefore lie either in the intentions of the would-be revolutionaries, or in the perceptions of the government being pressed to change, or both. Thus in the language of the governing classes which dominates the historical record, genuine revolutionaries intent on using force to bring about political change might be dismissed as mere rioters without political understanding or aims; while constitutionally-minded protesters unwilling to appeal to force might be condemned as wicked revolutionaries.

Although governments in Britain carried many reforms in the period 1789–1850, only three concerned what might be called 'the constitution'. In 1801 the Act of Union with Ireland came into effect as a result of government policy and so can properly be called a reform. In 1829 the Catholic Relief Act was granted by a reluctant Parliament in the face of widespread unrest in Ireland, so that would seem to make it revolutionary. In 1832, the first Reform Act was carried as government policy, but popular pressure played a part in events. It was a major constitutional reform or a constitutional revolution, depending on the emphasis given to the reasons why the measure was carried. On none of these occasions was the government forcibly overthrown.

To the Whigs the 1832 Reform Act was a revolution in the old sense – a conservative, corrective adjustment – and a reform in the new sense, conducted along traditional English lines of change through continuity, avoiding the French way of change through violent rupture. This perception of the superiority of reform over revolution was widely accepted by all classes in Britain by 1850, but this outcome was not at all obvious to the two generations who lived through the events between 1790 and 1850. Revolutionaries in those years were seeking change, either by putting pressure on governments or by looking to some undefined way of overthrowing them. Contrary to later Victorian liberal ideology, governments did not always grant reasonable reforms ungrudgingly and without resistance, and they constantly feared insurgencies from below. The equilibrium of the mid-nineteenth century was a compromise achieved through the experience of disequilibrium in the preceding sixty years.

Overshadowing all events during this period was the French revolution: not the neatly packaged event of historical theory but a messy, incoherent process, the direction and outcome of which were neither intended nor foreseen. This left contemporaries all too aware that an uprising might create its own revolutionary situation, as arguably happened again in Paris in 1830 or in several European capitals in 1848. Revolution in this period was an accident waiting to be caused – or prevented. So, how close did Britain come to revolution and how did the country avoid it? The rest of this chapter attempts to consider this question thematically by looking at the balance of conservative and revolutionary forces in the structures and institutions of British society, the outlook of the people whose leadership and support would have been necessary to turn a rising into a revolution, and the ideological and physical means available to those who wished to prevent them.

## The nature of the popular movement

In a strikingly powerful metaphor, Edmund Burke sought to belittle the supporters of revolution in 1790:

> Because half a dozen grasshoppers under a fern make the field ring with their importunate chink, while thousands of great cattle, repose beneath the shadow of the British oak, chew the cud and are silent, pray do not imagine that those who make the noise are the only inhabitants of the field; that, of course, they are many in number; or that, after all, they are other than the little, shrivelled, meagre, hopping, though loud and troublesome, insects of the hour.[5]

If Burke's polemic were as true as it was effective, then the revolutionary threat was an illusion, and historians who think otherwise have followed magistrates and politicians of the time in confusing noise with numbers. In this view, the political insurgents were small, untypical groups of troublemakers. Though they sometimes attracted wider support, this was unreliable and dependent on a downturn in the trade cycle or a rise in the price of bread. The popular movement throughout was largely peaceful. It was therefore caught in the paradox of seeking a revolutionary end by non-revolutionary means. At most it could appear revolutionary in order the frighten the government into concessions, but it had no response if the government refused to be frightened or was frightened only into suppressing rather than yielding to those who threatened it.

If true, this is a powerful argument, though it begs the questions of why the majority was constitutional and why the revolutionaries were not popular. It also implies a passive relationship between minorities and majorities rather than a dynamic interrelationship, and it assumes that revolutions must be made by majorities.

One theory of revolution in the nineteenth century, which can be traced back to Babeuf's 'Conspiracy of the Equals' in 1797, accepted that revolutions are the work of minorities. Governments no less than revolutionaries are minorities and so vulnerable to conspiratorial plots. English radicals were made aware of this when Bronterre O'Brien's translation of Buonarotti's *History of Babeuf's Conspiracy for Equality* (1828) was published in 1836. Although Marx's purpose in writing the *Communist Manifesto* was to reject this model of revolution in favour of raising the consciousness of the mass of the people – which is what he thought was happening in Chartism – the Marxist-Leninist approach has reinforced the idea that revolutions are created by a small revolutionary leadership. On this definition, revolutions do not have to be the work of majorities to be threatening or even successful.

# Why was there no revolution?

The reports produced by informers overwhelmingly referred to dangerous minorities. This evidence exposed a series of revolutionary conspiracies, from Robert Watt's plot in Edinburgh in 1794, which so alarmed the Committee of Secrecy, through Thistlewood's repeated schemes between 1817 and 1820 to the Chartist revolutionaries of 1848 with a new French revolution to emulate. The expectation of these conspirators was that there was a wide body of support in the country which would rise once they had commenced the deed. The government, from a more fearful perspective, shared this view. In their reports on individuals the informers were probably not wildly inaccurate, providing the detail which enabled the authorities to pick off the leaders and so extinguished their plots. Where they were not so reliable was in their estimates of wider support and here they drew on their own imaginations and, more importantly, the optimism of the revolutionary leaders. In this way spies and revolutionaries deluded themselves, each other and sometimes the government.

However, this lack of realism was its most dangerous aspect. It was recalled, with some unfair exaggeration, in the memoirs of a one-time Chartist, Benjamin Brierley. His context was a group of hand-loom weavers meeting to read the *Northern Star* in the village of Failsworth near Manchester on the eve of the 1842 strikes:

> Every Sunday morning these subscribers met at our house to hear what prospect there was of the expected 'smash-up' taking place. It was my task to read aloud so that all could hear at the same time; . . . A Republic was to take the place of the 'base, bloody, and brutal Whigs,' and the usurpers of all civil rights, the Lords. The Queen was to be dethroned, and the president of a Republic take her place. This would be a very easy task.[6]

Brierley's irony in the final sentence indicates, at least in retrospect, his scepticism on this point. Few men who rationally contemplated the odds of a successful revolution would ever start one. Those who thought seriously about the prospects for change – Thomas Hardy and Francis Place of the LCS; Henry Hunt on the edge of the Spencean post-war conspiracies; Feargus O'Connor in Chartism – knew the limits of their powers and worked within them. Those who did not were either *agents provocateurs* or fanatics, driven by frustration or desperation or filled with the millenarian hope of a new dawn that did not rely on numbers or rational human agency.

Much depended on how popular this minority of revolutionaries was: that is, how they related to 'the people', not in the Whig sense of those having or deserving the franchise but in its increasingly common meaning of those who were excluded from it, the 'masses' as opposed to the 'classes'.[7] Though there is little evidence to support the idea of a mass rising to start a revolution, there were certainly large numbers of discontented people who could have responded if the minority had been united and able to create and exploit a revolutionary situation. Magistrates and ministers alike were always alert to the potential dangers of the 'mobility', the inverse of the 'nobility', 'the disorderly and riotous part of the population'.[8] The word 'mob' conjures up the view of a crowd seen from the hustings, or from horseback, or the town-square balcony before the Riot Act was read: a dark, secret and seething anonymous sea of heads, ever in motion and liable to break out from time to time in tempestuous fury, lashing itself against the defences of law and order until its force was spent. The people, on the contrary, were good-hearted and deferential, loyal subjects of the King. But there was always the possibility, especially in times of high food prices and unemployment, that the high winds of 'trading agitators' might whip them up into a furious rabble, a mob. Those responsible for law and order could never be complacent about the reliability of 'the people'.

The aim of government propaganda was to maintain the idea that there was an identifiable minority of revolutionaries who were separate from the larger body of 'the people'. This distinction was emphasised, for example, by speakers from both parliamentary sides in the debate in the House of Commons on the Charter in 1839. As Lord John Russell, the Whig Home Secretary, stated in a rather convoluted speech,

> My own opinion is, that these are the exhortations of persons, several of them, no doubt, conscientious persons, but others very designing and insidious persons, wishing not the prosperity of the people, but exhorting the people, by those means most injurious to themselves, to produce a degree of discord – to produce a degree of confusion – to produce a degree of misery, the consequence of which would be to create a great alarm, that would be fatal, not only to the constitution as it now exists, not only to those rights which are now said to be monopolised by a particular class, but fatal to any established government.[9]

Here Russell was attempting to divide the naively idealistic from the malevolent, and both from the people, who needed protection from those who would agitate them for their own nefarious purposes.

The problem for the leaders, though, was not that they were unrepresentative of a great many of the people, but that they were divided among themselves and this severely limited their effectiveness in harnessing the discontents of the majority in a consistent and coherent way. Lack of leadership or clear political aims, rather than lack of potential numbers, meant that for most of the time the challenge presented to the government by the revolutionaries was to be one of law and order rather than political survival.

A major theoretical division existed between those who sought to amend the constitution to purge it of aristocratic corruption and make it more accountable to 'the people'; and those who wished to establish 'a republic', sometimes (like the Failsworth Chartists in Brierley's recollections) without any clear idea of what that might mean beyond forming a democratic government which would give 'the people' the laws they wanted. As James Epstein has argued, although Paine and many of his radical contemporaries, filled with enthusiasm for events in France in 1789 and imbued with the language of the Enlightenment, advocated a break with the past and a recognition of the natural rights of the people with the formation of a republic, others appreciated the strategic merits of adopting the conservative view of revolution as a restoration of traditional, historic rights, using the language of Burke to subvert his conclusions and argue for radical change. Thus constitutionalism became the language of revolution in a linguistic struggle with the propertied and enfranchised. The object was to present the latter not as defenders of the constitution but its enemies, subverting the usual argument employed against radical reformers.[10] Such a strategy depended upon a peaceful agitation, at least until the political classes could be shown to have violated the peace.

Feargus O'Connor's phrase, 'Peaceably if we may; forcibly if we must', may look like a rhetorical device for staying within the law while at the same time uttering a threat, but in fact the mainstream of radical reformers in Britain did prefer the peaceable and constitutional way not only through necessity but also as their chosen strategy. Even in the 1790s, advocates of Paine's thorough-going republicanism did not command the entire argument and in the nineteenth century they were in the minority. The petitions of the LCS

CITY COLLEGE
LEARNING RESOURCE CENTRE

against the Two Acts in 1795, written by John Thelwall and thoroughly approved by Francis Place, appealed to the House of Commons as 'the constitutional guardian of the people's liberties, and the champion of its rights and privileges', referring back to the reign of Edward III and, inevitably, 1688.[11] While such phrases addressed to the ideal Parliament may have revealed a desire to expose the shortcomings of the actual one, the constitutional language of the radicals should be taken seriously. The device of petitioning Parliament was urged by Major Cartwright and William Cobbett, and was central to Chartist strategy. The image which the majority of radicals wished to convey was that of a body defending the traditional rights of the people against the dangers of arbitrary government. In this respect they were at one with the Foxite Whigs in the 1790s and with Grey in 1831. The Whig 'betrayal' after 1832 was felt all the more bitterly because the Whigs had promoted themselves as defenders of the liberties of the people – until they themselves got power. Then with Irish coercion and the Poor Law Amendment Act, they legislated like Tories.

The determination of the majority of reformers to act peacefully pushed the revolutionaries to the margins of radical protest but it did not entirely isolate them. When the House of Commons rejected petitions, when *Habeas Corpus* was suspended or new Acts were rushed through Parliament to limit the people's liberties, the peaceful approach could become discredited and larger numbers were then persuaded that, to preserve the constitution, it was necessary to cross the narrow line between peaceful pressure and insurrection. As William Stevens reasoned, perhaps rather disingenuously, in 1818:

> until after the passing of the Suspension and other violent Acts,
> in the month of March 1817, he never heard any person propose,
> or hint at, any measure of resistance in arms on the part of the
> people; but, that, after those acts had been passed, he himself, as
> well as many hundreds of others, and, as he believes, many
> Thousands, said, that, as the Laws of the land were now
> destroyed, as there was now no safety for any man, and as the
> people were not allowed even to petition, it was time to *resist*, or,
> if not, to make up our minds to die slaves.[12]

Though leaders like Cobbett, Hunt and Feargus O'Connor usually preached peace, they could not always contain the logic of their own arguments or the forces they were unleashing. Other radicals, from John Baines, Thomas Bacon, James Wilson and Joseph Mitchell to John Frost and Peter Murray McDouall, could become convinced that the enfranchised classes had stepped beyond the limits of the constitution and that the peaceful approach was no longer adequate: then they were drawn into support for insurrection. The right to bear arms, enshrined in Magna Carta and the Common Law, was legal for defensive purposes. So the division between minority revolutionists and majority constitutionalists was never hard or fast. It was the moderate William Lovett who seconded the motion in the Chartist Convention in 1839 advising the people to arm because the government was putting down meetings by Proclamation which he held to be illegal.[13] A great deal of activity which the government feared might be revolutionary and which alarmed magistrates was, strictly speaking, perfectly legitimate. England was not under an arbitrary government and the legal powers available for the suppression, even of arming and drilling, were uncertain. The neat division into 'moral' and 'physical' force, like the division between agitators and people, was an oversimplification.

More significant in weakening the popular movement for reform were the differences between social classes. In George Rudé's opinion, middle-class leadership was needed for a revolution to be successful. As he observed, there was no revolution in 1831–32 because 'nobody *of importance* wanted one' [my italics]. In the Marxist model of revolution, the proletariat does not rise spontaneously but is led by a fragment of the *bourgeoisie*. This may have been possible in Ireland, with support from the United Irishmen and later the Confederates, but it did not happen in Britain, unless people such as Muir, Palmer, Cobbett, Hunt and O'Connor are made to fill the role.

As was pointed out in Chapter 2, there was an imprecise relationship between the language of class relating to socio-economic groupings and that referring to political positions.[14] The phrases 'middle class' and 'working class' were widely used by the 1830s, but more by leaders to project an image of themselves for polemical purposes than to offer social analysis of use to the historian. Those who were thought of as the middle class in Britain were a relatively small group, internally divided. The radical middle class was even smaller and dependent upon working-class support to make an impact – what Richard Cobden of the Anti-Corn Law League called 'something in our *rear* to frighten the Aristocracy'[15] – but middle-class radicals were prepared to lead the masses only on their own, non-revolutionary terms.[16] Probably before, and certainly after, 1832 most leaders of working-class opinion did not trust the middle classes. In 1832 and again in 1839, whatever Thomas Attwood might have threatened and Francis Place recorded for posterity, the middle-class political unions drew back from actual violence. The concession made by the Whigs to their supporters in 1832, extending the political nation to include moderates (the 'middle class') while isolating democrats (the 'working class'), removed any possibility of revolutionary leadership coming from the middle classes in Britain. The Anti-Corn Law League peered into the abyss in 1842, and hastily drew back.[17] By extending the property base of politics in 1832, stability was reinforced. Whereas in 1848 across Europe, revolutionary leadership was provided by liberals turning popular discontents against existing regimes, in England the same sort of people joined the special constabulary and turned out in Lord John Russell's massive counter-demonstration against what was portrayed as revolution.

## Geography and the problem of London

A further division which weakened the revolutionary movement was not of its own making. In July 1849 the Owenite and latter-day Chartist lecturer, George Jacob Holyoake, delivered a lecture in London on the question, 'Why have we had no revolution in England?' His answer was excessive individualism, by which he meant no common objects, no united organisation and no accepted leadership. Since he had spend the past few years trying to destroy all three, this may have been true of Chartism after 1848. But in offering his analysis he considered firstly three other reasons, which will be considered later in this chapter. His second was

> We have equality of towns. When Paris is conquered, France submits; but when London shall be possessed, there will be Birmingham, Liverpool, Manchester, Glasgow, Edinburgh to subdue. A revolution here could only be effected by a protracted civil war. A provisional government in London would be useless without a Cromwell.[18]

This is worth considering. Forgetting, as Holyoake apparently did, the role of the French provinces in 1789 and the revolutionary part played by the major textile centre of Lyon in the 1830s, from the standpoint of 1848 it did seem that French revolutions were actually political revolutions made in Paris. A comparison and contrast between London and Paris can be instructive.

London was much bigger than Paris and contained a larger percentage of the country's population: around a million inhabitants in 1801 and over two and a half million in 1851 – more than 10 per cent of the population of England. Paris was half this size in 1801 but held only about 2 per cent of the population of France and with a population of a million in 1851 held about 3 per cent at that date. Both were major manufacturing centres and both were centres of government. London ought to have been more important in England and in Britain as a whole but Holyoake was right that London could not speak for Britain in the way that Paris had come to speak for France. Whereas in 1801, Lyon was still larger than any provincial British town, in 1851 it was much smaller than Liverpool, Glasgow, Manchester, Birmingham or Leeds. Indeed, these provincial British cities were in the same league as many European capitals.[19] London was huge and yet only first among equals. Though it could be argued that this made life difficult for governments, they were able to overcome the problem of the dispersed nature of the British urban and industrial population more effectively than the would-be revolutionaries.

London best fitted the role of a European revolutionary capital in the 1790s, but with only the Foxite Whigs to play Jacobins to the LCS's sansculottes, there were many reasons why no revolutionary situation matured in the capital in these years: no bankrupt administration, no significant divisions within the political elite, no attempt to re-write the constitution in a way that encouraged every political opportunist to have his say, no actual military defeat and threatening foreign armies by land, no manipulation of the crowd in support of political faction. If London had been placed under these intolerable strains, the story might have been very different.

Holyoake's remarks about London in 1848 arose from the unusual situation of the capital taking the lead in serious revolutionary planning, but for much of the first half of the nineteenth century the reverse was true. The mobilisation of the discontented masses to exert pressure on the government was achieved not in London but 100–200 miles away. As the Blanketeers discovered in 1817, putting pressure on London at that distance was not easy. The Vice-Lieutenant and magistrates of the West Riding felt frustrated in 1812 that Lord Sidmouth in London did not truly appreciate the difficulty of maintaining law and order in the industrial districts as he did not have their first hand experience of the Luddites.[20] Had there been Luddites in the capital, they might have had more effect. This was appreciated by the London-based *Chartist* newspaper in 1839:

> Chartists, what are you now about? We hear, we see nothing of you – the metropolis scarcely knows of the existence of such a class of people. They are found only at our police-offices, and there they appear in twos and threes, without causing any more excitement than the arrest of an equal number of pickpockets. How is this? Is it that the Charter was a mere popular phantasy, which has been cried up and deserted with all the customary fickleness of a crowd? or is it that the people do not feel the evils of which they were accustomed to complain? It never can be the case that there are five hundred thousand workmen in London and its suburbs ardent to obtain a suffrage which will enable them to better their condition, and yet that a party of a few thousands cannot be got up to make a demonstration, or, what is still better, to smash a Whig or Tory meeting.
>
> That there is this number of workmen in the metropolis is certain enough. But are these men Chartists? If they are, why do they not show themselves so? . . . The fact is, that, be it from listlessness, ignorance, want of thought, incapacity to reason as to political causes and effects, or satisfaction with things as they are, the great majority of the working men of the metropolis are altogether indifferent as to representation. They feel certain evils, and they complain of them, but they do not apply themselves to consider whence they proceed.
>
> In the country, we believe it is far otherwise. The men of Birmingham are as one man – the hardy spirits of the north know no difference – the acute and reasoning Scotchmen have satisfied themselves where the evil lies. Throughout the provinces all is unanimity. We are sorry to have to report that in the metropolis, where the lead should have been taken, there is nothing doing; and unless the metropolis be set working, all agitation elsewhere is useless. It is here that the seat of government is. A demonstration in the streets of London comes before the very eyes of those who make the laws. An atmosphere of agitation here does not dissipate without first involving the two houses of legislation in

its influence. A hundred demonstrations in the country are only
heard of through the newspapers of the factions, which invariably describe them as contemptible, diminish the numbers, and
caricature the speeches.[21]

In this extract, there is a combination of frank admission of the failure of
early Chartism in London, a perhaps exaggerated view of the provincial
movement, and a proper appreciation of the centrality of London to any
effective political pressure group. One major reason why early Chartism
failed, both as a pressure group and as a revolutionary threat, was that
the source of its energy was not in the capital. London Chartism did not
really become well-established until after 1840. The failure of London
and the provinces to exert maximum pressure at the same time was one
reason for the failure of Chartism. The hope of attaining simultaneous
action across the country was never to be realised, yet this was the only
chance for a planned revolution to be effective.

## Loyalism and the silent majority

The assumption so far has been that structural weaknesses and divisions prevented the minority of revolutionaries from realising the
potential support of the masses of the people and using it to bring
pressure to bear on, or to overthrow, the existing institutions of
society. This is to ignore the efforts made by the governing classes to
secure or maintain the loyalty of the people – Burke's cattle content-
edly chewing the cud, rather than his more celebrated 'swinish multitude' of revolutionaries. Revolutions may be made by minorities but
they need the willing acquiescence of majorities, and this they failed
to win, not for want of trying but because the governing classes
proved themselves better at winning it.

In achieving this they were aided by several characteristics of the
popular mind. The first, detected by the *Chartist* in 1839, was indifference. Many people were committed to the daily task of survival. Any
further commitment to political action depended upon a conviction that
this was relevant to survival. The task of the radicals was to persuade
them of this. Cobbett's achievement, according to Samuel Bamford, was
that, 'He directed his readers to the true cause of their sufferings – mis-
government; and to its proper corrective – parliamentary reform.'[22]

Although riots aimed at an unpopular local personality (even the

King in London), might have an immediate political motivation, those who turned seriously to revolutionary activity did so only in reaction to the failure of parliamentary reform. They had to pass through quite a sophisticated process in order to reach the serious decision to use physical force against the existing political order. From his Conservative perspective, Benjamin Disraeli was highly sceptical about the probability of this, even in 1839. In his speech in the House of Commons on the Petition, he argued that 'Political rights had so much of an abstract character, their consequences acted so slightly on the multitude, that he did not believe they could ever be the origin of any great popular movement.'[23] Although this point was made in the context of an argument to show how the Whig attack on the civil rights of the people had changed this situation in the 1830s, the point about the minority appeal of abstract rights remains a valid one. Though the popularity of Paine's *Rights of Man* is more often asserted than demonstrated, such popularity as it enjoyed has to be put in context. Much of the evidence, including the alleged sale of 200,000 copies of Part 1 by 1793, comes from loyalist propaganda with a vested interest in tarring radicals with Paineite and French brushes.

The constitutionalist alternative to Paine to which many radicals turned, if only in self-defence, was open to a loyalist counter-attack because it employed the same language, images and concepts and was more effectively organised without hindrance from the law. As H. T. Dickinson has reminded us, 'The variety, the sheer volume and the social and geographical distribution of conservative propaganda was certainly much greater than that disseminated by the radicals in the years from 1789 to 1815.'[24]

Popular wrath was often directed against those seen to be locally responsible for the hardships of the people: the baker, the miller, the farmer, the hoarder, the profiteer, the factory owner or farmer who created unemployment by introducing new machinery, or the employer who reduced wages. As Edward Thompson argued, such direct actions were in themselves highly rational, aimed at redressing the market and re-establishing traditional practices, but they had a relevance which was easily understood.[25] When Cobbett urged the journeymen and labourers of Norfolk in 1816 to meet and petition for the redress of their grievances, 'and let it not enter into your minds, that Bakers, Butchers, Millers and Farmers are the cause of your sufferings', he was asking them to understand something much harder.[26] Tradition and history were a sounder basis for popular propaganda than abstract rights. Major Cartwright's language of 'Saxon liberties' remained more appealing than Paine's newer abstractions even though Paine presented them in graphic and at times humorous language which clearly made some impact. However, as we have seen, the defence of tradition could feed revolution and it could equally well open the popular mind to the arguments of conservatives.

The plural 'liberties' is important. Unlike the abstract 'liberty' to which the American Thomas Jefferson had appealed in the language of the Enlightenment and in which the French had followed him, liberties meant privileges or exemptions. The liberties of 'the freeborn Englishman' had concrete meaning: a patriot rejoiced in the liberties of the English, not granted to foreigners: roast beef, white bread and no wooden shoes at the most basic; Magna Carta and trial by jury at a more elevated level. But the word 'liberties', frequently coupled with 'patriotism', was ambiguous. To love one's country could mean both defending it against its traditional enemies – the Pope, Spain, France – and defending it against corruption and despotism, the enemies of freedom at home.[27] This view was developed in anti-Jacobite propaganda in the 1740s and in anti-French propaganda throughout the century, especially during the Seven Years' War. David Garrick's celebration of British military victories in 1759, 'Heart of Oak', may read like a recruiting song for the navy, but its contrast of free men and slaves was telling:

> Come cheer up, my lads, 'tis to glory we steer,
> To add something more to this wonderful year;
> To honour we call you, not press you like slaves,
> For who are so free as the sons of the waves?

Freedom and patriotism were also the themes of James Thomson's verses, set to music by Thomas Arne in 1740 in what was to become one of the most popular of patriotic songs:

> When Britain, first at Heaven's command,
> Arose from out the azure main,
> This was the charter, the charter of the land,
> And guardian angels sung this strain,
> Rule Britannia! Britannia rule the waves,
> Britons never will be slaves.

This charter of freedom, redolent of Magna Carta, preceded the People's Charter by a hundred years. Conservatives, loyalists, radicals and Chartists used a common vocabulary to compete for the hearts and minds of the people. A later verse from 'Rule Britannia' drew the image of the firmly rooted 'native oak' withstanding the storms of 'each foreign stroke'. This exploited a fruitful line in propaganda appealing to traditional xenophobic anti-French feeling. Propagandists readily returned to this on the outbreak of war with France in 1793, in loyalist tracts which scoffed at the French, and in didactic or amusing cartoons such as Thomas Rowlandson's 'The Contrast' and James Gillray's 'Fashion before Ease; or, A good Constitution sacrificed, for a fantastic Form', both of 1793.[28]

In the Rowlandson the viewer is offered a contrast between British Liberty and French Liberty': on the one hand, 'Religion, Morality, Loyalty, Obedience to the Laws, Independance [sic], Personal Security, Justice, Inheritance, Protection of Property, Industry, National Prosperity, and Happiness'; on the other hand, 'Atheism, Perjury, Rebelion [sic], Treason, Anarchy, Murder, Equality, Madness, Cruelty, Injustice, Treachery, Ingratitude, Idleness, Famine, National & Private Ruin, and Misery'. The print concludes by asking the unnecessary question 'Which is Best?'

In the Gillray, Britannia is being forced into a pair of stays made by Thomas Paine (who had been a stay-maker), while she clutches a British oak. This was a potent and widely used symbol, for the oak was not only the material out of which the navy's ships were built, but referred also to the symbol of the Stuart Restoration, recalling that Charles Stuart had hidden in an oak tree after his defeat at the battle of Worcester in October 1651. His birthday and the anniversary of his re-entry into London on 29 May 1660 was commemorated annually from 1664 with the wearing of sprigs of oak and special services in church. Burke was playing on this image in 1790 when his cattle lay in the shade of the British oak.

A third patriotic song, which eclipsed 'Rule Britannia' in the 1790s and attained the religious status of national 'anthem' was an anti-Jacobite song made popular in 1745. Although the words of the opening verse were much older, and had been sung (in French!) for Louis XIV in 1686, the words of a later verse were explicitly loyalist:

> O Lord our God, arise,
> Scatter his enemies,
> And make them fall;
> Confound their politics;
> Frustrate their knavish tricks;

On him our hopes are fix'd;
O save us all.[29]

When Benjamin Brierley came to reconstruct in fiction the political life of Failsworth in the 1840s, his symbol of loyalism was a character called Nokin, who scrawled 'Damn Tom Paine' and 'Honour the King' on the loom-house wall; and who went around singing 'Confound their politics, frustrate their knavish tricks'. Even so, Nokin became a Chartist, but only for the duration of the depression.[30]

When faced with the growth of popular societies and the circulation of seditious literature, the government cultivated these images and appealed to 'public opinion' for support.[31] In response to the Royal Proclamation of 1 May 1792, some 382 loyal addresses were sent in during the next three months, and with the first invasion scare towards the end of 1792, the governing classes again turned to this well of potential loyalism for support against those who favoured French innovation to home-spun liberties.[32] Pitt himself was wary of encouraging popular politics, even of a loyalist kind, but on 20 November 1792 with semi-official government support, John Reeves, who held the government post of Receiver of the Public Offices, started the Association for the Preservation of Liberty and Property against Republicans and Levellers to rally public opinion against the radicals. Over the next three months between 1,200 and 1,500 associations were founded to sign loyal addresses. Sheffield was one of the few places where the loyalists did not outnumber the radicals. It is true that the lead was taken by a rather higher social class – mayors, aldermen, councillors, clergymen and other local leaders – and that pressure could be exerted on people to sign, but for the most part the number of signatures gathered and the attendance at meetings suggests widespread support from the lesser ranks of society. In only eight places was the loyal address taken round every house so that non-signers (like William Blake in Lambeth) would become marked men.[33]

The loyalists proceeded by a combination of persuasion and bullying, with personal threats against known radicals, pressure on landlords not to permit radical meetings on pain of losing their licences, and intimidating processions and burnings of Paine in effigy.[34] This upsurge in loyalist activity was accompanied by the production of tracts to counter the 'seditious' literature of the radicals. These

CITY COLLEGE LEARNING RESOURCE CENTRE

included simple but effective chap-books, such as *One Pennyworth of Truth from Thomas Bull to his Brother John*, and Hannah More's *Village Politics; a dialogue between Jack Anvil the Blacksmith and Tom Hod the Mason; Addressed to All the Mechanics, Journeymen, and Day Labourers, in Great Britain*. Here the loyalist argument was simple and straightforward; the radical case was over-simplified and distorted – all radicals were levellers and thieves, idlers who wished to live by other people's industry – and naturally plain common sense was triumphant. Other literature appealed to straightforward class interest. A manifesto issued by the Loyal Associations of Manchester and Salford against the Unitarian radicals in 1795 described the latter as

> Hypocrites whose ears are *always shut* to the cry of *distress* – who oppress their servants – who exact with the GREATEST SEVERITY EXORBITANT RENTS FROM THEIR POOR TENANTS – who endeavour to compel the labouring poor to maintain the necessitous poor, and remove the burden from themselves, TO THEIR BOSOMS, the soft impulse of philanthropy is a stranger. – They who are continually seeking their own aggrandisement – incessantly panting after supremacy, and to acquire it, would see, with unconcern, their native soil DELUGED *with the Blood of their Countrymen*, know nothing of the animating glow of true Patriotism.[35]

This was dangerous talk, the violence of the language and demonstrations summoned up by the loyalists not only matching that of the radicals, but also setting them a precedent.

The function of this propaganda was partly to keep the mass of the people loyal, partly to boost the confidence and morale of the lesser property-owning classes, and partly to isolate and demoralise the radicals. By 1794 this last objective had been achieved with the radicals reduced to a beleaguered minority, but how far any permanent impact was made on the mass of the people – by either radicals or loyalists – is hard to tell. It may be that the most effective work was done in bolstering the middling group in society, who could identify with John Bull and his prejudices, and whose support was necessary to the traditional governing classes.

The initial impact made by the Reeves' Association was over by the spring of 1793 and, although the loyalists remained in the ascendancy until the Treason Trials of 1794, thereafter the trend seems to have been reversed. With the rise in food prices in 1795 and the growing unpopularity of the war, much popular opinion was now turning against the government. The Volunteer force, raised from March 1794 to provide additional local defence forces, drew on the loyalism of the middling and upper classes to produce cavalry units in the counties and urban infantry, but its recruiting owed its appeal to many factors, including its local base, its attractive uniform and opportunity for display, and also the fact that volunteering exempted a man from the militia ballot. Even so, local enthusiasm and voluntary subscriptions to pay for the force proved difficult to maintain in the longer term and in 1798 government funds had to be used to supplement local subscriptions. Anti-French feeling may have remained powerful, but so did opposition to a war that was blamed for high taxes and economic hardship.[36] John Bull may have been a patriotic figure, but he was one often portrayed as the victim of an unreasonable tax burden.[37] With the next grain crisis and even higher prices in 1799–1801 as the government sought unsuccessfully to end the war, popular loyalism were tested to the limit. Food rioting and industrial unrest on a major scale were the background to the suppression of the popular societies and the widespread political unrest that surfaced in the Despard plot. In these years it was by no means certain that the soundness of the people could be depended upon.[38]

This was to set the pattern for the early nineteenth century. There was undoubtedly some popular loyalism, but it was fickle and spasmodic: anti-French but also at times anti-ministerial. During times of hardship and in depressed sectors of the economy, revolutionary support was bred among men who felt they had little to lose. In 1812, the magistrates of the West Riding felt the situation so slipping out of control that they asked the government to introduce General Warrants and impose military law.[39] In 1812, 1817 and 1820 the widespread accumulation of arms in the population at large was greater than the right of 'constitutional self-defence' could warrant. In the industrial districts this amounted to far more than a minority-based London *coup d'état*. The same pattern was repeated in the Chartist years. Though it would be hard to claim at any time that the insurgents commanded the support of the majority, what ministers feared was that the government did not either and that events might therefore be decided by whichever side looked like winning. At this point, security became a practical and not an ideological matter.

The ambiguities of loyalism are illustrated in the 1830s by the loyalist crowd called out in 1832 to demonstrate against the Leeds Whigs and factory-owners as personified by Edward Baines of the *Leeds Mercury*. In the middle of the debate over the Reform Bill, the Leeds Tories took up the issue of factory reform in a bid to outflank the parliamentary reformers. This produced a working alliance between the radical *Leeds Patriot* and the Tory *Leeds Intelligencer*, building on the Tory–Radical compact forged by Richard Oastler and Michael Thomas Sadler. The occasion was the great 'Pilgrimage to York' by supporters of the factory movement at Easter 1832, a march attended by the sympathetic editor of the *Intelligencer* but vilified by the hostile Baines in the *Mercury*. His account appeared on the streets of Leeds on Saturday 28 April. Immediately, a crowd gathered and a copy of the *Mercury* was tied to a pole with a piece of black crepe and borne aloft as the crowd marched on the *Mercury* office where they burned the offending paper to the accompaniment of hisses, booings and groans.

That evening a far larger crowd assembled, bearing an effigy of Baines draped with banners proclaiming the words which William Cobbett had recently applied to the *Mercury* and its editor – 'The great Liar of the North'. Preceded by a brass band, the crowd marched past the *Mercury* office to the accompaniment of the 'Rogues March', then to the *Leeds Patriot* office where they gave three cheers, and then to the *Intelligencer* office where they gave three cheers and made the effigy bow down. They then marched to the homes of prominent supporters, including Sadler, where the band played 'God Save the King' and 'Rule Britannia' before returning to the *Mercury* office where they set fire to the effigy amid deafening shouts.[40] This immediately preceded the 'days of May' when Baines and the Leeds Political Union were supposed to be in the forefront of the revolution against the Duke of Wellington. Yet this same anger of a 'Rule Britannia' marching crowd – Britons never will be (factory) slaves – was a few years later to be turned against Poor Law guardians, and it led to Chartists marching and drilling on the moors in 1839, drawing boiler plugs in 1842 and defeating the incompetent and outnumbered Bradford police in 1848.

## The cohesion of social welfare

In his influential Ford lectures of 1983–84, Ian Christie offered an explanation of the avoidance of revolution in terms of social cohesion.[41] Undoubtedly the factors he pointed to were important, although at times he idealised social relationships and appeared to admit that what may have been true of the 1790s was not necessarily applicable in the nineteenth century. This was a society of ranks and orders, of deference and paternalism. Although such a society, as appealed to by Disraeli in his attack on the Whigs for causing Chartism in 1839, was always something of a fiction, there was some reality behind the myth, particularly in rural communities where the economic interests of landlords, farmers and labourers could be bound together in a social network of charity and paternalism. There was often much to be gained and little to be lost by deference to the squire and the parson, either through habit or rational calculation. A great deal of charity was dispensed to the lower orders in times of personal or national hardship, whether through Christian benevolence or self-interest is not really relevant. Much of society was maintained in equilibrium by a recognition of what the rich and influential owed to the poor and of what the poor deserved from the rich.

On 19 October 1831, a deputation waited upon the Duke of Newcastle with the following address, signed by 313 of his tenants on his Clumber estates in Nottinghamshire:

> We, the undersigned inhabitants . . . deeply regretting the attempts that have been made to destroy your grace's property, cannot find terms sufficiently strong to express our detestation of proceedings so revolting to every good feeling. Living, as we do, in the neighbourhood of your grace's residence, where your character and virtues are felt and appreciated, and sensible as we are of the comforts and advantages derived from so kind and liberal a landlord, we feel a real pleasure in coming forward to declare our respect for, and attachment to, your grace; and to offer our united services to protect your person, and that of every individual member of your family; and at the same time to assure your grace, that it is our unanimous determination to exert every energy in our power to prevent the destruction and plunder of your grace's property, and a repetition of outrages so flagrant and disgraceful to the county.[42]

Admittedly this was from the tenantry, not the peasantry, and it was not written with the unlettered hand of an agricultural labourer, but it nevertheless probably contains sentiments not wholly forced or false.

Similarly, in 1843, in the Yorkshire township of Slaithwaite which had been a regular centre of industrial unrest since William Horsfall was murdered by the Luddites in 1812, the landlord and lord of the manor, the fourth Earl of Dartmouth, visited his people in order to celebrate the coming of age of his eldest son by laying the foundation stone of a new Church of England Sunday School high on the moors to serve the scattered communities of weaver/farmers on land he had given the previous year. Two years later he was back to open it, and in 1852 he was expressing concern for handloom weavers who 'do not partake in the general prosperity of factory labour'. In 1840 his wife had become patron of a maternal society for lying-in women started by the vicar's wife. 'He responded promptly and liberally, though with much discrimination, to every appeal made to him, for the spiritual and educational improvement of the tenants of his estates.' For over a century of industrialisation, successive earls from the second to the fifth bestowed this kind of personal patronage on the people of the village.[43] Whatever the motives of the Earls of Dartmouth – and they were men who took their religious faith seriously – this kind of personal benevolence could only add a warmth to the economic relationship which tied tenants to their landlord and villagers to the lord of the manor.

In 1795, Henry Yarbrugh of Heslington near York rebuilt the ancient almshouses and gave land for a village school. The same year soup kitchens were started, funded by private subscriptions or subsidised from the poor rates. Enormous amounts of private charity went into the relief of distress and more was contributed through the poor rates. One estimate is that in the first half of 1795, the first crisis of the war years, some 15–40 per cent of the population received relief from private and public charity.[44]

Against this background the system of poor relief was modified, following the emergency decision of the Speenhamland magistrates in 1795 to pay relief in proportion to need and the price of bread. The crisis of 1799–1801 was even worse, and need outstripped the ability of rate payers to find adequate funds. In London the government had to make loans to the poorest parishes to prevent starvation. Parishes further from the seat of government were dealt with less promptly but the need was unavoidable.[45] Christie concludes that had the poor law 'not been in operation, then the degree of desperation can only be guessed'. Wells argues that the poor law was breaking under the strain, and that the degree of desperation was a real threat to social stability. The same could be said of the third great wartime crisis in 1811–12, when harvest failure coincided with trade depression. Whereas Poor Law expenditure in 1801 had been £4,017,871, in 1811 it rose 65 per cent to £6,665,105. Private charity amounted to at least as much again. A fifth of the population in most Lancashire towns was estimated to be in receipt of relief.[46] Though Poor Law expenditure then declined a little, it was back up to the 1811–13 level again in 1817 and peaked at £7,517,000 in 1818. The 1820s saw a decline to under £6 million, but this was still above the level of the first crisis in 1795, and in 1832 the total was back to over £7 million.[47]

Without this huge transfer of funds from rate payers to the poor, the social fabric might well have crumbled. But such enormous calls on taxation led to a reconsideration of the basis on which relief was awarded. New philosophical ideas challenged older religious notions of the duty of the rich to feed the poor by suggesting that hand-outs produced dependency and encouraged both idleness and low wages. This thinking led to the Poor Law Amendment Act of 1834. It looked like punishment in the countryside for the collapse of social deference in 1830.

To conservative thinkers, the spirit of *laissez-faire* that lay behind the new Poor Law was, in Thomas Carlyle's memorable phrase, 'an *abdication* on the part of the governors'.[48] Disraeli had used the same idea a few months earlier in the debate on the 1839 Petition in his argument that there was a 'sentiment on the part of the people of England, that their civil rights had been invaded' and that this was what had made Chartism a mass movement. By civil rights he meant the right of the destitute to look to their neighbours for relief in the expectation that those in authority would recognise their social duties. Disraeli may have been constructing a golden age under the pre-1832 constitution and the old poor law in order to criticise the Whig reformers, but the values embodied in that myth were ones widely shared and to that extent he was right. The obverse of the argument that the system of poor relief saved Britain from revolution in the period 1790–1820 is that the change in the system brought Britain close to revolution after 1837. The word 'Britain' is used deliberately because, although the poor law applied only to England and Wales, the less adequate systems in Scotland and Ireland offered the safety net of emigration to England. Even so, the widespread agrarian discontent in Ireland, exported to both Britain and the United States, did owe something to the lack of a resident aristocracy and structure of public welfare underpinning private charity.

In practice, the anger against the new Poor Law was directed against its threat rather than what actually happened. Whatever Disraeli might say and although it is true that poor law expenditure was cut back from the 1830s, so that even in the period 1839–42 it was lower than in any previous crisis since 1799–1801 despite a near doubling of the population, much of the old system of private charity and public relief outside the workhouse continued as before. In Nottingham, for example, the mayor, William Roworth, led the opposition to the building of a new workhouse, and when the Guardians applied for land on which to built one, the corporation refused permission.[49] Major-General Napier, in charge of the troops garrisoned in the north to keep the Chartists in control, observed in his journal in December 1839: 'Spoke to the mayor about a subscription: – the excellent mayor, Mr Roworth. He joins me in all my opinions as to the thrice-accursed new poor law, its bastiles, and its guardians. Lying title! They guard nothing, not even their own carcases, for they so outrage misery that if a civil war comes they will immediately be sacrificed.'[50]

Another voice, sympathetic to the poor though hostile to Chartism, came from the Domestic Missionary to the Poor in Manchester at the time of the Plug Riots in 1842. This was John Layhe, reporting from his journal entry for July 1842 to the Manchester middle class at the Cross Street Unitarian chapel:

> The demand for soup tickets continues unabated, and the very early hour at which many persons are accustomed to resort to the kitchen in Bale-street proves the extremity of their destitution. I was lately conversing with a poor man, who has a wife, three sons and a daughter, all of whom except the woman were then out of work, and he informed me that being unable to sleep or rest, he went for soup one morning so early as half-past one o'clock, and even then found 50 or 60 persons before him. At the time referred to in the above statement, though the more skilled of the hand-loom weavers and out-door labourers had pretty regular employment, yet many other classes were suffering unusual depression. Such was the case with factory operatives and mechanics, and there were numbers of dyers and spinners,

and the more common descriptions of weavers, who had long had nothing to do. I was myself acquainted with many individuals connected with these branches of industry, who had been almost without any work for periods varying from a few weeks to twelve months. When to all this is added the long-continued depreciation of wages, we shall be convinced that the measure of human endurance was filled to the brim.[51]

He added, 'At length this measure was exceeded, and the waters of civil strife and commotion threatened to overflow the land, and sweep away the institutions of society.' The strike and lock-out, though, made things worse, for the few who had work were now deprived of it. 'Yet these poor people are of remarkably peaceable habits,' he reassured his subscribers, 'and would have been glad to have worked if they had been allowed. In these circumstances, I rendered them some assistance, which they received with great thankfulness.' In all this one small charity distributed 3,000 soup tickets, as well as bedding and clothing.

Layhe's report shows why the idea of strikers holding out until the Charter was the law of the land was impracticable. It also shows how the view that unrest was the work of a minority exploiting the grievances of the majority could be used to win charitable sympathy for the majority. Though Layhe may have been aware that some of his subscribers might have wished to starve the strikers back to work, his emphasis was on the need to relieve those whose distress was no fault of their own. Motives are always hard to disentangle, and contemporaries probably could not do it even for themselves, but in Layhe's report – as in the novel which the wife of the secretary to the Mission, Elizabeth Gaskell, based on his report – compassion appears more important than social control.[52] Compassion had the effect of blunting those edges of class hostility which fed the anger and despair of Chartism. Similarly, the grateful recipient's motives are hard to isolate. The donor naturally heard or wanted to hear gratitude, but we cannot now tell whether sullen resentment was also present.

Layhe also observed how many working people were too proud to accept charity, and turned first to 'incurring debts, and withdrawing funds from benefit societies'. The friendly society was seen by Professor Christie as another of those institutions which helped bind society together,[53] but it also gave working men independence and lessons in organisation. In 1793 Rose's Act help separate these societies from trade societies by giving them a legal existence but the trade societies also continued to offer financial support to their members parallel to that offered by the friendly societies. They undoubtedly helped take the edge of distress and, if one regards distress as a major cause of revolutions, they may have correspondingly reduced the risk. But in so far as they encouraged the capacity for independence and organisation they did not – unlike the poor law – promote those ties of paternalism and deference which Tory thinkers regarded as essential to social stability.

## Religion

In 1913 the French historian, Elie Halévy, sought to explain 'the extraordinary stability which English society was destined to enjoy throughout a period of revolutions and crises'. His answer was that 'the *elite* of the working class, the hard-working and capable bourgeoisie, had been imbued by the evangelical movement with a spirit from which the established order had nothing to fear.'[54] Since then historians have both rejected and been attracted by this theory. It was given a twist by Edward Thompson for whom Methodism was a conservative force which indoctrinated the workers, gave them an alternative sense of community and belonging, and offered them a spiritual safety valve on Sundays and during periods of religious revival.[55] Halévy himself meant by 'Methodism' the whole evangelical movement in Church and Dissent; other historians have extended the theory to apply to other religious emphases as well. William Jones, curate at Nayland in Suffolk and author of the *John Bull* loyalist tracts, was a high churchman and a millenarian.[56] Hannah More, who followed up her *Village Politics* (1793) with the monthly *Cheap Repository Tracts*, issued from 1795 to 1797, was an Evangelical.[57]

Religion provided a powerful language and exerted a greater impact on the way people thought than the secular language of political debate. It dominated cultural life and the media of communication: the sermon and homily, Sunday and weekday schools, charities and popular reading matter. The Bible and *Pilgrim's Progress* were central to the self-awareness of many a working-class autodidact. This meant that religion often provided the ideological ground on which revolution and stability were contested. For the followers of Richard

Brothers in 1795, Robert Wedderburn in 1819, John Thoms in 1838 or Joseph Rayner Stephens in 1839, religion could release revolutionary language, remove mundane inhibitions and promote revolt. A favoured text, used by United Britons in 1801 and by Luddites in 1812,[58] was taken from Ezekiel 21, verses 25–7:

> And thou, profane wicked prince of Israel, whose day is come, when iniquity shall have an end, Thus saith the Lord God; Remove the diadem, and take off the crown: this shall not be the same: exalt him that is low, and abase him that is high. I will overturn, overturn, overturn it: and it shall be no more, until he comes whose right it is: and I will give it him.

This was the spirit, with its vision of the revolutionary wheel of fortune, which inspired Luddites and anti-Poor Law protesters, incited Spenceans in Wedderburn's chapel, and made political preachers so dangerous in south Wales.

Counter-revolutionaries appreciated the importance of religion in maintaining the social and political order and reinforcing the legitimacy of 'the powers that be'. When Thoms found that a gang of men working in a gravel pit near Sittingbourne would not join his band of disciples in 1838, his response was to dismiss them as 'a set of Methodists'.[59] John Wesley had been a Tory, opposed even to American independence, and after his death in 1791 Methodism continued to stress its loyalty. In 1792 the Conference resolved that

1  None of us shall, either in writing or in conversation, speak lightly or irreverently of the Government under which he lives.
2  We are to observe, that the oracles of God command us to be subject to the higher powers; and that honour to the king is there connected with the fear of God.[60]

This continued to be the official policy throughout the period, but as a developing party outside the established Church, employing itinerant preachers and spreading its message by unorthodox means, Methodism was not always seen in this light by the authorities. In 1811, Lord Sidmouth proposed a Bill which, among other things, would have prohibited itinerant preaching. The Methodists demonstrated their loyalty as a matter of survival and then gratitude.[61] The Reverend John Stephens, Wesleyan Methodist superintendent minister in Manchester in 1819, expelled 400 Manchester Methodists suspected of radicalism after the Peterloo massacre and published a sermon in defence of the magistrates.[62] The fact that there were so many Methodists whom he felt he had to expel indicates the ambiguity of the Methodist contribution to stability and conflict no less than the politics of Stephens's sixth child, Joseph Rayner Stephens. Samuel Bamford's father and uncle were the sons of a leading local Methodist in Middleton. They found Wesley's theology perfectly compatible with reading Paine's *Rights of Man* and joining a reading society to support parliamentary reform.[63]

The established Church was more reliable, and here the Evangelicals did make an important contribution. Their deeply pessimistic view of human sinfulness caused them to see the French Revolution both as a manifestation of evil and as a divine punishment for the sins of everyone, including the ruling classes of Britain. Their moral mission, therefore, should not be seen as a simple instrument of repressive politics, though it had that effect. Their mood is caught in a memoir of one of their number, the Reverend William Richardson of York:

> Though Mr Richardson avoided mixing with politics and parties, he was a true lover of his country, and omitted no suitable opportunity of enforcing the duties of loyalty and subordination, and of denouncing the too frequent disposition to 'murmur and complain,' as equally contrary to the express precepts and to the spirit of the Gospel.
> During the twenty years' wars of the French Revolution, he suffered great distress and anxiety of mind, on account of the spirit of revolt and blasphemy which extended over Europe.[64]

Following the de-Christianisation campaign in France and the publication of Paine's *The Age of Reason* (1795), the debate in Britain switched emphasis from the constitution to religion. Atheism was the bugbear. Religion underpinned the law and morality; without it, all that was sacred would count for nothing. Repentance and divine mercy were needed if Britain were to resist France. The Evangelicals were unusual in identifying the high-born as well as the low as needing this message, and in this they had the support of the pious King George III, if not of his rather lax and sceptical prime minister, William Pitt. Religion was not a front for repression, but a vital necessity if Britain were to be saved from revolution and the wrath to come.

It was in this mood that the leading Yorkshire Evangelical clergy-men of the Elland Clerical Society (founded 1767) received and approved in 1797 a resolution from a kindred spirit in Sheffield, sol-emnly declaring 'that the revolutionary spirit of these Καιροι Χαλεποι [Perilous Times] calls for new and extraordinary exertions & methods of grace to oppose it' and agreed to form a committee 'for the purpose of conducting the Circulation of cheap Tracts & pamphlets in order to counteract the pernicious principles that have been diffused amongst the lower orders of people'.[65]

Over the next few years tracts and sermons urged repentance, loyalty and subordination on the West Riding which was sinking ever deeper into that revolutionary abyss that culminated in Luddism. One of their number was Hammond Roberson, curate in the parish of Dewsbury. Remembered as the model for Mr Helstone in Charlotte Brontë's *Shirley* and his apparently callous attitude to the dying Luddites after the attack on Rawfolds mill in 1812, he was not only an energetic opponent of the Luddites but also a founder of Sunday schools, the builder at his own expense of Christ Church, Liversedge, of which he became incumbent in 1816, and 'a devoted and highly conscientious man whose motives were pure and elevated'.[66] Yet Roberson's character was all of a piece. His sermons, tracts, Sunday schools, churches and anti-Luddite activities were all aimed at the ele-vation of the people, the promulgation of morality and an end to that spirit of disloyalty and insubordination that brought Europe so close to tragedy between 1789 and 1815.

Through militant and conscientiously pious pastors like Roberson in the parishes, and politically appointed bishops in the House of Lords, the Church and its message were woven into the fabric of unreformed society in defence of religion and against rev-olution. As much by their support of charities and Sunday schools as by their ideological underpinning of the existing system of pol-itics, they helped create a society capable of weathering the storms of radicalism. Their impact was probably greatest on the morale and sense of purpose of the governing classes, nationally and locally; but it may be that their non-commissioned officers in the reserve armies of Methodism and Nonconformity made a greater impact on the middling sections of society. However they operated, the combined forces of religious revival may have called people's minds to higher things, softened the edges of social conflict and,

where they did contribute to radical organisation and consciousness, turned that into constitutional and non-revolutionary chan-
nels.

## The strength of the state

Modern revolutions are often described as overthrowing 'the state'
but this view usually assumes a Germanic model of what constitutes
'the state', as found in the philosophies of Hegel and Marx. This
abstract concept is hardly appropriate in a discussion of revolution in
late eighteenth-century Britain. The word 'state' is a derivative of
'estate' and originally had territorial implications. Then, by extension,
it referred to the legal and administrative machinery by which the territory was governed. The 'state' was therefore a legal abstraction, and
the word was used in this sense in the 1790s in contexts such as 'State
prisoners' and 'State Trials'. The machinery which made up the state
included the courts of law, the established church, the privy council,
the king's ministers and the supreme legislature – the king-in-parlia-
ment. The exact concept was vague, for Britain possessed no defining
constitution, which Edmund Burke regarded as a virtue and Thomas
Paine as a vice. A programme of reform which sought fundamental
change to any of these aspects of the state could be thought revolutionary. In fact, the word 'state' was rarely used: Paine preferred to
discuss 'systems of government' or 'constitutions'. What usually
appears to have been meant was the nature of the administration. The
personnel of the legal system might be swept away, Parliament might
be reformed, but apart from the church there was little hostility to the
institutions of the state as such.

The main object of hostility was the administration: the government; the king and his ministers. Revolution to overthrow 'the state'
could therefore mean little more than a violent alternative to a general
election for a people excluded from the normal political processes, in
order to destroy that corruption whereby the propertied classes were
parasitic upon the over-taxed poor. The king, his ministers, or even
the whole of Parliament were tangible symbols of government, and as
such objects of radical attack, but beyond them Britain was actually
governed not by a centralised bureaucracy such as modern revolutions are directed against, but by a diffuse, amateur, local, part-time

and numerous body of men who collectively substituted for what a later age would call 'the state'. At the start of the French Revolutionary War, the Treasury employed only seventeen clerks; the Home and Foreign Offices each had an establishment of nineteen, including the secretaries of state.[67] What central administration there was concerned internal and external security – although much of this was also local and amateur – and collecting the money to pay for it and the interest on loans raised to pay for past wars: what has been called 'the fiscal-military state'.[68]

The paradox of a small and apparently weak state that was actually strong and resilient has been explored by John Brewer. The British state was strong because it was militarily effective and relatively efficient at raising tax revenues. France was, by eighteenth-century criteria, a much wealthier country than Britain, yet the long series of wars with Britain bankrupted the Bourbons not the Hanoverians. Even the crisis of 1797, which Paine had anticipated in his *Decline and Fall of the English System of Finance* (1796) and expected to lead to rapid collapse, was surmounted with surprisingly little difficulty. Whatever Cobbett might say about paper money, it worked for Britain because of the underlying financial strength of the country. The diffuse nature of the largely amateur administration also meant that it was not as vulnerable as a centralised bureaucracy to the *coup d'état* approach to revolution. Local self-government may have weakened the central state but in so doing actually strengthened the capacity of the state to survive a crisis at the centre.

Another apparent weakness but actual strength lay in the rule of law. State power and authority were exercised in England through the law, which was made in the courts as well as in Parliament and was administered locally as well as nationally.[69] The 'rule of law' was widely accepted as the foundation of English liberties, and the different Scottish system held a similar position north of the border. Only in Ireland was there dissent about the legitimacy of the law, which always made Ireland a special case. In Britain, it was the law which restricted Parliament and prevented despotism. This weakened the theoretical powers of the executive but strengthened their legitimacy. Revolutionaries in Britain did not seek to overthrow the rule of law. They objected to specific laws, or the absence of them, and to those who administered the law in what was seen to be an 'unjust' way, but such conflict as occurred was within the framework of the law. The

CITY COLLEGE
LEARNING RESOURCE CENTRE

justification for bearing arms by appeal to Blackstone is a good example of this. Constitutionalism and respect for the law was reinforced when the jury system, which could be notoriously independent of government, led to the acquittals of Hardy and the rest in 1794, O'Connor in 1798, and Thistlewood and the Folly Hall insurgents in 1817. The safeguard of *Habeas Corpus* was seldom suspended, and then mainly in time of war; its suspension in 1817 was unusual. The innate constitutionalism of British radical protest blunted its revolutionary edge. Conversely, this meant that when the constitutional approach was frustrated, when particular laws were seen to be so unjust as to be unacceptable, when ministers made laws by Proclamation and not by Act of Parliament, or when the normal paths of legitimate protest were stopped by the suspension of *Habeas Corpus*, the moral and indeed constitutional justification for revolution was all the greater. It could be sanctioned by an appeal to 1688 or even 1642 which few conservatives could gainsay.[70]

The diffuse and amateur British state was also strong because of the people who administered it. The British aristocracy, like the British state, was the opposite of its public image. Apparently an open elite, cascading its younger sons down into the gentry and drawing its daughters-in-law and their money up from wealthy merchant families, in fact the mobility of the upper reaches of the social order was more a matter of recycling through the same small number of titled families than a genuine openness of access. The occasional lawyer or churchman might ease his way upwards from the professions to the House of Lords, and a career might be made in politics or a position bought with money made in India or finance and commerce (and, even more rarely, industry) but these were the exceptions. The result was that Britain was administered by an elite of families from the peerage and titled gentry who dominated positions in every aspect of national and local government at every significant level.

Furthermore, by socialisation in a common education dominated by Eton or Westminster and then Christ Church, Oxford, or Trinity or St John's, Cambridge, followed by marriage into one another's families, the peerage and its relations formed a homogenised elite.[71] They provided around a fifth of the membership of the House of Commons but their connections reached beyond politics to other significant institutions, notably the higher ranks of the armed forces. The key figure in the administration of law and order locally was the Lord

Lieutenant, who almost invariably in England was a peer or the son of a peer. He was at the apex of county society and wielded important patronage, nominating local magistrates and officers in the militia.[72] Though the numbers of peers increased dramatically after 1784, rising from 189 in 1780 to 267 in 1800, most of these new creations came from old peerage families.[73] Beyond the peerage families, among the titled aristocracy at large and down the social scale to the baronets, much of the argument remains true. At the county level the gentry supplied the Deputy Lieutenants and Sheriffs, they dominated the magistracy and filled the lesser commissioned ranks in the armed forces. Many of them through intermarriage were also more or less distantly related to peerage families.[74] In 1818 four-fifths of MPs were elected from the landed elite of gentry or aristocracy.[75]

The economic interests of this elite were as broad as their social base was narrow. Aristocratic landlords exploited, directly or indirectly, the mineral wealth of their estates; wealthy commercial and industrial families bought estates and merged into the gentry at the lower levels, and then by further well-placed marriages their links to the greater county families were established. In this way the governing elite could both remain relatively small and closed, and yet at the same time be part of the mainstream of wider gentry and commercial society. They were part of the single, seamless fabric of society. Below them they controlled a network of patronage which reached down through their tenants and employees to tradesmen dependent on the local 'big house' for custom. Though Cobbett might dismiss this as part of 'Old Corruption' it was much more and remained an important characteristic of British society well into the nineteenth century. It faltered but recovered in 1832, having shed its less acceptable characteristics. When Robert Peel judged that the Corn Laws were bringing the system into disrepute, he repealed them – aided by the most aristocratic section of the legislature, the Whigs. From the 1820s onwards the British elite showed a remarkable ability to reform its institutions and move from a fiscal–military state to an administrative state capable of meeting the needs of an increasingly complex commercial and industrial society.[76] The third reason given by the Chartist, G. J. Holyoake, for the lack of revolution in England in 1848 was, 'The mixed interest of our commercial nobility and the people.'[77]

The significance of this elite is the unity of direction and purpose it gave to British society. If revolutions are caused when the elite is divided, the opportunities in Britain were few. If there were a hint of weakness or dissent, that was quickly disposed of. When the Duke of Norfolk unwisely toasted 'Our Sovereign, the Majesty of the People' at Fox's birthday celebration in 1798, Pitt dismissed him from the lord lieutenancy of the West Riding.[78] When his successor, Earl Fitzwilliam, supported a county meeting in 1819 to protest at the Peterloo massacre, he too was dismissed.[79] Both men were Whigs who saw themselves as defenders of English liberties and the rule of law. If there was to be a revolution, it would be one to protect liberty as in 1688, and they would lead it. When they bid to do so in 1832, Wellington drew back rather than risk civil conflict.

Revolutions are also made when the army rebels. Revolutionaries need troops, which must come from within the existing armed forces or from abroad. The British army was not divided vertically by region or tribe, but horizontally by social class. Because the same elite which controlled the army controlled everything else, there was unlikely to be a military *coup*, or a revolution led by disgruntled regiments. As John Cannon has reasonably asked, 'What in the eighteenth century, could army officers have rebelled against and, if they had taken over, how could they have constructed a society more congenial to their own aristocratic views and interests?'[80]

## The authority of the law

The legal hand of the British system of justice was deceptively light. Acceptance of the rule of law and the independence of the jury system meant that arbitrary justice was thought neither desirable nor possible. There were relatively few political trials, and many of these ended in an acquittal including, spectacularly, the trial of Hardy and others in 1794. Fox's Libel Act of 1792 gave a measure of protection in seditious libel cases. The Two Acts of 1795, despite their potential, were rarely used. The government did not usually interfere in the work of local magistrates who were on the front line of administering justice, and frequently left them to their own devices and complaining at the lack of support they received from the centre.[81] Nevertheless, the law was effective. Exemplary punishments, some of them harsh, were exacted. The outcomes of the Scottish treason trials of 1793 and 1794 under the different Scottish legal system, contrast with those in

England at this time, but even in Scotland Lord Braxfield's use of transportation against Muir, Palmer, Skirving, Gerrald and Margarot was dubious but legal.[82]

The device of proceeding by *ex-officio* information circumvented unreliable grand juries. Under an *ex-officio* information filed by the Attorney General, there was no Grand Jury to give a case a prelimi-nary hearing; the accused need not be informed of the charges against him (or, very rarely, her); there was no need to bring the accused to trial, and if they could not afford bail they might be imprisoned without charge and without trial. Even if a case did come to trial, and even if normal procedures were followed or the case were dropped, a poor bookseller could be ruined and thus silenced without any need to prove guilt. The very threat of such proceedings was often enough.

The Attorney General could also call for a special jury to be appointed. These were not chosen at random and could be vetted by the prosecution in advance. In Scotland, juries were selected by the court and the presiding judge, no challenges were allowed, and majority verdicts were accepted. As a result of these limitations on the jury system in both parts of Britain, in the 1790s the majority of trials for politically-related offences, other than the treason trials, resulted in convictions.[83] Clive Emsley's estimate of 200 prosecutions for treason and sedition in the 1790s has been challenged as an underes-timate, but his overall point remains: that Pitt's 'Terror' was based not so much on the new legislation introduced in the 1790s as on the regular processes of law available to the authorities at any time they cared to use them. Despite spectacular failures, repeated in William Hone's trial for libel in 1817 when the jury refused to convict, this remained true and the law was used to punish rioters, demonstrators, libellers, publishers and insurgents throughout the period of this book. But even an important case like the trial of Smith O'Brien for sedition in May 1848 could fail when Catholics on the jury refused to produce a unanimous verdict of guilty, unlike the case of John Mitchel who was convicted by a carefully packed jury.[84]

Not all prosecutions were initiated by the law officers of the crown or local magistrates. One feature of the loyalist reaction against the radicals was the creation of private prosecution societies. In response to a Royal Proclamation in June 1787 for the encouragement of piety and virtue, and for preventing and punishing vice, profaneness and immorality, William Wilberforce set up what was known as the Proclamation Society. One of its tasks was, in the words of the Proclamation, the suppression 'all loose and licentious prints, books and publications, dispersing poison to the minds of the young and unwary; and to punish the publishers and vendors thereof'.[85] Among its successes was the prosecution of Paine's *The Age of Reason* in 1797. This society later merged with a parallel society, created in 1802, entitled the 'Society for the Suppression of Vice and the encouragement of religion and virtue, throughout the United Kingdom, to consist of members of the Established Church' – known to radicals as the 'Vice Society'. By the end of 1803 it had over eight hundred members and nearly seven hundred convictions. These were for 'moral' offences, but since in the evangelical view of the world morality underpinned the civil order, these could include 'political' offences. As the secretary explained in the disturbed year of 1817, 'The influences of religious obligation seem much on the decline among the lower orders of society, to which is probably attributable much of that impatience under civil restraint which is the characteristic feature of the times.'[86] This purpose was taken over more explicitly in 1820 by the 'Constitutional Association for Opposing the Progress of Disloyal and Seditious Principles', founded with offices in Bridge Street, Blackfriars (hence its alternative name, 'the Bridge Street Gang') by 20 peers, 40 MPs, 9 bishops and 97 clergy. The Bridge Street Gang operated by prosecuting booksellers in order to disrupt their businesses and land them with heavy costs irrespective of whether a conviction was secured. During 1820–22 they obtained only four convictions, one of which resulted in a sentence – on Mary Ann Carlile, wife of the republican publisher, Richard Carlile who was already in gaol for republishing Paine's *The Age of Reason* as a result of a Vice Society prosecution.[87]

The government found these private prosecutions convenient, for they distanced ministers from measures of which they could approve privately but did not wish to endorse officially. The impartiality of the rule of law was important and ministers had to balance the need for security with reforms to improve the way the law worked and how it was perceived. Lord Sidmouth, in his earlier days as Henry Addington, Speaker of the House of Commons, had consoled himself following the acquittal of Hardy in 1794 with the thought that 'It is of more consequence to maintain the credit of a mild and unprejudiced administration of justice than ever to convict a Jacobin.'[88]

In 1812, as Home Secretary in the middle of the Luddite panic, he refused the urgent demands of the Vice-Lieutenant and magistrates of the West Riding for the issue of General Warrants so they could raid homes for arms because he did not see 'under present circumstances, cause for adopting the strong measure of a forcible seizure, nor for resorting to any measure, that does not derive its effect from the Law as it now stands'.[89] Subsequent reforms at the Home Office under Robert Peel extended this policy of emphasising the impartiality of the rule of law. An important change introduced by his ministry in 1842 removed from the justices in Quarter Sessions to the Assizes a number of cases, including those involving punishment by transportation, unlawful oaths, blasphemous and seditious libel, arson and most unlawful combinations and conspiracies, which had figured large in prosecutions against those involved in disturbances and worse over the previous half century.[90]

The determination of governments to maintain the impartiality of the law illustrates the extent to which most conservatives and many revolutionaries had consciously elected to confine their operations within constitutional limits until such time as the other side should break them. The threat of revolution on constitutionalist grounds might therefore be seen as one reason why restraints were observed by successive British governments; but equally the fact of such constitutionalism on the part of the authorities is one reason why the revolutionaries were themselves constrained in the main to constitutional methods. Both sides accepted, as it were, the rules of the game, written in a common language of constitutional liberties.[91]

In practice, however, there were players on both sides who did not appear to accept the rules. A minority of revolutionaries, like Paine, rejected the language of historical rights and by the 1830s were beginning to be attracted by the alternative language of socio-economic conflict; and a minority of magistrates and armed civilians in the yeomanry were impatient with the blatant exploitation of constitutionalist language by subversive troublemakers intent only on seizing property which they did not own. Either of these could upset the delicate balance which helped prevent outbreaks of revolution.

The law was still subject to the vagaries of individual judges. Those tried in 1842 before Special Commissions presided over by Baron Abinger were dealt with by a judge who appeared to think that supporting the Charter was itself a political offence; but then, as plain

Mr James Scarlett, he had led the prosecution of Henry Hunt after Peterloo.[92] In contrast is Lord Chief Justice Tindal who recommended the commutation of the life sentences on Frost, Williams and Jones in 1840.[93] By the 1840s, the government and its law officers, if not all judges and magistrates, had realised the strength of justice tempered with mercy. In the wake of the Chartist disturbances of 1848, most sentences passed were for periods of between six months and two years. That avoided making martyrs, but took troublemakers out of circulation for long enough to ensure that the forces of law and order would prevail. Moderation and restraint by the authorities deprived would-be revolutionaries of their moral case for rebellion.

## The forces of order

Under the Lord Lieutenant of the county, the next effective person responsible for the maintenance of law and order was the Justice of the Peace in England and Wales, and the Sheriff in Scotland where the Sheriff Principal was usually the Lord Lieutenant, while the Sheriff Depute and his Sheriff Substitutes exercised the law and order role left to magistrates south of the border.[94] The role of the magistrate, according to an Act of the reign of Edward III, was 'to restrain offenders, rioters and all other barrators, and to pursue, arrest, take and chastise them according to their trespass and offence, and then cause them to be imprisoned and duly punished'.[95] When necessary in his judgement, he could suspend civil law and hand over to the military by reading the Riot Act of 1715.

> Our Sovereign Lord the King chargeth and commandeth all Persons, being assembled, immediately to disperse themselves, and peaceably to depart to their Habitations, or to their lawful Business, upon the Pains contained in the Act made in the first year of King George, for preventing Tumults and riotous Assemblies. God Save the King.[96]

This Act could be applied whenever twelve or more persons were 'unlawfully, riotously and tumultuously assembled', and following this proclamation, anyone remaining after one hour, whatever his or her intentions or actions, was guilty of an offence.

The Duke of Wellington felt that the magistrates were much

maligned but in fact made the difference between England and France in 1830:

> We have mobs; we have riots; we have broken windows and broken heads; and much injury done to, and destruction of, property. But we never fail to find the Justice of the Peace faithful to his trust, making the most energetic, the most moderate that circumstances will permit, but at the same time the most effectual and successful exertions to put an end to the mischief.[97]

On the other hand, Francis Lindley Wood feared in 1812 that magistrates were, as in Ireland, reaching the end of their tether and might refuse to serve;[98] and in 1839, Major-General Napier grumbled at magistrates who chose to go grouse-shooting in August 1839 in the middle of the Chartist crisis.[99]

In the eighteenth century, the forces available to the magistrates were limited. Parish constables were part-time officials concerned only with collecting local taxes and dealing with petty crimes and perhaps the odd instance of drunken disorder. Magistrates might pay informers to supply information useful for maintaining the peace and this role was performed by the police employed by stipendiary magistrates appointed in London under the 1792 Middlesex Justices' Act, but in cases of major unrest they had to resort to the military. Their powers included issuing search warrants, forbidding meetings, and calling upon the militia, yeomanry or regular army for support.

The most ancient auxiliary force on which the magistrates could call was the *posse comitatus* or *levée en masse*, the whole body of adult males in the county called out by the sheriff in the event of a riot. This was both impractical and largely inoperative by the end of the eighteenth century, despite its resurrection with the Levée en Masse Act of 1803.[100] Theoretically, under the provisions for Watch and Ward every citizen could be called upon to assist the authorities, and an attempt was made to revive this in 1811–12, but it was preferable to swear in 'the most respectable members of the community' as special constables and in an emergency this was usually the first line of defence.[101]

The other ancient resource available to magistrates was the county militia, reformed in 1757. This provided for a levy on every parish, chosen by lot if insufficient numbers volunteered, to produce a corps of men who were to be trained (hence they were sometimes called 'train bands') and serve for three years in county regiments which could be called out in the event of 'actual or imminent danger'. Militiamen were to be paid.[102] Under pressure of the French Revolutionary and Napoleonic Wars, several changes were made to the militia: in 1796, the Supplementary Militia and the Provisional cavalry were created. The former increased the levy beyond what many local men found sustainable and it was very unpopular. The latter was not a success, and gave way to the Volunteers. In 1808 the Local Militia was formed to serve only in their own areas and release the Regular Militia for wider service. After the war, the militia sank into relative insignificance.[103]

This was not true of the Volunteers, first formed during the invasion scare of 1794 to rally loyalist opinion to the government and marginalise the Foxite opposition. As such it was always something of a political force, employed to maintain order at home as well as providing a defence against foreign invasion. In the absence of the latter, the only action they saw was as domestic police. Although the Volunteer Infantry were important during the war, it was the Volunteer Cavalry, or Yeomanry, who were to continue important in peace time. Possession of a horse determined the social rank and status of the Yeomanry, described by one military historian as 'full of life and vigour, less as complete regiments than as troops and squadrons of tenant farmers and their sons, acting under command of their landlords and their landlords' sons for the preservation of internal order'.[104] As the Vice-Lieutenant of the West Riding wrote in June 1812, 'no force seems to me so much to be depended upon as the yeomanry cavalry'.[105] When magistrates felt the need, beyond these auxiliary part-time forces were the Fencibles – full-time troops on garrison duty in Britain – and the regular army.

The numbers of troops of various kinds were formidable, but their efficiency was variable. Recruiting for the militia could itself cause riots, especially in 1796 following the Supplementary Militia Act. Yorkshire was the worst county affected, but there were anti-recruitment riots also in Lincolnshire, Bedfordshire, Cambridgeshire, Hertfordshire and Northamptonshire. Regular troops had to be used to restore order.[106] Such was the reaction in Scotland in 1797, when the militia was introduced for the first time, that the commander-in-chief felt that his forces were inadequate to deal with widespread simultaneous disturbances. In East and West Lothian, Stirlingshire, Ayrshire,

Lanarkshire and indeed right across south, central and eastern Scotland from Dumfries to Inverness, riots broke out.[107] At Dalry in Ayrshire, the Liberty Tree was planted. At Tranent in East Lothian, the Riot Act was read on 29 August 1797 and the troops opened fire, killing twelve people. As a result of these riots across Scotland, eighty people were subsequently charged with riot, two of them also being charged with sedition: eight men were transported.

These disturbances were happening only a few weeks after the navy mutinied in England and, as in that case, there was a suspicion of Jacobin involvement. The minister at Campsie, Mr Leslie, was doubtless right to 'perceive some of the old Jacobin Societies using every effort to alarm the farmers and the Country people with mis-representations about the wording of the Militia Act'. The Duke of Montrose suspected that those behind the disturbances were 'the set of men who were active with Muir &c'.[108] A closer examination of the militia riots does suggest some truth in this, linking the disturbances to the formation of the United Scotsmen societies in the same places.[109] To set against this were the loyal addresses by men protest-ing against the principle of the militia but offering to volunteer for military service. The reason no militia had been created for Scotland in 1757 had been fear of arming Jacobites. Forty years later, there was a danger of arming Jacobins. For this reason Pitt's government was wary of loyalists who were armed, throughout Britain, unless they also had a stake in the property they were called upon to defend.

The reaction of militiamen to food riots again shows the unreli-ability of drawing men from the same social class as those whom they were to control. With a fixed food allowance of fivepence a day, mili-tiamen were vulnerable to rises in the price of food such as happened in 1795. Riots occurred across the south coast. In Lewes, the Oxfordshire militia marched on Seaford and Newhaven with fixed bayonets to seize provisions which they sold at reduced prices: as a result, four of them were executed and several more flogged. At Canterbury, the Volunteers had to be called out to control the South Hampshire Militia.[110] In the worse crisis of 1800–01, Volunteers and Regulars were used to guard grain stocks and disperse riots, but as with the militia the Volunteer Infantry proved less than reliable.[111] In Dartmouth, the Volunteers mutinied, telling their officers: 'that Gover[nmen]t had been applied to long & nothing done for them, therefore it was high time they should do something for themselves to prevent their Families from starving.'[112] For this reason, magistrates came to rely heavily on the Volunteer Cavalry, backed up by the Regular Army.

The extent of this dependency became clear during the Luddite disturbances of 1811–12. The magistrates began by swearing in special constables by the hundred: 600 in Nottingham at the end of 1811; 1,500 in the Salford Hundred of Lancashire – 10 per cent of all adult males – in April 1812, and another 400 in Bolton. An attempt was made to revive Watch and Ward, but this was largely unsuccessful and voluntary associations were felt to be a more appropriate way for property owners to protect their own property. This proved insufficient in the winter of 1811–12, and so the authorities had to turn to the militia, the yeomanry and regular troops. In May 1812, arrangements were made to garrison 3,000 infantry and 500 cavalry near Nottingham, and in Lancashire and Cheshire, General Maitland had at his command 79 companies of infantry, 18 troops of horse and two detachments of artillery – amounting to 5,500 infantry and 1,400 cavalry. In the West Riding, General Grey had 1,000 infantry and 800 cavalry. But even with so large a number of troops, the army could not be everywhere at once or guard every factory. All they could hope to do was to supplement local self-defence, and hope to surprise or overawe Luddite gangs by garrisoning the towns and scouring the countryside with highly mobile troops.[113]

Military cut-backs after the war meant that by 1817, when social tension had again reached wartime heights, the entire British army available for effective service in Britain and Ireland probably amounted to only 16,000 soldiers. The yeomanry, with 17,818 was to be the mainstay of public order, supplemented by the 11,000 pensioners called up in the emergency of 1819.[114] The disastrously undisciplined performance of the yeomanry at St Peter's Field, Manchester, on 16 August 1819 exposed the weakness of relying upon a part-time, armed civilian force to maintain order, particularly in large towns. Thereafter when dealing with localised disturbances, magistrates looked to regular troops to support their special constables. Even in 1831, it was the Hussars who were called on in Derby and Nottingham (as they had been, along with the yeomanry, at Peterloo), and the Dragoons and Dragoon Guards in Bristol. In south Wales in 1831, detachments of the East Glamorgan Yeomanry, the 93rd Highlanders and the 3rd Dragoon Guards were all involved. In April

1839, when General Napier wished to put the yeomanry on permanent duty, the Whig Prime Minister and Home Secretary, Melbourne and Russell, declined to do so. Napier noted in his Journal on 15 August – Napoleon's birthday as well as the eve of Peterloo – 'If the Chartists want a fight, they can be indulged without yeomen, who are over-zealous for cutting and slashing.'[115]

For the Tories, Sir James Graham continued this preference for regular troops. His reasons were partly financial – the yeomanry were paid only when they were called out but regular troops had to be paid anyway; partly political – he appreciated the need not to call out farmers at harvest time; and partly tactical – he knew that the yeomanry was hated and its appearance would be as likely to cause a riot as prevent one.[116] But where disturbances were widespread, as in the 'Swing' counties in 1830, and again in the industrial districts in 1839, 1842 and 1848, traditional forces had to be employed, including the yeomanry and voluntary associations. The military, though, was always intended to be the second line of defence. Magistrates were supposed to maintain order by calling on civilians – in voluntary associations, as special constables and, increasingly in the nineteenth century, as regular policemen.

In London the double issue of crime and the maintenance of order led the Home Office under Robert Peel to introduce the Metropolitan Police in 1829. This did not at first supersede existing police arrangements; nor was it necessarily better. William Popay, a police sergeant, was accused in 1833 of having infiltrated the National Union of the Working Classes as an *agent provocateur*; and at Copenhagen Fields in the same year a baton charge against the crowd resulted in the death of a constable. At the subsequent inquest, the coroner's jury returned a verdict of 'justifiable homicide'. Though quasi-military in organisation and discipline, the new London police was a civilian force, its constables were usually armed only with batons and, unlike the yeomanry and regular soldiers with their colourful uniforms, they dressed to look like civilians.[117] With an average strength of 3,389 during 1834–38,[118] the new police only slowly made an impact on the metropolis and, by example, on ideas about policing elsewhere. In 1835, the Municipal Corporations Act required corporate boroughs to establish police forces, but Birmingham and Manchester were incorporated only in 1838 and Bradford in 1847. When Birmingham needed police in 1839, controversially the Home Office sent down a force of metropolitan policemen on the train.

Outside the corporate boroughs, county magistrates were given the option of appointing a police force by the Rural Police Acts of 1839 and 1840. On grounds of cost, not all did so and there was no clear correlation with areas of Chartist strength: Lancashire adopted the Act; the West Riding did not. Their reasoning in Yorkshire was clear: 'for common times and purposes they conceive the present force sufficient, and that upon occasions of Outbreak or riot, such as we have unfortunately seen, no addition to the Police force, which can be contemplated, would be sufficient for their protection'.[119]

This meant that magistrates preferred to rely on the army. The Northern District, based on Nottingham, was put under the charge of Major-General Charles Napier in April 1839. He was a cousin of Charles James Fox and politically a radical, whose condemnation of Feargus O'Connor's brand of Chartism was matched only by his contempt for local magistrates. His fear was not revolution, but widespread disturbances. He sought to prevent these by concentrating his forces and overawing his opponents, on the grounds that prevention was better than cure. If large-scale disturbances broke out, there would be deaths among the rioters and this he wished to avoid. His approach probably suited Whig Home Secretaries, Lord John Russell and Lord Normanby, whose Liberalism was fortified by their paying insufficient attention to detail, but the Tory Sir James Graham was different: Napier was sent to India in September 1841. During the summer of 1842 both the Northern and Midland Districts were put under the overall control of Lieutenant-General Sir Thomas Arbuthnot, based in Manchester. He worked closely with the Home Secretary and the Commander-in-Chief, the Duke of Wellington. The Home Office remained in overall control however, even in 1848 when the Duke advanced his own schemes for the defence of London, parallel to those of the government.[120]

The effectiveness of the army was important in the maintenance of order. In retrospect, we know that on each occasion when an armed rising was planned or actually occurred it was suppressed, even though the number of would-be insurgents outnumbered those available to defeat them. This was partly because of the efficiency of the government's intelligence systems. The structure and effectiveness of the informer system built up in the 1790s has already been discussed in Chapter 1.[121] Despite some decline in efficiency in the nineteenth century and the reluctance of peacetime governments to spend money on informers, and despite the exaggeration contained in many of the informers' reports, they, nevertheless, remained essential. At every level the government had to sift the wheat from the chaff for important clues about the plans of 'the disaffected'. During the Luddite disturbances, Earl Fitwilliam was infuriatingly calm most of the time, but capable of resolute action when necessary. The same was true of Napier, who refused to be panicked by the magistrates and preferred to use soldiers to check the information supplied by them. The problems experienced in Yorkshire in 1812 and in south Wales in the autumn of 1839, arose when traditional sources of information dried up.[122] Usually, however, the effectiveness of the government lay not in its superior armed forces but in its superior intelligence sources. Most of the plots from 1794 to 1848 were exposed by spies. As the schemes matured, the government knew as much about them as the plotters. Sometimes the government probably over-reacted to the information gathered, but in 1839 Russell at the Home Office almost certainly under-reacted to the clear signs available to him during the summer from south Wales. The Newport rising suggests the wisdom of over-reaction. The policy of forestalling insurrection generally worked.

When there were open conflicts, these were suppressed by small numbers of troops. This was sometimes a matter of luck, particularly with the weather, but the authorities made their own luck through superior organisation and forethought. When Napier took charge of the Northern District in 1839 he did not have enough troops to suppress a Chartist rising. He out-thought the Chartists rather than out-fought them. His policy was to keep his troops together in sufficiently large numbers not to risk conflict. He set out his ideas in a letter to his subordinate in Manchester, Colonel Wemyss, in April 1839:

> With regards to detachments, my mind is made up to have as few as possible. . . . I lay down as an axiom, and our first, greatest principle, that the queen's troops must not be overthrown anywhere, because the effect in the three kingdoms would be fearful. If only a corporal's guard were cut off it would be 'total defeat of the troops' ere it reached London Edinburgh and Dublin; and before the contradiction arrived the disaffected, in moral exaltation of supposed victory, would be in arms. This is more especially to be apprehended in Ireland, where rivers of blood would flow.

Napier here showed his understanding of the importance of play-acting in the maintenance of order, where the control of the majority by the minority was based on a successfully maintained illusion. The fact was that there were never enough troops to enforce order by physical power alone, and by 1839 successive government cut-backs had left the army and yeomanry much reduced in numbers. Napier continued his letter:

> Now let us look at the other side. Suppose from want of soldiers a rising takes place in some town; suppose the worst, and nothing can exceed what happened at Bristol . . . What did Bristol amount to? Only individual loss. The troops were victorious the instant they were put in motion and all the world knew it was a riot; it produced no national evil; it had no public results, though one of the largest towns in the empire was nearly laid in ashes.[123]

Here was another version of Holyoake's 'equality of towns' argument. Napier's overall sense was sound, though his argument was exaggerated. In 1842 at Salterhebble a small detachment of cavalry had been defeated, more because of the terrain than the smallness of their numbers, but this had not led to a rising largely because the Plug Rioters were not seeking one. On the other hand, even a small detachment of thirty-two soldiers in a good defensive position were able to deal with the thousands pitted against them at Newport.

Napier was right. With only about sixty soldiers in Newport, there was no alternative: it was a high risk brought about by neglect of earlier warnings, and if the troops at the Westgate had been defeated, then south Wales in 1839 might have looked very different from Bristol in 1831. If necessary Napier was prepared to sacrifice the police to preserve the army. This was not a point of view shared by the magistrates but, as he pointed out to the magistrates of Halifax in 1839, 'The cavalry at Halifax are quartered in the very worst and most dangerous manner. Forty-two troopers in twenty-one distant billets! Fifty resolute Chartists might disarm and destroy the whole in ten minutes.'[124] This had been the strategy discussed at Folly Hall in 1817. But Halifax was dependent on its soldiers: it was not a corporate borough until 1848 and there was no rural police.

By 1848 the position of the forces of law and order was immeasurably strengthened. Firstly, the small number of troops had been made more effective by the establishment of the railway network.

Already by 1839 Napier was able to move some troops by train, but when the national network was established the logistical situation was transformed. As Sir James Willoughby Gordon, the Quartermaster General, explained to a select committee in 1844:

> you send a battalion of 1,000 men from London to Manchester in nine hours; that same battalion marching would take 17 days; and they arrive at the end of nine hours just as fresh, or nearly so, as when they started. By moving troops to and fro by that mode of conveyance, you do most important service to the public, so much so that without that conveyance, you could not have done one tenth part of the work that it was required of the troops to do, and necessarily to do, in the year 1842.[125]

The second development was the London police. Their handling of crowds in the 1830s had been poor and ineffective, but by 1848 they had learned a great deal about crowd control. Not only were they able to confront the peaceful demonstration on 10 April with firmness and without provocation, but they also survived the much more testing time during the summer evenings of May, June and July.

The short answer about the effectiveness of the troops is to see what happened when they came into conflict with rioters and insurgents when numbers alone would have suggested defeat. At Folly Hall and Pentrich, the insurgent forces ran away at the sight of troops; even at Bonnymuir and Merthyr Tydfil where the insurgents stood their ground and fought, they were easily defeated. At even a suspicion that troops might be coming, as at Grange Moor in 1820, the revolutionaries melted into the night. It is not that they were cowards but, for the most part, they were realists. When they were not, as in Bossenden Wood in 1838, they were overcome.

One reason for this lies not in the strength of the army, the weaknesses of which have been discussed and which were all too obvious to nervous commanding officers, but in the greater weakness of the insurgents. Two aspects of this can be considered here: first, their tactics. One of the few works on military tactics that the would-be revolutionaries used was Colonel Macerone's *Defensive Instructions for the People*. The use of pikes as recommended by him may have been suitable for street fighting against cavalry in the narrow rookeries of London's Seven Dials, and a knowledge of recent revolutionary history in France had taught people about barricades. As Napier

CITY COLLEGE LEARNING RESOURCE CENTRE

observed, in urban warfare 'cavalry can do little better than get out of it with all possible speed', and leave it to the infantrymen with their rifles.[126] But in open warfare the pike was useless. For a start, as Napier explained, a six-foot pike was not long enough.[127] Secondly, he noted in his journal as he prepared to take up his command,

> I expect to have very few soldiers and many enemies: hence, if we deal with pikemen my intent is to put cavalry on their flanks, making my infantry retire as the pikemen advance. If they halt to face the cavalry, the infantry shall resume fire, for if the cavalry charge pikemen in order the cavalry will be defeated; the pike must be opposed by the musquet and bayonet, in which the soldiers must be taught to have confidence: it is the master weapon.[128]

Napier went on to say that he would use buckshot not bullets, in order to wound but not kill. The Chartist tactic, as at Newport, was the headlong charge. The naivety of this was recaptured many years later by Benjamin Brierley as he recalled the rebellious readers of the *Northern Star* in his father's house in Failsworth as he ground their pikes on his father's stone: 'My father did not encourage these "physical forceist" ideas. Having been at Waterloo, he knew what fighting meant, especially on battle fields where they could not run away.'[129]

The lack of military expertise was telling, which is why the insurgents in every decade looked to desertions from the army to swell their cause. The danger with the militia and the volunteer infantry in the 1790s is that they gave men a military training, though not officers or weapons. The period of greatest military threat was therefore likely to come during the war and, especially, after the war when large numbers of soldiers were discharged into civilian society where they suffered unemployment and hunger. One of the most worrying aspects of the Despard plot in 1802 was the involvement of guardsmen. When Alexander Somerville of the Scots Greys wrote to a Birmingham paper in 1832 that, although the soldiers would put down riots and defend property, 'against the liberties of our country we would never, never, never raise an arm', he was court-martialled and flogged.[130] More humanely, when Major-General Napier heard that there were many Chartists among the riflemen, he wanted to send for their leader to reason with him on the grounds that he shared his political opinions but differed only over method.[131] Military men and insurgents alike understood the critical importance of army loyalty. With few exceptions, the common soldiers, despite their affinity with the protesters and the repeated hopes of would-be insurgents, remained loyal – or, at least, obedient – to their officers and their regiments.

Although in the nine months following the Newport Rising, the 45th Regiment of Foot suffered over a hundred desertions, all had stood firm on 4 November. As one of the Chartist leaders had advised, 'the only way to succeed is to attack and remove those who command them'.[132] Even this underestimated the loyalty of many soldiers. Despard was betrayed when a soldier who had been approached to join the plot reported back to an army agent who 'gave him advice as to what he was to do' – so he became a spy.[133] Although there was always a danger of subordination when soldiers drank with civilians in public houses, Napier turned this to his advantage by encouraging his men to drink with ex-soldiers and get them to boast of their plans and then report them back to him.[134]

If the soldiers had been won over, they would have brought not only their expertise but also their weapons. Despite all the arming and drilling that went on throughout the half century between the 1790s and 1840s, the would-be insurgents lacked weapons. They made pikes by the thousand because they could not get anything else. They had no response to the rifle but to run away. The first reason that G. J. Holyoake gave in 1849 for the lack of revolution in England was that 'our populace are unused to arms'.[135] Had he but known it, G. J. Harney, the Marat of the English revolution, had written to Friedrich Engels in 1846 along similar lines:

> The English people will not adopt Cooper's slavish notions about peace and non-resistance but neither would they act upon the opposite doctrine. They applaud it at public meetings, but that is all. Notwithstanding all the talk in 1839 about 'arming,' the people did not arm, and they will not arm. A long immunity from the presence of war in their own country and the long suspension of the militia has created a general distaste for arms, which year by year is becoming more extensive and more intense. The *body* of the English people, without becoming a slavish people, are becoming an eminently pacific people.

Then, Harney forgot himself for a moment as national pride in the British army took over.

I do not say that our fighting propensities are gone, on the contrary I believe that the trained English soldiery is the most powerful soldiery in the world, that is, that a given number will, ninety times out of a hundred, vanquish a similar number of the *trained troops* of any nation in the world. (I hope I shall not offend your Prussian nationality.) Wanting, however, military training, the English *people* are the most unmilitary, indeed anti-military people on the face of the earth. To attempt a 'physical-force' agitation at the present time would be productive of no good but on the contrary of some evil – the evil of exciting suspicion against the agitators. I do not suppose that the great changes which will come in this country will come altogether without violence, but organized combats such as we may look for in France, Germany, Italy and Spain, cannot take place in this country. To organize, to conspire a revolution in this country would be a vain and foolish project and the men who with their eyes open could take part in so absurd an attempt would be worse than foolish, would be highly culpable.[136]

Britain did not have a conscript army and, apart from the Yeomanry Cavalry, it did not have a large number of men trained in arms. This state of affairs was not new, despite the temporary impact of enlistment during the French Revolutionary and Napoleonic Wars, and can be traced back to the decision to disarm the general population in the reign of Charles II and to the Game Laws from 1671 onwards which restricted who was to hunt, and empowered gamekeepers to search for and impound guns and other sporting gear that might be used for taking illicit game.[137] Britain was increasingly a de-militarised society, despite all the vaunted 'right to bear arms'. In all the actual risings there was a woeful lack of serious weaponry. Pikes and agricultural implements far outnumbered guns. The first object of an insurrection was to acquire weapons: in Sheffield in 1812, John Blackwell's attack was on the local militia armoury; the Spa Fields rising of 1816 attacked gun shops on the way to the arsenal at the Tower of London. The Luddite strategy in 1812 was to threaten individual property owners into giving up their weapons; so much so that 'well affected people' were refusing to hand their arms over to the authorities because they feared for their property if they had nothing left to hand over to the Luddite gangs.[138] When the authorities wanted to know the extent of arming in the 1790s, they watched the levels of production and sales by arms manufacturers in Birmingham and elsewhere.[139] It is not known how many of the half million or so stands of arms ordered in Birmingham for 'people not connected with government' in the latter part of 1792 were intended for illicit purposes. But the alarmist second Report of the Committee of Secrecy in 1794 thought, 'The number of firelocks actually provided, as far as it has been discovered, may seem inconsiderable for the execution of any design' and then went on to discuss the manufacture and stockpiling of pikes at much greater length.[140]

Two generations later, a return of arms sold in London during the first six months of 1848 shows that 122 guns and 162 pistols went to 'Mechanics, Labourers etc. who are believed to be, and others known to be, Chartists' while three times that number went to the much smaller class of 'Gentlemen, Respectable Tradesmen, Gamekeepers etc.'[141] Though Sheridan was no doubt exercising dramatic licence in 1795 when he described the supposed conspiracy as possessing 'an arsenal furnished with one pike and nine rusty muskets',[142] half a century later Major-General Napier, who took the Chartist threat very seriously, was probably not being over complacent in December 1839 when he wrote

> An anonymous letter come, with a Chartist plan. Poor creatures, their threats of attack are miserable. With half a cartridge, and half a pike, with no money, no discipline, no skilful leaders, they would attack men with leaders money and discipline, well armed, and having sixty rounds a man. Poor men![143]

Back in August he had confined to his journal:

> The plot thickens. Meetings increase and are so violent, and arms so abound, I know not what to think. . . . Poor people! They will suffer. They have set all England against them and their physical force: – fools! We have the physical force, not they. . . . Poor men! Poor men! How little they know of physical force.[144]

## Conclusion

Explanations in history are never certain. As Herbert Butterfield observed, the only safe thing we can say is that the whole of the present has come out of the whole of the complex past.[145] How that happened is for historical speculation and there will never be agreement. The accidental and the contingent, the unique combination of events at a particular time, will determine an outcome in a situation created by many factors, and that situation is never static. The easy contrasts of reform or revolution, physical or moral force, constitutional or illegal behaviour, belong to propaganda not historical analysis. The understanding which people had of their situation at different times was ever changing. How individuals behaved, and whether enough of them were persuaded to behave in the same way, varied according to circumstances. Undoubtedly, for most of the time most of the people were loyal, law abiding, contented, quiescent, subdued, apathetic, sullen. Most popular leaders for most of the time sought constitutional means to improve the political, economic and social position of the people: they believed in historical liberties and accepted the rule of law. There were many reasons for this 'normal' situation: some positive, such as an unquestioning acceptance of prevailing ideology and of things as they are, and a rejection of change and innovation which might threaten what they already enjoyed; some negative, such as an awareness that the dominant ideology was underpinned by political, economic and military power.

Readings of the period 1790–1850 which see a comfortable and natural harmony in society do not seem to me to fit the evidence. When one has allowed for exaggeration, scaremongering, and panic born of ignorance or malice, one is left with sufficient evidence of tension to realise that the idea of revolutionary change in Britain cannot be dismissed out of hand. If the ship of state appears in retrospect to have been sailing like a modern liner smoothly through the seas, stabilised against the storms (though the complacent should remember the *Titanic*), at the time the governing classes felt they were in a small, oak-built ship-of-the-line, buffeted by storms and easily driven off course or prevented from making a safe landing.

The government was composed of neither fools nor knaves – as Samuel Bamford discovered to his surprise when he was hauled before the Privy Council in 1817.[146] Their duty was to maintain the ship of state in defence of liberty and property. Reformers who challenged this view in the name of liberty and individual rights wished to blow it off course. How they were to do this depended on the options open to them. Throughout the period, the option of revolution through insurgency always remained a possibility. Indeed, from Whig politicians to popular demagogues, there were many men who believed that the only way to achieve change was to force ministers to legislate revolution from above by threatening it from below. For most of the time, the forces for stability and change were in balance, but it was an artificial equilibrium maintained with difficulty during years of unprecedented social and economic change.

Occasionally the balance was upset. Revolution from below came closest when popular leaders despaired of peaceful constitutional change. The device of petitioning was discredited when petitions were not heard. The situation was most dangerous when larger numbers of people in one or more parts of the country no longer felt tied by the bonds of conventional loyalty. This could happen for a number of reasons: desperate hunger brought about by high food prices, low wages and unemployment; threats to liberty caused by dubiously legal recruitment practices to the armed forces; novel legislation threatening traditional values; heightened expectations of change induced by violent changes in governments overseas; hopes of the millennium. All these and more could, separately but more usually in combination, produce instability and gave opportunity to those who believed there was no other way to achieve change but by leading the people in revolution.

It is at this point that the practicalities of such actions should be considered by the historian. The argument of this concluding chapter has been that, although the failure of potential revolution was not a foregone conclusion and although stability was usually maintained more by ideological than by physical force, ultimately the government of Britain never lost the will, power or the means of controlling by physical force those who wished to force change by violent action.

Britain *was* different. This is the easy explanation for the failure of revolution, but the challenge is to explain *why*. The distinctiveness of Britain was not ordained 'at heaven's command', but was the creation of men who, building on some historical differences in institutions and traditions, were determined that the course of British history should be different from that of Europe in the age of revolutions. A sense of pride in constitutional liberties and of the capacity of the political system to evolve without revolution assisted the maintenance of stability for most of the time and ensured a smoothness and continuity in political change which was not known in countries with more autocratic and less flexible institutions. In 1849, G. J. Holyoake told his audience of Chartists, 'We have a proverb that "they manage these things better in France." I trust the distinction will be ours of saying that "we manage these things better in England".'[147]

The complacency of Victorian liberalism was already setting in but it was a view which, like stability itself, was created not inborn. The phrase 'whig history' is used too liberally to denigrate all histories that depend on the idea of constitutional progress. During the period 1790–1850, those who wished to change the system learned from the failures of their predecessors and in that sense progressed. They saw that it was not possible for a nation to free itself purely by an act of will. Garibaldi was to learn that with the failure of Mazzini's dreams for Italy in 1849. So too did George Julian Harney. Despite his letter to Engels in 1846, in March 1848 his editorial in the *Northern Star* shows him still hoping for revolutionary change in England on the coat-tails of revolution in France. But, in November 1849, as he surveyed the wreck of the continental revolutions and the dark winter which had followed the 'springtime of the peoples', he wrote the obituary of serious revolutionary aspirations in Britain:

> Perhaps the events on the Continent, within the last year, are the strongest argument that could be adduced in favour of an unceasing, gradual, peaceable, and resolute aggressive popular movement. The revolutionary earthquake which shook thrones to the dust, and scattered kings, queens, royal dukes and duchesses, princes and nobles, like sea birds in a storm, has passed away. What are its present results? The old tyrannies restored in almost every country where Liberty achieved a brief and fleeting triumph. . . . The meteor has flashed, dazzled and disappeared, leaving profounder darkness behind it. That in the course of nature another convulsive upheaving of the forcibly repressed, but universal discontent which exists in these countries, will occur again, there can be no doubt – but is there any reason to believe with better results, if the conflicting parties are similarly composed? The old rulers of the world have been trained to the exercise of force and fraud. They understand thoroughly the full use of these weapons. The people have neither the education nor the means to contend with them on their own battle-field. They should be wise, therefore and choose one more favourable for the development of the powers they unquestionably possess. The strength of an unorganised majority is no match for that of a well-disciplined and well-armed minority. What then? ORGANISE THE MAJORITY. How? Popular progress in

# Why was there no revolution?

England supplies an answer. Inch by inch the ground has been forced from the oligarchy; every advantage thus slowly won has been as sturdily retained, and with each successive advance the power of the people grows stronger – that of their adversaries less, Can there be any doubt as to the ultimate issue?

The spirit of gradual reform had of necessity triumphed over the will to revolution. Arguing against an extremist reform strategy in the 1860s, the Manchester Owenite and Chartist, Robert Cooper, reflected on the lessons he had learned in the 1840s: faced with 'extreme proceedings . . . the government would be instigated to put down our meetings, and, if need be, incarcerate our leaders, leaving the people once more a prey to disappointment and suffering'.[148] He was not the first to have reached this conclusion. If the threat of justified revolution constrained British governments to pay more than lip-service to constitutionalism and the rule of law, the realities of government force ultimately taught most reformers the practical as well as theoretical virtues of constitutionalism and peaceful agitation for reform within the law. By 1850, Britain had learned to be different through what the *Northern Star* called 'dear-bought past experience'.[149]

## Notes

1 See above, p. 7.
2 S. Prickett, *England and the French Revolution* (London, Macmillan, 1989), pp. 2–5; Williams, *Keywords* – 'Revolution'.
3 *OED* – 'Revolution'
4 Quoted and translated by P. Wende, '1848: Reform or Revolution' pp. 152–3, in Blanning and Wende (eds), *Reform in Great Britain and Germany*, pp. 145–57.
5 E. Burke, *Reflection on the Revolution in France*. Everyman edition (London, Dent, 1964), p. 82. The same device of belittling was used in loyalist propaganda by persistent references to Thomas Paine as 'Tom'.
6 B. Brierley, *Home Memories, and Recollections of a Life* (Manchester, Heywood, 1886), p. 23.
7 D. Thompson, 'Who were "the People" in 1842?', in M. Chase and I. Dyck (eds), *Living and Learning* (Aldershot, Scolar Press, 1996), pp. 118–32; Vernon, *Politics and the People*, pp. 302–3.
8 *OED* – 'Mob'
9 *Hansard's Parliamentary Debates*, House of Commons, 12 July 1839, col. 245.
10 J. A. Epstein, '"Our real constitution": trial, defence and radical memory in the Age of Revolution' in Vernon, *Re-reading the Constitution*, pp. 22–51; also Epstein, *Radical Expression*, pp. 3–28.
11 Thale (ed.), *LCS*, pp. 322–7.

12   Deposition of William Stevens, *Cobbett's Weekly Political Register*, 33:18 (16 May 1818), col. 553.

13   *Northern Star*, 18 May 1839

14   See above, pp. 70–1.

15   Manchester Central Library, J B. Smith MSS, R. Cobden to J. B. Smith, 4 December 1841, as quoted in L. Brown, 'The Chartists and the Anti-Corn Law League', p. 348 in A. Briggs (ed.), *Chartist Studies* (London, Macmillan, 1959, reprinted 1965), pp. 342–71.

16   Fulcher, 'The English people and their constitution', p. 78.

17   McCord, *Anti-Corn Law League*, pp. 108–36.

18   G. J. Holyoake, 'Why have we had no revolution in England?', *Reasoner*, 7:1 (4 July 1849), p. 1.

19   B. R. Mitchell, *European Historical Statistics, 1750–1970* (London, Macmillan, 1978), Tables A1 and A2.

20   PRO, HO 40/1(8), fos 17–19, F. L. Wood to Earl Fitzwilliam, 17 June 1812.

21   'Prospects of our Cause', *Chartist*, 30 June 1839.

22   Bamford, *Passages*, p. 7.

23   *Hansard's Parliamentary Debates*, House of Commons, 12 July 1839, col. 246.

24   H. T. Dickinson, 'Popular Conservatism and Militant Loyalism, 1789–1815', p. 110 in H. T. Dickinson (ed.), *Britain and the French Revolution, 1789–1815* (London, Macmillan, 1989), pp. 103–25. For the intellectual defence of the conservative position, see also his *Liberty and Property*, pp. 270–318 and A. D. Harvey, *Britain in the Early Nineteenth Century*, pp. 106–14.

25   E. P. Thompson, 'The Moral Economy of the English Crowd in the Eighteenth Century' and 'The Moral Economy Reviewed' in *Customs in Common* (London, Penguin Books, 1993), pp. 185–258 and 259–351.

26   *Cobbett's Weekly Political Register*, 20:21, (23 November 1816), col. 672.

27   H. Cunningham, 'The Language of Patriotism, 1750–1914', *History Workshop Journal*, 12 (Autumn 1981), pp. 8–33, and the subsequent debate in 14 (Autumn 1982), p. 179, and 16 (Autumn 1983), pp. 189–90.

28   M. D. George, *English Political Caricature, 1793–1832: A Study in Opinion and Propaganda* (Oxford, Clarendon Press, 1959), pp. 2–3 and Plate 1.

29   *Brewer's Dictionary of Phrase and Fable*, 14th edition (London, Cassell, 1992), entries under 'Heart of Oak', 'National Anthem' and 'Rule Britannia'. See also Colley, *Britons*, pp. 43–4.

30   B. Brierley, *Old Radicals and Young Reformers: A Sketch for the Times* (Manchester, Heywood, 1860), pp. 8–9.

31   For a discussion of this changing concept, 'public opinion', as varied as the allied concept of 'the people', see D Wahrman, 'Public Opinion, violence and the limits of constitutional politics' in Vernon, *Re-reading the Constitution*, pp. 83–122.

32   D. Eastwood, 'Patriotism and the English state in the 1790s', pp. 154–7, in Philp (ed.), *French Revolution*, pp. 146–68.

33   R. R. Dozier, *For King, Constitution and Country. The English Loyalists and the French Revolution* (Lexington, University Press of Kentucky, 1983), pp. 55–75; Dickinson, 'Popular Conservatism', pp. 114–16. My thanks to Michael Phillips of the University of York for the information about Blake in Lambeth.

34   A. Booth, 'Popular loyalism and public violence in the north-west of England, 1790–1800', *Social History*, 8:3 (October 1983), pp. 295–313.

35 'Meeting of Delegates of the Loyal Associations of Manchester and Salford', *Manchester Mercury*, 10 February 1795.

36 Eastwood, 'Patriotism', pp. 158–61.

37 M. Taylor, 'John Bull and the iconography of public opinion in England, *c.* 1712–1929', p. 104, *Past & Present*, 134 (February 1992), pp. 93–128.

38 R. Wells, 'English society and revolutionary politics in the 1790s: the case for insurrection', pp. 215–26, in Philp (ed.), *French Revolution*, pp. 188–226.

39 PRO, HO 40/1(8), fos 7–9, Francis Lindley Wood to Earl Fitzwilliam, 11 June 1812.

40 *Leeds Intelligencer*, 3 May 1832; *Leeds Mercury*, 28 April, 5 May 1832.

41 Christie, *Stress and Stability*.

42 *Annual Register* (1831), Chronicle for 19 October 1831, cols. 165–6.

43 C. A. Hulbert, *Annals of the Church in Slaithwaite* (London, Longman, 1864), pp. 178, 181, 223; and *Annals of the Church and Parish of Almondbury, Yorkshire* (London, Longmans, 1882), p. 212.

44 R. Wells, *Wretched Faces: Famine in Wartime England, 1793–1801* (Gloucester, Sutton, 1988), p. 295.

45 Wells, *Wretched Faces*, p. 313.

46 Darvall, *Popular Disturbances*, pp. 19–20.

47 B. R. Mitchell, *Abstract of British Historical Statistics* (Cambridge, Cambridge University Press, 1962), p. 410.

48 T. Carlyle, 'Chartism' (1839), p. 198 in *Selected Essays* (London, Dent 1915, reprinted 1972), pp. 165–238.

49 Edsall, *The Anti-Poor Law Movement*, pp. 202–3.

50 Journal, 3 December 1839, printed in W. Napier, *The Life and Opinions of General Sir Charles James Napier*, 4 vols., second edition (London, John Murray, 1857), vol. 2, pp. 93–4 (hereafter *Napier*).

51 Report of John Layhe, 30 April 1843, to the Annual Meeting of the Manchester Ministry to the Poor, *Ninth Report to the Ministry of the Poor* (Manchester, Forrest, 1843), pp. 7–8.

52 E. C. Gaskell, *Mary Barton: A Tale of Manchester Life* (London, Chapman & Hall, 1848).

53 Christie, *Stress and Stability*, pp. 126–30.

54 Halévy, *England in 1815*, pp. 387, 425.

55 Thompson, *The Making*, pp. 385–440.

56 R. Hole, 'English Tracts and Sermons as media of debate on the French Revolution, 1789–99', pp. 19–29 in Philp (ed.), *French Revolution*, pp. 18–37.

57 R. Hole (ed.), *Selected Writings of Hannah More* (London, Pickering, 1996), pp. xii–xiii.

58 Wells, *Insurrection*, p. 200; Dinwiddy, *Radicalism and Reform*, p. 388.

59 Reay, *Last Rising of the Agricultural Labourers*, pp. 146–7.

60 Conference XLIX (1792), in *Minutes of the Methodist Conference*, 3 vols (London, Blanchard, 1813), vol. 1, p. 260.

61 D. Hempton, *Methodism and Politics in British Society, 1750–1850* (London, Hutchinson, 1984), pp. 98–104.

62 M. S. Edwards, *Purge this Realm. A Life of Joseph Rayner Stephens* (London, Epworth, 1994), p. 22.

63 S. Bamford, *Early Days* [1849], ed. W. H. Chaloner (London, Cass, 1967) pp. 42–3.

CITY COLLEGE
LEARNING RESOURCE CENTRE

64   *A Brief Memoir of the late Revd William Richardson, Sub-Chanter of York Cathedral, &c*, second edition (York, Wolstenholme, 1822), p. 53.

65   West Yorkshire Archive Service, Wakefield, C 84/1, Records of the meetings of the Elland Clerical Society, 1795–1898, entries for 5/6 October 1797 and 26/27 April 1798. I am grateful to Mr R. L. Peach of Bootham School and Prof. A. H. Sommerstein of the University of Nottingham for helping me identify the Greek phrase taken from 2 Timothy 3:1, where the context is apocalyptic.

66   F. Peel, *Spen Valley: Past & Present* (Heckmondwike, Senior & Co., 1893), pp. 236, 396–9.

67   Emsley, *British Society*, p. 9.

68   Brewer, *The Sinews of Power* (London, Unwin Hyman, 1989), pp. xvii–xx.

69   Brewer and Styles (eds), *Ungovernable People*, pp. 13–20.

70   On popular constitutionalism, see the essays in Vernon, *Re-reading the Constitution*, by Epstein, Fulcher and Wahrman, pp. 3–122.

71   J. Cannon, *Aristocratic Century: The Peerage of Eighteenth-century England* (Cambridge, Cambridge University Press, 1984), pp. 34–59, 113.

72   Cannon, *Aristocratic Century*, pp. 118–23.

73   Cannon, *Aristocratic Century*, pp. 20–5.

74   These points can be substantiated by reference to any listing of county families, such as J. Foster, *Pedigrees of the County Families of Yorkshire*, 3 vols (London, Head, 1874).

75   I. R. Christie, *British 'Non-Élite' MPs, 1715–1820* (Oxford, Clarendon Press, 1995), p. 206; see also A. D. Harvey, *Britain in the Early Nineteenth Century*, pp. 6–37.

76   P. Harling and P. Mandler, 'From "Fiscal-Military" State to Laissez-faire State, 1760–1850', *Journal of British Studies*, 32:2 (April 1993), pp. 44–70.

77   *Reasoner*, 7:162 (4 July 1849), p. 1.

78   Emsley, *British Society*, p. 67.

79   Smith, *Whig Principles*, pp. 346–7.

80   Cannon, *Aristocratic Century*, p. 125.

81   C. Emsley, 'An aspect of Pitt's "Terror": prosecutions for sedition during the 1790s', pp. 155–163, *Social History*, 6:2 (May 1981), pp. 155–84.

82   Meikle, *Scotland and the French Revolution*, pp. 134–6, 144–5; Epstein, '"Our Real Constitution"', pp. 34–5.

83   Emsley, 'An aspect of Pitt's "Terror"', pp. 163–75.

84   Saville, *1848*, p. 133.

85   W. H. Wickwar, *The Struggle for the Freedom of the Press, 1819–1832* (London, Allen & Unwin, 1928), pp. 35–6.

86   Wickwar, *Struggle for the Freedom*, pp. 35–7.

87   Wickwar, *Struggle for the Freedom*, pp. 180–205; *Republican*, 11:26 (1 July 1825), pp. 818–20.

88   Devon CRO, Sidmouth Papers, 1794/OZ 43, Henry Addington to Hiley Addington, 8 November 1794, as quoted in Emsley, 'An aspect of Pitt's "Terror"', p. 175.

89   BIHR, Hickleton MSS, A4/7, Earl Fitzwilliam to F. L. Wood, 15 June 1812.

90   5 Victoria, cap 315, An Act to define the Jurisdiction of Justices in General and Quarter Sessions.

91   Vernon, *Politics and the People*, pp. 295–307; G. Stedman Jones, 'Rethinking

Chartism', in *Languages of Class: Studies in English Working Class History, 1832–1982* (Cambridge, Cambridge University Press, 1983), pp. 90–178.

92  Jenkins, *General Strike*, pp. 223, 229–32.

93  Jones, *Last Rising*, p. 197.

94  Mather, *Public Order*, pp. 47–8.

95  34 Edward III, cap. 1, quoted in R. Vogler, *Reading the Riot Act: The Magistracy, the Police and the Army in Civil Disorder* (Milton Keynes, Open University, 1991), p. 13.

96  1 George I, cap. 5, quoted in R. Vogler, *Reading the Riot Act*, p. 1.

97  Wellesley (ed), *Despatches*, vol. 8, p. 225.

98  PRO, HO 40/1(8), fos 17–19, F L. Wood to Earl Fitzwilliam, 17 June 1812.

99  C. J. Napier to Colonel Wemyss, 16 August 1839, printed in *Napier* vol. 2, p. 79.

100  Mather, *Public Order*, p. 47; J. W. Fortescue, *A History of the British Army*, 13 vols. (London, Macmillan, 1899–1930), vol. 7, pp. 205–7.

101  Darvall, *Popular Disturbances*, pp. 252–4.

102  J. R. Western, *The English Militia in the Eighteenth Century* (London, Routledge and Kegan Paul, 1965), pp. 127–45.

103  Fortescue, *British Army*, vol. 4, pp. 888–9; vol. 5, pp. 198–207; vol. 6, pp. 180–3; vol. 7, pp. 34–5; vol. 11, p. 43; Emsley, *British Society*, pp. 53–5.

104  Fortescue, *British Army*, vol. 7, pp. 199–222; vol. 11, p. 43; J. R. Western, 'The Volunteer Movement as an anti-revolutionary force, 1793–1801', *English Historical Review* 71 (1956), pp. 603–14.

105  BIHR, Hickleton MSS, A4/7, F. L. Wood to F. Lumley, 10 June 1812 [copy].

106  Western, *English Militia*, pp. 273–302.

107  PRO, HO 102/14, fo. 216, Rev J. Lapsie to Henry Dundas, 28 August 1797.

108  PRO, HO 102/15, fo. 78, Lord Melrose to Duke of Portland, 7 September 1797.

109  Logue, *Popular Disturbances in Scotland*, pp. 109–13.

110  J. Stevenson, 'Food Riots in England, 1792–1818', pp. 47–8 in R. Quinault and J. Stevenson (eds), *Popular Protest and Public Order*, pp. 33–74.

111  Wells, *Wretched Faces*, pp. 120–32.

112  Quoted in Wells, *Wretched Faces*, p. 154.

113  Darvall, *Popular Disturbances*, pp. 250–73.

114  Fortescue, *British Army*, vol. 11, pp. 46–64; Mather, *Public Order*, p. 143; J. Stevenson, 'Social Control and the Prevention of Riots in England, 1789–1829', pp. 37–8 in A. P. Donajgrodzki (ed.), *Social Control in Nineteenth Century Britain* (London, Croom Helm, 1977), pp. 27–50.

115  Journal, 15 August 1839, in *Napier* vol. 2, p. 73.

116  C. J. Napier to S. M. Phillipps, 25 April 1839 and C. J. Napier to the Under-Secretary, 11 May 1839, in *Napier* vol. 2, pp. 20, 32; Mather, *Public Order*, pp. 35, 146–7.

117  C. Emsley, *The English Police. A political and social history*, second edition (Harlow, Longman, 1991), p. 29.

118  Mather, *Public Order*, p. 97. In 1833, there were only 211 police in Marylebone compared with 256 under the old system – Emsley, *English Police*, p. 27.

119  PRO, HO 45/264, fos 288–9, Lord Wharncliffe to Sir James Graham, 3 October 1842; Mather, *Public Order*, pp. 130–1.

120  Mather, *Public Order*, pp. 153–6; Goodway, *London Chartism*, pp. 147–9.

121 See above, p. 26.

122 BIHR, Hickleton MSS, A4/7, F. L. Wood to F. Lumley, 10 June 1812 [copy]; Jones, *Last Rising*, pp. 97–8.

123 C. J. Napier to Colonel Wemyss, 22 April 1839, in *Napier* vol. 2, pp. 13–14.

124 C. J. Napier to the magistrates of the West Riding, 24 April 1839, in *Napier* vol. 2, p. 16.

125 PP (1844), 318, *Fifth Report from the Select Committee on Railways*, 24 May 1844: evidence of Sir J. W. Gordon, 1 March 1844, Q. 1995.

126 C. J. Napier to Sir Hew Ross, 7 December 1839, in *Napier* vol. 2, p. 94.

127 Journal, 30 March 1839, in *Napier* vol. 2, p. 7.

128 Journal, March 1839, in *Napier* vol. 2, p. 4.

129 Brierley, *Home Memories*, p. 24.

130 A. Somerville, *The Autobiography of a Working Man* [1848], new edition (London, Turnstile Press, 1951), p. 159.

131 C. J. Napier to W. Napier, July 1839, in *Napier* vol. 2, pp. 54–5. Lord John Russell forbade the experiment, for fear of what the papers might say.

132 Wilks, *South Wales*, pp. 151–2, quoting from Ap Id Anfryn [Gwilym Hughes], *The Late Dr Price (of Llantrisant). The Famous Arch-Druid* (Cardiff, 1890), p. 10.

133 *State Trials at Large: The Whole Proceedings on the Trials of Col Despard, and the other State Prisoners, before a Special Commission, at the New Sessions House, Horsemonger Lane, Southwark, Feb. 7 and 9, 1803* (London, R. Bent & John Mudie, [1803]), p. 27.

134 Journal, 18 April 1839, in *Napier* vol. 2, p. 11.

135 *Reasoner* 7:162, (4 July 1849), p. 1.

136 G. J. Harney to F. Engels, 30 March 1846, reprinted in F. G. Black and R. M. Black (eds), *The Harney Papers* (Assen, Van Gorcum & Comp., 1969), p. 240.

137 Western, *English Militia*, pp. 71–2.

138 PRO, HO 45/1(8), fo 7–9, F. L. Wood to Earl Fitzwilliam, 11 June 1812.

139 Dozier, *For King, Constitution and Country*, pp. 40–4, 186–7.

140 'Second Report of the Secret Committee of the House of Lords Respecting Seditious Practices, *Cobbett's Parliamentary History*, House of Lords, 7 June 1794, cols. 891–2.

141 Mather, *Public Order*, p. 19.

142 *Annual Register* (1795), History of Europe, p. 156. For a fuller version of this quotation, see Debate on Sheridan's motion for repeal of the Habeas Corpus Suspension Act, *Cobbett's Parliamentary History*, House of Commons, 5 January 1795, col. 1066.

143 Journal, 1 December 1839, in *Napier* vol. 2, p. 98.

144 Journal, 6 August 1839, in *Napier* vol. 2, p. 69.

145 H Butterfield, *The Whig Interpretation of History* [1931], reprinted (London, G. Bell, 1968), p. 19.

146 Bamford, *Passages*, pp. 105–8.

147 *Reasoner*, 7:162 (4 July 1849), p. 1.

148 Tyne and Wear Archives, Joseph Cowen Papers, TWAS 634/C1738, Robert Cooper to Joseph Cowen, 28 July 1862.

149 *Northern Star*, 17 November 1849.

# Appendix: wheat and bread prices, 1790–1850

| Year | Wheat s. d. | Bread d. | Year | Wheat s. d. | Bread d. | Year | Wheat s. d. | Bread d. |
|------|-------------|----------|------|-------------|----------|------|-------------|----------|
| 1790 | 54 9 | 7.0 | 1811 | 95 3 | 14.0 | 1832 | 58 8 | 10.0 |
| 1791 | 48 7 | 6.3 | 1812 | 126 6 | 17.0 | 1833 | 52 11 | 8.5 |
| 1792 | 43 0 | 5.9 | 1813 | 109 9 | 15.7 | 1834 | 46 2 | 8.0 |
| 1793 | 49 3 | 6.8 | 1814 | 74 4 | 11.4 | 1835 | 39 4 | 7.0 |
| 1794 | 52 3 | 7.0 | 1815 | 65 7 | 10.4 | 1836 | 48 6 | 8.0 |
| 1795 | 75 2 | 9.6 | 1816 | 78 6 | 16.8 | 1837 | 55 10 | 8.5 |
| 1796 | 78 7 | 9.7 | 1817 | 96 11 | 13.3 | 1838 | 64 7 | 10.0 |
| 1797 | 53 9 | 7.6 | 1818 | 86 3 | 11.6 | 1839 | 70 8 | 10.0 |
| 1798 | 51 10 | 7.7 | 1819 | 74 6 | 11.5 | 1840 | 66 4 | 10.0 |
| 1799 | 69 0 | 9.6 | 1820 | 67 10 | 10.1 | 1841 | 64 4 | 9.0 |
| 1800 | 113 10 | 15.3 | 1821 | 56 1 | 9.5 | 1842 | 57 3 | 9.5 |
| 1801 | 119 6 | 15.5 | 1822 | 44 7 | 9.5 | 1843 | 50 1 | 7.5 |
| 1802 | 69 10 | 9.5 | 1823 | 53 4 | 10.3 | 1844 | 51 3 | 8.5 |
| 1803 | 58 10 | 8.7 | 1824 | 63 11 | 10.5 | 1845 | 50 10 | 7.5 |
| 1804 | 62 3 | 9.7 | 1825 | 68 6 | 10.5 | 1846 | 54 8 | 8.5 |
| 1805 | 89 9 | 13.1 | 1826 | 58 8 | 9.5 | 1847 | 69 9 | 11.5 |
| 1806 | 79 1 | 11.7 | 1827 | 58 6 | 9.5 | 1848 | 50 6 | 7.5 |
| 1807 | 75 4 | 10.8 | 1828 | 52 11 | 9.5 | 1849 | 44 3 | 7.0 |
| 1808 | 81 4 | 11.6 | 1829 | 46 2 | 10.5 | 1850 | 40 3 | 6.75 |
| 1809 | 97 4 | 13.7 | 1830 | 64 3 | 10.5 | | | |
| 1810 | 106 5 | 14.7 | 1831 | 66 4 | 10.0 | | | |

*Source*:   B. R. Mitchell, *Abstract of British Historical Statistics* (Cambridge, Cambridge University Press, 1962), pp. 488–9 and 498. Wheat prices are per Imperial Quarter (448 pounds weight or 203.4 kg) taken from statistical returns from a large number of towns throughout Britain (and Ireland after 1800). Bread prices are for a 4 pound (1.8 kg) wheaten loaf in London (see Mitchell for details). Prices are expressed in pre-decimal currency: conversion: 1 shilling (s) = 12 pennies (d) = 5 pence.

# Select bibliography

Ashton, O., Fyson, R. and Roberts, S. (eds), *The Chartist Legacy* (Rendlesham, Merlin, 1999).

Belchem, J., *'Orator' Hunt: Henry Hunt and English Working-class Radicalism* (Oxford, Clarendon Press, 1985).

Belchem, J., 'Nationalism, republicanism and exile: Irish emigrants and the revolutions of 1848', *Past & Present*, 146 (February 1995), pp. 103–35.

Booth, A., 'Popular loyalism and public violence in the north-west of England, 1790–1800', *Social History*, 8:3 (October 1983), pp. 295–313.

Christie, I. R., *Stress and Stability in Late-Eighteenth Century Britain* (Oxford, Oxford University Press, 1984).

Church, R. A. and Chapman, S. D., 'Gravener Henson and the making of the English working class', in E. L. Jones and G. E. Mingay (eds), *Land, Labour and Population in the Industrial Revolution* (London, Arnold, 1967), pp. 131–61.

Cole, G. D. H., *British Working Class Movements: Select Documents, 1789–1875* (London, Macmillan, 1965).

Colley, L., *Britons: Forging the Nation, 1707–1837* (London and New Haven, Yale University Press, 1992).

Darvall, F. O., *Popular Disturbances and Public Order in Regency England, being an Account of the Luddite and other Disorders in England during the Years 1811–1817 and of the Attitude and Activity of the Authorities* (London, Oxford University Press, 1934).

Dickinson, H. T., *Liberty and Property: Political Ideology in Eighteenth-century Britain* (London, Weidenfeld & Nicholson, 1977), paperback edition (London, Methuen, 1979).

Dickinson, H. T., *British Radicalism and the French Revolution, 1789–1815* (Oxford, Blackwell, 1985).

Dickinson, H. T. (ed.), *Britain and the French Revolution, 1789–1815* (London, Macmillan, 1989).

Dinwiddy, J. R., 'The "Black Lamp" in Yorkshire, 1801–1802', *Past & Present*, 64 (August 1974), pp. 113–23.

Dinwiddy, J. R., *Radicalism and Reform in Britain, 1780–1850* (London, Hambledon Press, 1992).

Dozier, R. R., *For King, Constitution and Country: The English Loyalists and the French Revolution* (Lexington, University Press of Kentucky, 1983).

# Select bibliography

Edsall, N. C., *The Anti-Poor Law Movement, 1834–1844* (Manchester, Manchester University Press, 1971).

Elliott, M., 'The "Despard Conspiracy" reconsidered', *Past & Present*, 75 (May 1977), pp. 46–61.

Elliott, M., *Partners in Revolution: The United Irishmen and France* (London and New Haven, Yale University Press, 1982).

Ellis, P. B. and Mac a' Ghobhainn, S., *The Scottish Insurrection of 1820* (London, Gollancz, 1970), re-issued (London, Pluto Press, 1989).

Emsley, C., 'The London "Insurrection" of December 1792: fact, fiction, or fantasy?', *Journal of British Studies*, 17:2 (Spring 1978), pp. 66–86.

Emsley, C., *British Society and the French Wars, 1793–1815* (London, Macmillan, 1979).

Emsley, C., 'The Home Office and its sources of information and investigation, 1791–1801', *English Historical Review*, 94 (1979), pp. 532–61.

Emsley, C., 'An aspect of Pitt's "Terror": prosecutions for sedition during the 1790s', *Social History*, 6:2 (May 1981), pp. 155–84.

Emsley, C., 'Repression, "terror" and the rule of law in England during the decade of the French Revolution', *English Historical Review* 100 (1985), pp. 801–25.

Emsley, C., *The English Police: A Political and Social History*, second edition (Harlow, Longman, 1991).

Epstein, J., *The Lion of Freedom: Feargus O'Connor and the Chartist Movement, 1832–1842* (London, Croom Helm, 1982).

Epstein, J., *Radical Expression: Political Language, Ritual, and Symbol in England, 1790–1850* (New York and Oxford, Oxford University Press, 1994).

Gammage, R. G., *History of the Chartist Movement, 1837–1854*, second edition [1894], reprinted (New York, Kelley, 1969).

Goodway, D., *London Chartism* (Cambridge, Cambridge University Press, 1982).

Goodwin, A., *The Friends of Liberty: The English Democratic Movement in the Age of the French Revolution* (London, Hutchinson, 1979).

Hobsbawm, E. J. and Rudé, G., *Captain Swing* (London, Lawrence & Wishart, 1969).

Hone, J. A., *For the Cause of Truth: Radicalism in London, 1796–1821* (Oxford, Oxford University Press, 1982).

Jenkins, M., *The General Strike of 1842* (London, Lawrence & Wishart, 1980).

Jones, C. (ed.), *Britain and Revolutionary France: Conflict, Subversion and Propaganda*, Exeter Studies in History No. 5 (Exeter, University of Exeter, 1983).

Jones, D. V. J., *Before Rebecca* (London, Allen Lane, 1973).

Jones, D. V. J., *Chartism and the Chartists* (London, Allen Lane, 1975).

Jones, D. V. J., *The Last Rising: The Newport Insurrection of 1839* (Oxford, Clarendon Press, 1985).

Logue, K. J., *Popular Disturbances in Scotland, 1780–1815* (Edinburgh, Donald, 1979).

McCalman, I., *Radical Underworld: Prophets, Revolutionaries and Pornographers in London, 1795–1840* (Cambridge, Cambridge University Press, 1988).

Mather, F. C., *Public Order in the Age of the Chartists* (Manchester, Manchester University Press, 1959).

Meikle, H. W., *Scotland and the French Revolution* (Edinburgh, Maclehose, 1912), reprinted (New York, Augustus Kelley, 1969).

O'Gorman, F., *The Whig Party and the French Revolution* (London, Macmillan, 1967).

Parssinen, T. M., 'The Revolutionary Party in London, 1816–20'. *Bulletin of the Institute of Historical Research*, 45:111 (May 1972), pp. 266–82.

# Select bibliography

Peacock, A. J., *Bread or Blood: A Study of the Agrarian Riots in East Anglia in 1816* (London, Gollancz, 1965).

Peacock, A. J., *Bradford Chartism, 1838–1840* (York, St Anthony's Press, 1969).

Philp, M. (ed.), *The French Revolution and British Popular Politics* (Cambridge, Cambridge University Press, 1991).

Pickering, P. A., *Chartism and the Chartists in Manchester and Salford* (London, Macmillan, 1995).

Pollard, S. and Holmes, C. (eds), *Essays in the Economic and Social History of South Yorkshire* (Sheffield, South Yorkshire County Council, 1976).

Prothero, I., *Artisans and Politics in Early Nineteenth-Century London: John Gast and his Times* (Folkestone, Dawson, 1979), republished (London, Methuen, 1981).

Read, D., *Peterloo. The 'Massacre' and its Background* (Manchester, Manchester University Press, 1958).

Reay, B., *The Last Rising of the Agricultural Labourers: Rural Life and Protest in Nineteenth-Century England* (Oxford, Clarendon Press, 1990).

Reid, R., *Land of Lost Content. The Luddite Revolt, 1812* (London, Heinemann, 1986).

Rowe, D. J. (ed.), *London Radicalism, 1830–1843* (London, London Record Society, 1970).

Rudé, G., 'English Rural and Urban Disturbances 1830–1831', *Past & Present*, 37 (July 1967), pp. 87–102.

Rudé, G., 'Why was there no revolution in England in 1830 or 1848?', in Kossok, M. (ed.), *Studien über die Revolution* (Berlin, 1969), reprinted in H. J. Kaye (ed.), *The Face of the Crowd* (Atlantic Highlands, Humanities Press International, 1988), pp. 148–63.

Saville, J., *1848* (Cambridge, Cambridge University Press, 1987).

Schoyen, A. R., *The Chartist Challenge* (London, Heinemann, 1958).

Smith, A. W., 'Irish Rebels and English radicals, 1798–1820'. *Past & Present*, 7 (April 1955), pp. 78–85.

Smith, E. A., *Whig Principles and Party Politics: Earl Fitzwilliam and the Whig Party, 1748–1833* (Manchester, Manchester University Press, 1975).

Stevens, J., *England's Last Revolution: Pentrich, 1817* (Buxton, Moorland Publishing Company, 1977).

Stevenson, J., *Popular Disturbances in England, 1700–1870* (London, Longman, 1979).

Stevenson, J. (ed.), *London in the Age of Reform* (Oxford, Blackwell, 1977).

Stevenson, J. and Quinault, R. (eds), *Popular Protest and Public Order* (London, Allen & Unwin, 1974), pp. 115–40.

Thale, M. (ed.), *Selections from the Papers of the London Corresponding Society, 1792–1799* (Cambridge, Cambridge University Press, 1983).

Thomis, M. I., *The Luddites: Machine-Breaking in Regency England* (Newton Abbot, David & Charles, 1970).

Thomis, M. I and Holt, P., *Threats of Revolution, 1789–1848* (London, Macmillan, 1977).

Thompson, D., *The Chartists* (London, Temple Smith, 1984).

Thompson, D. and Epstein, J. (eds), *The Chartist Experience* (London, Macmillan, 1982).

Thompson, E. P., *The Making of the English Working Class* (London, Gollancz, 1963), Penguin edition (Harmondsworth, 1968).

Thompson, E. P., *Customs in Common* (London, Penguin, 1993).

# Select bibliography

Vernon, J., *Politics and the People: A Study in English Political Culture, c. 1815–1867* (Cambridge, Cambridge University Press, 1993).

Vernon, J. (ed.), *Re-reading the Constitution: New Narratives in the Political History of England's Long Nineteenth Century* (Cambridge, Cambridge University Press, 1996).

Wells, R., 'Rural Rebels in Southern England in the 1830s', in C. Emsley and J. Walvin (eds), *Artisans, Peasants and Proletarians, 1760–1860* (London, Croom Helm, 1985), pp. 124–65.

Wells, R., *Insurrection: The British Experience, 1795–1803* (Gloucester, Sutton, 1986).

Wells, R., *Wretched Faces: Famine in Wartime England, 1793–1801* (Gloucester, Sutton, 1988).

Western, J. R., 'The Volunteer Movement as an anti-revolutionary force, 1793–1801', *English Historical Review*, 71 (1956), pp. 603–14.

Wilks, I., *South Wales and the Rising of 1839: Class Struggle as Armed Struggle* (London, Croom Helm, 1984).

Williams, G. A., *The Merthyr Rising* (London, Croom Helm, 1978).

Worrall, D., *Radical Culture: Discourse, Resistance and Surveillance, 1790–1820* (Hemel Hempstead, Harvester Wheatsheaf, 1992).

Wright, D. G., *The Chartist Risings in Bradford* (Bradford, Bradford Libraries, 1977).

# Index

Note: 'n.' after a page reference indicates the number of a note on that page.

# Index

Beaumont, Augustus Hardin (Tyneside radical) 94

Benbow, William (Lancashire radical) 46–7, 76, 78, 79, 82, 101, 113

Beniowski, Major Bartolomiej (Polish refugee) 105

Bent, Charles (Lancashire informer) 34–5, 63n.56

Bent, John (Lancashire informer) 6, 39, 41, 42, 63n.56

Berkshire 83

Binns, John (Irish and LCS radical) 24, 27, 29–30, 34

Birley, Hugh Hornby (Lancashire mill owner) 116

Birmingham 14, 93, 95, 101, 102, 105, 148, 149, 150, 181, 186, 188–9
Political Union 69, 71–4, 93, 102, 112
riots (1839) 101–2

Blackburn (Lancashire) 36, 116

Black Country 95

Blackstone, Sir William (English jurist) 102, 170

Blackwell, John (Sheffield radical) 58, 59–60, 188

Blackwood (Monmouthshire) 104, 106

Blaina (Monmouthshire) 104

Blakey, Robert (editor of *Northern Liberator*) 95, 109

Blandford (Dorset) 85

'Blanketeers' 47, 149

Bolton (Lancashire) 35, 36, 101, 116, 180

Bone, John (LCS radical) 28

Bonnymuir rising (1820) 56–7, 66n.115, 185

Bossenden Wood rising (1838) 86–8, 185

Boughton (Kent) 86

Bradford (West Riding) 38, 95, 96, 97, 105, 108, 181
riots (1840) 108–11; (1842) 117; (1848) 128, 131–3, 134, 158

Brandreth, Jeremiah (Pentrich rebel) 50–1, 59

Brayshaw, James (Leeds radical) 55–6

bread prices 2, 3, 22, 36, 37, 39, 42, 59–60, 83, 96, 113, 116, 123, 124, 142, 153, 160, 199

Brierley, Benjamin (Failsworth radical) 143, 145, 155, 186

Briggs, William (Halifax magistrate) 119–20

Bright, John (Radical MP) 114

Bristol 14, 77, 106–7
riots (1831) 67, 73, 78, 79, 82, 88, 180, 184

Brothers, Richard (millenarian prophet) 45, 164–5

Brougham and Vaux, Henry Peter Brougham, first Baron (Whig lawyer; Lord Chancellor, 1830–34) 39, 99

Burdett, Sir Francis (Whig MP) 33, 43, 45, 62n.42

Burke, Edmund (Whig MP and anti-revolutionary propagandist) 13, 14, 15, 139, 141–2, 145, 151, 154, 168

Burnley (Lancashire) 53

Burns, William (Dundee Chartist) 108, 109

Burslem (Staffordshire) 117

Bussey, Peter (Bradford Chartist) 105–6, 108–10, 112

Cambridgeshire 83, 178

Camden, John Jeffreys Pratt, second Earl and first Marquis (Lord Lieutenant of Ireland, 1796–98 and of Kent, 1808–40) 89

Campsie (Stirlingshire) 179

Canterbury 86, 179

Carlile, Richard (radical publisher) 76–7, 85, 174

Carlisle 122

Carmarthen 81

Carron ironworks (Falkirk) 57, 95

Cartwright, Major John (radical leader) 43, 47, 146, 153

Cartwright, William (Yorkshire mill owner) 38

Cashman, John (Spa Fields rioter) 54, 65n.108

Castle, John (*agent provocateur*) 46

Catholics 22, 24, 25, 31, 173
Emancipation 34, 67, 68–9, 140

Cato Street conspiracy (1820) 54–5, 88

charity 159–63, 167

Chartism 2, 3, 4, 6, 47, 59, 69, 88, 89, 92–142 *passim*, 143, 145, 146, 147, 148, 150–1, 153–5, 157, 158, 159, 161, 162–3, 171, 176, 177, 181, 182, 183–4, 186–7, 189, 191, 193

CITY COLLEGE LEARNING RESOURCE CENTRE

# Index

Cheetham, William (United Englishman) 34
Cheshire 31, 34, 36, 40–1, 44, 53, 83, 95–7, 115, 117, 180
Chester 122
Church and King riots (1791–92) 14–15
Clarendon, George William Frederick Villiers, fourth Earl (Lord Lieutenant of Ireland, 1847–52) 128
class 4, 8, 35, 43, 47, 70–2, 75, 76, 79–82, 104, 113–15, 120, 123, 144, 147–8, 155, 156, 162–4, 172, 179, 189
Clayton, John (Sheffield Chartist) 111
Clydach (Brecknockshire) 104
Cobbett, William (radical journalist and MP) 43, 45, 47, 48, 85, 100, 146–7, 151, 152, 158, 169, 171
Cockayne, John (informer) 21
Coigly (O'Coigly), Rev. James (Irish revolutionary) 24–5, 29–30, 32–3
Collins, John (Birmingham Chartist) 102, 112
Constitutional Association for Opposing the Progress of Disloyal and Seditious Principles 174
constitutionalism 1–2, 6–9, 13, 23, 52, 68, 74, 89, 93, 96, 101–3, 108, 112, 122–3, 140–1, 142, 145–7, 152, 170, 175, 190–3
Convention
(1790s) 17–21, 61n.6
    Chartist 79, 93–5, 100–5, 108, 110, 112–13, 125, 129, 147
Cookson, Craven (Barnsley radical) 60, 66n.125
Cooper, James Thomas (Hampshire radical) 85
Cooper, Thomas (Leicester Chartist) 117, 187
corn laws 42, 171
    see also Anti-Corn Law League
Corresponding Societies Act (1799) 25
Courtenay, Sir William see Thoms, John
Crabtree, Joseph (Barnsley Chartist) 105
Cumberland 85
Cumberland, Ernest Augustus, Duke of (fifth son of George III) 73

Dalry (Ayrshire) 179
Dartmouth (Devonshire) 179
Dartmouth, William Legge, fourth Earl 160
Davidson, William (Spencean radical) 51, 55
death penalty 1, 14, 15, 20, 24, 25, 29, 38, 40, 50, 55, 57, 65n.108, 83–4, 111, 130, 179
Defenders (Irish terrorists) 24, 27, 29
Derby 14, 73, 180
Derbyshire 31, 50, 83, 95
Despard, Colonel Edward Marcus (Irish revolutionary) 25, 28, 29, 34–5, 44, 45, 48, 51, 59, 60, 62n.42, 157, 186–7
Devyr, Thomas Ainge (Newcastle radical) 95
Dewsbury (West Riding) 38, 110–11, 167
Disraeli, Benjamin (Tory MP) 3, 152, 159, 161–2
Dissenters see Unitarian Dissenters
Dixon, James (United Englishman) 31
Dorchester 86
Dorset 83, 85, 86
Doubleday, Thomas (Newcastle radical) 95
Dowlais (Glamorgan) 81
Downie, David (Scottish radical) 20
Dublin 19–20, 24, 28–9, 32, 42, 128–9, 183
Duckett, William (United Irishman) 34
Duffy, Charles Gavan (Irish nationalist) 128
Dukinfield (Cheshire) 115
Dunbartonshire 56
Dundas, Henry (Home Secretary, 1791–94) 19
Dundee 16–17, 108–9, 129
Dunkirk (Kent) 86

Ebbw Vale (Monmouthshire) 104, 106
Edinburgh 17–20, 31, 110, 124, 129, 138n.69, 143, 148, 183
education 2, 87, 92, 160, 170, 192
    schools 160, 164, 167
Edwards, George (agent provocateur) 54–5, 56
elections 67, 68, 69, 85, 86, 97, 112, 123, 168
    see also riots, election

206

# Index

# Index

# Index

# Index

# Index

# Index

# Index

Dawson 3/96

KU-573-226

# Reform of Post-16 Education
# and Training in England and Wales

HANDSWORTH COLLEGE

T00058

WITHDRAWN

# THE REFORM OF
# POST-16
# EDUCATION AND
# TRAINING IN
# ENGLAND AND
# WALES

Edited by
William Richardson
John Woolhouse
David Finegold

LONGMAN

*Published by* Longman Information & Reference
Longman Group UK Limited, 6th Floor, Westgate House, The High,
Harlow, Essex CM20 1YR, England and Associated Companies
throughout the world.
Telephone: Harlow(0279) 442601
Fax: Harlow(0279) 444501
Telex: 81491 Padlog

© Longman Group UK Limited, 1993

All rights reserved. No part of this publication may be reproduced, stored
in a retrieval system, or transmitted in any form or by any means,
electronic, mechanical, photocopying, recording or otherwise, without
either the prior written permission of the Publishers or a licence permitting
restricted copying issued by the Copyright Licensing Agency Ltd, 90
Tottenham Court Rd, London WP1 9HE

A catalogue record for this book is available from The British Library

ISBN 0-582-20928-5

374·942 T00058

HANDSWORTH COLLEGE
LIBRARY SERVICE

Printed in Great Britain by Antony Rowe Ltd, Chippenham, Wiltshire

# Contents

# Contributors

## Max Burgess

Max Burgess is a BTEC regional Education Adviser in the north east of England. His main role is to act as a first contact for existing or potential teaching centres which require information or advice about BTEC curriculum and qualitative issues. In line with BTEC policy a focal point of his work is to contribute to the promotion and development of BTEC GNVQ and NVQ.

## Keith Evans

Keith Evans is currently Senior Research Fellow at the North Wales Institute of Higher Education. He was Director of Education for the County of Clwyd from 1983 to 1992. His experience includes teaching in secondary modern and comprehensive schools, in further education and in higher education. Before entering LEA administration, he was an Executive Producer (Education) with HTV Wales and the West of England. He has also served as a member of the original Board of 'Training and Enterprise', the North East Wales TEC.

## David Finegold

David Finegold is a policy analyst at the Rand Corporation, Santa Monica, California, specialising in international comparisons of countries' education, training and industrial systems. His books include *Skills and Competitiveness* (Oxford University Press, forthcoming) and *Something Borrowed Something Blue* (Oxford, Triangle Books, 2 Vols, 1993). He is currently completing a four country comparison of the machine tool industry.

## Prue Huddleston

Prue Huddleston is Senior Research Fellow in the Centre for Education and Industry, University of Warwick. Previously she taught for many years within further education and with adult and community groups. Her research interests include: the implementation of NVQs; the development of vocational programmes in schools; and teacher secondments to business. She has been involved in a number of national evaluation programmes of education-business links.

## Gilbert Jessup

Gilbert Jessup has been Deputy Chief Executive and Director of Research and Development at the National Council for Vocational Qualifications since 1987. He has played a central role in developing the NVQ model of qualifications, was responsible for introducing the National Record of Vocational Achievement and is currently directing the GNVQ development programme. He is an honorary professor at Nottingham University.

## Philippa Leggate

Philippa Leggate was brought up in East Africa, returning to England for secondary and higher education. During 1975–85 she worked at the Bahrain School before becoming founding Principal of the American British Academy in the Sultanate of Oman in 1986. Since then she has been Middle East representative, Africa and Middle east regional director, and finally, Director of the International Baccalaureate for England. In 1993 she was appointed Head of the Overseas Children's School, Colombo, Sri Lanka.

## Andrew Morris

Andrew Morris entered further education as a lecturer after having completed a PhD in biophysics. During 1991–93 he was seconded by Islington Education Authority to work on curriculum development at the Post-16 Education Centre of the London Institute of Education. Whilst there he directed a project funded by the Paul Hamlyn Foundation which has subsequently developed into the Hamlyn/CILNTEC Post-16 Unified Curriculum Project. He became deputy director of Islington Federal College at its inception in 1993.

## David Raffe

David Raffe is Professional of Sociology and co-Director of the Centre for Educational Sociology at the University of Edinburgh. His research interests include secondary and further education, training and the labour market. His current research includes a study of modular innovations in vocational education in different European countries, an OECD project on young people's pathways, research on participation in post-compulsory education, and a feasibility study for a European school-leavers' survey. He is chair of the European Science Foundation Network on Transitions in Youth, which is seeking to develop the use of school-leavers and transition surveys for comparative research. Several of his recent papers have addressed issues raised in *A British Baccalauréat* (IPPR, 1990), of which he was co-author.

## Bob Rainbow

Bob Rainbow is co-ordinator for the Wessex Project, a post he has held for four years. Prior to that he worked with the Somerset TVEI scheme developing modular courses for the 14–19 age group. Recently he has taken on responsibility for a post-16 curriculum programme in collaboration with the University of Bath and he is also developing GNVQ teaching materials for publication.

## William Richardson

William Richardson is Senior Research Fellow at the Centre for Education and Industry, University of Warwick. His research interests are divided between the religious politics of late Tudor England and the relationship, in the contemporary period, of education systems to work processes. He is currently writing a book on the political, economic and cultural role of the education system in twentieth century England.

## Ken Spours

Ken Spours is Director of TVEI in Tower Hamlets and a consultant to the Post-16 Education Centre, Institute of Education, University of London. He was a co-author of the IPPR report *A British Baccalauréat* (*1990*) and is currently working on a report examining participation, attainment and 'value added' in post-16 education and training.

## Lorna Unwin

Lorna Unwin is a lecturer in flexible learning at the University of Sheffield and a part-time tutor for the Open University. She has taught in further and adult education and carried out a number of evaluations and research projects related to post-16 education and training.

## John Woolhouse

John Woolhouse is Professor of Education at the University of Warwick, Director of the Centre for Education and Industry, and Acting Director of the Vocational Education and Training Institute. He has 25 years experience in industry and in international management consultancy, and was director of the Technical and Vocational Education Initiative for five years, before taking up his present appointment at Warwick in 1988.

# Foreword

This book has been written to provide a critical analysis of the current arrangements for the education and training of the 16–19 age group in England and Wales.

Chapters 1, 2, and 10 provide complementary perspectives on what may be termed questions of 'high' policy. These chapters, it is hoped, will be of interest to several 'readerships' including teachers, training specialists and employers, as well as to those who are actively engaged in formulating and implementing policies. In Chapter 3 David Raffe gives a comparative perspective from Scotland. In the middle section of the book, Chapters 4 to 6 deal specifically with the reform of qualifications, whilst Chapters 7, 8 and 9 provide case studies of issues confronting the further education sector, education-business partnerships and Training and Enterprise Councils.

The editors would like to thank contributors to the University of Warwick's Vocational Education and Training Forum, especially Helen Rainbird and Ewart Keep, for stimulating discussion of many of the issues raised in this book. The support of the Forum by the Employment Department from 1989 to 1992 is gratefully acknowledged, as is the Economic and Social Research Council's funding of a research seminar programme at Warwick on 16–19 education and training (grant no. A45126400285). We also record with thanks the hard work of Bobbie Easterlow in preparing the manuscript.

William Richardson
John Woolhouse
David Finegold

*University of Warwick,*
*September 1992*

# PART I
# THE CONTEXT

# 1 The 16–19 education and training debate: 'deciding factors' in the British public policy process

## William Richardson

On 7 June 1988 Professor Gordon Higginson of Southampton University held a press conference to introduce the report of his official committee of enquiry into the future of the advanced (A) level examination in England and Wales. The document recommended a set of changes — the streamlining of syllabi, broader courses, the assessment of students skills — and was widely applauded in the national and educational press. Yet, by the end of the same day, the Secretary of State at the Department of Education and Science (DES) had publicly dismissed the committee's report. Professor Higginson was given only a few minutes' warning that the work carried out by his committee over the previous year was to be immediately and summarily rejected by the government department which had commissioned it (DES/WO, 1988, Crequer, 1988).

The Higginson Committee was the fourth official body since 1970 to recommend changes to A levels and, once more, the reform of academic examinations undertaken at the age of 18 had been postponed. By 1988, however, widespread dissatisfaction at the government's reliance upon the *status quo*, coupled with the public *debacle* of the Higginson episode, served to unleash an unprecedented policy debate. Moreover, the debate increased in intensity during the three years in which the government considered its position.[1] This chapter examines that debate. How was it conducted? What reform proposals were tabled, and by whom? Which were the deciding factors that determined the outcome? Has the end result been a policy resolution or, merely, a further postponement of overdue reform?

The chapter is designed both to provide a context for the contributions which follow and to offer a case study of the 'deciding factors' characteristic of the British policy process (Greenaway et al., 1992).[2] It is divided into three sections. The first supplies a narrative commentary of the public debate surrounding 16–19 education and training reform during 1987–91. Four phases are identified and the main policy themes are introduced chronologically;[3] this narrative is then followed by a short discussion and a postscript which briefly describes the period of initial policy implementation, from the publication in May 1991 of the government's 16–19 White Paper, to the general election of April 1992. The second part of the chapter is an analysis of the conduct of the 16–19 debate. This analysis forms a case study from which, in the final section, conclusions are drawn about the nature of the education and training policy process in England and Wales.

## The 16–19 education and training debate, 1987–92

---

**Figure 1**: Principal events influencing 16–19 education and training policy in England and Wales, 1987–92

---

| March 1987 | Higginson Committee convened |
|---|---|
| June 1988 | Higginson Committee reports |
| July 1988 | Education Reform Act receives royal assent |
| August 1988 | GCSEs awarded to 16-year-olds for the first time |
| December 1988 | Department of Employment announces the creation of TECs |
| February 1989 | Kenneth Baker (DES) call for 'core studies' post-16 (position reversed October 1991) |
| August 1989 | SEAC report on 16–19 core studies |
| October 1989 | CBI publishes *Towards a Skill Revolution* |
| April 1990 | Training Credits piloted in 11 TECs/LECs |
| June 1990 | HMC calls for retention of traditional A levels |
| July 1990 | IPPR publishes *A British Baccalaureate* |
| August 1990 | Non-governmental National Commission on Education launched |
| November 1990 | Fall of Margaret Thatcher |
| December 1990 | Government lifts restriction on schools offering BTEC courses |

| March 1991 | 'Poll tax' review forces early announcement of government plans to centralise FE sector funding |
| April 1991 | Labour Party publishes *Today's Education and Training* |
| May 1991 | Government published three white papers including *Education and Training for the 21st Century* |
| July 1991 | *Ministers, TECs and the TUC pledge commitment to 'world class' education and training targets* |
| July 1991 | *John Major announces his desire to see reductions in GCSE coursework* |
| October 1991 | *Queen's speech announces the establishment of an independent FE sector and the abolition of the 'binary line' in higher education* |
| December 1991 | *Completion of the TEC network* |
| January 1992 | *John Major launches GNVQs* |
| March 1992 | *Further and Higher Education Act receives royal assent* |
| March–April 1992 | *General election campaign and Conservative victory* |

**Phase (i): Momentum for change stifled (mid-1987–December 1988)**

In March 1987 the Higginson Committee was charged with considering changes to the teaching and assessment of A level examinations. Whilst the committee was sitting, legislation for a national curriculum for the age group 5–16 was being prepared, and fifth year students in secondary schools (National Curriculum Year 11) undertook courses for the first time. Both these reform initiatives, coupled with widely reported and broadly supported indications that the Higginson committee of enquiry would be recommending significant changes to A level arrangements, led the policy community to anticipate government reform.

However, this expectation was confounded by the government's comprehensive rejection of the Higginson committee's proposals in June 1988. Both of the official reasons given related to the policy process itself: that there was too much reform already in progress, and that Higginson's recommendations would 'queer the pitch' of the newly introduced A/S level examination (Crequer, 1988).[4] Such an explanation, coupled with the suggestion that Mrs Thatcher had, at an early stage, narrowed the committee's brief to prohibit the outright abolition of A levels, fuelled a belief within the education and training community that necessary change had been forestalled for political reasons and the committee members' time needlessly wasted.

Policy coherence was also brought into question as institutions began to point to the widened dissimilarity between curriculum and teaching methods for public examinations at 16 (GCSE) and at 18 (A level). Meanwhile, pressure was mounting on the government to ensure that all 16-year-olds who leave school for employment receive training. Specifically, widespread criticism was voiced over the lack of training provision by employers and the apparent low motivation of individuals to demand training (TA/DE, 1989).

As yet, the tackling of the youth training 'problem' through the provision of a planned, coherent reform of qualifications for the whole 16–19 age group was not part of the debate. Instead, in December 1988, the Department of Employment announced that the government's reform of the employer-based training component of the post-16 'problem' would be through a voluntarist approach on the part of employers. A network of local, employer-led Training and Enterprise Councils (TECs) would be charged with the responsibility for the national training effort (DE, 1988).

The TECs would have at their disposal the emerging structure of occupationally-specific national vocational qualifications (NVQs — launched in September 1986 following the White Paper *Working Together — Education and Training*: HMSO; 1986) and, at this early stage, a vaguely defined goal of the TECs was to devise local policies 'to ensure that vocational education and training arrangements meet the needs of employers and young people' (DE; 1988, para 6.15).

The creation of TECs had one significant effect on the education and training policy process. The views of employers about education reform — including post-16 qualifications — would, in future, carry considerably more authority than before and thus have the potential to circumscribe central government training policies and their local operation.

**Phase (ii): First stirrings: core skills and broader courses (January 1989–May 1990)**

Six months after the rejection of the Higginson proposals, the government signalled, through a speech by Kenneth Baker in February 1989, that it wished to reopen the question of syllabus reform for 16–19 year olds. The Secondary Examinations and Assessment Council (SEAC) was asked to consult on the matter and in August (when the education system is, effectively, 'shut') it reported the same inadequacies of A levels as had Higginson's committee: courses had 'a narrow academic orientation . . . over burdened content . . . and an inadequate range of assessment methods' (Wilby, 1989).

Several independent organisations over the following two months (the Confederation of British Industry (CBI), British Petroleum (BP), British Association for the Advancement of Science (BAAS)) drew similar conclusions and discussed the implications of such inadequacies for a related policy area which was beginning to fall under closer scrutiny — that of increasing access to higher education. This reform momentum was reinforced in November when DES ministers re-emphasised the need for 'core skills' and asked the National Curriculum Council (NCC) to propose recommendations.

The NCC report duly appeared five months later, in April 1990, accompanied within the month by others from the National Council for Vocational Qualifications (NCVQ), the Royal Society of Arts (RSA) and the Policy Studies Institute (PSI) which all served to broaden the specific focus of the access debate to encompass credit transfer between academic and vocational courses and increased participation in public examinations at the age of eighteen.

To this point the progress of the public debate had been unanimous in its call for change, the only brake seeming to come from the government's own timetable for manageable reform. The Conservatives' one definite commitment, thus far, was to announce the considerable reduction of A level syllabi (a Higginson recommendation, DES/WO, 1988, paras: 9.4–9.5) which, from 1994, would be centrally controlled.

## Phase (iii): Contention: standards versus breadth (June 1990-November 1990

June and July 1990 saw a flood of public pronouncements on the now related policy questions of A level reform, vocational provision and increased access to higher education.

The leaked draft of SEAC's report on A level skills assessment suggested that the government's main advisory body was considering recommending fundamental changes to the structure of examinations. Nevertheless, of more immediate impact were two developments, one of which was important to conservative interests within government, the other of which was to become influential among progressive groups seeking structural reform of the post-16 system.

First, the Headmasters' Conference (HMC) of independent schools called an extraordinary meeting which resolved that the development of alternative examinations such as A/S levels should not be at the expense of existing A levels. These, it was claimed, were already in danger of having their standards eroded (MacLeod, 1990a). This

HMC position was to become that adopted by government ministers — most trenchantly by 'no turning back group' member, Michael Fallon — as the pressure to modify A levels substantially continued to grow. The following month, in July 1990, the Institute for Public Policy Research (IPPR, 1990a) published a radical proposal for the abolition of A levels in favour of a unitary 'advanced diploma' combining intellectual, practical and work-based learning.

The two options presented by HMC and the IPPR — on the one hand, to develop wider access through courses alongside existing A levels and, on the other, to create a unitary system of qualifications at the age of eighteen — came to define the basic structural alternatives of policy reform. In the ensuing months many interest groups within the education and training system declared their own reform proposals at a point on the continuum between these two poles (see Appendix 1).

With the government intent on proceeding cautiously with consultation into the feasibility of core skills whilst retaining the structure of existing A levels, official figures published over the summer on participation rates presented an ambiguous picture. Analysts of participation levels in higher education could not agree on reasons for the unexpectedly high increase in applications for the following autumn. In addition, comment on published A level and GCSE results registered disappointment at the decline in maths and physics candidates, and expressed both scepticism and optimism that the small percentage rise in absolute passes represented increased standards of attainment.

Meanwhile, signs had emerged in June 1990 of the first stirrings of concerted lobbying from the further education (FE) sector aimed at projecting FE colleges as the core sector in a coherent expansion policy, a development enhanced by an exchange of ministers between the Department of Employment (DE) and the DES where the newly arrived Tim Eggar began to champion the role of FE.

Following the skirmishes during the summer about the structure of a reformed qualification system, the delayed publication of SEAC's report on A level assessment in September re-awakened the debate about curriculum and teaching methods, and their effect on 'standards' (Clare, 1990, Richardson, 1991:20). SEAC's proposals that GCSE-style course work with 'core skills' should be compulsory in A level, that all candidates should take at least two A levels and that credit transfers might be feasible between A levels and NVQs exposed a continuing lack of clarity as to which reform elements were designed to secure particular policy goals. Increased course work was interpreted by some as a tool to increase higher education access and A level participation; by others it was seen as a device that would lower A level standards and, consequently, make university entrance more difficult if selection criteria remained constant.

A further dimension of the debate was stimulated in August and September 1990 by four separate reports — from the National Institute of Economic and Social Research (NIESR), the Institute of Manpower Studies (IMS), the House of Lords and IPPR — which focused attention upon the relationship of proposed reforms of academic qualifications and employer training to the operation of qualifications in the youth labour market. This renewed attention on reforms of academic and vocational qualifications for the whole age group 16–19, whether in full-time education or in employment, was now set to become a rallying point at the main political party conferences in October. Both Neil Kinnock and Margaret Thatcher vowed to place education and training at the heart of manifesto policy. As part of the government's marketing of its policy, Michael Howard re-announced the first major programme to have been developed through TECs, that of training credits designed to stimulate a competitive market between employers to provide training based upon the purchasing power of vouchers, cashable by individual employees or youth trainees.

During the autumn, the controversy around current educational standards, and the ability of proposed reforms to improve them, intensified. Sir Claus Moser capitalised on the mood by announcing that, despite government indifference, he would be going ahead with plans for the British Association for the Advancement of Science to mount a 'national commission' on education reform. Over the following weeks several leading organisations (the National Curriculum Council (NCC), the Joint Matriculation Board (JMB), the National Association of Head Teachers (NAHT), the HMC, the secretaries of the GCSE boards, the RSA, the Adult Literacy and Basic Skills Unit (ALBSU), the Policy Studies Institute (PSI)) launched public attacks on features of the existing system or on SEAC's reform proposals for post-16 education.

The government itself seemed wrong-footed by SEAC's recommendations on core skills. These had not established clearly how increased participation would result from its proposals, and seemed to threaten the standards of traditional A levels. Mrs Thatcher gave assurances that A Levels were still in safe hands while Michael Fallon at the DES complained that the SEAC recommendations had gone 'very much further than . . . was originally intended' (Wood, 1990, Nash, 1990c).

During October and into November 1990 the question of A level standards continued to be the most emotive element of debate. The political parties, however, were also beginning to focus detailed attention on the question of how to raise the esteem of vocational qualifications. For the government, Tim Eggar called for the delivery of Business and Technology Education Council (BTEC) courses alongside academic study whilst Jack Straw (Labour) visited France to observe the increase in access being achieved through the baccalaureate system. By early November John MacGregor (DES) was indicating the government's preference for A/S levels to be sat at the age of seventeen as an intermediate exam (as recommended by HMC) and not as a final exam at eighteen (as recommended by SEAC), with a diversity of vocational and A level courses available in the sixth form.

Then, on 22 November 1990, all policy proposals were suddenly thrown into disarray by the fall of Margaret Thatcher.

## Phase (iv): 'Reform' floodgates opened (December 1990–May 1991)

The hiatus in the post-16 policy debate following the dramatic appointment of John Major as Prime Minister eased in mid-December 1990. As part of the groundwork for a new emphasis on the merits of vocational study, Tim Eggar (DES) announced the lifting of government restrictions on the provision of BTEC courses in schools.

The thrust of official policy remained obscure, however. The Conservative party leadership struggle had led to a second change of the Secretary of State for Education within a year. A leak of SEAC's revised recommendations for A level assessment based on its autumn consultation appeared to reverse its September 1990 report (itself a considerable revision of a previous position) and now strongly reflected the concerns of HMC and the former Prime Minister by retaining A levels in their existing form. This approach was endorsed in January 1991 by Kenneth Clarke, the new Secretary of State, despite a public rebuttal by Sir Brian Nicholson, the chairman of the CBI's Vocational Education Task Force. Nicholson criticised SEAC's new stance and called instead for the inclusion of assessments of capability and core skills as part of A level courses.

During the first ten weeks of the new year public interest in the post-16 issue returned to the high level of the previous autumn. A House of Commons select committee announced an enquiry into the 'mess' of 16–19 education and why performance in England and Wales was relatively poorer than that in Scotland and Ireland, and a new shoal of reports and statements were issued by public groups (Her Majesty's Inspectorate of schools (HMI), the Institute of Economic Affairs (IEA), the DES, Leicester University, the Associated Examining Board (AEB), the Association of Polytechnic and College Teachers (APCT)) on aspects of the post-16 question.

Specifically, the policy community was awaiting the formal presentation of SEAC's proposals on A level assessment to the Secretary of State and his subsequent public response which, it was believed, would outline firm government proposals. In early March both Kenneth Clarke and his deputy secretary at the DES intimated the government's developing stance in public speeches: policy would increasingly stress mechanisms designed to raise the esteem of vocational study to the same plane as the academic and, by this means, would leave A levels as a distinct pathway to higher education.

The normal processes of education policy making were then dramatically interrupted by the official leaking and subsequent announcement of major changes to the funding structure of post-16 education and training precipitated by the need to reduce local expenditure as part of the Poll Tax review. Included in the announcements was the promise of a new White Paper on post-16 reform, to be jointly published by the DES and the DE.

The scene was now set for a wave of speculation from the press and intensified, renewed lobbying, both from those remaining interest groups, organisations and individuals whose views were not already in the public domain, and from those who sought a second or third salvo (RSA, PSI, the Association of Principles of Sixth Form Colleges (APVIC), Sir Claus Moser, HRH Prince Charles, HMC, Alan Smithers/NCVQ, the Association of Colleges of Further and Higher Education (ACFHE)). Meanwhile, the Labour Party formally announced its intention to abolish A levels in favour of a unitary system of qualifications, and the government conducted widely reported private negotiations with many of the agencies responsible for post-16 provision (DES, DE, NCVQ, the Scottish Vocational Education Council (SCOTVEC), BTEC, RSA, the City and Guilds London Institute (CGLI), TECs, the Advisory Council on Science and Technology (ACOST), the Royal Society (RS)) prior to the unveiling of its detailed proposals.

A distinctive feature of the heightened activity in advance of the publication of the White Paper was what ministers acknowledged to be an unprecedented level of co-operation between the DES and the DE, despite reported tension over how central a role TECs would play in the reconstituted careers service and FE funding structure. Also notable was growing confidence within the NCVQ that, with government commitment to increased status for vocational study, the policy climate would allow the National Council to bring longer-standing qualifications such as those of the BTEC, the RSA and the CGLI under its umbrella.

On 20 May 1991 John Major and five cabinet ministers launched three White Papers, including *Education and Training for the 21st Century*. These laid out the government's account of progress to date and provided policy proposals for the future of British post-16 education and training. This phase of the public policy process, which had begun with the establishment the Higginson Committee four years earlier, appeared to have reached its culmination (notwithstanding the many areas of proposed legislation left open for official 'consultation'). But, as commentators were quick to point out, it was impossible to know whether the policy resolution arrived at would survive a general election, due within thirteen months or less. If not, opposition parties were committed to radically different proposals for 16–19 education and training.

**Discussion: The content of the debate**

As a conclusion to this narrative commentary of the development and content of the 16–19 education and training debate, a number of points may be made.

In the first place, it is evident that in the context of post-16 reform, it proved considerably easier to agree on policy goals than policy measures. Furthermore, an increasing number of reform goals enjoyed consistent support. In order of appearance they were: the reform of courses leading to the greater full-time participation of 16–19 year olds in education and training; intervention to ensure training in employment for 16–19 year olds; a greater use of credit transfer between courses; increased access to higher education; measures to increase the status of vocational qualifications; and the renewal of the further education sector.

Second, it is clear that the content of education reform proposals have proved notably more controversial than that of training proposals. For example, after three years of intense debate there remained, in 1991, widespread disagreement amongst academics, practitioners and policy makers about the role and nature of 'core skills' provision in courses and of their potential contribution to widely promoted policy goals. Meanwhile, the content of employer-based training for 16–19 year olds received little attention outside a small academic circle and appeared, by comparison, to have been accepted as an instrumental activity which, of itself, furthers the goals of industrial and employment policy. Where controversy existed in this area, it was centred around the economics of training delivery. An explanation for this contrast is that the core skills question has been generally regarded as part of the debate about 'standards' in a publicly funded education system, whilst the adequacy of training content has traditionally been regarded as a private, commercial function of individual employers.

Third, and more generally, it is noticeable how the content of the debate led to the inexorable blurring of the traditional boundaries of education policy, training policy and employment policy. These processes, and the fortunes of policy bodies associated with them, are discussed more fully in the remainder of this chapter. Before moving to this analysis, the next section provides a brief description of developments in the 16–19 field during the period leading to the general election in April 1992.

## Postscript: The early stages of implementation

The White Paper on 16–19 issues, *Education and Training for the 21st Century* (DES/DE, 1991a), marked the end of the policy debate, moving the government and associated interest groups into the initial stages of a period of policy implementation. Despite pre-election uncertainty, the government tabled the Further and Higher Education bill in November 1991. Before this, however, several developments signalled the consolidation of Conservative Party intentions. In July the government joined with TECs and the Trades Union Congress (TUC) (the latter sharing a platform with the Conservatives for the first time since 1986) to launch the CBI's 'world class' education and training targets. In the education sphere, John Major caused a storm the same month by announcing his desire to see the element of GCSE examinations assessed by coursework reduced to 20 per cent. The controversy over this statement — subsequently rubber stamped by SEAC in September — was to reach a crescendo at the end of the year; many educationalists regarded the move as retrogressive (see Spours, Chapter 6, below), and some observed that it reinforced traditional study at A level.

Whilst the GCSE row rumbled, higher education institutions were busy anticipating the abolition of the 'binary line' between universities and polytechnics announced in the White Paper on higher education (DES/DE, 1991b). The Committee of Principles and Vice Chancellors (CVCP), in particular, was encouraging them all to adopt modular curricula and so create a national credit accumulation and transfer system. Many institutions agreed to this in principle during 1991. Modular credit proposals were also being formulated for the 16–19 age group by the Further Education Unit (FEU) with many analysts believing that the continuing expansion both of the post-16 and higher education sectors could best be underpinned by this kind of curriculum reform.

The path of policy implementation in training policy ran less smoothly from the government's point of view. Specifically, continued recession and climbing unemployment was, by the autumn of 1991, placing a funding squeeze on TECs' training programme budgets and increasing the queues of young people waiting for Youth Training (YT) places. In the weeks before the election some TECs

broke ranks to lay the blame largely at employment minister Michael
Howard's door — a move which was interpreted both as one in a series
of eruptions of TEC discontent at the tight leash on which the
government kept them, as well as a negotiating strategy on the TECs'
part prior to discussions with the government about their budgetary
funding for 1992/93. With the general election rapidly approaching,
the Further and Higher Education Act was secured in March 1992, in
advance of an election campaign which saw the Conservatives
returned to power the following month.

## The conduct of the 16–19 education and training debate

### The context for policy change

A public policy debate as lengthy and wide ranging as that
surrounding the reform of 16–19 education and training in England
and Wales during 1988–91 requires a foundation. This was provided
in 1984 by the influential IMS report *Competence and Competition*,
which acted as rallying call to modernise the existing system.
Specifically, it marshalled evidence which was subsequently to unite
all participants in the education and training policy community in the
assertion that low rates of participation in full time education and
training beyond the minimum school leaving age were detrimental to
Britain's economic well-being.

A general acceptance of the need to modernise, based upon the
example of arrangements in competitor countries whose systems were
held to be more efficient, was only a first step in the policy process,
however. The 16–19 education and training debate in England and
Wales illustrated very clearly how divisions appeared as soon as
consensus over the need to change was translated into specific
'reform' proposals tabled by individuals, interest groups and political
parties.

The single most contentious question surrounded the role of A
levels in a future education and training system. This central issue has
tended to create a polarity which still (1992) defines the terms of
debate. At one extreme, arguments were presented to retain A levels
in their present form so that measures to increase participation would
have to rely solely upon the increased effectiveness of vocational
provision (DES/DE; 1991a). At the other pole, the academic-
vocational 'divide' was swept away and replaced by an overarching
qualification mixing components of intellectual, practical and work-
based learning (IPPR; 1990a). Politically, as well as pedagogically, the
A level examination and its relationship to the rest of the 16–19 system

continues (1992) to represent a central, emotive issue raising dichotomies of: academic method *versus* vocational and applied study; the independent sector *versus* the state sector of schooling; tradition *versus* change; an elite *versus* a mass system of higher education; a clearly defined pathway to higher education *versus* a new logic determining access; the maintenance of 'standards' *versus* 'untried' methods of assessment.

A second feature of the 16–19 debate was a new interest in the interrelated nature of causes for Britain's low participation problem. Specifically, this sought to relate to each other analyses of curriculum issues, the role and structure of educational institutions and examinations, the operation of the youth labour market, and the role of incentives in public policy intervention. In terms of policy generation, the effect of this process was to broaden the scope of post-16 reform from the narrow, A level focus of the Higginson Committee's terms of reference to encompass vocational qualification structures, the opportunities for credit transfer between the two 'tracks', training credits and, most recently, the reform of the funding of further and higher education (all issues discussed in more detail by contributors to the present volume).

At the level of national government and the civil service, this perception of a complex set of issues led to a measure of inter-departmental co-operation in contrast to traditions of indifference and rivalry (THES; 1991).[5] It is to be noted, however, that this co-operation, whilst indicating a more sophisticated approach to policy-making, proved significantly less powerful in the British education and training policy process than a more recognisable convention — that of polarised interest groups, bolstered by ideological differences between the political parties, generating competing proposals. If the retention of A Levels was the central point at issue in the educational part of the debate, the re-introduction of a training levy upon employers was the focus of dispute between rival groups' policies for training.

**The role of interest groups and 'opinion formers'**

The education and training system in England and Wales is notoriously fragmented and, being an 'extended' policy community, is subject to the competing demands of multiple interest groups (Greenaway et al., 1992: 58). The 16–19 debate illustrates this fully and Appendix 1 lists the appearance in under two years (July 1989–May 1991) of 52 separate sets of recommendations for 16–19 reform.

The fragmentation evident in the education and training policy community has a particular effect on the policy process. On the one hand, it may be used by politicians as evidence of lack of professionalism on the part of the educators. In this light, the National Curriculum may be regarded as an official antidote to incoherent and individualistic curriculum provision. Similarly, the tendency of the system to fragment (encouraged by market pressures) has been held to be responsible for a multiplicity of competing qualifications — both vocational and academic — and to have impaired the ability of individual students and their parents to discern an *optimum* pathway through the system. The first specific change that the Conservative government felt able to make, in the aftermath of its blanket rejection of the Higginson report, was the adoption, in August 1989, of one of its proposals — the rationalisation of A level syllabi. This move was replicated in the vocational sphere through an announcement in the White Paper of May 1991 (DES/DE; 1991a, Vol. 1, para. 3.10) that, in future, NVQs would be the only qualifications available in schools and colleges. In both sectors, the Thatcher/Major administration was, once more, accompanying market-oriented proposals for reform of the education and training system with clear regulation of its operation.[6]

The diversity of organised education opinion has, in contrast, been justified as beneficial. It is held to indicate a vigorous profession, working in a field where conclusive evidence of effectiveness is unavailable. In this context, the need for SEAC to have to consult with over four thousand interested parties over changes to methods of A level assessment is seen as effective consultation and the appropriate means of ensuring that the policy process is influenced both down from the top and up from the bottom of the system (see, for example, Burgess, this volume). In a period before the full implementation of a National Curriculum and teacher appraisal, such techniques may also be seen as serving an important consensus-generating role and acting as a 'safety valve' in central policy generation. Moreover, in some right wing circles, a diversity of provision has also been commended as encouraging the development of internal market disciplines within the education service.

In a policy field of such diversity as that of education and training, each interest group and 'think tank' felt driven to make its own distinctive pronouncement on post-16 reform. Notwithstanding, it is notable how particularly influential three of the several dozen contributions proved to be.

The intervention of the independent schools through the vehicle of the HMC in June 1990 (MacLeod, 1990a) and repeatedly thereafter, proved particularly influential with the government. Most conclusively, the contention of the HMC that A levels represented a guarantee of standards of excellence remained unchallenged in the government's view and was carried through into the 1991 White Paper on education and training and the 1992 election campaign (Davies,

1992). For a period, the government also toyed with HMC proposals for an intermediate, modular exam to be sat at the age of seventeen as a way of broadening access to sixth form study (an idea subsequently supported by two of the headteacher unions, SHA and NAHT).

Of a completely different hue was the IPPR's proposals of July 1990, which lucidly established the case for a radical alternative to the HMC's stance — a full unitary system of qualifications from the age of 16, loosely inspired by the baccalaureate model (IPPR, 1990a). This report enjoyed wide influence in education circles, even if not all those groups which followed its tenor went so far as to propose the abolition of the 'dual track' — the majority preferring instead to recommend widespread credit transfer between the two pathways (see Appendix 1). Whilst it was to be expected that the Labour Party would use the IPPR report as the basis of its policy proposals, a measure of the authority of the IPPR's work was the admission by the Secretary of State John MacGregor, in August 1990, that the government was actively looking at adopting selected IPPR ideas. This was subsequently confirmed when the 1991 White Paper announced — in a completely different form to that envisaged by the IPPR — the adoption of an umbrella qualification of 'Advanced Diploma' for 18 year olds (DES/DE; 1991a; Vol. 1, para 4.4) and employed in its rhetoric, references to a unified system which would offer a 'blend of qualifications' (*ibid*. paras. 4.1–4.7).

The third highly influential contribution to the 16–19 debate was the proposal to establish training credits, cashable by 16 and 17 year olds in employment, with training providers. Detailed plans were proposed by the CBI's Vocational Education Task Force in October 1989, and were piloted in a modified form by ten TECs and one LEC from 1990, before being proposed for national extension to all 16 and 17-year-old school leavers during 1991–96 (DES/DE; 1991a, Vol. 1, para. 6.9). The IPPR's alternative approach to the question of youth and adult training was a more detailed justification of its case for a training levy (IPPR; 1990a, 1990b). Despite being formally adopted by the Labour Party, this proposal enjoyed considerably less influence than did rival training policies which argued for the deployment of incentives. In the employer context the mechanism of central regulation was decidedly out of fashion.

Which were those characteristics that seem to have determined the particular influence of the HMC, the IPPR, and the CBI in defining the co-ordinates of the 16–19 policy debate?

In training policy, the CBI adopted thoughtful proposals which capitalised both on the current interest in consumer (i.e. trainee) intervention and which re-emphasised employers' traditional dislike of centrally imposed regulation in their affairs. The strength of the CBI's position was, in addition, bolstered by the development of

complementary Conservative employer-led policies for national
training and the seemingly continuing inability of the TUC — which
cautiously rejected a levy and tentatively endorsed credits (1989) — to
promote its training strategy in an effective, challenging way.

In education policy, the HMC was able to exert its accustomed
influence over Conservative administrations by well-timed and
effective interventions in the policy debate (during June 1990–May
1991), by symbolising standards of educational excellence, and by
raising fears and uncertainties over new examination methods.
Kenneth Clarke spoke for the HMC's position in an interview in May
1991, asserting that anyone who could afford it would obviously
prefer to put their children through fee-paying schools because of
their 'more formalised approach to teaching . . . and measurement of
results by academic achievement'; furthermore, A levels were 'the
simplest and most effective part of the [post-16] system' (*Independent*,
1991a). The IPPR, on the other hand, had been able to marshal a
strong team of writers for its *British Baccalaureate* report who had
before them an attractive brief to argue for structural reform in an
education and training system which large numbers of practitioners
and academics believed to be in need of comprehensive updating.

In the case of the *British Baccalaureate* it was the strength of the case
and the quality of the argument which enabled the IPPR to appeal to a
wide spectrum of educational opinion beyond any role the Institute
might have in generating policy ideas for the political 'left'. More
debatable is how effectively the HMC and CBI could have carried
their arguments to a Labour government or an administration
including the Liberal Democrats. It would appear from the policy
proposals launched by the Labour party (LP, 1991a and b) that, on
the contrary, it would have relied heavily upon the IPPR. The Liberal
Democrats' proposals, meanwhile, had already anticipated and were
later to echo IPPR ideas (SLD, 1988; LD: 1989, 1990a, 1990b).

When set against the political momentum enjoyed by the CBI and
the prominence and influence of individuals fielded by HMC and the
IPPR, the role of interest groups representing narrower platforms,
such as the teacher unions and specialist curriculum groups, is seen to
be that of camp followers (see Appendix 1). A more significant source
of influence in the debate more generally has been claimed for the
various 'opinion formers' whose presence is currently
institutionalised in the British education and training policy scene. In
the 16–19 debate the figures of Sir John Cassels, Sir Christopher Ball,
Sir Claus Moser, John Rae, Stuart Sexton and Stuart Maclure have
been conspicuous (Richardson, 1991:46). The function of such
individuals seems to be largely as self-appointed or peer-appointed
hunter-gatherers of policy options. Stuart Sexton's Education Unit
and Institute for Economic Affairs activities, tailor-made for the

et office committee chaired by the prime
bove the uncertain reefs of departmental
high status and singular brief — that of the
wer — the Council was able to remain aloof
16–19 debate and, in the process, cause
ent departments: by indiscreet circulation
ts which dissented from departmental
embers of the Council and their contractors
rets Act!); and by issuing public proposals
fications which were later flatly refuted in
igher education (ACOST, 1991; DES/DE;

select committees were also able to
isters and official education and training
a House of Lords committee concluded
tarist training policy had failed, and went
ent's resistance to EC training directives
naintained, had been viewed by the
than as an investment (HL, 1990). Four
' committee on Education, Science and
, would conduct an enquiry into what it
ducation and training, with reference to
cultures similar to our own' (TES, 1991).
ommittees, in common with others in
be seen as largely calling to account the
policy areas of legitimate public concern.
dable scandal, however, this regulatory
e of an 'opinion forming', longer term
likely to lead to specific changes of policy
ate of the enquiries of the Commons
lect committees are vulnerable to short-
ing taken detailed evidence on the 16–19
refrained from providing a critical
hed, in the run up to the 1992 general
d oral evidence from its enquiry (HC,

**and of government**

education and training policy process,
parties and of the government, both in
ion and in the determination of policy

s, the government has dominated the
al Democrat party's reform package was

presiding Conservative government, have been extremely effective in directly influencing the policy process; his recommendations for the education system (O'Leary, 1991) match the subsequent content of the White Paper *Education and Training for the 21st Century* more closely than any other proposals referred to in Appendix 1. Also notable was John Major's judgement, in April 1991, that Sir Claus Moser's impending 'National Commission' into British education had now gathered sufficient momentum that further government resistance to it would be counter-productive (Crequer, 1991).

The influence of other 'opinion formers' upon policy making has been less politically explicit and, consequently, harder to gauge. Taken together, however, the reports that they have produced between them have provided useful briefing material for ministers, and ammunition for cadet opinion formers who attend seminars at the PSI and RSA. The function of such reports lies mid-way between the mass dissemination products of the CBI and IPPR and the closed networks of clubs and seminar groups where 'high level' soundings are taken and alliances formed among the generators of education and training policy.

## The role of empirical research

An interesting feature of the 16–19 debate is that it lasted sufficiently long for related empirical research to be commissioned and published, and that it was sufficiently tentative and open for the research potentially to inform policy choices. This was true in two specific areas.

The first set of research was conducted at Manchester University by Alan Smithers and Pamela Robinson. In August 1990 they reported on teacher supply in the sciences. This was followed in May 1991 with work on the supply of candidates with vocational qualifications into higher education, their subsequent degree performance and the barriers to access and achievement encountered by such individuals (Smithers and Robinson, 1990; Smithers, 1991). Meanwhile, related work on access to higher education had been reported by Professor John Gilbert at Reading University the previous October (Nash, 1990b). In public, Professor Smithers was careful to present his findings in isolation from any policy conclusions that might be drawn from them, although he was reported as being in favour of the creation of greater coherence within the education and training system through extensive credit transfer between vocational and academic study.[7] This middle course was not reflected in the headline proposals subsequently unveiled by the Labour and Conservative parties, due to the potent effect of traditional A levels upon the parties — the Conservative instinct being for their retention, the Labour instinct for their abolition. Closer inspection of Labour's plans (Judd, 1991a; LP, 1991a and b), however, indicated that credit transfer might, of necessity, need to be the first stage in a policy of gradual reform.

A second area of research informing the 16–19 debate prior to the publication of the 1991 White Paper was studies of the impact of 'core skills' upon education and training attainment. In October 1990 the Training Agency published the results of a study, led by Alison Wolf at the London Institute of Education, indicating that problem-solving training not specifically related to occupational competence enhanced individuals' skills. Seven months later, in May 1991, a study at King's College, London reported that pupils in receipt of a short 'thinking skills' course at the age of 11–13 were considerably (up to three times) more likely to gain top grades at GCSE three years later (Wolf et al., 1990; Adey et al., 1991).

Evidence from both research projects began appearing well before the government's White Paper was drafted, but not in time, apparently, to influence the section headed 'Modern Qualifications', where traditional A level study was reasserted 'without the need for radical change to a highly regarded, tried and tested examination system' (DES/DE: 1991a, Vol. 1, para. 3.15). By now government ministers had successively presented three contradictory official stances on 'core skills'[8] As a result, the adoption of firm new evidence on the benefits of such study being specifically timetabled and so requiring a yet further reversal, in the teeth of HMC opposition, was not to be contemplated. In subsequent proposals (DES, 1991) this situation remained unchanged, with government moves toward the development of a 'core' syllabus for 16 year olds within the Ordinary Diploma relating to a set of subjects rather than the cognitive skills which link them (see also Spours, Chapter 6.)

## The role of government bodies and select committees

The research reported by King's College on 11–13 year olds and by Alison Wolf's team on problem-solving work in occupational training was of direct relevance to the discussions over curriculum modernisation in which SEAC, NCC, NCVQ, HMI and ACOST had been engaged. These official government bodies were not always in agreement with each other on post-16 issues, however. The specific outcome of both the King's College and the Wolf teams' research, for example, endorsed NCVQ's recommendations for separate problem-solving programmes of study, and cast doubt upon HMI, FEU, BTEC and NCC preferences for the insertion of core skills study in each A level curriculum.

More generally, the fortunes of advisory bodies ebbed and flowed during the course of the 16–19 debate, depending upon their degree of

converg
For in
Nation
been b
which
pupils

SEA
policy
own
SEAC
as a
indep
an ov
Mich
(Rich
consi
1990
that
gove
(Jacl
had
este
was

T
sou
full
imp
occ
voc
the
un
cha
(R
co
qu
ga
1,
g
g
p
tl
tl
c

working direct to a cabi
minister, it could float a
ministerial whim. With its
supply of scientific manpo
from wider issues in the
embarrassment to governm
of consultation documer
policies (Nash, 1990a — m
have to sign the Official Se
for broader academic quali
the 1991 White Paper on h
1991b, para. 16)

All-party parliamentary
challenge government mir
policy. In September 1990
that the government's volu
on to criticise the governm
which, the committee r
government as a cost rather
months later the Common
Arts announced that it, too
called the 'mess' of 16–19
more successful systems in
The role of these select
different policy fields, may
government of the day over
In all but the most unavoi
function appears to be mo
endeavour than one which is
direction. Moreover, the
committee illustrates how s
term political pressures. Ha
question, the committee
commentary when it publis
election, selected written a
1991a).[9]

## The role of political parties

Finally, in this review of the
there is the role of opposition
the process of policy format
decisions.

In the 16–19 policy proce
opposition parties. The Liber

first announced in August 1988 and reinforced with three further documents during 1989–90 (SLD, 1988; LD: 1989, 1990a, 1990b). Despite unveiling proposals two years ahead of the other two parties and including decisive, radical policies this package generated very little attention, perhaps because its recommendations appeared in insufficient ideological contrast to the polarised positions of the two main parties. The timing of its two most innovative publications, both in August, no doubt helped to contribute to the lack of impact.

Labour policy, inevitably, generated more public interest. During 1989–90, the comprehensive Labour Party policy review commanded considerable public attention. Nevertheless, despite the high visibility of the party's internal reform process, shadow cabinet members proved surprisingly diffident about providing detailed proposals on topical issues such as the restructuring and assessment of A levels. The view was widely held by political commentators that this reticence was due to a vacuum in independent left-of-centre policy analysis. It was the plugging of this gap that had led to the formation of the IPPR in 1988. One result of this development was that by the autumn of 1990, with Mrs Thatcher's style of government coming under increasing criticism and with commentators identifying education and training policy as 'natural' strong ground for Labour, Neil Kinnock was able to vow with some confidence that education and training would form the heart of the party's election manifesto. Accordingly, in his party conference speech in October, he outlined, in general terms, policies for increased access to higher education for both academic and vocational students and his party's intention to introduce a training levy upon employers. Both policies were indebted to more detailed proposals outlined in the initial two papers on education and training which had so far appeared from the IPPR.

A Labour party policy momentum could now be constructed and shadow spokesman Jack Straw set off on a study tour of the French baccalaureate system, a visit which had the effect of generating additional exposure for the IPPR's headline concept for post-16 reform. By March 1991 the Labour party had determined on the policy goal of abolishing A levels altogether and, in April, in an attempt to pre-empt the government's forthcoming White Paper, plans were unveiled which detailed the gradual dismantling of the current 'two track' system. A first step would entail implementing the Higginson Committee's proposals for a norm of five advanced level studies per student, to be followed later by the move to a fully modular, unitary qualification system. This proposal, under which all students would study for an 'Advanced Certificate', once more closely amplified the recommendations made by the IPPR in *The British Baccalauréat* (IPPR, 1990a; Judd, 1991a; LP, 1991a).

In terms of influencing the policy debate or the conduct of the policy process in 16–19 education and training, it cannot be maintained that the Labour Party, of itself, achieved a clear impact as its ideas were heavily reliant upon the IPPR's academic authors. Over education policy more widely, the Conservatives' powerful appeal to parental and pupil 'choice' was not successfully countered through, for example, potent policies tapping public fears of the social consequences of the opting out of schools. Neither did the Labour Party's commendation of an employer training levy appear to carry the potential populist appeal of the Conservatives' enthusiastic backing for training credits.

The radical, alternative policies for 16–19 education and training that Labour adopted, such as the substantial modification of A levels, were challengingly argued by the IPPR authors, widely supported in education circles and welcomed in the broadsheet press. Nevertheless, the pace and tenor of the 16–19 debate was largely conducted at the Conservatives' pace and on their terms. Even with the government on the ropes over its internal leadership difficulties in late 1990, and Poll Tax troubles in early 1991, the post-16 policy debate, surely a strong Labour card, demonstrated how difficult it was for the Labour opposition — perhaps any British opposition party — to seize the initiative on specific, non-economic policy issues from the government of the day. As if to exemplify this latter point in the education and training context, an NOP poll in June 1991 showed not only that 78 per cent of those interviewed believed that Britain was worse at educating and training its young people than Germany and Japan, but also that one third doubted that a government of any political party could reverse the situation (*The Independent*; 1991b).[10]

Perhaps the clearest example of government control over the 16–19 public policy process during 1988–91, even at the expense of exposing its own confused inconsistency, arose over the question of 'core skills' in A level study. Here, successive policy recommendations of SEAC — the official body designated to consult with educationalists — dutifully reflected two reversals of government policy (Richardson, 1991:51). It would seem likely that a contributory cause of this inconsistency — up to November 1990 — was the occasional but decisive intervention of Mrs Thatcher in education affairs. A newspaper interview of April 1990 (*Sunday Telegraph*; 1990) was widely interpreted as undermining the DES's implementation of the National Curriculum and six months later, following SEAC's proposals in favour of core skills, the Prime Minister moved quickly to assure the HMC that she ruled out any plans to 'undermine the most excellent A level examination' (MacLeod, 1990b; Wood, 1990).

Colourful reinforcement of the Prime Minister's line was provided by junior DES minister Michael Fallon, unofficially the education spokesman for the right wing 'no turning back group'. Following his arrival at the DES in the cabinet reshuffle of July 1990, his public comments on A level standards seemed designed to ensure that the existing examination was maintained and that the Secretary of State John MacGregor — increasingly coming under public scrutiny by Mrs Thatcher's supporters as a closet 'wet' — was not allowed room to deviate from the desired path. Further evidence for the influence of junior ministers was the increasing credit accorded to Tim Eggar and Robert Jackson for building bridges to overcome the traditional antagonism between the DES and the DE, and for Eggar's success in moderating the customarily patrician DES style of policy making and raising his department's interest in developing a more incisive set of policies for further education (Richardson, 1991:52). The examples of Michael Fallon and Tim Eggar both illustrate, in different ways, the considerable potential influence of forceful individual ministers in determining not only the content of policy but the tone of debate surrounding its development. It would seem likely that this phenomenon was reinforced by the instability in policy-making inherent in three different Secretaries of State holding office at the DES with in a 16-month period.

More powerfully, however, the incongruity of the public policy process is well illustrated by the way in which, after three years of detailed, specialised debate, the government's education and training policy reform for 16 to 19 years olds was finally occasioned by its Poll Tax review and the urgent need to alter the balance of local and central public spending (MacLeod, 1991a). Once committed, in March 1991, to the restructuring of further education funding — a complicated administrative change requiring legislation — the Conservative government elected to bring forward proposals on the restructuring of higher education planned for the following autumn, and to present a comprehensive package of education and training measures even though, in important areas of policy such as higher education research funding, there had been insufficient time to arrive at considered and coherent proposals.

As in other areas of Conservative education policy, the relationship between political ideology, political expediency and policy coherence was an important dynamic in 16–19 policy making. For example, the expediency implicit in the decision to support the HMC's rejection of core skills left unresolved the tension between GCSE and A level teaching and curriculum methods. In a different context, the ideology implicit in the prohibition of LEA representation on the governing bodies of the new, independent FE colleges, of sixth form colleges and of their funding councils in favour of strong TEC membership (DES/ DE; 1991a, Vol. 1, paras. 4.1, 4.4, 5.5–7, 5.9) appeared to meet increasing calls by FE institutions to be released from LEA constraints. Yet it gambled on local TECs not only being able to supply a regional and national framework for employer-based training, but that their more active involvement in the FE sector would prove at least as effective and coherent as that of the LEAs they were replacing.

**Implementing policy**

Debating and formulating policy is one aspect of the policy process; implementing proposals is a second aspect, giving rise to a different political climate and calling for different rules of engagement. The parliamentary majority which British governments usually enjoy allows them an easier passage in policy implementation than that available in many overseas political systems. The 16–19 education and training legislation proposed for England and Wales in 1991, however, had to be implemented in a climate of some uncertainty. Primarily, this related to the imminence of a general election (within 13 months at most), but some indication of the shallow foundations of the 16–19 reform proposals came from the government itself. Even before the publication of *Education and Training for the 21st Century*, Kenneth Clarke was displaying a political style which, in its assumptions and method, hinted at the Conservatives' uncertainty about their chosen project. Their preferred option of maintaining a 'dual track' curriculum for 16 to 19 year olds (see Spours, Chapter 6) led, inevitably, to the retention of dual institutions. Moreover, it was intended that vocational institutions would have their status raised by freedom from LEA control and through a unitary system of vocational qualifications. However, Clarke's belief that, given sufficient means, the majority of parents would prefer to send their children to private schools (with traditional sixth forms), and that the main technique required to raise the status of vocational education for the remainder was to 'repeat the message over and over until it gets across' (*Independent*, 1991a; Jackson, 1991), suggested that, after three years of detailed debate on policy options, the policy process through which solutions are chosen had yet to attain a sophistication beyond the rudimentary.

Nevertheless, the most effective political weapon can be the blunt instrument, particularly if the opposition is weak. Kenneth Clarke remained at the DES for a further year until the election, continuing to define meretricious education policy in terms of loosened teacher control over the system. In this he was joined increasingly by John Major who, in July 1991, criticised the GCSE examination by assigning its origins to the 'canker' of 1960s 'fashionable theory' and called for a reduction in the element of GCSE assessment by coursework (Hughes, 1991 — a move which, in turn, would strengthen the position of traditional A levels).[11] Major's speech to staff of the Centre for Policy Studies at the *Cafe Royale* — apparently the first devoted solely to education by a prime minister since that of James Callaghan at Ruskin college in 1976 — caught officials at the DES and at SEAC off-guard, in a manner similar to Margaret Thatcher's announcement in parliament in 1982 of the creation of the Technical and Vocational Education Initiative (TVEI) (Judd, 1991b; Dale, 1985: 41). By June 1992, with the Conservatives safely returned to office, Major was beginning to make Thatcher's occasional interventions in education policy appear *ad hoc* and unfocused.[12] Addressing the Adam Smith Institute, he declared his intention 'to end for good — and I mean for good — the giant left wing experiment in levelling down'. Three weeks later he told back bench Conservatives: 'we know we've got it right when the teachers' unions attack our reforms' (*Independent*, 1992d; Hughes, 1992).

This direct style — reinforced by John Major's personal, leading role in developing education policy *via* the Downing Street policy unit — signalled an increasingly tight hold by the government over the implementation of education and training policy. Whereas Margaret Thatcher's interventions had served to unsettle the NCC and SEAC, both bodies had their chief executives removed in July 1991 to be replaced with a manager from British Petroleum and a former head of the Downing Street policy unit respectively (Hughes, 1992; Nash, 1991b; Nash and Hackett, 1991).[13] Moreover, the continuing rise of the NCVQ was confirmed when Major personally launched GNVQs in January 1992 (Clement, 1992a). A further consequence of the government's tightened control was the continuing difficulty of the Labour Party in setting the agenda or pace of education and training policy discussion or gaining the upper hand. Thus, whilst education issues, in particular, remained of major political significance,[14] Labour's July 1991 document, *Qualified Optimism: Post 16 Education and Training Reform in England and Wales*, passed almost unnoticed. Furthermore, several policy decisions indicated that Labour was unsure of its response to the Conservatives' relentless emphasis on consumer choice: it reversed its policy of opposing separate education provision for gifted children; it announced that, if elected, it would delay (rather than reverse) Conservative plans to reduce GCSE coursework; and, under election campaign scrutiny over its fiscal policies, it was forced to convert a 'pledge' to provide a training guarantee to school leavers, to an 'aim' (Hughill, 1991; *The Independent*, 1992a; Bevins, 1992). Most probably, the many voters who indicated the importance of education at the outset of the campaign reverted to economic concerns and a mistrust of Labour fiscal management on polling day — although it seems likely that a large majority of teachers voted Labour.[15]

During June 1991–April 1992 the education and training policy process was inevitably dominated by the forthcoming election. As a consequence, the 16–19 debate was temporarily extended, even though the 1991 White Paper had signalled the government's policy choices. However, none of the political parties offered fresh 16–19 proposals during the campaign, and the former flood of policy documents from researchers, interest groups and 'opinion formers' dried up almost completely. Characteristically, Alan Smithers and Pamela Robinson's work continued, resulting in a useful 'numerical picture' of the key 16–19 issues, and the Further Education Unit (FEU) produced a 16–19 curriculum document which was widely welcomed by the IPPR's *British Baccalaureate* supporters.[16] These solitary reports, coupled with a right-wing counterblast from the Centre for Policy Studies indicated that the earlier policy formation stage of the 16–19 reform process had all but ended (Smithers and Robinson, 1992; FEU, 1992; Pilkington, 1991).[17]

In its place, attention now switched to implementation issues arising from the choices made by the government in the 1991 White Paper, *Education and Training for the 21st Century*, and it is with these that the contributors to this volume are particularly concerned (see especially Chapters 2, 6–10). Meanwhile, it is too early to draw detailed conclusions about the process of policy implementation that can stand comparison with analysis of the policy germination, formulation and decision-making phases of the 16–19 education and training policy case. To reach a fuller understanding of the entire policy process, further work will be required for, as Greenaway, Smith and Street (1992) point out: 'most accounts of the British political system treat implementation as an afterthought [yet it] is not a less important stage in the policy-making process than that of taking decisions [and] it is just as political' (p. 239).

## Conclusion: deciding factors in the 16–19 policy debate

The 16–19 reform debate in England and Wales during 1987–91 offers an unusually good opportunity to examine: the complex interplay of ideas, institutions, vested interests and ideologies that lie below the surface of national education and training provision; how these become agitated during the upheaval of anticipated policy change; and how the priorities of the presiding government can shape and influence the outcome of events.

Perhaps because of the extent of the academic, education 'practitioner' and policy communities drawn into as complex a project as the overhaul of the national education and training system for 16 to

19 year olds, the specialist debate during the period August 1989 to late March 1991 was both spirited and inconclusive. Government supporters could point to the conduct of the debate as a model of consultative policy making; government detractors could claim that it illustrated the administration's sense of uncertainty and indecision, particularly in the area of 'core skills' and assessment. The disinterested policy analyst could observe that the policy process itself seemed well designed both to 'cool out' the tensions and rivalries expressed by professional interest groups, and to accommodate the benign influence of patrician, opinion-forming public figures.[18] Only when the urgent measures required to bring down the level of the 1991/92 community ('poll tax') charges settled the government on a course of FE funding reform, were all the elements of the debate finally drawn together: the Labour Party published *Today's Education and Training* and the government issued comprehensive proposals for legislation in *Education and Training for the 21st Century, Higher Education: A New Framework* and *Access and Opportunity: A Strategy for Education and Training* (DES/DE; 1991a, b; SO; 1991). Even at this late stage, the high level of public interest in the reforms ensured that the various drafts of the White Papers, the private horse-trading between civil service departments and negotiations between civil servants and outside bodies such as the NCVQ and the TECs were widely reported (Richardson, 1991:54).

Emerging most clearly from the analysis in this chapter is the conclusion that, despite the complexities referred to, the HMC and the IPPR between them defined the core of the debate in June–July 1990, supplemented by the influence of the CBI's promotion of the training voucher idea. The Conservative government of the day found much to applaud in the proposals of the CBI and HMC, and sufficiently recognised the quality of the IPPR analysis to appropriate some of its terminology. In comparison with these three organisations, the contribution to the debate of the majority of the 32 other interest groups, non-governmental bodies and individuals summarised in Appendix 1 was of little significance except in perpetuating the fragmented nature of the education and training policy scene. Perhaps only Stuart Sexton and Sir Claus Moser's team could take satisfaction that they, like the IPPR, CBI and HMC, had made sufficient impact on the policy process to influence policy outcomes.[19]

The Conservative policy that emerged may be described as one of homogeneous differentiation. It proposed separate pathways and institutions for the 16 to 19 age group whilst maintaining that the 'two tracks' would be bridged for the first time by a parity of esteem brought about by the umbrella qualification labelled 'advanced diploma'. Beneath its surface, this policy is an instinctive appeal to the *status quo*, to familiarity and, it may be argued, to continuing social differentiation based upon educational background and qualification. Labour's policy sought to dismantle this dual structure. It offered voters the gamble that the momentum and effectiveness of new padagogies emphasising core skills and self-learning in the FE sector, in some schools and in some companies, backed by research into cognition such as that discussed earlier, would prove strong enough to ensure that a new unitary system could be made to work.

The policies of the two main parties are sharply divergent. Can it be concluded, therefore, that in the case of education and training, the public policy process has been ineffective in tackling the problems identified in the debate? Yes, insofar as the various institutions and pedagogies that currently thrive within the education and training system are inescapably politicised when wider efficiency and equality considerations impact upon them. Because the social sciences describe the workings of the education and training system so imprecisely and because, in England and Wales, there is such a strong hierarchical tradition of educational attainment linked to social class, commonly agreed policy goals are, in the policy formulation phase of the public policy process, transformed into ideological policy measures. Furthermore, whilst some measure of conflict in public policy is inevitable, it appears to be particularly acute in the case of English education and training policy.

Under such conditions, no 'ideal' education and training system can be agreed upon.[20] Moreover, achieving even broad areas of consensus within the policy community becomes more difficult as its constituent groups become polarised. Consequently, and at a relatively superficial level, whilst the tentative measures, counter-measures and legislative proposals reviewed in this chapter illustrate that the 16–19 debate during 1988–91 tended toward an open style of policy formulation, a persistent and divisive characteristic was the habitual 'discourse of derision' (Ball, 1990) adopted by the government toward the 'education establishment'.

More fundamentally, however, the legacy of education as a mirror of social division is sufficiently strong (and institutionalised in the two main political parties) and the empirical understanding upon which current policy reforms have been constructed is sufficiently weak, to ensure — for the present — the political battleground upon which education and training policy decisions are made and the ideological climate within which they are implemented. The debilitating consequences of this policy environment for the coherent modernisation of education and training practice are explored in the following chapters.

# Notes

1 See Ken Spours, Chapter 4, this volume, for a brief *resumé* of earlier periods in the development of 14–19 qualifications in England and Wales.

2 For a different but complementary approach to analysing education policy-making, see Ball, 1990, especially Chapter 1 which, like the present discussion, deals with what Margaret Archer (1981) has called 'high' educational politics.

3 Much fuller details of all the developments listed in this section may be found in Richardson, 1991.

4 Unspecified sources for the narrative in this section are taken from contemporary press coverage in: *The Independent, The Daily Telegraph, The* (London) *Times, The Independent on Sunday, The Times Educational Supplement*, and *The Times Higher Educational Supplement*. See Richardson, 1991, for full details.

5 In the run up to the 1992 general election, however, co-operation once more reverted to the norm of competition and ministerial power-struggle, Clement, 1992b.

6 Many analysts have observed this phenomenon. See, for example, Chitty, 1989; Finegold, 1992.

7 In a more detailed subsequent study, Smithers and Robinson (1992) seem to support the strengthening of existing A levels alongside new technical and vocational pathways of qualification.

8 As detailed in press coverage between June 1988 and November, 1990 and itemised in Richardson, 1991: 47.

9 Select committees are not always so supine. The Commons employment committee published reports in July 1991 and May 1992 both of which were critical of aspects of the government's relations with TECs, government training schemes, 16–19 qualifications and the National Curriculum (HC, 1991b; *Independent*, 1992c).

10 In contrast to education and training policy, it may be argued that, during the winter of 1990/91, Labour was able to wrest the initiative from the government over NHS affairs with policies of less substance than those put forward in *Today's Education and Training* (LP, 1991a). Nevertheless, when the general election came, economic issues re-asserted themselves as the primary focus of the campaign in its later stages.

11 A National Opinion Poll (28.7.91) of parents of children aged 11 to 16 showed 49 per cent disagreeing with Major's announcement and 37 per cent agreeing (Judd, 1991b). In supporting Major, Clarke complained of the 'large, essentially uncontrolled element of teacher assessment in GCSE' and enthusiastically endorsed November 1991 plans for the introduction of four separate GCSE papers, differentiated according to pupil ability: 'it encourages streaming, which I'm all in favour of' (quoted in *The Independent*, 25 September and 21 November, 1991). During the election campaign Clarke ridiculed Labour's proposals to create an Education Standards Commission due to its likely composition of 'the usual old gang of the education world' (Davies, 1992).

12 Major had launched the Conservatives' education policies in a separate document the day before the two main parties' general manifestos were published (Bevins and Hughes, 1992).

13 In its 1992 schools White Paper the government announced that it was to merge the NCC and SEAC (TES, 1992).

14 In the first week of the election campaign voters placed education second only to health as an election issue. When asked 'Which party do you trust to take the right decision about education/schools?', the response was: Conservative, 30 per cent; Labour, 41 per cent; Liberal Democrat, 14 per cent; don't know, 15 per cent (NOP, 1992).

15 See *Independent*, 1992b and Judd, 1992. The government's eighth pamphlet in a series called 'You Can't Trust labour', *Labour and Education: Lowering Standards* may have swayed — or at least reassured — some voters (Davies, 1992).
16 *British Baccalauréat* supporters were also heartened by the appearance of the Howie Report in Scotland, in March 1992 (see Raffe, Chapter 3, this volume).
17 Education and Training policy formation was now focused, respectively, upon the course work question in GCSE, an issue which set virtually the entire teaching profession against the government, and upon government training programmes, particularly Youth Training (YT) which attracted repeated criticism from the Labour Party as well as from trades unions, the Unemployment Unit, the National Audit Office and the House of Commons select committee on employment. Official Employment Department / careers service figures leaked the week before the election showed a waiting list of 50,882 school leavers for YT places in November 1991, (Hyder and Marks, 1992). On top of this, long running tensions between the government and the TECs over their political control and financing continued to attract attention. See *The Independent*: 8 May; 18, 20 June; 9 July; 20, 28, 31 October; 7 November; 9, 17 December 1991; 8 February; 3 April; 1992.
18 For a different expression of this point, see Greenaway *et al.*, 1992: 58.
19 It will be noted that in this analysis of education and training policy-making, non-governmental bodies defined the issues. This concurs with the main finding of Greenaway, Smith and Street's case studies that 'the formal political system was rarely of any importance in the decision making process', (1992: 238).
20 Such as that which 'rational actor' models of decision-making might ideally suggest. Rather, the 16–19 reform process would seem to be a classic example of 'disjointed incrementalism' (Greenaway et al., 1992: 26). Although written before the appearance of Greenaway, Smith and Street's book, the analysis in this chapter could serve very well as an additional case study to their own on 'deciding factors' in British politics.

# References

ACOST (1991) *Science and technology education and employment*, Advisory Council on Science and Technology, The Cabinet Office, London.
Adey P. Shayer M. and Yates C. (1991) *Better learning*, London, Kings College, University of London.
Archer M. (1981) 'Education politics: a model for their analysis', in Broadfoot P., Brock C. and Tulasiewicz W. (eds.), *Politics and educational change*, London, Croom Helm.
Ball S. (1990) *Politics and policy making in education: explorations in policy sociology*, London, Routledge.
Bevins, A. (1992) 'Training pledge diluted by Blair', *The Independent*, 25 March.
Bevins, A. and Hughes, C. (1992) 'PM pledges school "revolution"', *The Independent*, 18 March.
Blackburne, L. (1992) 'Major promises to cure inner-city ills', *Times Educational Supplement*, 19 June.
CBI (1989) *Towards a skills revolution* Confederation of British Industry, London.
Chiity C. (1989) *Towards a new education system: the victory of the new right?*, Lewes, Falmer Press.
Clare, J. (1990) 'A-level exam to be brought into line with GCSEs', *Daily Telegraph*, 5 September.
Clement, B. (1992a) 'Major gives support to vocational training', *The Independent*, 24 January.
Clement, B. (1992b) 'Ministers at odds over Employment Department's future', *The Independent*, 4 February.

Crequer, N. (1991) 'Major supports idea of education system enquiry', *The Independent*, 3 May.

Crequer, N. (1988) 'Baker opposes "leaner but tougher" syllabuses', *The Independent*, 8 June.

Dale R. (1985) 'The background and inception of the Technical and Vocational Initiative', in Dale R. (ed.), *Education, training and employment: towards a new vocationalism?* Oxford, Pergamon Press.

Davies, P. (1992) 'Clarke says Labour may abandon exams at 16', *The Independent*, 15 February.

DE (1988) *Employment for the 1990s* Department of Employment, London, HMSO.

DE/DES/SO/WO (1986) *Working together — education and training* Department of Employment / Department of Education and Science / Scottish Office / Welsh Office, London, HMSO.

DES (1991) *Ordinary and Advanced Diplomas* [consultative document], London, Department of Education and Science.

DES/DE (1991a) *Education and training for the 21st century*, Department of Education and Science/Department of Employment (2 Vols.), London, HMSO.

DES/DE (1991b) *Higher education: a new framework*, Department of Education and Science/Department of Employment, London, HMSO.

DES/WO (1988) *Advancing A levels* (The Higginson Report), Department of Education and Science/Welsh Office, London, HMSO.

FEU (1992) *A basis for credit?*, London, Further Education Unit.

Finegold, D. (1992) 'The Low Skill Equilibrium: an institutional analysis of Britain's education and training failure', unpublished D. Phil., University of Oxford.

Greenaway J., Smith S. and Street J. (1992) *Deciding factors in British politics: a case study approach*, London, Routledge.

Gunn S. (1992) 'Old school tie still rules the roost', *The Times*, 2 May.

HC (1991a) *Education and training for the 21st century* [House of Commons select committee on education, science and arts, 6th report], London, HMSO.

HC (1991b) *TECs and vocational training* [House of Commons select committee on employment 5th report], London, HMSO.

HC (1992) *Industrial change: retraining and redeployment* [report of the House of Commons select committee on employment], London: HMSO.

HL (1990) *Vocational training and re-training* [House of Lords select committee on the European communities, 21st report], London, HMSO

Hughes, C. (1992) 'Major taking tough stance on education', *The Independent*, 4 July.

Hughes, C. (1991) 'Major signals tougher GCSE', *The Independent*, 10 July.

Hughill, B. (1991) 'Labour U-turn will put gifted pupils on fast track to success', *The Observer*, 27 October.

Hyder, K., and Marks, K. (1992) 'Youth Training guarantees not being honoured', *The Independent*, 3 April.

IMS (1984) *Competence and competition*, Brighton, Institute of Manpower Studies.

Independent, The (1992a) 'GCSE pledge', 6 February, London.

Independent, The (1992b) 'Teachers swing against Tories after "too hasty" school reforms', 30 March, London.

Independent, The (1992c) 'MPs say job training schemes are failing', 8 May, London.

Independent, The (1992d) 'Major outlines plans for "privatisation of choice"', June 17, p6.

Independent, The (1991a) 'Startling the county halls' [interview with Kenneth Clarke], 2 May, London.

Independent, The (1991b) 'Little faith in British education, poll shows', 8 June, London.

IPPR (1990a) Finegold D. et al., *A British Baccalaureat; ending the division between education and training*, London, Institute for Public Policy Research.

IPPR (1990b) Miliband D., *Learning by Right*, London, Institute of Public Policy Research.

Jackson, M. (1991) 'Clarke calls for two paths to college', *Times Educational Supplement*, 8 March, London.

Jackson, M. (1990), Award body's funds run out', *Times Educational Supplement*, 15 June, London.

Judd, J. (1992) 'Frustrated teachers turn their backs on the Tories', *The Independent*, 25 February, London.

Judd, J. (1991a), "Continental" exam plan for sixth form', *Independent on Sunday*', 24 March, London.

Judd, J. (1991b) 'Major's plan for GCSE "unfair to girls"', *The Independent*, 28 July, London.

LD (1989) *Britain's industrial future*, London, The Liberal Democrats Party.

LD (1990a) *Higher education: investing in our future*, London, Liberal Democrats Party.

LD (1990b) *Putting Pupils first*, London, The Liberal Democrats Party.

LP (1991a) *Today's Education and Training*, The Labour Party, London.

LP (1991b) *Qualified optimism: post 16 education and training reform in England and Wales*, London, The Labour Party.

MacLeod, D. (1991a) 'Councils lose control of college', *The Independent*, 22 March, London.

MacLeod, D. (1991b) 'Clarke foiled again over penalties for poor spelling', *The Independent*, 17 May, London.

MacLeod, D. (1990a) 'Independent heads call for "easier" A-levels', *The Independent*, 13 June, London.

MacLeod, D. (1990b) 'Heads criticise A-level reform proposals', *The Independent*, 29 July, London.

Nash, I. (1992) 'Alliance calls for A level reform', *Times Educational Supplement*, 14 February.

Nash, I. (1991a) 'Chance to learn a trade at 14', *Times Educational Supplement*, 22 March, London.

Nash, I. (1991b) 'A relaxed defender of the faith', *Times Educational Supplement*, 26 July, London.

Nash I. (1990a) 'Rebel advisers demand science A level reform', *Times Educational Supplement*, 13 July, London.

Nash I. (1990b) 'Arts-science mix "a waste of effort" at A level', *Times Educational Supplement*, 12 October, London.

Nash I. (1990c) 'Government row looms after Fallon attack', *Times Educational Supplement*, 29 October, London.

Nash I., and Hackett G. (1991) 'NCC chief takes early retirement', *Times Educational Supplement*, 12 July, London.

NOP (1992) National Opinion Poll Survey, *The Independent*, 19 March, London.

O'Leary, J. (1991) 'New plan for A level reforms', *The Times*, 2 February, London.

Pilkington P. (1991) *End egalitarian delusion: different education for different talents*, London, Centre for Policy Studies.

Richardson, W. (1991) *Education and training post-16: options for reform and the policy process in England and Wales*, Coventry, University of Warwick VET Forum.

SLD (1988) *The learning society*, Social and Liberal Democrats Party, London.

Smithers A. (1991) *The vocational route into higher education*, Manchester, University of Manchester.

Smithers A. and Robinson P. (1990) *Teacher provision in the sciences*, Manchester, University of Manchester.

Smithers A. and Robinson P. (1992) *Beyond compulsory schooling*, London, Council for Industry and Higher Education.

SO (1991) *Access and opportunity: a strategy for education and training*, Scottish Office, London, HMSO.

*Sunday Telegraph* (1990) 'Core curriculum for a civilised society', interview with Mrs Thatcher, 15 April.

TA/DE (1989) *Training in Britain*, Sheffield, Training Agency/Department of Employment.

*TES* (1992) 'Patten ushers in era of opting out', *Times Educational Supplement*, 31 July, London.

*TES* (1991) 'MPs to enquire into 16–19 "mess"', *Times Educational Supplement*, 25 January, London.

*THES* (1991) 'Whitehall's marriage of convenience', *Times Higher Educational Supplement*, 22 March 1991.

Wilby, P. (1989) 'MacGregor to regulate A level syllabuses', *The Independent*, 23 August, London.

Wood, N. (1990) 'Thatcher rules out A level reforms', *The Times*, 24 October, London.

Wolf A. et al. (1990) *Learning in context: patterns of skills transfer and training implications*, Sheffield, Training Agency.

# Appendix 1

## Summary chart of the recommendations of leading organisations and interest groups for post-16 reform, 1988–91

| Policy Group/ Date | Retain A levels (existing 'dual track' system) | Broaden A levels content (e.g. core skills) | Extensive credit transfer within 'dual track' | Inter- mediate qual. at age 17 | Abolish A levels (full 'unitary' system) | Training credit | Training levy |
|---|---|---|---|---|---|---|---|
| Higginson 6.88 | | ✓ | | | | | |
| SLD 8.88 | | ✓ | ✓ | | | | ✓ |
| HMI 7.89 | | ✓ | | | | | |
| LD 8.89 | | | | | | | ✓ |
| SEAC 8.89 | | ✓ | | | | | |
| TUC 8.89 | | | | | ✓ | | |
| BAAS 9.89 | | ✓ | | | | | |
| BP 9.89 | | | ✓ | | | | |
| RSA 10.89 | ✓* | | | | | | |
| CBI 10.89 | | ✓ | | | ✓ | | |
| SEAC 11.89 | | ✓ | | | | | |
| IP 2.90 | | ✓ | | | | | |
| AEB 3.90 | | | | ✓ | | | |
| NCC 4.90 | | ✓ | | | | | |
| NCVQ 4.90 | | | ✓ | | | | |
| PSI 4.90 | ✓ | | | | | | |
| RSA 5.90 | ✓* | | | | | | |
| CVCP 5.90 | | ✓ | | | | | |
| AUT 5.90 | | ✓ | ✓* | | | | |
| HMC 6.90 | ✓ | | | ✓ | | | |
| SEAC 6.90 | | ✓ | ✓ | | | | |
| IPPR 7.90 | | | | | ✓ | ✓ | |
| PAT 7.90 | ✓ | | | | | | |
| ACOST 7.90 | | ✓ | | | | | |
| SHA 7.90 | | | | ✓ | | | |

| Policy Group/ Date | Retain A levels (existing 'dual track' system) | Broaden A levels content (e.g. core skills) | Extensive credit transfer within 'dual track' | Inter-mediate qual. at age 17 | Abolish A levels (full 'unitary' system) | Training credit | Training levy |
|---|---|---|---|---|---|---|---|
| NIESR 8.90 | | | √ | | | | |
| LD 8.90 | | | | | √ | | √ |
| SEAC 9.90 | | √ | √* | | | | |
| HoL 9.90 | √* | | | | | | |
| IPPR 9.90 | | | | | | | √ |
| JMB 10.90 | | | √* | | | | |
| HMC 10.90 | √ | | | | | | |
| AUT 10.90 | | | | | √ | | |
| CPS 11.90 | √ | | | | | | |
| JR 11.90 | | | | | √ | | |
| NAHT 11.90 | | √ | √ | √ | | | |
| IEA 11.90 | √ | | | | | | |
| SEAC 12.90 | √ | | | | | | |
| FEU 12.90 | | | √ | | | | |
| CBI 1.91 | | √ | | | | | |
| ASE 1.91 | | | √ | | | | |
| EU 2.91 | √ | | | | | | |
| AEB 2.91 | √ | | | | | | |
| APCT 3.91 | | | | | √ | | |
| CVCP 4.91 | | √ | √ | | | | |
| PSI 4.91 | | | | | | √ | √* |
| APVI 4.91 | | | √ | | | | |
| RSA 4.91 | | √* | √* | | √* | | |
| LP 4.91 | | | | | √ | | √ |

| Policy Group/ Date | Retain A levels (existing 'dual track' system) | Broaden A levels content (e.g. core skills) | Extensive credit transfer within 'dual track' | Inter- mediate qual. at age 17 | Abolish A levels (full 'unitary' system) | Training credit | Training levy |
|---|---|---|---|---|---|---|---|
| ACOST 4.91 | | √ | √ | | | | |
| SMITHERS/ NCVQ 5.91 | | | √ | | | | |
| HMC 5.91 | √ | | | | | | |
| RS 5.91 | | | | | √ | | |
| **DES/DE 5.91** | √ | | | | | √ | |

Details of all the recommendations made by organisations listed in this appendix may be found in Richardson, 1991.

Key:

| | |
|---|---|
| ACOST | Advisory Council on Science and Technology |
| AEB | Associated Examining Board |
| APCT | Association of Polytechnic and College Teachers |
| APVIC | Association of Principles of Sixth Form Colleges |
| ASE | Association for Science Education |
| AUT | Association of University Teachers |
| BAAS | British Association for the Advancement of Science |
| BP | British Petroleum |
| CBI | Confederation of British Industry |
| CPS | Centre for Policy Studies |
| CVCP | Committee of Vice-Chancellors and Principals |
| DE | Department of Employment |
| DES | Department of Education and Science |
| EU | Education Unit (Stuart Sexton) |
| FEU | Further Education Unit |
| HoL | House of Lords |
| HMC | Headmasters' Conference |
| HMI | Her Majesty's Inspectorate (of Schools) |
| IEA | Institute of Economic Affairs |
| IP | Institute of Physics |
| IPPR | Institute for Public Policy Research |
| JMB | Joint Matriculation Board |
| JR | Mr John Rae |
| LD | Liberal Democrats Party |
| LP | Labour Party |
| NAHT | National Association of Head Teachers |
| NCC | National Curriculum Council |
| NCVQ | National Council for Vocational Qualifications |
| NIESR | National Institute of Economic and Social Research |
| PAT | Professional Association of Teachers |
| PSI | Policy Studies Institute |
| RS | Royal Society |

| RSA | Royal Society for the Encouragement of Arts, Manufactures and Commerce |
| SEAC | Schools Examinations and Assessment Council |
| SHA | Secondary Heads Association |
| SLD | Social and Liberal Democrat Party |
| SO | Scottish Office |
| TUC | Trades Union Congress |

*Recommendations by implication or for further evaluation

# 2 The emerging post-16 system: analysis and critique

## David Finegold

In the last three years, Britain has experienced an unprecedented growth in participation in post-compulsory education and training (ET). This chapter will begin by exploring the reasons for this increase in staying-on rates and then argue that despite recent improvements, Britain still faces a major ET deficit relative to its main competitors. The government is attempting to solve this problem through the creation of a radical new post-16 marketplace. After outlining the key components of the 'market model', I will suggest some of the difficulties Britain faces in closing the skills gap.

### Why the growth in staying-on rates?

Up until 1988, Britain was one of the only advanced industrial countries (AICs) where a majority of 16 year olds left education at the first opportunity. In just two years, however, staying-on rates increased to 58 per cent, with the estimates for 1991–92 at close to 65 per cent. Looking at the whole age group, the government statistics show that more than 90 per cent are in some form of education or training. Growth in higher education enrolments has been equally impressive, with the government projecting that by the year 2000 one in three of all young people in England and Wales will continue in education after 18 (and more than 40 per cent in Scotland), compared with an average of just 12 per cent between 1980 and 1987.

The reasons for this sudden surge in participation rates are still not clear, but there are a number of contributing factors:

1. **Higher examination pass rates**

   The single best predictor of whether young people will continue in post-compulsory education is their examination success at 16. The introduction of the GCSE, including continuous assessment and coursework, has significantly increased the percentage of 16 year olds gaining five or more examination pass marks (Jesson and Gray, 1991). While GCSEs have thus increased the pool of students with good results who are likely to remain in full-time education, the introduction of the new exam cannot explain why more students with marks which previously would have led them to leave school are now staying on in greater numbers.

2. **Bums on seats**

   The surge in staying-on rates has coincided with a sharp drop in the size of the age cohort (shrinking by 28 per cent between 1985 and 1995) and the change in the funding of schools and colleges which ties their resources more closely to the number of students. This has given institutions a doubly strong incentive to compete with each other to get 'bums on seats'.

3. **More educated parents**

   In the mid-1980s the DES mistakenly predicted a fall in the numbers entering HE because of demographic decline. Part of the reason for this error was the failure to take into account the uneven nature of this decline across the class structure; as a result of the post-Robbins Report expansion of HE in the 1960s, there has actually been an increase in the number of young people with at least one parent who has participated in FE or HE, a key influence on the educational choices of their children.

4. **Pull from new post-compulsory courses**

   The introduction of vocational courses from BTEC and City & Guilds, along with the national extension of TVEI, have provided young people with new alternatives to A levels. These new courses have been made more attractive by the large growth in HE places, accompanied by HE-FE compacts and other programmes to expand access for those with non-traditional qualifications.

5. **Shifts in the labour market**

   There have been both short- and long-term shifts in the youth labour market that have improved the incentives for young people to remain in education. Major structural changes in the economy — e.g. the shift from manufacturing to services, the introduction of new technologies, the increase in international competition — have forced companies to restructure their operations, reducing the supply of apprenticeships and the jobs available to school-leavers with little or no qualifications. In addition, the 'demographic time bomb' prompted many large employers to choose part-time workers and/or women returners in preference to young people. These trends have been accelerated in the last few years by the prolonged recession and the removal of under-18s from eligibility for benefits, a combination which may have caused young people to stay in education because of the absence of attractive alternatives.

## Has Britain solved its ET problems?

While the increase in staying-on rates, if not the rate of increase, is likely to continue because of such factors as the greater education of the previous generation, knock-on effects from HE expansion and shifts in the youth labour market, there is a danger in extrapolating from the recent figures. As the fall in the number of 16 year olds comes to an end and the economy recovers, many individuals may prefer jobs to remaining in education. Nowhere is this more apparent than in teacher training, where government claims that shortages have been solved must be treated with scepticism, since many of those enrolled on courses have no intention of entering the profession. In addition, the HE projections assume that the system can continue to expand at its current rate without any major additions to capacity. Even, if the target is met through franchising arrangements with FE colleges, part-time 16–18 year old students and trainees, who are worth less to the colleges, are likely to be squeezed from the post-compulsory system.

Furthermore, increases in staying-on rates should not be equated with improvements in skill levels. The figures for full- and part-time participation rates of 16 year olds hide a number of deficiencies in the current system (Raffe, 1992): the statistics include evening courses which may be of brief duration and rarely lead to qualifications; the main part-time route, Youth Training, does not offer the breadth and quality of skills provided in the Germanic countries' dual systems, with only 38 per cent of trainees obtaining any qualification in 1991, most at a very low skill level. As for the full-time route, the new funding formula has put pressure on schools to keep 16 year olds in the sixth form regardless of whether the courses on offer are the best options for the individual. This has led to concern about the independence of the careers education and guidance on offer to young people, a growing number of whom are resitting GCSEs, starting but not completing A levels or taking broad vocational courses that hold no currency in the labour market.

The improvements in UK staying-on rates must also be viewed against the more sustained growth in educational investment in the UK's main competitors. Not only do other AICs — such as the US, Japan and Sweden — still have more than twice as many 16–18 year olds remaining in education (85+ per cent) as Britain (38 per cent), but newly industrialised countries, such as South Korea already have more students continuing into HE (36 per cent) than the British Government's targets for the year 2000. And South Korea will not be standing still, as it invests heavily in new skills as part of a concerted strategy to move into higher quality, higher value-added world markets. A recent poll showed that more than 80 per cent of South Korean parents expect their children to be in HE in the next decade (Porter, 1990).

If we look in more detail at UK education and training statistics (see Table 2.1), they reveal a consistent pattern: the top 15–20 per cent of the age group (in terms of academic ability) do relatively well in the English system, reaching a high level of attainment by the end of schooling, getting a generous subsidy to continue into HE and then receiving the vast bulk of the training provided by employers. For the rest of the population, however, the situation is reversed, with relatively poor attainment levels pre-16 and little incentive to remain in education and training. As a consequence, most leave the system poorly qualified with limited opportunities to improve their skills throughout their working lives.

**Table 2.1:** Participation rates in full time education

|  | UK | Germany | Sweden | USA | Japan |
|---|---|---|---|---|---|
| **Participation rates in full-time education. (% 1987)** |  |  |  |  |  |
| 16 years old | 50 | 71 | 91 | 95 | 92 |
| 16-18 year-olds | 35 | 49 | 76 | 80 | 77 |
| **New entrant rate to higher education (1987)** | 37 | 30 | 40 | 31 | 52 |
| **Management – % with degree or professional qualification (1987)** | 20 | 60 | N/A | 85 | 85 |
| Sources: DFE, OECD. |  |  |  |  |  |

## Understanding the skills problem

Why does Britain fail to provide the majority of its population with the same level of skills as its main rival. Before suggesting a possible explanation, let me dispel a couple of myths prevalent in recent policy debates:

1. **The education and training system is to blame**
   The Black Papers and James Callaghan's Ruskin College speech launched the much-repeated argument that the British ET system is failing to meet the needs of an advanced industrial economy. While there are unquestionably major deficiencies in the British ET system, the focus on the supply-side has obscured the two-way nature of the problem, ignoring the extent to which inadequate demand for skills from British employers is at least equally to blame for lack of investment in ET. This 'disastrous paradox' was identified by the Balfour Committee in 1929:

   > British industry was desperately short of well-educated and skilled personnel of all kinds compared with its rivals; . . . and yet, this fraction [of skilled workers] was actually more than British industry wished to employ (in Barnett, 1986, 212).

   And it is still evident today; a 1991 comparison of British and German engineering firms, for example, found that the UK companies had a significantly less educated and trained workforce and yet managers stated: 'we're still more dependent on shop-floor skills than we would like' (Campbell and Warner, 1991, 15).

2. **The problem is British attitudes**
   Historians, such as Martin Wiener (1981) and Corelli Barnett (1986), have made the influential argument that Britain's relatively poor economic performance can be traced to a distinctive set of English values, such as an 'anti-industrial spirit' and the 'cult of the practical man'. While they are right to point to the deep historical roots of the problem, it is a mistake to attribute Britain's difficulties to the national cultural characteristics; rather, there is growing evidence to suggest that seemingly irrational attitudes, such as the decision of many young people to leave education at 16 or managers, reluctance to train the majority of their workforce, can be seen as rational responses to the incentives they face.

By altering these incentives it is possible to change attitudes, as the Ford EDAP scheme has clearly demonstrated. When the company offered workers £200 to spend on an educational course to be taken in their free time, it expected, based on its experience with the programme in the US, that about five per cent of employees would participate. In fact, more than half of the work force has taken up the opportunity for further learning, contradicting any notion that the British working class is inherently hostile to education.

## The low-skill equilibrium

To understand the reasons for Britain's relative skills failure I have developed a new framework for analysing the relationship between education and training systems and the economy in the AICs (Finegold, 1992a and c). It begins with the distinctive characteristics of the investment in higher-level skills (e.g. the long payback period, the danger that a company which invests in training may have their skilled workers poached by competitors). For each characteristic, it then identifies the institutional factors — such as the structure of financial markets, the industrial relations and qualifications systems, employer organisations, etc. — that can create incentives or disincentives for the three main investors in skills (individuals, company managers and government policy-makers) to follow the high-skill path. In the British case, an historically-evolved set of institutions, which can be traced back to the Industrial Revolution and the development of a captive trading empire, has combined to trap the economy in a *low-skill equilibrium* in which the majority of enterprises staffed by poorly trained managers and workers produce low-quality goods and services (Finegold and Soskice, 1988).

Applying this framework to young people who are deciding whether to invest in education and training (ET) after compulsory schooling, we can begin to see why many individuals choose to leave education at the first opportunity. The concentration of UK-based companies in low value-added product and service markets using low-skill forms of work organisation sends signals to the majority of young people that it does not pay them to invest in higher-level skills. The relatively low supply of skills, both in the existing workforce and those emerging from the ET system, however, creates further disincentives for companies to pursue a high-skill strategy.

This disincentive to invest in ET is reinforced by one of the distinctive features of the UK's skills-creation system — the continued existence of a youth labour market that offers 16 and 17 year olds relatively well-paid, adult status jobs with little or no formal training. In its 1991 White Paper (DE, DES, 1991), the government refused to impose any education and training requirement on the 16 to 18 age group for fear that this would deter employers from offering young people jobs. The question is whether it is in either the individual's or country's interest for school leavers to enter jobs with no future.

Likewise, the way in which the costs of building higher level skills are distributed among the three main investors in Britain has served to restrict the number of places on offer. At the 16–18 phase, the relatively high wages of British apprentices increases the cost to employers and hence makes them reluctant to invest in creating general skills. The problem is magnified in the training of technicians, where an even greater portion of the costs falls on individuals and their employers, unlike France and Germany where the state covers all or most of the off-the-job training costs (Steedman et al., 1991); the National Institute for Economic and Social Research has estimated that the net cost to an employer of training a single technician, who might then leave the firm, was £14,000 (ibid).

Conversely, in higher education, the British government bears a far higher percentage of the costs for each full-time student than in other AICs, causing the Treasury to keep a tight hold on the supply of places. At the same time, however, the state provides no assistance to individuals who are studying for degrees through far more cost-effective routes, such as part-time or distance-learning.

## The new VET marketplace

The government hopes to improve the incentives for young people to invest in education and training by creating a new post-16 ET marketplace. The post-16 reforms begun during Mrs Thatcher's third term and continued by John Major's government are not as clear cut as the comprehensive 1988 Education Reform Act which released market forces in the compulsory education system, but they are no less radical. The following sections will review the various elements of the post-16 reforms which extend the Conservatives' efforts to create what Freedland (1988, 3) dubs a 'market analogue' in the ET system:

> a structure in which the provision of educational services could be controlled by mechanisms as sensitive to considerations of efficiency and cost-effectiveness as the government conceives market forces themselves to be.

The public sector 'market analogue' parallels the financial flexibility strategy common in many large British companies (Finegold, 1992a). Just as top managers seek to improve company responsiveness by setting clear targets for operating units, introducing cost accounting systems and competitive pressures to ensure the targets are met, and pursuing greater wage and numerical (the freedom to hire and fire workers) flexibility, so too the pre- and post-16 ET reforms are striving to raise educational attainment by creating:

1. clear indicators of performance and efficiency;
2. sources of pressure to maximise efficiency; and
3. flexibility of response to those pressures (Freeland, 1988, 5)

**Empowering the consumer**

The state's main youth training programme — YTS — underwent major reform in response to the shifting economic and demographic situation in the latter part of the 1980s. These changes satisfied the government's underlying aims of reducing state involvement in training while making provision more dependent on market mechanisms. YTS, hailed by then MSC Director Geoffrey Holland as Britain's 'last hope' for youth training when it was upgraded to two years in 1985 (Keep and Mayhew, 1992), fell out of favour in Mrs Thatcher's third term. The first change came just after the 1987 election, when the Secretary of State of Employment, Norman Fowler, announced that in the coming year the government would legislate to disqualify young people who refused a place on YTS from eligibility for supplementary benefit (Wintour, 1987, 36). Fowler's success in making YTS compulsory, in contrast with Norman Tebbit's 1981 failure, reflected the diminished levels of youth unemployment, as the government could now plausibly argue that a training place was available for all school-leavers who were not in employment or full-time education (ibid).

More radical reforms were still to come, however, as the February 1988 White Paper *Training for Employment* stated: '. . . the changing circumstances of the youth labour market require the scope and role of YTS to be kept under review' (DE, 1988, para 6.12). A formal Youth Training Group was set up within the TA to conduct this review under the chairmanship of the new Training Agency Director, Roger Dawe. The confidential report of this Group, completed in May 1989, concluded that YTS should be replaced by a new 'model', called 'Youth Training' (YT). Among the areas where YTS was perceived to be inadequate were:

> the levels of qualifications gained, attractiveness to employers and young people where the labour market is tightening, providing quality training for 17-year-old leavers, increasing the volume of higher skill training, and catering for the needs of small and medium sized enterprises (TA, 1989, 6).

The report in effect acknowledged that YTS had never been able to overcome its low status as a programme for the unemployed, leaving 360,000 16 and 17 year olds in employment with no real training (ibid).

The report outlined the twin objectives of improving the quality and quantity of youth training — as measured in the number of school leavers, particularly those in employment, receiving training and the percentage of those achieving higher-level qualifications — while decreasing the Exchequer's expenditure from YTS levels. In order to accomplish these seemingly conflicting objectives it proposed 'to make the "market" in training work better' (ibid, 7). The new Youth Training 'model' — it lacked the detail of a typical MSC 'scheme' — relied on demographic decline to act as a lever for altering the behaviour of employers and individuals. Following CBI recommendations (CBI, 1989), the government was to phase out paying an allowance for trainees under the rationale that in increasingly tight labour markets employers would be competing to take on young people. The YT budget would then be used to give managers an incentive to provide quality training for their young employees by giving a grant for every young person that achieved a recognised qualification.

Michael Howard, who succeeded Fowler as Secretary of State for Employment took this 'market model' for youth training one step further in 1990 when he announced the launch of 11 local pilot programmes to test the other major element of the CBI's proposals: the 'individual training credit' or voucher (CBI, 1989, 33). The idea, similar to the logic underlying the proposals for vouchers in the compulsory education system, was to make individuals more demanding consumers of training while encouraging competition among the providers by giving 16 year olds a credit to cover the costs of training up to at least NVQ Level II (see Unwin, this volume for more detail). They could redeem this voucher wherever they chose — with an employer or in an FE college. 'With an individual credit', argued the CBI (ibid), 'young people would, for the first time, have consciously to choose not to enhance their skills.' The credit concept is to be extended nationally by 1996 (DE, DES, 1991).

**Increased institutional responsiveness**

Just as the 1988 Education Reform Act created incentives for schools to compete for students in the new educational marketplace — through measures such as local management of schools (LMS) and opting out — so too the government is encouraging colleges to become more responsive to the needs of the newly empowered post-16 consumers by giving these institutions independent status effective in 1993. The decision to remove sixth-form colleges, as well as tertiary colleges and colleges of further education, from local authority control was announced in the May 1991 White Paper, *Education and Training for the 21st Century* (DE, DES, 1991) and came as a surprise to many in the education sector. All of the colleges will receive resources directly from a new FE Funding Council headed by William Stubbs, who seems likely to apply a version of the successful funding formula he devised in creating incentives for polytechnics to recruit record numbers of students (Stubbs, 1992).

**Increased employer power**

The third, and perhaps most dramatic element in the move towards a post-16 marketplace was the decision to transfer the control of the state's £2.5 billion in training programme from the national Training Agency (formerly the Manpower Services Commission) to a group of new, local employer-led Training and Enterprise Councils (TECs). The network of 82 TECs and 20 Local Enterprise Companies (LECs) in Scotland, with budgets ranging from £5–50 million, replaced the TA's Area Manpower Boards (AMBs), the relatively weak tripartite organisations that had held nominal responsibility for overseeing the operation of TA programmes (see King and Schnack, 1990). The TECs were presented as 'a locally-based system . . . a rare opportunity to restructure, from ground up, the nation's approach to job growth and human development, to enterprise and training' (Department of Employment, 1989, 3,4).

The inspiration for TECs came from US Private Industry Councils (PICs) and the German chambers of commerce (Bailey, 1993). The TEC proposals took the principle of devolving control over government initiatives to the private sector far further than was attempted through PICs in the US, however. Virtually all of national training budget was delegated to the Councils, although roughly 90 per cent of their funds were specifically earmarked for YT and Employment Training. The powers given to the employers on TECs were an attempt by government to attract the leaders of the local business community on to the Councils — only chief executives or managing directors are able to become board members — a factor that was seen as critical in the more successful PICs (Stratton, 1989, 22).

The TECs are the most recent in a series of efforts by the Thatcher Government to mobilise local employers to play a greater role in the ET field. Earlier experiments — such as Local Collaborative Projects and Local Employer Networks — had largely failed to strengthen the relatively weak chambers of commerce (Leadbeater, 1987, II.I), although some of these groups were to serve as the core of the new TECs. While the TECs have far greater resources and a much higher profile than their precursors, they are in keeping with the Thatcher Government's general desire to return to Britain's voluntarist training tradition.

The TECs also further the government's aim of reducing the size of the state sector. The staff of the TA's Area Offices — around 3000 civil servants — were seconded to the TECs for three years, after which only a small percentage were expected to return to the government (Clement, 1991b, 7). This phased reduction in the size of the TA could have been even more abrupt if Fowler had had his way, according to one TA official:

> Whereas the Secretary of State might have preferred to set up TECs with new personnel, which would then have absorbed functions from existing TA Area Offices, senior civil servants modified this approach (Shepherd, 1990, 5).

**Performance indicators**

The system that TECs are to oversee is to be outcome, rather than input-driven (DE, 1990). The government is gradually removing the criteria for the delivery of training (e.g. where it should take place or how long it should be); in their place, the government has endorsed the CBI's set of National Education and Training Targets, taking the attainment of qualifications as evidence that individuals have acquired the desired level of competence. The Conservatives have also decided that there should be a single currency for the whole system, mandating that all vocational qualifications should conform to the National Vocational Qualifications framework (DES, DE, 1991). As with the National Curriculum, NVQs serve as an example of the Thatcher government's 'paradoxical project' — a centralisation of power to remedy market failure that later enables the state to play a less interventionist role, by reducing the monitoring of training provision (Hall, 1986; Finegold, 1992a).

## The danger of market failure

While it is still too early to assess the effectiveness of the government's post-16 reforms, each element in the 'market analogue' approach suffers from serious deficiencies, which will be reviewed in the following sections. In addition, fundamental weaknesses in the national ET policy-making process raise major questions about the capacity of Britain to break out of the low-skill equilibrium.

**Credits — where to spend them**

As Unwin (this volume) observes, the first round of training credit pilots has been beset by problems, most notably poor timing. The blueprint for training credits was drawn up by the CBI in 1988 at a time when the economy was booming and 'the demographic time bomb' was the dominant issue; young people were in short supply and armed with vouchers, they would, in theory, be in a position to choose the job which offered the best training. By the time credits were introduced, however, the bomb had been defused by the recession, and it was jobs that were scarce, diminishing the opportunities for young people to use their credits. Other factors which helped account for the failure of credits to empower individuals, evident from the low low take-up rate in most pilot areas, were: the fact that credits, with few exceptions, were confined only to school leavers, thereby perpetuating the artificial divide between full and part-time study and the image of failure that dogged YTS; along with the inability of the credit mechanism to alter the traditional modes of delivery in colleges and private training providers (Howells, 1992). These difficulties were compounded by the government, which gave the pilots inadequate time to develop their schemes. This error is in danger of being repeated as the national extension of the initiative was announced before the results of the first pilot were known, and the second round pilots were obliged to begin their planning without the benefit of the extensive evaluations conducted on the first round schemes (ibid).

**Independent institutions — fighting for fewer students**

While freeing schools and colleges to compete in the marketplace for the diminishing number of 16 and 17 year olds may succeed in increasing the percentage of young people who remain in post-compulsory education, it is not clear that it will have a positive impact on the quality of provision. The independence of colleges and ability of schools to opt out of local authority control has not only made it difficult to remove the excess capacity in the system caused by falling roles, but it has also jeopardised those developments that seem most able to deliver the government's aims of 'bridging the academic and vocational divide' and creating 'parity of esteem' between A levels and the new General NVQs (DES, DE, 1991). The consortia of schools and colleges set up under the Technical and Vocational Education Initiative (TVEI) are under a double threat, as the Initiative's funds begin to run out in 1993 and some schools that remain within an LEA are reluctant to co-operate with others that have gone for grant-maintained status or colleges which are offering a large array of A levels. Likewise, local plans to establish tertiary colleges or tertiary systems that offer young people the widest mix of academic and vocational routes are virtually impossible to implement in the new environment.

**TECs — toothless tigers?**

The problems surrounding TECs constitute the third major weakness with the government's market model. Company chairmen were attracted onto TECs by the promise of substantial resources which they could use to create a high-skill local economy. What they actually received were budgets — cut by up to 25 per cent in the first year— most of which were earmarked to train the unemployed and least qualified young people. In addition, TECs have not been equipped with the tools necessary to tranform the incentives to train. Unlike German or French chambers of commerce, they do not represent all the employers in their areas, and may have difficulty addressing the concerns of small firms. And they lack either the carrot of large discretionary funds or the stick of a training levy to sanction those companies who fail to pay for their share of education and training costs.

One positive, though unintended, consequence of TECs is the creation of a potentially powerful new lobby in favour of greater expenditure on training (Peck, 1991). With unemployment rising sharply, the government can ill afford to have its main vehicle for training the jobless fail and this gives the TECs a strong lever to bargain for extra funds and freedom. Though there are signs that TECs are beginning to use this power, thus far they do not appear to have had much influence on national policy. If they should become an effective lobbying group, however, the government could be placed in a quandary: if TECs are given the greater budgetary and staffing freedom they desire, then the already serious concerns of the Treasury over accountability — entrusting public money to non-elected, non-representative private companies — would be magnified (Bailey, 1993); however, if TECs' remit is not broadened then the government faces the political embarrassment of losing the commitment of hundreds of employers to the education and training system.

## NVQs — uncertain outcomes

Another problem with the market model is that the outcome which drives the whole system — NVQs — is not, at least at present, up to the task. Already several years behind schedule, the industry lead bodies responsible for drawing up these new qualifications have been given the near impossible task of reconciling the low existing skill requirements of British employers with the education and training needs of 16 to 19 year olds for the next century. In retailing, for example, one company estimated that the additional cost of preparing its new workers for an NVQ level 2 was less than £30. It had no interest in training them to take the next step up the qualification ladder, however, because broader vocational training wasn't needed for the jobs on offer and employees who obtained the qualification were seen to be more likely to leave the firm.

By creating new general NVQs the government hopes to give vocational qualifications equal status with A levels by embracing them all under a single 'advanced diploma' (see Jessup, this volume). But while the White Paper *Education and Training for the 21st Century* (DES, DE, 1991) adopts the rhetoric of 'a fully-integrated education and training system', first proposed in the IPPR's *A British Baccalauréat* (Finegold et al., 1990), it offers no substantive measures for bridging the academic-vocational divide. On the contrary, the government's moves to restrict coursework in A levels, along with the way in which GNVQs appear to be developing, may make it more difficult to carry forward the many local efforts to create common modular frameworks (see Morris, Burgess, Rainbow, this volume). If instead, GNVQs are an attempt to create a separate, but equal track to A levels, then, as Huddleston's study (this volume) makes clear, large amounts of additional resources will be required to transform the organisation of institutions and prepare college staff and employers for the new forms of teaching and assessment entailed in the competence-based approach to teaching and learning. Even then, so long as A levels remain intact, offering the best qualified 16 year olds the clearest route to higher education and rewarding jobs, vocational qualifications are likely to continue to be perceived as second best.

## Tensions in the national ET policy process

Perhaps the largest obstacle which the reforms face has been created by the government itself through its failure to define a clear strategy and set of objectives for the post-16 system; instead, there are at least four separate aims of government policy (Stubbs, 1992; DE, 1989; DES; DE; 1991):

1.  to increase staying-on rates in full-time education;
2.  to meet the CBI's national education and training targets;
3.  to deliver the 'guarantee' of a training place to all 16 and 17 year old school-leavers;
4.  to reduce the state's share of ET expenditure.

While it might appear that at least the first three of these objectives are compatible, in practice they come into conflict at the local level. One tension has already been referred to — the pressure on schools to retain sixth-formers (goal 1), which may not offer the individuals the most desirable or efficient means to improve their qualifications (goal 2). Likewise, the pressure to generate the quantity of training places necessary to deliver the guarantee has taken precedence over the grand mission of creating a high-quality, high-skill economy which had been used to lure chief executives on to the TEC boards. This conflict has been reflected in the TECs' budgets, which are predominantly tied to the delivery of training programmes for the low-skilled or unemployed. The problem was magnified by the large cuts in state funding for training programmes in each of the TECs' first three annual budgets at a time when the recession was increasing the demand for places (Clement, 1991a).

These budget cuts are symptomatic of a major defect in the British ET policy process: its short-term orientation. This short-termism was reinforced during the 1980s by the close association between training and unemployment and the Prime Minister's practice of rapidly rotating ministers, with each new Secretary of State striving to make his mark with a new set of initiatives. The result was that in the first two terms of the Thatcher Government 25 new employment and training initiatives were launched and 22 were cancelled, leading to a severe case of reform overload at the local level that has not subsided with the change of leadership.

On the contrary, there is a risk that the tensions within the government's post-16 policies will be magnified as the FE Funding Council comes into operation. Based on the early statements of the FEFC's Director (Stubbs, 1992), it appears that the government will be running two contradictory reform strategies in tandem — the Department of Education using the FEFC to oversee a centrally administered funding system, where colleges are rewarded for increasing student numbers (inputs), alongside the Department of Employment's attempts to put into place a locally-driven, output-related funding mechanism for TECs (Finegold, 1992b).

This seemingly irrational situation is the product of a second major weakness in the policy-making structure — the absence of co-ordination of education, training and labour market policy either within or between departments. Britain stands alone among the main European nations for its failure to establish a well-financed, independent organisation that is able to develop and evaluate policy in this rapidly changing field.

If Britain is to build on the recent improvements in staying-on rates and break out of the low-skill equilibrium then the government must, as a first step, develop a single, coherent national policy structure focused on the needs of all 16 to 19 year olds.

# References

Bailey, T. (1993) 'The Mission of TECs and Private Sector Involvement in Training,' in Finegold et al. (eds), *Something Borrowed, Something Blue?*, Oxford, Triangle Books.

Barnett, C. (1986) *The Audit of War*, London, Macmillan.

Campbell, A. and Warner, M. (1991) 'Training Strategies and Micro-Electronics in the Engineering Industries of the UK and Germany,' in Ryan, P. (ed), *International Comparisions of Vocational Education and Training for Intermediate Skills*, London, Falmer.

Clement, B. (1991a) 'Link Between TECs and Government Breaking Down', *The Independent*, 9 July, p.4.

Clement, B. (1991b) 'Training Councils Staff Set to Strike', *The Independent*, 3 December, p.7.

Confederation of British Industry (CBI) (1989) *Towards a Skills Revolution*, London, CBI.

DES, DE et al. (1991) *Education and Training for the 21st Century*, London, HMSO, Cmnd 1536.

DE (1988) *Training for Employement*, London, HMSO, Cmnd 316, February.

DE (1989) *TECs: A Prospectus for the 1990s*, London, DE.

Finegold, D. (1992a); The Low-Skill Equilibrium: An Institutional Analysis of Britain's Education and Training Failure; unpublished D. Phil. theme University of Oxford.

Finegold, D. (1992b) 'TECs and Education', Unpublished report for the National Training Task Force, June.

Finegold, D. (1992c) *The Low-Skill Equilibrium*, National Commission on Education Briefing Paper No. 5.

Finegold et al, (1990) *A British Baccaularéat*, London, Institute for Public Policy Research.

Finegold, D. and Soskice, D. (1988) 'The Failure of Training in Britain: Analysis and Prescription', *Oxford Review of Economic Policy*, 2, 2.

Freedland, M. (1988) 'The Education Reform Bill 1987', paper presented at Law/Labour Relations Seminar, Oxford University, 18 January.

Hall, P. (1986) *Governing the Economy*, Oxford, Polity Press.

Howells, D. (1992) 'Training Credits', Background Paper for Training Credits Workshop, Birmingham 10–11 June.

Jesson, and Gray, J. (1991) *Boosting Post-16 Participation in England and Wales*, QQSE Research Group, Sheffield University, May.

Keep, E. and Mayhew, K. (1992) 'Missing: Presumed Skilled', paper presented at LSE Centre for Economic Performance, 10 March.

Leadbeater, C. (1988) 'Employer Networks Need Further Cash for Survival', *Financial Times* 5 April, p.12.

Peck, J. (1991) 'The Politics of Training in Britain', *Capital and Class*, 44, Summer, pp. 23–34.

Porter, M. (1990) *The Competitive Advantage of Nations*, London, Macmillan.

Raffe, D. (1992) *Participation of 16–18 Year Olds in Education and Training*, NCE Briefing Paper No.3, May.

Shepherd, W. (1990) 'Perspectives on TECs', paper presented at VET Forum Seminar, University of Warwick, June.

Steedman, H. et al., (1991) 'Intermediate Skill in the Workplace', *National Institute Economic Review*, May, pp. 60–76.

Stratton, C. (1989) 'TECs and PICs', in Bennett, B. (ed), *TECs and Vocational Education and Training*, LSE, Department of Geography.

Stubbs, W. (1992) 'The FEFC and TECs', talk at the Training Credits Workshop, Birmingham, 10–11 June.

Training Agency (1989) 'Review of the Youth Training Scheme and Proposals for Youth Training', [internal report], Sheffield, TA, May.

Wiener, M. (1989) *English Culture and the Decline of the Industrial Spirit*, Cambridge, Cambridge University Press.

Wintour, P. (1987) 'No Benefit for Jobless Youths Who Refuse YTS', *The Guardian*, 23 June, p.36.

# 3 The changing Scottish scene: implications for south of the border

## David Raffe

## Introduction

The English have rediscovered Scotland. In the last few years debates on 'British' or English and Welsh post-compulsory education have displayed a renewed awareness that things are organised differently north of the Border, and that England and Wales may have something to learn from Scotland. This awareness is reflected in press reports, in radio and television documentaries, in reports such as *A British Baccalauréat* (IPPR 1990), *Beyond GCSE* (RS 1991) and *Learning Pays* (Ball 1991), in Sir Claus Moser's 1990 speech to the British Association and in the current work of the National Commission on Education.

There is a strong case for England and Wales seeking to learn from Scotland. The differences in education and training systems, and in their social, labour-market, economic and political contexts, are smaller than in the case of overseas comparisons; where institutional differences exist it is easier to infer their effects from comparative study because the 'other things' are more nearly 'equal' (Raffe, 1991). But there are dangers. Too often international comparisons are simply dredged for evidence to support preconceived ideas (Keep, 1991, Goodman, 1992); comparisons with Scotland are probably no exception. Moreover, the level of knowledge of the Scottish system among educationists south of the border is generally low; when

Scotland is held up as an example to England and Wales it is often a stereotyped and inaccurate view of Scotland that is presented.

If any useful lessons are to be learnt from the comparison, Scotland must be more than a distorting mirror for English prejudices; the Scottish system, and Scottish debates, must be understood in their own terms. In the next section of this chapter, The Scottish system: an overview, I briefly describe the system. In the section on themes in 16–18s debates in Scotland I summarise some of the main themes of current debates about post-compulsory education in Scotland. In the next section, Current reform proposals, I describe recent policy initiatives or proposals, including the Howie Report (SOED, 1992) on upper secondary education, published in March 1992. Finally, in the last section I suggest some implications for England and Wales.

## The Scottish system: an overview

### The 'mixed model': institutions and government

Post-compulsory education and training in Scotland, as elsewhere in the UK, is provided through what the OECD (1985) has termed a 'mixed model'. That is, the full-time sector is small and narrow in scope, compared with other OECD countries, but it is complemented by a more diverse and informal sector of part-time and work-based education and training.

The mixed model presents Scottish 16 year olds with the same four main choices as their peers south of the border: to study full-time in further education (FE); to study full-time at school; to enter part-time or work-based training, most of which is employer-led and supported by Youth Training or Training Credits; or to leave education and training (see Figure 3.1). However, there are differences. Scotland lacks the institutional diversity of English post-compulsory education, and Sixth Form Colleges and Tertiary Colleges are almost unknown. Few enter full-time FE at 16, and those who do so study a narrower, more exclusively vocational range of courses. The vast majority of 16 year olds who continue full-time education in Scotland stay at the same school; in England and Wales the proportion is less than a half. Consortia of schools and colleges working together to deliver post-compulsory curriculum in partnership have been more widespread in Scotland than in most parts of England and Wales.

The mixed model is also reflected in the separate government of education and of training, respectively through education and employment departments of central government, and locally through education authorities (EAs) and local enterprise companies (LECs, analogous to TECs in England and Wales). However in Scotland this separation has had an additional national dimension. Education has been administered by the Scottish Office Education Department (SOED), while training policy has been made at a Great Britain level by the Employment Department or its agencies. Especially during the 1980s, Scottish education policy was preoccupied by the need to accommodate 'British' training policies designed for English circumstances and in response to English problems (Raffe, 1991). In principle this has changed since 1990, when responsibility for training in Scotland passed to a new body, Scottish Enterprise (together with Highlands and Islands Enterprise). However so far Scottish Enterprise has shown little interest either in reforming the structure of education and training or in developing national training initiatives independently of the broader British framework (Scottish Enterprise, 1991). The Scottish White Paper *Access and Opportunity*, published in May 1991, showed few signs of an emerging distinctive Scottish training strategy (Scottish Office, 1991: see current reform proposals section below). Most of its proposals were borrowed from the White Paper for England and Wales published at the same time; the influence of Scottish Enterprise was conspicuously absent. The date of publication of the White Paper reflected an English timetable not a Scottish one; seven months from the expected submission of the Howie Report was an absurd time to propose further changes which would either pre-empt Howie's proposals or would need to be changed to accommodate them.

**Courses and qualifications**

Further differences appear in respect of the courses taken. Most full-time FE students in this age group study programmes of National Certificate (NC) modules. About half of YTS trainees took NC modules (the proportion is probably higher under YT with its 'output-related' funding, although figures are scarce). A majority of post-compulsory school students take some NC modules, usually alongside academic courses. The NC was introduced in 1984; all non-advanced vocational courses were replaced by a single national framework of (notionally) 40-hour modules, designed to a standard specification, assessed by a single certificate. The NC accompanied reforms of curriculum, pedagogy and assessment, intended primarily to revitalise FE, although modules are also available at school and increasingly at private training centres. The NC was a response to the problems of coherence inherent in the mixed model. It rationalised vocational qualifications, provided a standard framework for pedagogy and assessment and provided lines of progression for students who could take modules in a variety of different institutions and by different modes or methods of study. It also enabled the SOED to maintain a degree of control over schemes such as TVEI and YTS controlled from south of the border. Modules are criterion-referenced and specified primarily in terms of learning outcomes; they are individually assessed and certificated. Initially programmes or groups of modules received no formal recognition except in respect of the individual modules. Group awards, most significantly Scottish Vocational Qualifications (SVQs), were introduced in 1990. SVQs are directly equivalent to NVQs south of the border; they must incorporate occupational standards specified by industry lead bodies, their assessment should reflect the conditions of the workplace, and they are composed of modules or units. Many SVQs are composed of NC modules, but they may also be based on separate workplace-assessed units and/or Higher National Units (the components of modular HNDs).

The post-compulsory stages of secondary school are the fifth and sixth years (S5 and S6). However for the first term of each session S5 also includes 'winter leavers', about one in seven of each year group, who are too young to leave after S4 but who leave at the first opportunity in the December of S5. Their curriculum tends to be dominated by NC modules, which can be combined to make short programmes leading to national certification.

**Figure 3.1:** Post-compulsory education and training in Scotland

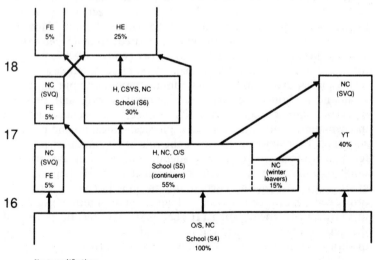

Key to qualifications

| | | | |
|---|---|---|---|
| H | Higher grade | O/S | Ordinary or Standard grade |
| CSYS | Certificate of Sixth Year Studies | NC | National Certificate (modules) |
| SVQ | Scottish Vocational Qualification | | |

Note: Percentages approximate (see text for discussion of participation rates).

Nearly six in ten of each year group are 'S5 continuers', who stay on voluntarily to the end of S5 or beyond. At least informally, their curriculum is modular, with a variety of types of courses, mostly short but some flexible in duration, which can be taken in various combinations (Croxford, Howieson and Raffe 1991a). At the centre of this system is the Higher, traditionally a one-year course, and the main entrance qualification for higher education. A 'high-flying' student might take four or five Highers subjects in S5. However many S5 continuers — 54 per cent in 1988/9 — attempt fewer than four Highers in S5, and the proportion doing so is increasing with the growing number of 'less academic' students in S5, and with the trend for schools to offer the Higher as a two-year option for students who do not achieve the highest grades at Standard grade in S4. Other courses attempted by S5 continuers include Ordinary and Standard grade and NC modules. Ordinary and Standard grades are the nearest equivalents to O level and GCSE respectively, and are attempted for the first time in S4. However they have dominated the curriculum of many S5 students, especially the less academic, although they are now declining in importance in S5. Standard grade, which has been phased in to replace Ordinary grade, is a more process-based course which is less suited either to re-sits or to crash courses in S5, and students are increasingly pressed to take NC modules instead.

The growth of NC participation in schools, especially in S5, has been one of the striking developments in recent years. The NC was designed primarily for FE, although it was expected to provide a useful basis for the curriculum of S5 winter leavers. However participation among S5 continuers also soared, from 15 per cent in 1984/5, the first year of the NC, to 51 per cent in 1988/9, with the trend still strongly upward. The main NC subjects at school are in the technological area (business and administration, computing, home economics, engineering, built environment, caring and personal services). Other significant NC subjects at school include mathematics, communication, arts, physical education and personal and social development. However the role of NC modules at school tends to be secondary to that of academic courses. They are variously used to fill gaps in a curriculum dominated by Highers (or O/S grades), to broaden the curriculum, to add 'interest' courses, to provide alternative certification to Highers or an intermediate target in S5 for those contemplating a Higher in S6, or to certificate areas of the curriculum (such as physical or religious education) for which qualifications had not previously been awarded (Croxford, Howieson and Raffe, 1991a).

About half the continuers — around three in ten of each year group — leave at the end of S5. A small but symbolically important minority (some one in twenty of each year group) enters higher education directly from S5. The other leavers variously enter YT, employment or FE. Most of those who stay on to S6 plan to enter higher education. In S6 they may study combinations of Highers (whether new subjects, re-sits, or subjects studied over two years), NC modules (typically in subjects such as computing or typing which might be useful in higher education), or Certificate of Sixth Year Studies courses (pre-university courses to permit greater depth of study and to develop habits of individual learning).

## Participation

Scotland is widely perceived in England and Wales to have higher rates of full-time participation. At first glance the differences may appear striking. In 1990 70 per cent of maintained school students entered S5 (SOED, 1992, Table A1); allowing for independent schools would bring this figure to 71 per cent. By contrast, of the English age group eligible to leave school in 1989, only 35 per cent were at school in January 1990 (DES, 1991). Similar figures have frequently been used in the media, or by protagonists in English debates, to convey an impression of Scottish superiority. But they are misleading. Scottish participation appears less impressive when we take account of four factors.

First, the 71 per cent figure includes under-age pupils for whom compulsory schooling continues to the December of S5; the 'voluntary' staying-on rate which excludes those who leave in December (the winter leavers) is only 58 per cent. Second, only about 5–8 per cent of each year group in Scotland enters full-time FE after S4 (precise estimates vary), compared with 18 per cent of 16 year olds in England; including full-time FE further narrows the gap, to about 63–66 per cent against 53 per cent. Third, Scottish and English year groups cover different age ranges. While Scottish S4 is the nearest equivalent to English fifth year, Scottish S4 pupils are some six months younger on average than English fifth-year pupils. The comparisons described above are based on young people at comparable stages, but whose average ages differ; age-based comparisons would show *lower* participation at 16-plus in Scotland than in England and Wales. On the other hand, comparisons based on stage may be more appropriate, since participation is only of value in relation to the levels of attainment that are reached. Fourth, the Scottish advantage at the S5 (or equivalent) stage tends to disappear at the S6 stage. Thirty per cent of the year group entered S6 in 1990; together with full-time further or higher education this yields a Scottish participation rate of some 38 per cent at this stage, compared with 38 per cent of 17 year olds in England in January 1990.

Full-time participation at '18' — the post-S6 stage — tends to be much higher than in England. This largely reflects the higher proportion of young Scots entering full-time HE (25 per cent in 1989/90, compared with 17 per cent in Britain as a whole). This in turn may reflect the fact that many more stayers-on in Scotland take 'mainstream' school courses which lead to higher education. More than four in ten young people take Highers while only a quarter attempt A level south of the Border.

Forty-five per cent of a recent cohort entered YTS, although some of these stayed on it only briefly. Comparable figures for YT are not available, but would probably show a decline in participation. As in England and Wales, only a few young workers in non-YT jobs receive significant amounts of part-time education or training, and they tend to be well-qualified males in particular industries such as engineering (Croxford, Howieson and Raffe, 1991b).

## Themes in 16–18s debates in Scotland

In current Scottish debates about 16–18s education and training one finds themes that are essentially UK-wide (notably the need for skills to support economic regeneration) and themes that are more specifically Scottish. The latter were given new focus in March 1990 when the Howie Committee was appointed to review courses, assessment and certification in S5 and S6. However the blend of UK and Scottish themes in educational debates is complicated by the fact that Scottishness is itself a theme. In Howie's own words:

> 'One of the key questions in our letter requesting evidence [to the Committee] concerned the importance of comparability of Scottish qualifications with those of (a) England, and (b) Europe. The answers were very revealing of Scottish attitudes: roughly speaking they could be described as: (a) not at all and (b) very important.' (Howie, 1991 p.2).

That said, the polarisation which characterises English debates (essentially around the maintenance, reform or abolition of the A level) is strikingly absent. Scotland is closer to a consensus on educational policy, or at least on its broad objectives, and fewer people react to policy suggestions on predetermined political lines. However while participants in educational debates in Scotland can not easily be divided into conservatives and radicals, it is possible to identify *arguments* that are respectively for and against the *status quo*.

## Arguments in favour of the *status quo*

At least five arguments have been used in defence of the existing system:

1.  Participation
    The higher participation in Scotland (in terms of stages) is attributed to the availability of a certificated exit point at 17, and to the greater 'modularity' of Scottish courses. Compared with England, it is easier for stayers-on in Scotland to keep their options open, to remain in touch with the academic mainstream and to pursue short-term targets. Howie is known to be sceptical about comparisons with England, since compared with almost any other European country Scottish participation is low. However the point of the comparison with England is not to provide yardsticks, but to identify features of the education system that may encourage participation; the comparison with England 'controls' for social and labour-market contexts, and suggests that participation is promoted by the more open structure of Scottish courses.

2.  Weaker academic–vocational boundary
    The Scottish system encourages more mixing of academic and vocational courses by 16 to 18 year olds, either concurrently (combining Highers and NC modules at school) or over time (many students take one largely academic post-compulsory year at school before entering vocational education or training). In this respect Scotland is distinct from most other European systems, not just from England. However academic and vocational courses do not mix on equal terms (see below); this argument tends to be used, not to defend the *status quo* as such, but rather to identify strengths of the present system on which reforms should build (for example, that they should build on existing modularity to develop a more integrated system).

3.  'If it works, don't fix it'
    Business interests, and many educationists, are concerned about the disorientation and confusion that would accompany further radical reforms, especially following so soon after reforms of 14–16 courses (Standard grade) and of 16-plus vocational education (the NC).

4.  The strengths of the NC
    Any radical reform, and particularly one which limited the 'modularity' of the academic courses with which NC modules dovetail, could have adverse effects on the NC, both at school and in college or YT (through knock-on effects on participation and

progression). The NC is seen to have provided much-needed coherence in vocational education; it is generally popular among students and employers (although it still suffers from insufficient employer awareness and recognition); and any 'bittiness' in the modular curriculum could be corrected through more incremental reforms (such as 'clusters' and general SVQs — see last section, below).

5.  The four-year degree
    This argument is none the less powerful for being largely tacit. It is feared that reform of school courses, and especially a lengthening of the Higher to two years and a removal of the exit point at 17, would undermine the case for four-year honours degree courses. Were the issue resolved on purely educational grounds Scotland would have little to fear. Most European systems have degree courses of four years (or longer) following secondary school courses which extend at least to 18 years; the aberrant English case reflects the extreme specialisation of A levels, which no one proposes to copy. However Scots fear that a Treasury intent on cutting spending might take a narrower, more anglocentric view.

**Arguments for change**

We can also identify at least five arguments for change.

1.  Content and pedagogy of Highers: the 'two-term dash'
    The one-year Higher often involves just two terms of teaching; this restricts curriculum coverage and imposes a teacher-led, 'pressure-cooker' pedagogy which offers little time for independent learning or more open-ended forms of study. These weaknesses particularly affect students who go on to higher education, where they may find themselves less prepared than A-level-qualified students either for the content of degree courses or for the methods of study. While many of these courses could be criticised for pitching their expectations in terms of A-level specialists from the south, the standards reached in most secondary school courses in Scotland are lower than in the corresponding school courses in most other European countries.
2.  Coverage and choice in the school curriculum
    Despite the Scottish reputation for breadth, the curriculum of most S5 and S6 students is relatively narrow. Even students taking five Highers cover a narrower range of subjects than their continental counterparts; and most students take fewer than five Highers. The range of NC modules offered by schools, and the choices of modules made by students, are perceived to lack

coherence or educational justification. They are too dependent on availability of staff and resources within schools, on poorly guided student choices and on the constraints and exigencies of timetabling. The problem is aggravated by the secondary role of the NC in schools, typically to 'fill gaps' in a curriculum dominated by academic courses.

3.  The low success rate of 'less academic' stayers-on
    More than half of students completing S5 achieve one Higher or less (SOED 1992, Figure 3.7). While this partly reflects the wide range in the number of Highers attempted in S5, it also reflects the very low success rates among students attempting just one or two Highers. Paradoxically, these include many of the same students whose participation may have been encouraged by the greater accessibility of the Higher and its availability as a one-year course. The Howie Committee identified an 'uneven gradient of difficulty throughout school education', with the Higher representing too big a step after S4 for 'less academic' students. However the Committee's analysis largely overlooked the increasing tendency for such students to take Highers over two years, and it totally ignored Ordinary or Standard grade presentations in S5 (still a very substantial phenomenon during the period covered by the Committee's data). On the other hand it correctly identified a problem of low completion rates for NC modules in S5, which may partly reflect their low status within schools (see below and Croxford et al., 1991a, 1991b).

4.  Academic/vocational divisions
    While there is more mixing of academic and vocational courses in Scottish schools than in most other systems, they do not mix on equal terms. Academic courses have higher status, and the sharp contrast between Highers and NC in pedagogy, assessment and certification reinforces the differences. The 'mixing' of academic and vocational courses may even accentuate the low status of the latter; most young people gain their first taste of vocational education in a context where its low status is underlined by the juxtaposition with academic courses. The failure in 1984 to include Highers in the modular reform limited the ability of the NC framework to impose coherence on the system. Underlying this argument for change is a broader criticism of the 'mixed model'.

5.  Quality and quantity of youth training
    Youth Training and other employer-based training are criticised, as elsewhere in Britain, for their narrowness, for focusing too much on employers' own and immediate needs, for providing few opportunities and inducements to progression, and for being variable in quantity and quality. Until recently Scotland, with an

education-led system of modules in place, was less vulnerable to these criticisms than England and Wales. However occupational standards are now set by the same lead bodies as in the rest of the UK; although many SVQs are comprised of NC modules, and therefore already part of a more coherent national system, it is difficult for SVQs to be radically 'broader' or different in approach from NVQs.

**A consensus?**

As might be expected, these criticisms do not point consistently towards a single direction of policy change. Nevertheless an analysis of submissions to the Howie Commission from 25 key bodies suggested that

> there is a widespread consensus on the key issues. In particular, there is virtually unanimous support for a system that retains a fifth-year exit point, and a substantial majority wants the certification available at the end of sixth year also to be available at the end of fifth year. Many submissions stress the importance of the one-plus-one structure to the higher levels of participation that Scotland enjoys. The other major point of agreement amongst submissions is that a reformed system should endeavour in some way to combine vocational and academic elements within a single system of assessment, and not in the type of two-track solution that government policy envisaged for England and Wales. Many suggest that this could best be achieved through modularisation of the remaining (school) parts of non-advanced post-compulsory education, though such modules would not necessarily follow Scotvec National Certificate modules in their time allocations or in their use of criterion-referenced internal assessment (McPherson, 1992 pp. 126–27).

# Current reform proposals

## Access and opportunity

*Access and Opportunity* (Scottish Office, 1991). This White Paper was published in May 1991. Its main proposals affecting 16–18s were:

–   **The nationalisation of FE**. FE colleges are to be removed from local authority control and given self-governing status under the Scottish Office. (In contrast to English colleges, Scottish colleges will have no FE Funding Council as a buffer, but the Secretary of State has powers to create such a body when appropriate.) Scottish opinion on the change is mixed, but the local co-ordination of 16–18 provision is likely to suffer. The effect may be greater in Scotland than south of the border, because more young people move between school and college during the post-compulsory stage, and because there is a stronger tradition of school-college co-operation. Such co-operation will become even more important if the Howie proposals (see below) are implemented.

– **Training credits**. As in England and Wales, these are to be extended to all of Scotland by 1996. However they will be restricted to 16 and 17 year old school leavers. The first Scottish pilot (in Grampian) made credits available to 18 year old leavers as well, on the grounds that this accorded better with Scottish participation patterns and provided less disincentive to staying on.

– **General SVQs**. These are to be introduced in 1992, on similar lines to general NVQs. They are aimed primarily at full-time students, and are intended to provide progression links with higher education as well as with occupation-specific SVQs. A more recent consultative paper has proposed that GSVQs at levels 2 and 3 be developed in five occupational areas, and that they should incorporate core skills, require 12 credits (modules) for each award, have core and optional modules, and be based largely on existing Scotvec provision (Scotvec, 1991). GSVQs respond to problems that Scotland shares with England, notably the weak structural position of broad-based vocational education; but the solution — of creating yet another stream — is a characteristically English one.

### Clusters of modules

The Scottish Consultative Committee on the Curriculum is developing 'clusters' of three modules, equivalent in length to a Higher, for school pupils. This is in response to the frequent fragmentation and incoherence of the NC in schools. Details have not been published at the time of writing, but it is expected that the clusters will be at an intermediate level between Standard grade and Higher, and that some of them will be convertible to GSVQs by adding further modules.

### The Howie Report

The Howie Report was published in March 1992. It rejected an integrated modular solution, as some submissions had advocated:

> The needs of school students are far more homogeneous than are those of adults and, being generally free from employment and

domestic commitments, students have less need for flexible
access systems. (SOED, 1992 para 5.19)

In a meeting at Edinburgh University, after the report was published,
Howie said that an entirely modular system 'would have been feasible'
but was rejected for one fundamental reason: that 'modularity does
not sit easily with external assessment'.

The report described the existing system as 'excessively' flexible
(*ibid*. para 4.28). The 'current system . . . in which all S5/S6 students
are on a common pathway dominated by Highers', should be
replaced. In trying to find a single pathway for all, we provide a
satisfactory pathway for very few' (*ibid*. para 5.3). The Howie
Committee proposed a two-track system, with a more demanding
three-year course leading to a Scottish Bacculauréat (ScotBac), and a
two-year course leading to a Scottish Certificate (ScotCert) Part 1 after
one year, and Part 2 after two years. There would be 'guided self-
selection' of students to courses, with up to 40 per cent of each year
group expected to attempt the ScotBac. Both courses would start at
15: the first two secondary years were felt to be a period when many
pupils marked time, and the Committee suggested that Standard
grade could be brought forward to S3 with only modest disruption.

There would be common elements in ScotBac and ScotCert. Both
would embrace general and vocational education, with the same
framework of core skills; both would lead to the award of group
certificates, assessed by a mixture of internal and external methods,
with different levels of attainment recorded. Both would lead to
employment or higher education. There would be opportunities for
transfer. However, ScotBac would be developed from existing
Highers and CSYS courses, modified to reflect the continental
principle of 'lines', with two broad lines (arts and sciences) and
sub-lines within each (including two with a vocational slant). ScotCert
would be based on new and existing Scotvec modules, with the
addition of 'integrative modules' and new elements of external
assessment. There would be ten ScotCert awards based on broad
occupational sectors and two with a more general educational
orientation. The Committee anticipated that ScotCert would often be
provided by schools and colleges in collaboration. It also proposed
that ScotCert be 'amalgamated' with levels 2 and 3 GSVQs (*ibid*. para
7.5), but since GSVQs were only announced at a late stage in the
Committee's deliberations, it had no opportunity to discuss the
details. At first sight the amalgamation would appear problematic; if a
two-year less demanding course led to GSVQ level 3 or its equivalent,
while a three-year more demanding course led to ScotBac, this would
make a nonsense of the attempt in England and Wales, through the

Advanced Diploma, to establish equivalence between the two types of qualification.

Initial reactions to the report have been broadly positive. There is a receptive climate for change, and an appreciation of the report's reassertion of a European identity for Scottish education. However the proposed changes to compulsory education — at last beginning to settle down after a decade of flux — may have been politically unwise. Bringing Standard grade forward by one year would probably involve more disruption than the report recognised; and the proposed earlier age of selection, and the likely backwash effects on lower-secondary and even primary education, may be unpopular. (Under the Howie proposals the youngest members of each year group would embark on ScotBac or ScotCert at the age of 14 years and 5 months.)

If the Howie proposals are implemented, their success or failure will depend on the ScotCert which is likely to prove the weakest element of the strategy. There are no British precedents for a general/ vocational course, aimed at students who fail to reach the standards of entry to academic courses, having high external status. The Howie Committee, in its enthusiasm for continental models, may have neglected the very different labour-market contexts of continental systems where there is a stronger demand for qualifications at a range of levels. Employers would need to change their recruitment practices and selection criteria for the ScotCert to provide a reliable route to employment. The opportunities for progression from ScotCert to higher education will also be restricted — mainly to HNCs and HNDs. The use of NC modules as the building blocks for ScotCert will open up some progression routes, but it will also confirm the low status of the ScotCert within schools. There will be visible differences in pedagogy and assessment to reinforce this status gap, and transfer between the two tracks might prove difficult in practice. Yet the success of the ScotCert in attracting large numbers of students is essential for the Howie proposals. One can picture three possible scenarios: a 'French scenario', in which a majority of students attempt the ScotBac, leading to a more heterogeneous student group than it was designed for, and for which it is less equipped to cater than the present set of courses; an 'English scenario', in which total participation remains low because students have to choose between a course whose standards are too demanding for many or a course whose extrinsic value is doubtful; and a 'Danish scenario' in which both tracks attract substantial numbers of students (although in Denmark too there is concern about academic drift). To realise the Danish scenario in Scotland would require intervention in areas (such as the labour market, training and further and higher education) that were not covered by Howie's remit.

## Implications for England and Wales

Scottish developments have at least three types of implications for England and Wales. First, a 'British' education and training policy community should ideally be equally well-informed about education and training in all parts of Britain. This may be unrealistic, but it is entailed by the unitary system of government in which education/ training policy for each part of the UK is made by the central UK government. (This point is lost on many non-Scottish MPs who wish to retain their right to legislate on Scottish affairs but do not recognise the corollary duty to be well informed about these same affairs.)

Second, further implications arise from Scotland's continuing position as another country within the EC and, probably, within the UK. Young people with Scottish qualifications will continue to apply for jobs and higher education in England and Wales, and vice versa. Language and other ties will ensure that these links remain closer than those with other EC countries.

Third, England and Wales can learn from Scottish experience. The Scottish system has much in common with the systems south of the border, and cultural, social, labour-market and political contexts are broadly similar; there is therefore more scope either for direct borrowing, or for drawing inferences from comparing the systems where they do differ, than in the case of comparisons with overseas countries. For example, the greater co-ordination of policy and provision in Scotland has been cited as an example for England and Wales to follow on a regional basis (McNay, 1991). The Higher has been held up as a model for a one-year AS level, and the greater 'modularity' of Scottish post-compulsory school courses has been seen to provide lessons, if not a precise model, for the English. There may also be much to be learnt from the Scottish experience of school-college partnerships, although as far as I am aware these have never been evaluated at a national level.

### Lessons for a unified system

Currently the most significant lessons that England and Wales can learn from Scotland concern the strategic direction of future reform, and in particular the development of a unified model of education and training on the lines of the *British Baccalauréat* proposals (IPPR 1990). Two features of the Scottish system exemplify aspects of this model. First, the National Certificate is an example of a modular framework which permits flexibility of delivery and a diversity of providers within a unified, coherent system with progression lines built in. Second, although the NC and Higher are separate, the whole system of post-compulsory courses is to an extent 'modular'. Scotland demonstrates that a structure of courses which is relatively open and flexible, and based upon relatively small units, can be a basis for boosting participation and attainment, and for weakening the boundary between academic and vocational study. The Scottish system, in effect, occupies an intermediate position on the continuum which stretches from the divided and inflexible English system at one end to the unified and flexible *British Baccalauréat* model at the other.

However a successful unified system must solve a number of practical problems. These include:

- how to ensure that students follow programmes of modules which are coherent and worthwhile and which lead somewhere, without losing flexibility;
- how to maintain value-pluralism, and in particular avoid academic drift;
- how to maintain coherence in a system with diverse providers and contexts for learning.

All three problems are illuminated by the Scottish experience.

The English and Welsh system imposes a division between academic and vocational study which is both stark and arbitrary, based on gender, geography and status rather than inherently 'educational' considerations. While Scotland avoids this stark and arbitrary division among students, there is an arbitrariness about the way each student's programme of study is decided, especially at school (Percy, 1990, SOED, 1992). The available options are too dependent on contingencies of staffing and resources. Student choices are often poorly guided and based on questionable criteria. The curriculum of many school stayers, especially the 'less academic', tends to be fragmented and to lack coherence; their attainments are often unsatisfactory; their opportunities for subsequent progression are poor.

There are at least three practical lessons from this. First, effective guidance is essential in a unified modular system; in many Scottish authorities post-16 guidance has had too low a priority, despite evidence that the traditional support from parents and peers is less effective. Second, group certificates can be a basis for imposing coherence on modular programmes; 'clusters' and GSVQs are responses to the problems outlined above. However, unless they are carefully designed, group awards could reduce the flexibility of choices — forcing young people into academic or vocational tracks. Moreover the idea of a group certificate has been resisted in Scotland on the grounds that it would reduce the value of intermediate attainments and thereby reduce incentives to participate. Third, a unified modular system must be designed as such; it cannot simply be assembled from pre-existing components designed for very different purposes. This leads on to the second practical problem which a unified system must solve.

A unified system will require special efforts to develop and sustain the value-pluralism appropriate to mass participation. Comprehensive systems tend to encourage academic drift (Squires, 1989). The dominant values in any sector of education tend to reflect the expected destinations of its students (compare, for example, apprenticeships with pre-university courses). But if a unified system enables all young people to keep their options open then all parts of the system potentially lead to the same destinations; their values become more uniform and are typically most influenced by higher-status destinations such as higher education.

The Scottish system 'works' by allowing more young people, particularly middle-attainers, to keep their options open and to continue to have access to high-status academic courses, especially Highers. This tends to sustain the predominance of academic values, since most students still have their sights set on courses (at school or in higher education) governed by those values. The weak boundary between academic and vocational education paradoxically makes it harder to develop an alternative value-system based around vocational education, whose low status is reinforced. The curriculum of many 'less academic' stayers is a fragmented mixture of courses designed for the academic minority, re-sits, and lower-status courses to fill in the gaps. The system is top-heavy. Scotland's relative advantage is greatest in respect of qualifications for, and entry to, higher education. Recent projections suggest that 46 per cent of the age group will enter full-time higher education by 2000, and if current graduation rates are maintained Scotland will rank among the best-educated European countries at this level. However the problem lies elsewhere. Too few young people leave the system with intermediate levels of attainment; few young people, except for those progressing to higher education, continue in education or training beyond 17 or 18 years (Croxford, Howieson and Raffe, 1991b); vocational qualifications at this level lack status; and opportunities beyond 16 still tend to be polarised between those leading to higher education and those involving early entry to the labour market.

There may be two practical lessons from this. The first is that a unified system must be fully integrated, and it cannot be developed simply by adding new elements to a system of courses designed for the academic minority. (It may be more practical to design a unified system from the middle outwards, starting with the needs of middle-attaining students). In Scotland the continued separation of the Higher and the NC (and the failure adequately to reform the Higher), has reinforced the low status of vocational education and prevented a fully integrated system from developing; instead, less academic students are fed with the crumbs from the rich man's table. The second lesson is that reforms of 16–18s education can only work if they are complemented by reforms of the 'context' — in particular of higher education, youth training and the labour market, which create incentives for participation through their recruitment practices and selection criteria. The low status of the NC in Scotland partly reflects the reluctance of universities to accept an internally assessed and criterion-referenced certificate for entry purposes; but it also reflects the failure of the labour market to reward broad-based vocational qualifications, particularly those gained by staying on in full-time education (Raffe, 1988). A unified system for 16–18s must lead to destinations in employment as well as higher education; for this reason we put considerable emphasis in the *British Baccalauréat* on parallel reforms of the labour market that would make the unified certificate a normal entrance requirement for many jobs (IPPR, 1990).

The third practical problem for a unified system is how to combine coherence with diversity. The NC exemplifies a particular strategy for this. It accepts the diversity of providers and of institutional contexts for learning that is inherent in the mixed model; but it promotes coherence through a single national system of modules designed to a standard framework, to give co-ordinated and rationalised curriculum coverage and horizontal and vertical lines of progression. In England and Wales, the NCVQ is working towards a similar model (Jessup, 1991), although it faces stronger centrifugal forces, such as the plurality of awarding bodies, wide regional differences and the differing approaches of lead bodies. The NC approach can be seen as a distinctive strategy for comprehensive education: one that relies on reform of courses, curricula and certificates, rather than institutional reorganisation.

The NC experience draws attention to several limitations of this approach. In the first place, it suggests that the 'outcomes' approach can only influence participation and attainment to the extent that the certified outcomes have value in the eyes of potential students. The introduction of the NC has not substantially changed levels or patterns of participation; young people have continued to respond to the incentives and opportunities associated with the institutional context — employment, YT, FE and so on — rather than those associated with the modular framework superimposed on it (Croxford, Howieson and Raffe, 1991b). Simply providing a flexible framework for pursuing qualifications will only encourage participation to the extent that the qualifications are worth pursuing; and in Scotland, as in England, vocational qualifications at this level have relatively low status and market value.

Moreover, the 'outcomes' model as a basis for coherence rests heavily on the validity and credibility of assessment; the modular currency can easily become debased. For example, in a study of a recent cohort we identified young people who left school with NC qualifications and took further modules in FE or YTS; a majority were required to repeat at least one of the modules they had already completed, either because of rigidities in the college timetable or because colleges did not respect modules achieved at school as valid indicators of competence (*ibid.*). More generally, the Scottish experience suggests that it is difficult for a single framework of qualifications to be equally suited to the demands of what I have called the internal and external modes — respectively employer-sponsored provision geared to the demands of the internal labour market, and education-led (mainly full-time) provision which anticipates selection in the external labour market (Raffe, 1992). The two modes demand different styles of organisation and certification of courses; the NC appears to be closer to the demands of the internal mode, but faces difficulties arising from its attempt to straddle the two.

An effective and coherent system requires attention to 'inputs' (processes and delivery systems) as well as 'outcomes'; a useful start would be to defer industry- and market-led provision to 18-plus, since it has proved incapable in Britain of providing an adequate general education and training of the kind needed by 16–18 year olds, or of sitting alongside 'education-led' provision in a coherent system for the age group.

**Lessons from Howie**

Finally, the Howie debate — and, perhaps, the Howie proposals in practice — will have numerous implications for England and Wales. Scotland could provide a reminder that it is possible to change long-established and cherished institutions. It may try out a new model, influenced by dual-track continental systems; but it would do so in a context of constraints (notably those arising from the labour market and the functions of qualifications) that are distinctively British. Whether or not the Howie reforms provide a model for England and Wales, they would provide further evidence on how education systems 'work' in the British context, and on the changes in that context that would make them work more effectively.

# Acknowledgements

The author acknowledges the financial support of the UK Economic and Social Research Council.

# References

Ball, C. (1991) *Learning pays*, Royal Society of Arts.

Croxford, L., Howieson, C. and Raffe, D. (1991a) 'National Certificate Modules in the S5 Curriculum,' *Scottish Educational Review* 23(2): 78–92.

Croxford, L., Howieson, C. and Raffe, D. (1991b) *Young people's experience of National Certificate modules*, Centre for Educational Sociology, University of Edinburgh.

Department of Education and Science (1991) 'Educational and economic activity of young people aged 16–18 years in England from 1974/5 to 1989/90', *Statistical Bulletin 13/91*.

Goodman, R. (1992) 'Japan — Pupil Turned Teacher?' Phillips, D. (ed) *Lessons of cross-national comparisons in education*, Oxford Studies in Comparative Education, Vol 1; Triangle Books.

Howie, J. (1991) 'Review of Education 16–18 in Scotland: European Comparisons', address to CBI Conference on *The 16–19 white paper: green light for a blueprint?*

Institute for Public Policy Research (1990) *A British 'Baccalauréat': ending the division between education and training*.

Jessup, G. (1991) *Outcomes: NVQs and the emerging model of education and training*, Falmer.

Keep, E. (1991) 'The grass looked greener: some thoughts on the influence of comparative vocational training research on the UK policy debate,' Ryan P (ed) *International comparisons of vocational education and training for intermediate skills*, Falmer.

McNay, I. (1991) 'Co-operation Co-ordination and Quality in Employers and Education Partnerships: A Role for the Regions', Raggatt, P. and Unwin, L. (eds) *Change and Intervention: Vocational Education and Training*, Falmer.

McPherson, A. (1992) 'The Howie Committee on Post-Compulsory Schooling,' Paterson, L. and McCrone, D. (eds) *Scottish Government Yearbook 1992, Unit for the Study of Government in Scotland*, University of Edinburgh.

Organisation for Economic Co-operation and Development (1985) *Education and Training after Basic Schooling*, Paris.

Percy, S. (1990) *Options and Opportunities: A Study of Subject Choice in S5 and S6 in Two Rural Secondary Schools*, Unpublished MEd Dissertation, Department of Education, University of Edinburgh.

Raffe, D. (1988) 'Going with the grain: youth training in transition,' Brown, S. and Wake, R. (eds) *Education in Transition*, Scottish Council for Research in Education.

Raffe, D. (1991) 'Scotland v England: The Place of "Home Internationals" in Comparative Research', Ryan, P. (ed) *International Comparisons of Vocational Education and Training for Intermediate Skills*, Falmer.

Raffe, D. (1992) 'Beyond the "Mixed Model": Social Research and the Case for Reform of 16–18s Education in Britain,' Crouch, C. and Heath, A. (eds) *Social Research and Social Reform: Essays in Honour of A H Halsey*, Oxford University Press.

Royal Society (1991) *Beyond GCSE*.

Scottish Enterprise (1991) *Strategies for the 1990s*.

Scottish Office (1991) *Access and Opportunity: A Strategy for Education and Training*, Cm 1530, HMSO.

Scottish Office Education Department (1992) *Upper Secondary Education in Scotland: Report of the Committee to Review Curriculum and Examinations in the fifth and sixth years of Secondary Education in Scotland*, HMSO (Howie Report).

Scottish Vocational Education Council (Scotvec) (1991) *General Scottish Vocational Qualifications: A Consultation Paper*.

Squires, G. (1989) *Pathways for Learning*, OECD, Paris.

# PART II
# QUALIFICATIONS

LIBRARY
HANDSWORTH COLLEGE
SOHO ROAD
BIRMINGHAM
B21 9DP

# 4 The recent background to qualifications reform in England and Wales

## Ken Spours

### Three phases in the recent development of 14–19 qualifications

The impact of recent changes in qualifications for the 14–19 age group will be determined not only by the content of the proposals but the ways in which they relate to the wider education and training policy-context. In England and Wales this appears to be dominated by the prestige of academic qualifications, the relatively low status of vocational qualifications and low-skill demands made by many British employers. It will be argued that these contextual factors mean that qualifications play a role in reinforcing what has been termed the 'low skills equilibrium'. But there have also been positive changes such as the gradual rise in examination attainment and increased post-16 staying-on rates. The chapter also evaluates how this changing and contradictory policy environment could affect the future direction of the reform of qualifications.

There have been several periods since the mid-1970s when the issue of 14–19 qualifications and their context have become an important area of education and training (ET) policy discussion and development. They appear to fall broadly into three phases.

First is the period of the 'new vocationalism' in the late 1970s/early 1980s which saw the development of pre-vocational certification such as the Certificate of Pre-Vocational Education (CPVE), in response to widespread youth unemployment and the lack of opportunities for a majority of students in the academic part of the post-16 ET system.[1] While there was an unprecedented growth in vocational youth training at this time, the leading edge of ET curriculum development was undoubtedly in the pre-vocational phase of provision.[2]

The second phase of qualification reform ranges from the mid-1980s to 1990. This is the period which saw the emergence of international comparisons of education and training.[3] In response, the 'new vocationalism' moved away from a preoccupation with youth unemployment towards the development of a more rationalised system of vocational qualifications, particularly that associated with the work of National Council for Vocational Qualifications (NCVQ). In addition, the mid-1980s witnessed attempts to diversify the academic curriculum, first through the introduction of GCSE, then in A levels through the 'core skills' debate, the introduction of advanced supplementary (AS) level examinations and the work of the Higginson Committee (HMSO, 1988). Furthermore, this period was marked by considerable innovation in modular developments — both within the Technical Vocational Education Initiative (TVEI) and through initiatives such as the modular A level Wessex Project (see Rainbow, this volume).

The third phase is that in which we currently find ourselves. Its principal feature is the aim of government to develop a 'dual track' of academic and vocational qualifications for the post-16 age group through the retrenchment of the academic and the broadening of the vocational routes through the ET system. During this third phase many initiatives of the second period are being reversed and the landscape is full of complexity and uncertainty. In terms of qualifications, recent reform efforts have been marked by four main developments.

- The restriction of the amount of assessed course-work in GCSE and A levels marks an end to the process of reforming and diversifying the academic track. The reversal can be seen as a policy designed to halt the gradual changes which have taken place in academic syllabuses and delivery practices.[4]
- A reduction in the role of occupationally-specific national vocational qualifications (NVQs) for the 16–19 age group due to the scheduled introduction of general national vocational qualifications (GNVQs).
- An end to the era of post-16 pre-vocational qualifications such as CPVE and the intended creation of over-arching national

qualifications (the Ordinary Diploma and the Advanced
Diploma) which perpetuate the 'dual track'.
- The emergence of a case for a unified qualifications system
  exemplified by proposals for a 'British Baccalauréat' (IPPR,
  1990).

## Current contexts for change in post-16 qualifications

The development of qualifications and the way in which these are
implemented have been affected by important contextual changes
affecting the post-16 ET system. The UK's persistent economic
problems of recession and the low-skills demands made of training
and education by employers (Finegold, 1992) have had a significant
impact on the development of vocational qualifications.
Furthermore, the government's belief in the virtues of free market
competition between education institutions, the impact of the local
management of schools (LMS) and the creation of a new sector of
colleges of further education independent of local education authority
control is affecting the ways in which qualification reforms are
implemented. Most immediate and significant, however, are the
dramatic rises in England and Wales of post-16 staying-on rates (see
Finegold, this volume) and the need to provide a ladder of progression
for the 75 per cent of students outside the A level track.

### Changes in post-16 participation

The period since 1990 has witnessed a rapid rise in the full-time
staying-on rate at the age of 16 to over 67 per cent (*Independent*, 1992).
This is occurring in inner-city areas as well as in areas that,
traditionally, have greater rates of participation. However, this
increase in participation is also exacerbating long-standing problems
of low attainment and barriers to progression:[5]

- the attitudes of students to staying-on may still be negative and
  many would prefer to be in the labour market — these students
  have been termed 'discouraged workers';[6]
- many students are on one-year courses and are staying-on to
  compensate for under-achievement pre-16;
- the number staying-on beyond 17 is much lower (around 40 per
  cent) than that at 16, highlighting problems of course retention,
  progression to higher courses and further achievement post-17.

Increased participation of this kind which lacks significant
increases in levels of achievement and qualification is the result of a

lowering in the demand for youth labour due to recession compounded by a lack of qualitative change in post-16 provision and its resulting qualifications. One of the most tangible effects of increases in post-16 participation is an unprecedented increase in demand for entry to pre-vocational and vocational courses. In many areas these are in short supply and students are being turned away. Moreover, it is becoming increasingly apparent that the provision of 16–19 education and training is set to experience similar conditions to those which have evolved in polytechnics over the last few years — quantitative expansion in participation without significant additional resources to support it. The effects of this on the post-16 sector are likely to be mixed. On the positive side, an increase in full-time participation has stimulated the development of GNVQs as a means of accommodating those students who cannot or choose not to participate in the academic track and who do not wish to experience occupationally-specific NVQs. At the same time, however, quality of delivery is at risk as class sizes increase and resources for learner-support diminish. We may face a situation in which more students participate and more drop out.

**Current policies which favour market and organisational competition**

The central thrust of current government reform is the introduction of market-oriented policies to both schools and colleges. One of the aims here is to increase the capacity of the system to recruit and retain students and so absorb higher levels of participation, by sharpening institutional competition.

   In the schools sector the main policy thrust is to encourage competition between schools for parental hearts and minds through the publication of raw test scores. In the post-16 arena there appears to be a different policy strategy which accepts that differentiation has already taken place and that the academic track of sixth form A levels should be preserved and not diluted. The effect is one of excluding three quarters of all 16 year-olds from the academic track and, instead, providing for their 'quantitative qualification' through the vocational route, either full or part-time. In contrast to schools policy, the main issue in the post-compulsory sector is not parental choice but the driving down of further education (FE) unit costs and the maximisation of outputs (students and qualifications). The intended policy of the Further Education Funding Council (FEFC) only to fund the expansion of college buildings when they have already achieved 160 per cent capacity is a confirmation of this approach. Furthermore, the FEFC has future plans which may include output-

driven funding of colleges measured by the rate of award of NVQs or
GNVQs to students.

Institutional competition is not confined to schools and colleges but
also involves the main examining and validating bodies (EVBs) — the
Business and Technology Education Council (BTEC), the City and
Guilds London Institute (CGLI) and the Royal Society of Arts (RSA).
Their job is to sell qualifications to providing institutions, while
operating within the NVQ framework. The question here is whether
such a diverse array of certification will serve to undermine external
recognition of the NCVQ's qualifications framework. Although
vocational qualifications will all be designed to conform to a particular
NVQ level, they will be given different titles by the respective EVBs
and this, no doubt, will perpetuate the practice of previous periods of
qualifications reform whereby different types of certification are
ranked by institutions to meet the highly differentiated needs of
participating students. Meanwhile, all vocational qualifications
remain overshadowed by academic awards which enjoy greater public
exposure and prestige. The process of aggressive marketing of
vocational qualifications by the EVBs, the tendency of institutions to
rank awards and a time-lag in recognition may all serve to generate less
public understanding of vocational awards than if there was an
arrangement such as in Scotland where a single vocational
qualification (the Scottish National Certificate) is awarded by a single
validating body — the Scottish Vocational Education Council
(SCOTVEC).

A further effect of the policy of market competition may be to
undermine the effectiveness of the existing 'dual track' system within
and between individual institutions. Sixth forms are often too small to
offer reasonable educational choice post-16 and, in many cases, do not
have a range of certification capable of attracting a diverse, two-year
cohort. At the same time, FE colleges newly detached from LEAs
now have their own preoccupations with controlling unit costs. In this
increasingly fragmented scenario, it is difficult to see how incentives
for institutional collaboration will arise which ensure progression
between levels within institutions and from one institution to another
such as is necessary to encourage sustained participation to the age of
18.

The stimulus of diversity and competition among providers
harbours other important policy contradictions. The introduction of
open enrolment in the Education Reform Act (1988) has driven many
schools to want to preserve a prestigious academic sixth form for the
sake of image but at the expense of adequate investment in vocational
provision post-16. The incorporation of the FE sector, on the other
hand, drives colleges to want a fast-learning student intake to reduce
course costs, especially if future funding is to be tied to NVQ or

GNVQ outcomes. Quite clearly, schools and colleges need to co-operate over plans for student progression which meet the needs of both fast and slow learners. But what is emerging is competition for the most cost-effective students — those on the academic track or the GNVQ track full-time (at NVQ level 2 and above) who will be most likely to boost institutions' output statistics. The school sector, meanwhile, will continue to stress selection and be relatively inefficient in meeting a wider variety of needs.

It seems probable that market competition between institutions will reproduce their different and divisive traditions. This is not an arrangement which, of itself, can make for 'parity of esteem' in the implementation of qualifications.

**Qualifications and the 'low-skills equilibrium'**

A third and important contextual factor influencing the direction and impact of current qualification reform is the relationship between qualifications and the economy. Ministers and officials from the NCVQ have talked of developing the most flexible system of vocational qualifications in the world (Howard, 1992). Finegold and Soskice (1988) argue, however, that such a qualifications structure can be seen as part of a 'low-skill equilibrium' in which a reinforcing relationship between low quality/low cost production in the UK and low skill and low-level training demands, act together to prevent the development of high-skill demands in the workplace or in education and training.[7] NVQs have many features of a low-skill approach to qualifications — their narrow occupational focus, a concentration on the segmentation of tasks rather than their inter-relationship and their subordination of the role of broad vocational knowledge. They focus upon the immediate operational demands of training rather than what have been described as longer-term, 'over arching capabilities'.[8]

The role of qualifications in maintaining the low-skill equilibrium is located in the uniquely regressive relationship between qualifications and the labour market in England and Wales. Employers have tended both to support highly selective academic qualifications (such as A levels) as the simplest and most understandable means of screening, selecting and recruiting candidates, and to adopt narrow vocationally-specific qualifications (such as NVQs), as the quickest and most basic means of qualifying the workforce. They have not always been fully supportive of broader vocational qualifications and many remain sceptical of government attempts to seek their support for GNVQs. Traditionally, many employers have preferred to poach trained talent rather than train their own workforce.

In response to the lack of employer interest in quality vocational qualifications the government has placed its belief in the power of consumers (in this case trainees) to demand quality education and training through the development of a system of training credits (see Unwin, this volume). To be fully effective, however, this strategy requires an efficient training market — a situation which, for various reasons, has never pertained. In a recession there simply is not the supply of jobs with training; in periods of growth when there are jobs and training scheme places available they often fail to meet aspirations. In the South East, in particular, there has been little faith in Youth Training and no more than 6 per cent of the cohort are involved. Rather than enter the labour market, most young people are choosing to stay-on in full-time education though, in practice, 16–19 year olds cannot find appropriate places in FE colleges and are proceeding to training schemes as a second or third choice.

This is not the whole picture, however, and there are groups of more progressive employers, supported by the Confederation of British Industries (CBI) and some Training and Enterprise Councils (TECs), which recognise the need for a high-skill approach to education and training. Their policies include support for the reform of A levels, more elaborated reporting of students' achievement, broader vocational preparation in schools and colleges, increased levels of access to higher education (HE) and delays in recruitment until 18. Such an approach does not under-value the need for basic occupational skills in young people; it sees the need to go beyond this if we are to train for the future. In a nutshell, this means moving away from a demand-led approach to education and training to look at the problem of improving quality from the supply-side — the education and training provision itself and those institutions delivering it.

## Issues in the debate about qualifications

The policy background sketched out in the preceding pages has created specific conditions within which the curriculum reforms described in the case studies in Chapter 5 have to operate. Such initiatives, however, need also to be assessed in the context of a set of long-running issues which have informed the debate about post-16 qualifications over the past 20 years. This has focused successively on three important deficiencies in the operation of post-16 qualifications.

### The problem of credential inflation

First there arose the discussion of the problem of 'credential inflation' (Dore, 1976). This describes a situation in which increasing numbers of students are acquiring qualifications but where an equivalent increase in the number of high skilled jobs or higher education places is not occurring. As a result, the qualifications demanded for entry to specific jobs inflate and there develops a qualifications treadmill. The phenomenon of credential inflation was reflected during the 1970s in the popular but erroneous assertion that an applicant to become a road sweeper required five O levels. This kind of discussion was prominent in the period immediately after the educational expansion of the 1960s. Moreover, it is an argument likely to make a come-back. The government's aim of increasing participation in HE to 35 per cent by the end of the century will introduce problems of credential inflation if the number of higher skilled jobs available is not radically increased. The effect of credential inflation is to produce reversals in the number of young people increasing their level of qualification due to disillusionment at their not being able to see guarantees of rewards for their effort in terms of deferred wages.

## 'Tertiary tripartism' and the stratification of qualifications

The debate about qualifications during most of the 1980s resulted from analyses of the 'new vocationalism' and focused upon the consequences of creating new types of qualifications for underachievers or the youth unemployed. It observed that new qualifications such as CPVE had much lower status than either academic or traditional vocational qualifications. The new array of qualifications was also paralleled by different routes for differing sections of the student cohort — academic, technical/vocational and pre-vocational — with little mobility between them. This proliferation of qualifications and training arrangements, it was argued, meant that the old division of secondary schools into grammar, technical and secondary modern was being reproduced in provision for post-compulsory age students. These new forms of division were termed 'tertiary tripartism' (Ransome, 1984).

Studies in the later 1980s tended to focus upon the practical problems of promoting progression between different types of qualifications and the pressure for reforms generated by this approach eventually led to the call for a more common or integrated modular system in post-16 education and training (Post-16 Centre, 1988; Post-16 Centre, 1989; Spours, 1991). The debate about stratification, status and progression, remains very relevant, however, when analysing attempts to reform qualifications systems by adding new arrangements or by attempting to integrate existing ones (see Chapters 5 and 6).

## The relationship between labour markets and qualifications

A third focus of concern about qualifications arose in the late 1980s. This concentrated on the inter-relationship between labour markets and qualifications and pointed to: the practice of British employers of early recruitment; the low level demands made of qualifications by low-skill production practices; and continued employer support for selective academic qualifications. It highlighted the peculiarities of the home situation in comparison with continental systems of post-16 education and training in which the English arrangements were described as exhibiting an 'early selection/low participation system'. This debate also highlighted a new dimension to the discussion — the relationship between qualifications, education and training policies, and economic strategy (Finegold and Soskice, 1988).[9] Eventually a group of analysts with differing but complementary perspectives in the qualifications debate teamed up to call for a unified 'late selection/high participation system' (IPPR, 1990).

# Qualifications and the 'curriculum of the future'

It is possible to argue that a new strand of analysis is just beginning which centres on the relationship between the quality of post-16 participation, the nature of qualifications and the future demands of the economy and society.[10] This analysis points to the need for over-arching capabilities, new types of knowledge and skill and a system which promotes 'learning organisations' suited to meet future national economic needs (Prospect Centre, 1991).

In recent debates about the content of post-16 education and training there has been a consistent argument advocating the need for breadth of learning in contrast to existing, narrow forms of specialisation in post-16 qualifications. While agreeing with the criticism of narrow and divisive specialisation, the analysis enshrined in the 'curriculum of the future' recognises that specialisation is an integral part of modern society but argues for learning specialisation of a more flexible and less divisive form. It further argues that the post-16 curriculum should encourage: the development of specialist knowledge and skill which can support and encourage new developments in production and society (e.g. the organisation of firms for flexible specialist production); the development of broad skill (transferability); and critical analysis (connectiveness). Whilst there is an acceptance of breadth in the range of subjects taught, the 'curriculum of the future' argues that there has to be a new quality within and relationship between specialist subjects, as elements of the curriculum actively seek to reflect changes in productive life and society.[11] It uses new and future industrial models as a starting point for conceptualising the curriculum in the same way as Chris Hayes at the Prospect Centre (1991) has used them to understand future patterns of educational organisation. The 'curriculum of the future' points to a unified and modular qualifications system as the prime means of developing the kind of flexibility and connectiveness which can provide for students' future learning and qualification requirements.

The changing context against which post-16 education and training is provided helps us to understand the conditions to which both the government and its critics are responding and to assess the nature and contribution of specific initiatives such as those described in Chapter 5. The central question is whether current reforms will modify 16–19 provision such that it more closely meets future economic and social needs or whether they will merely serve to ensure that the system remains a prisoner of its past. This question is considered in Chapter 6.

# Notes

1   The term 'new vocationalism' was developed by VET researchers in the early 1980s (e.g. D. Finn, C. Chitty, D. Gleeson and P. Cohen) to describe a new policy emphasis upon vocational training. It is generally recognised that this era began with James Callaghan's speech at Ruskin College in 1976.

2   The pre-vocational innovations stemmed from organisations such as the Further Education Unit (FEU) which produced important publications such as *A Basis for Choice* (1979) and *Vocational Preparation* (1981).

3   Two reports in the mid-1980s helped to change the climate of debate about education and training and introduce the international dimension: C. Hayes and N. Fonda *Competence and Competition* (MSC, 1984) and OECD *A Challenge to Complacency* (1985).

4   In recent years there have been a series of gradual changes in A level syllabuses which are well documented in Watts, 1991.

5   The problem of high participation and low achievement occuring simultaneously is explored further in Spours, forthcoming.

6   ESRC research project on post-16 participation based at Centre for Education and Industry, University of Warwick. The concept of the reluctant participant has also been explored in two recent television programmes *Every Child in Britain* (Channel 4 — 26 October 1991) and *Staying Power* (BBC2 — 14 January 1992). There is some evidence, however, that attitudes to staying-on are changing, not least because of recession and a suggestion that the debate around increased participation is beginning to permeate popular consciousness and affect the decisions of young people (see Spours, forthcoming).

7   This analysis has since been further developed by Finegold (1991). Here he likens the low-skill equilibrium to economic short-termism in company policies in the UK. See also Finegold, this volume.

8   See also Jessup, this volume. The concept of 'overcharging capability' has been developed by Prospect Centre in three collaborative projects between FE colleges and employers (reported in Prospect Centre, 1991).

9   Other critics of the system of post-16 education and training such as Sir
    Christopher Ball (*Profitable Learning*, RSA, January 1992) have stressed
    incentives designed to stimulate individuals' learning rather than reform of the
    qualifications system.
10  Young and Spours (1992) focus on implications of the debate about 'post-fordist'
    developments in production for developments in qualifications.
11  This argument takes further ideas on vocationalsim and academic learning
    outlined in Spours and Young, 1990.

# References

Dore, Ron (1976) *The Diploma Disease*, Allen Unwin.
Finegold, D. (1991) 'Institutional Incentives Towards a High Skill Equilibrium', P.
    Ryan (ed.) *International Comparisons of Vocational Education and Training for
    Intermediate Skills*, Falmer Press.
Finegold, D. and Soskice, D. (1988) 'Failure of Training in Britain: Analysis and
    Prescription', *Oxford Review of Economic Policy*, 4, 3, Autumn, pp.21–53.
HMSO (1988) *Advancing A-Levels*, (The Higginson Report), HMSO.
Howard, Michael (1992) 'Radical Reform of Education Gathers Pace', Department of
    Employment Press Notice, 23 January.
*Independent*, 1992 'More stay at school after 16', 16 July.
Institute of Public Policy Research (IPPR) (1990) *A British Baccalauréat: Ending the
    Division between Education and Training*.
Post-16 Education Centre (1988) *A Curricular Comparison of CPVE and BTEC First
    Diploma*, Working Paper No.3.
Post-16 Education Centre (1989) *Modularisation and Progression*, Working Paper No.6.
Prospect Centre (1991) *Growing An Innovative Workforce: Forward Looking Education
    and Training for Forward Looking Business*, November.
Ranson, S. (1984) 'Towards a New Tertiary Tripartism', P. Broadfoot *Selection
    Certification and Control*, Falmer Press.
Spours, K., forthcoming (1993) *Issues of post-16 participation: Evidence from the inner-
    city borough of Tower Hamlets*.
Spours, K. (1991) 'Politics of Progression: Problems and Strategies in the 14–19
    Curriculum', Clyde Chitty (ed.) *Post-16 Education: Studies in Access and
    Achievement*, Kogan Page.
Spours, K. and Young, M. (1990) 'Beyond Vocationalism', D. Gleeson (ed.) *Training
    and its Alternatives*, Open University Press.
Watts, A. G. (1991) 'Work-Related Learning and the A-Level Curriculum', School
    Curriculum Industry Partnership (SCIP), University of Warwick [mimeo].
Young, M. and Spours, K. (1992) 'A Curriculum of the Future', draft discussion
    paper, Post-16 Education Centre, Institute of Education, London.

# 5 New models of 16–19 provision: case histories and emerging frameworks

## CASE HISTORIES

---
### Case history A
### Modular A and AS Levels: The Wessex Project
### *Bob Rainbow*
---

The Wessex Project is a collaboration between five adjacent English local education authorities (LEAs) and the Associated Examining Board (AEB). The aim of the Project is to develop a number of modular advanced (A) and advanced supplementary (AS) level examinations which incorporate several unusual and innovative features. The scheme was initiated by teachers and advisory staff and has continued to be a 'grass-roots' development, funded from a variety of local and national sources. Despite its local nature, its influence and reputation have been national. The Wessex A levels have been given limited pilot status by the School Examinations and Assessment Council (SEAC) and currently 78 schools and colleges of every type within the state sector are involved. Twelve modular A level examinations are being piloted and a total of about 3,500 students are taking part in the scheme. The collaboration began in 1987 and will formally end in July 1993.

The Project stemmed from a recognition by teachers that change was needed in post-16 examinations and, particularly, in the way in which A levels were taught if education was to meet the needs of students in the 1990s and beyond. Working in teams, teachers, advisers and others across the five LEAs came together to devise a suite of modular A and AS examinations which shared a broad structure and philosophy. The structure of each A level syllabus consists of a core and four modules. An AS consists of a slimmer core and two modules. Each A/AS syllabus is accompanied by a collection of student and teacher materials designed to support more flexible approaches to learning and greater student autonomy.

## Aims

Four broad aims can be determined in the development of the Wessex A and AS level modular structure and it is hoped that the fulfilment of these will result in higher participation rates, greater flexibility and increased opportunities for post-16 students. The aims are:

1. to provide curriculum continuity from the general certificate of secondary education (GCSE) and the National Curriculum, both of which have demanded new approaches to teaching, learning and assessment;
2. to broaden the base of A level by placing increased emphasis on skill and experience compared with content and thus to integrate more effectively some aspects of the Technical and Vocational Education Initiative (TVEI) criteria in A level provision;
3. to create a suite of modules so that A level students not only have continued access to strictly 'subject' based A levels with traditional titles, but can achieve breadth of study by taking modules across subject areas/boundaries — permissible patterns of linkage being specified in advance;
4. to provide not only an opportunity to incorporate AS provision within A level, but also to facilitate bridge-building between A level and equivalent vocational qualifications (the module design specifies a notional 45 hours of study — equivalent to a GNVQ unit — and the assessment criteria are consistent with many of those used in vocational courses).

The TVEI criteria referred to in (2) above relate to the desire to incorporate a range of key experiences and skills into a student's course of study. These can be summarised as:

– a requirement that the student's development be profiled in areas of numeracy, communication, information technology, self-study skills, and personal development;
– the opportunity for the student to undertake an appropriate work/community-related experience;

– the provision of careers guidance and counselling as an integral part of the programme of study;
– a requirement that the student's programme of study contains a specific vocational or work-related focus and an educational breadth which counters any tendency towards a narrow specialisation.

These last two points are of particular importance when set against the overall aim of the Wessex Project to maintain the national currency of an A level qualification, but to broaden its base by making the programmes of study increasingly vocationally relevant. Thus, it has been the intention of the project to meet the needs of students for entry into higher education, whilst developing a range of A level provision which caters for other types of post-A level activity and easier transfer between A level and equivalent vocational courses.

## Structure of the scheme

When the Project began (initially in Somerset alone) in 1986/87 it was decided that the aspect of post-compulsory education most in need of change was A level. The changes in GCSE examinations, the introduction of TVEI, the Educational Reform Act (1988) and the introduction of a National Curriculum, together with changes in higher education had all served to isolate A levels which were increasingly perceived as narrow and demotivating for many of the students who took them. Failure rates were high and opportunities to transfer to more appropriate vocational courses remote. Assessment solely at the end of a two year course — based on written examination papers which mainly tested the recall of knowledge — seemed both limited and limiting. Teachers were looking for examinations which placed greater emphasis on understanding and skills and less on the recall of knowledge. They wanted to develop A levels which would provide regular feedback to students of their achievements. The Project therefore concentrated, in the first instance, on generating revised A level syllabuses and it was soon decided that the flexibility which was required could only be achieved by the establishment of a modular structure.

The Wessex project did not, however, adopt a conventional modular model for its scheme. From the outset it was concerned to promote progression and continuity through A level courses, believing that learning at this level is not readily divided into discrete units which can be taken without due regard for what has gone before and what follows. Many modular schemes have stumbled on this issue, and have resorted to official or unofficial imposition of a

Figure 5.1:

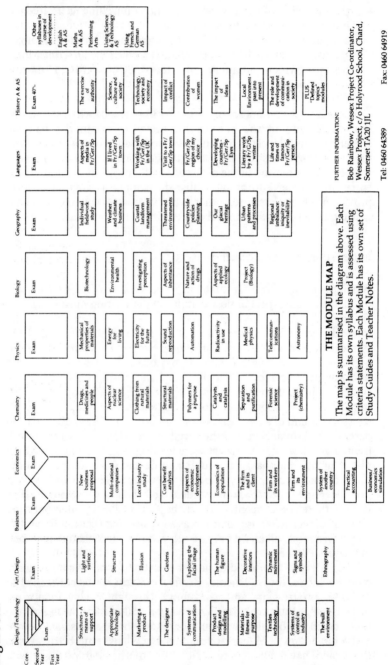

sequence on the modules. The Wessex Project has constructed its course in two parts which have different but complementary functions. The progressive development of knowledge, understanding and skills in each A level is provided by its **core**, which accounts for 60 per cent of course time and forms the 'stem' around which the course is built; core studies continue for the whole of the two years of the course. Attached to the core, is a bank of **modules** from which the student studies four, each worth 10 per cent of the final award. The modules are chosen within rules attached to each core; some modules are very specific to a particular subject whilst others can operate with several different cores. All modules provide opportunities for detailed study, student-centred work, and the study of relevant issues and themes; in addition, some modules enable work to take place across the curriculum rather than being confined to a single (traditional) subject.

Wessex AS courses are half the duration of an A level course, but operate at the same standard. They also consist of a core, taking up 60 per cent of the course time. Two modules drawn from the same bank as those for A level courses, are attached — each worth 20 per cent of the AS course.

Currently the following syllabuses are being piloted:

> biology, chemistry, physics, design and technology, art and design, French, German, Spanish, business studies, economics, geography and history.

Syllabuses have also been developed, but not piloted, in English, mathematics, and the performing arts. Figure 5.1 illustrates the suite of Wessex courses currently being piloted and the scope of the module bank.

## Assessment issues

Assessment and the maintenance of 'standards' at A level is the single, most fundamental, concern facing the Wessex Project. Do Wessex examinations ensure that the rigour and standards of A level are being upheld? There is little doubt that Wessex courses have stimulated and motivated teachers and their students: 'the Evaluators were particularly impressed by the students' general enthusiasm for the Wessex approach, although it does need to be acknowledged that it does not appeal to every student' (Bath, 1991). Her Majesty's Inspectorate (HMI) also commented in its inspection of a large sixth form college offering a full suite of Wessex subjects, that 'the quality of lessons which formed part of modular [Wessex] syllabuses with coursework was significantly better than that associated with other courses' (HMI, 1990). Students do well on Wessex courses; the pass rates are high and a satisfactory proportion of students achieve at grades A and B. The key problem lies in trying to equate the 'quality' expected of a student sitting a conventional written examination paper at the end of the second year of a course with the quality of work produced as coursework carried out during the course. This issue is complex and not easily resolved, as will be illustrated below.

Traditionally, student attainment at A level has mainly been assessed by external written examinations and teachers have had minimal involvement in this process. This is in sharp contrast to vocational courses which are accredited predominantly by continuous assessment made during the course by teachers using published grading/marking criteria. In the current education policy climate in England and Wales it is not possible to break away entirely from externally assessed, norm-referenced A level examinations. The Wessex Project has, therefore, attempted to treat the assessment of each subject on its own merits and arrive at an acceptable compromise. Where external assessment (that is, assessment operated by the examination board) is required, it is part of the core. However, *all* modules are assessed as coursework by teachers and moderated by the examining board. They are assessed using criterion-referenced methods.

A proportion of the modules involve students in work outside their school or college — in commerce, industry or the community, or in relating what they are doing in the classroom to the outside world. The intention is that, as a result, they have a broader experience and learn to become more independent in their learning. Wessex modules incorporate and assess the sorts of 'core skills' and experiences which were subsequently to be developed by the National Curriculum Council (NCC, 1990), strongly endorsed by the Confederation of British Industries (CBI, 1989) and incorporated in the proposals for general national vocational qualifications (GNVQs) (NCVQ, 1991). In many ways the demands of modules, whilst breaking new ground at A level, were a logical extension of what students had been doing within TVEI schemes, or in GCSE courses. Whether this will continue to be the case following recent proposals by the government to impose strict limits on coursework accreditation and place greater emphasis on the learning of facts, remains to be seen.

The recording of students' attainment through the core and the modules is arrived at separately. Results for work on modules are awarded for achievement based on criteria published in the syllabuses. This is an uncommon provision at A level, but one which is in step with National Curriculum methodology. The reporting of results as they are achieved during the course has a powerful motivating effect on most students with external evaluators reporting that 'the benefits of continuous assessment were whole-heartedly supported by the students and the teachers' (Bath, 1991, p. 13) — and is of considerable benefit for students when they attend interviews for higher education or work. It is widely reported that students on Wessex courses perform well at interview because they are able to discuss the detailed assignments they have undertaken in modules. They are also able to take to the interview a sizeable portfolio of work.

For each module title, a student guide and a teacher guide have been produced which indicate a range of activities that would be appropriate for both individual and group work. The relationship between these activities and the criteria for their assessment is also explicit. The following list will serve to illustrate the range of module titles available:

> drugs, medicines and people; biotechnology; forensic science; environmental health; energy for living; aspects of nuclear science; appropriate technology; the designer; illusion; the human figure; the weather and climate; business; threatened environments; a new business proposal; multi-national companies; working with a foreign language in the UK; the exercise of authority; the impact of ideas in history.

All Wessex syllabuses are assessed in two ways.

-   There is an *externally* assessed component amounting, in most cases, to 50 per cent–60 per cent of the final award. This normally takes the form of a fairly conventional written examination. The examination board is responsible for setting and marking the papers and conventional marking schemes are used to assess the work.
-   There is an *internally* assessed, externally moderated component (the modules) amounting to 40 per cent of the award. This normally takes the form of a portfolio of work which is marked by the teacher and moderated by inspection.

Generally speaking, the externally set examination papers proceed smoothly. In most cases Wessex syllabuses share the same or similar examination papers to the AEB's mode 1 equivalent and Wessex candidates perform at a comparable standard. Modules are more problematic, however. All Wessex modules are treated as coursework and use grade-related criteria in order to assess core skills and this procedure has given rise to four main concerns.

-   Is the function and the quantity of coursework in A/AS examinations appropriate?

- Is the use of explicit, grade-related criteria and an outcome-led approach to assessment at A level appropriate?
- Are the assessment of 'core skills' at A level and the relationship between the assessment of skills and subject content (knowledge) appropriate?
- Does the apparent success of candidates in modules indicate that assessment of this kind insufficiently differentiates between students?

Because of the design of Wessex courses, each of these issues is inter-related; furthermore, any one issue may attract criticism from observers. For example, coursework is often perceived as being too easy, too time consuming, too expensive, difficult to assess and moderate, unreliable and largely inappropriate at this level. These perceptions have led the present government and its advisers to express reservations about the coursework content of GCSE and A level. Set against this, evaluation of the Wessex scheme suggests that coursework motivates students and is capable of producing work of the highest quality. However, the evaluation stresses the need to accompany syllabuses with clear and unambiguous guidance about assessment criteria and the nature of the outcomes required of students. Evidence from the evaluation also confirms that:

- certain skills and abilities cannot be assessed simply using conventional written examinations, and that coursework is the only realistic and suitable way of assessing these;
- higher education and employers value students who have acquired skills such as problem solving and the ability to work both alone and with others;
- the inclusion of coursework at A level frequently improves the quality of the relationship between teachers and students;
- coursework motivates students and this, in turn, leads to higher expectations and a better quality of work from the outset of the course (Bath, 1991).

There is considerable debate associated with the feasibility of assessing core skills in A/AS examinations. The government's most recent view concerning such skills is somewhat ambiguous. On the one hand, it considers that their assessment by conventional examination is too difficult while, on the other, it is argued that they should be embedded, where appropriate, within all syllabuses. The Wessex Project has taken the view that core skills can only be successfully assessed as coursework, and are of such importance that they deserve formal recognition within the assessment framework of the examination. In addition, the Project would argue that core skills can only be effectively developed within the context of the subject/ discipline being studied. They should not be treated as 'bolt-on' extras.

## Teaching styles and learning styles

Many claims have been made for post-16 modular examinations. They are said to provide greater flexibility and improve motivation. It is argued that 'bite-sized chunks' of learning for which credit is given on completion, can be a powerful incentive for students frequently daunted by the prospect of being required to remember a large body of facts over a period of two years. While modular structures offer these potential benefits, their introduction does not necessarily lead to a significant change in teaching and learning styles.

A prime concern of the Wessex Project has been to foster such changes. It is a declared aim that students should be trained to work more independently and, in short, learn how to learn. Syllabuses, and the assessment objectives and criteria within them, have been designed to encourage such changes. The Bath University evaluation of the Project and HMI reports confirm that this strategy has been largely successful. Once students are made fully aware of what they are required to do (the learning outcomes), how their work will be assesed, and the criteria being used for assessment, they quickly learn how to improve their performance. In this achievement-led model of assessment (as opposed to the failure-based system which typifies most A levels), the teacher's role as counsellor is crucial. Teachers are able to advise and encourage students during the module so that individuals can reach their full potential. Ironically, the very success of this approach may be the Project's undoing if critics of criterion-referred examinations prevail. For them, the Wessex statistics of students' results which show a bunching of students in the upper bands and an overall high pass rate are evidence of 'grade inflation'.

The achievements of the Wessex Project are substantial, however. Through the introduction of grade-related criteria, it has broken new ground in the assessment of A levels and can demonstrate the assessment of core skills using grade-related criteria, in varied and stimulating contexts, is feasible. The pilot also shows that, in order to maintain consistently high standards, examination syllabuses need to be expressed in terms of outcomes. The link between knowledge, understanding and skills needs to be clear and explicit, and teachers require considerable guidance on the assessment of coursework at this level. In this light, all Wessex syllabuses require re-drafting so that such findings can be incorporated in new courses.

Turning to the question of teaching styles, Wessex project officers would argue that there has been a tendency in the past to 'over teach' at A level. Teachers, concerned to get through large amounts of content, have tended to rely on copious note-taking by students in preparation for their final examinations. Throughout traditional courses, regular tasks and tests are used to reinforce the need to remember facts and to acquire the techniques required to pass written examinations. The criteria assessment, as set out in syllabuses, frequently mitigates against a change towards teaching styles which place greater responsibility on the learner for his/her own learning. The relatively low status given in most A levels to the development and assessment of skills such as problem solving and oral communication also works against the development of more flexible approaches to teaching. The use of student-centred approaches, where the teacher's role is that of tutor and facilitator rather than dispenser of knowledge, is considered by many teachers to be too risky. There is little incentive to change when well tried 'chalk and talk' methods have proved successful hitherto.

The assessment of Wessex modules is designed to bring about change by requiring students to undertake research and other activities on their own and with other students. Many modules also focus on the applications of the subject in the 'real world' so that investigations take on an immediacy and relevance untypical of most academic courses at this level. The assessment criteria for modules support this process and are based on five skills statements.[1] These are the student's ability to:

- seek out and retrieve relevant information;
- design and plan an investigation/enquiry;
- carry out an investigation/enquiry using appropriate techniques/ approaches;
- evaluate/critically appraise the results of the investigation/ enquiry;
- communicate effectively in a variety of appropriate forms.

The intention is that the nature of the activities, the abilities being assessed, and the criteria used, should promote learning through research, self-reliance and problem-solving. Assessment is, therefore, rooted in criteria which describe the nature of performance required in terms of learning objectives. This provides the incentive for students to achieve and also the incentive required by teachers in order to alter the way in which they teach.

# The policy relevance of the Wessex Project

## Breaking down 'subject' barriers

It was the intention of the project that, as it grew, so the module bank would grow and, with it, the opportunity to use modules in an inter-disciplinary way. To some extent this has been the case but, overall, this aspect of the pilot has met with limited success. While it is possible to attach certain modules to more than one subject (for example, the module 'forensic science' can be used for either biology or chemistry) teachers have been reluctant to venture into territory explored in modules which are less familiar to them. The Bath evaluation does, however, point out that teachers will consider making such modules available once they feel they are more familiar and more confident with the course as a whole. Where 'inter-disciplinary' modules have been used they have usually been successful and welcomed by students in post-compulsory education and should not be underestimated as a means of increasing motivation and participation. Modules that appeal to individual interests and ambitions are highly prized and do much to motivate learners.

The process of adding modules to the 'bank', thereby increasing choice, has become increasingly difficult and time-consuming as the scheme progressed, however. All modules require the approval of the SEAC before they can be used within the examination, so the project's original intention to encourage centres to generate their own modules is no longer feasible. The process for obtaining approval is extremely cumbersome and time consuming. It can involve considerable expense since SEAC committees require to see both draft syllabuses and the teaching materials that may accompany them. Additional problems are posed for inter-disciplinary modules as these may require separate vetting by more than one subject panel. On more than one occasion, concern has been expressed about the possible dilution of a 'subject' when an inter-disciplinary module has been used. Although both higher education and industry are required to exploit the strengths of inter-disciplinary team work to tackle today's complex multi-disciplinary problems, there still appears to be deep suspicion of this approach at A level. It is, of course, common-place in vocational courses.

## Academic vocational bridge building

The government seeks to promote 'equal esteem for the academic and vocational qualifications and clearer and more accessible paths between them' (DES/DE/WO, 1991 para. 1.5). Both structurally and philosophically, Wessex A levels were designed to encourage closer harmony between academic and vocational qualifications and this enabled the project to introduce (with SEAC approval) a small scale bridging exercise in science at the Gloucester College of Arts and Technology (GLOSCAT). The scheme involved (1992) a common, integrated Business and Technology Education Council (BTEC)-A level first year course at the end of which students chose whether to study for A level or the BTEC National Diploma in science in the second year. By the end of the first year, students were able to assess their strengths, weaknesses and preferred way of working, and therefore were able, with careful counselling from their tutor, to make an informed choice whether to follow a BTEC route or an A level route in the second year. In either case, they retained the credits that had been accumulated during the first year as a contribution to both types of qualification.

Evaluation of the first year of the pilot indicates that students have enjoyed the approach and have found the applied nature of the work stimulating (GLOSCAT, 1991). Local employers welcomed the initiative as they hoped it would produce employees who combined the strengths of those with academic and vocational qualifications. However, the perception remains among students that the BTEC qualification is inferior to A level. As a result, several students who had been counselled to follow BTEC in their second year chose not to do so.

It is the view of the Wessex Project that the BTEC/A level link was only made possible because the project's A levels are significantly different from conventional A level examinations in that they contain a relatively large element of coursework. The project's assessment criteria are similar to those of BTEC and the teaching methods of both qualifications were well matched, with an emphasis on applied study. If, as government is proposing, coursework is to be severely limited and the assessment of A levels is to rely mainly on traditional examinations, then attempts at bridge-building will become increasingly artificial, if not impossible.

**Credit accumulation and credit transfer**

Modular examinations, whether academic or vocational, have a distinct advantage over non-modular courses. They enable the learner to earn credit for what he/she has achieved and this can be accumulated in small blocks. Modules may be retaken if needs be and credit can be carried forward over a number of years. While there has been opportunity in both Wessex A levels and BTEC awards for credit accumulation, opportunity to transfer credit between the two qualification systems is strictly limited as both systems are 'closed'.

After lengthy negotiation with both awarding bodies, some small concessions were made to allow credit transfer at GLOSCAT, but this was only a partial transfer. Government proposals for over-arching Advanced Diplomas and GNVQs perpetuate the notion of parallel, but separate, tracks (see also, Spours, this volume). A national framework for credit accumulation and transfer on the other hand, would change this by creating a common currency (a 'credit') and common building blocks ('units') for all qualifications. Credit accumulation would then become a reality and there would be true parity of esteem between academic and vocational qualifications and genuine opportunities to transfer credits between them.

## Conclusion

Students taking Wessex examinations have reacted well to the demands made upon them, although this is often true of pilot schemes. The first three groups to receive their final A level grades performed well. Much of the favourable reaction is attributable to the motivation of students which arises from opportunities for them to be more responsible for their own learning, from immediate feedback they receive about their achievements in modules and from their development of essential skills. At the same time, there have been problems associated with the interpretation and application of marking criteria and with workloads for some students. Also, not all teachers have been equally successful in adapting to a new kind of A level.

The examinations pose interesting problems for the examination boards. One of the implications of the assessment package is that teachers have a substantial — indeed, essential — role to play as assessors, as student achievement is often embodied in activities which, for practical reasons, moderators are unable to observe. This has led to a shift in emphasis away from the AEB as an external arbiter to its role as a partner in the process of assessment. This is surely a healthier role, but is it one that government or other examination boards will tolerate? It is encouraging that approval has been given for a new AEB A and AS level mathematics syllabus which was originally developed by the Wessex Project but not piloted. The syllabus retains much of the 'Wessex' philosophy and structure and has been available nationally since 1992.

The Wessex Project represents a response to a set of rapidly changing circumstances in English education. It is not a static project, however, and one of the practical problems it faces lies in persuading those in authority that organised flexibility of response within a project, accompanied by proper evaluation, is a profitable way of advancing education. Unfortunately, one of the consequences of the increased centralisation of education in England and Wales is a reduction in this flexibility.

## Notes

1. All Wessex subjects broadly adhere to there skills statements although these are some variations according to the particular requirements of individual subjects.
   Further information about the Wessex project may be obtained from: Bob Rainbow, Holyrood Community School, Chard, Somerset, TA20 1JL.

## References

Bath (1991) Evaluation report on the Wessex Project, University of Bath (available from the Wessex Office).

CBI (1989) *Towards a skills revolution*. Report of the Vocational Education and Training Task Force, Confederation of British Industry.

CBI (1991) Survey of students' attitudes: 17 and 18 year olds going on to higher education (Gallop Survey), Confederation of British Industry.

DES/DE/WO (1991) *Education and training for the 21st century*, Department of Education and Science, Department of Employment, Welsh Office, HMSO.

GLOSCAT (1991) 'Interim report on the Wessex-BTEC science project', the Wessex Project.

HMI (1990) *Report on the inspection of St Brendan's Sixth Form College, Bristol*, Her Majesty's Inspectorate, Department of Education and Science.

NCC (1990) *Core Skills 16–19*, National Curriculum Council.

NCVQ (1991) *General National Vocational Qualifications — Proposals for the New Qualifications, A Consultation Paper*. National Council for Vocational Qualifications.

---

**Case history B**
**Linking BTEC and A/AS Levels**
*Max Burgess*

---

## Introduction

The malaise which affects the provision of post-16, further and higher education in England, Wales and Northern Ireland has been well debated and documented. The statistics given in Figure 5.2 illustrate the focal point of concern — that the percentage participation of 16–18 year olds in full-time education and training in this country is very low compared with leading economic competitors.

**Figure** 5.2 Education and training statistics

| *Full-time education and training* | Staying on rates | | | |
|---|---|---|---|---|
| | *16 yr olds* | *17 yr olds* | *18 yr olds* | *16–18 yr olds* |
| UK (1988) | 50% | 35% | 20% | 35% |
| W. Germany (1987) | 69% | 43% | 33% | 47% |
| France (1986) | 78% | 68% | 52% | 66% |
| USA (1986) | 94% | 87% | 55% | 79% |
| Japan (1988) | 92% | 89% | 50% | 77% |

Source: DES (1990)

| School leavers' highest qualifications | *UK* | *France* | *W. Germany* |
|---|---|---|---|
| University entrance level (2 or more 'A' levels) | 15% | 35% | 30% |
| Intermediate level (1 'A' level and below) | 40% | 55% | 60% |
| Low level school leaver (below 'O' level) | 35% | – | – |
| No qualifications | 10% | 10% | 10% |

Source: CBI (1989, 18)

---

It is a widespread view that these statistics are the result of education provision which; in England and Wales, is based on early selection and low participation: 'A levels are seen as too narrow, specialised and old fashioned; vocational training is, in general, regarded as too job specific, low level and ill co-ordinated' (IPPR, 1990).

The system is thus divided and many years of social conditioning have produced a common public attitude along the lines that 'if you are clever you do A levels, if not, you do something else'. Moreover, the cost to students of A level failure is very high. There is, however an emergent movement which exhorts those educators to bridge this academic/vocational divide and bring about 'parity of esteem' between the academic and the vocational. This requires, *inter alia*, arrangements for credit transfer and/or credit accumulation between the academic and vocational areas.

Traditionally, the delivery of education has been didactic, with the tutor at the centre of the learning process and with the body of knowledge to be taught delivered in subjects. Often this was not a process which students and pupils perceived as being meaningful and relevant to their needs. The publication in 1979 of the FEU document *A Basis for Choice* was, perhaps, the event which brought to the centre of the stage ideas about student-centred approaches to learning — a process with practical, work-related outcomes which is underpinned by a focus on students' personal development.

Currently, post-16 provision revolves around academic courses leading to GCSE and A level and vocational courses, predominantly those at technician level in industry and those offering progression toward certification in the professions. Only limited vocational provision is available in schools, as many schools do not constitute a unit of resource of sufficient breadth or depth to sustain a full range of vocational awards.

The nature of provision post-16 is often described as a jungle with a welter of different awards being offered by different awarding bodies. Politically, commitment has been made towards thinning the undergrowth, particularly through the establishment of the National Council for Vocational Qualifications (NCVQ). The introduction of NVQ levels common across awarding bodies (see Jessup, this volume) has been a step forward but the setting up by the Council of around 160 lead bodies to identify sector-specific standards has, once more, threatened to increase the extent and complexity of the jungle.

This process typifies the one characteristic which all attempts to improve post-16 provision appear to share: the danger that each reform attempt may become no more than an element added to the existing system. Such increased complexity is often accompanied by claims that the added elements complement existing arrangements and that bridges and ladders are plentiful and convenient to implement. It is this incrementalism — and the status divide between academic and vocational courses — that constitutes the nub of the 'post-16 problem'.

Development work undertaken by the Business and Technology Education Council (BTEC) in recent years has been underpinned by two principles against which weaknesses in existing provision may be assessed, individual's needs and broader economic needs addressed, and reorganisation of post-16 education and training attempted. These two principles are:

- the identification and implementation of a *single learning process* for post-16 students; and
- the achievement of *outcomes* by those taking part which allow *freedom of choice* in relation to further career or education and training pathways.

These principles continue to represent a major goal for the reform of post-16 education and training. Clearly, however, such fundamental change will not be achieved in one simple step. The remainder of this case study is an account of how, during 1990-92, development work at BTEC supported a number of projects which assisted in moving post-16 provision closer to its longer-term goal.

## Linking BTEC and A/AS levels: some examples of development work

At one time, A levels and BTEC awards were regarded as entirely incompatible. This was in no sense an acrimonious situation but, rather, one which derived from the separate philosophies upon which each was based. A level pedagogy remains primarily tutor-centred, with the body of knowledge to be taught delivered in subjects. BTEC methodology, meanwhile, has traditionally been student centred, with the body of knowledge delivered in an integrated fashion. Over recent years, however, this clear cut division of method and delivery has begun to blur. Some of this is due to pressure on the system from 'below' generated by teachers; other changes have come from 'above' and have been government inspired.

One strand of development has been promoted by teachers who, in an *ad hoc* way, began considering modularising the A level curriculum in order to overcome some of its alleged limitations. The most well known outcome of this is the Wessex A level scheme (see Rainbow, this volume). Concurrently, programmes centrally funded through the technical and vocational education initiative (TVEI) have been introduced to the post-16 curriculum in which 'work-relatedness' and personal development are vital elements. Moreover, a strong similarity has emerged between the curriculum 'entitlement' implicit in TVEI methodology and the BTEC specification for 'commonskills'. Where the modular approach and/or TVEI influenced the learning process through which A level students were moving, there became possible a relationship between BTEC and A levels which had hitherto seemed impossible. These developments have, in turn, been reinforced by concern in government about low post-16 participation rates and the acknowledgement that measures should be introduced to bridge the academic-vocational divide.

A third element, alongside these 'bottom up' and 'top down' developments, was the adoption by BTEC of the 'Y' model — used to argue that a system where choice could be delayed to the age of 17 was desireable. This contrasts with the 'V' model where an irrevocable choice between the academic and vocational routes is made at 16, and where some young people choose to opt out of the system altogether. The 'V' and 'Y' models are illustrated in Figure 5.3.

**Figure 5.3:** The V and Y models

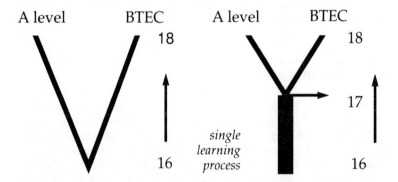

The 'Y' model incorporated the two fundamental reforming principles stated above — it provided a single learning process and outcomes ('credits') which could allow students to choose between a further year of study leading to the award of a BTEC National Diploma or A levels.

The four local examples which follow illustrate development work undertaken during 1990-92 in linking BTEC with A/AS levels, illustrating instances where the three strands, of teacher pressure, government interest and BTEC intervention had begun to come together.

**The Wessex/BTEC Science Project**

The basic structure and broad aims of this project, based at the Gloucester College of Arts and Technology (GLOSCAT), have already been outlined (Rainbow, this volume). The following paragraphs describe the project in more detail and with specific reference to the 'Y' model concept.

Curriculum development took place during the spring and summer of 1990 resulting in a pilot being implemented from September that year. No praise is too high for the Principal and staff of GLOSCAT for the speedy and effective creation of a single learning process from two sets of curricula. The specific aims of the initiative agreed by the college, the Associated Examination Board, the Wessex Project and BTEC were:

- to develop a unit-based curriculum for a common first year post-16 and to explore the feasibility of common delivery, assessment and accreditation of this curriculum;
- to provide individual counselling to students about the choice in the second year;
- to permit progression of students to the second year — either to study for A levels or the BTEC National Diploma in science, with student choice being deferred until the end of the first year;
- to provide a foundation for further development of the post-16 curriculum along similar lines.

These aims were the practical expression of the broad objectives shared by the wider Wessex A level project and by the BTEC National Diploma in Science. Integral to the Wessex approach were four curriculum objectives: the use of methods of assessment and delivery which provide continuity of experience from the 14–16 curriculum to post-16 students; the broadening of the base of A level by placing increasing emphasis on students' skills and experiences; the provision to students of courses which offer greater breadth of study; and the building of links between academic and vocational courses (Bath, 1991).

The guidelines for the design of BTEC National courses in Science, meanwhile, were based on fundamental aims shared by all BTEC courses:

> to provide a sound, intellectually demanding vocational learning experience for employees and potential employees, so that they can — in their own, employers' and nation's interests — develop the competences necessary for their work.

In addition to satisfying this basic aim, BTEC National courses in Science sought, simultaneously, to: provide an educational foundation for a range of careers and continuing education courses;

encourage students to use the knowledge, skills and understanding gained from the various parts of the course; and enhance motivation and personal qualities, including a positive attitude to working in industry and the public sector.

The broad objectives which the Wessex project and BTEC awards shared suggests a significant commonality of purpose around the development of knowledge, understanding and skills in students. In particular, the modular structure of A levels designed by the Wessex project met the criterion usual for vocational courses such as those offered by the BTEC — it could be offered in an applied, work-orientated context and it emphasised the development of personal and scientific skills.

The BTEC/Wessex/GLOSCAT scheme satisfied the two BTEC fundamental operating principles described at the beginning of this case study in several ways:

– credit transfer was an integral part of the single learning process built in during the students' first post-16 year;
– because options were kept open, the learning experience more closely met the needs of the learner;
– broadened opportunity was expected to increase motivation, inform students' choices, improve staying-on rates and bridge the academic/vocational divide.

## The Brent/East Sussex Project

This initiative was established by BTEC following the implementation of the Wessex/GLOSCAT project. Its objective was to develop the single learning process of the 'Y' model, this time in the domain of business studies. The parties to the development were advisers from the two local education authorities (LEAs), joined subsequently by a representative of the Leigh City Technology College (CTC), Dartford. Curriculum mapping and development was carried out in a similar way to that of the GLOSCAT scheme through a series of staff workshops. The intention was to incorporate A levels in business studies, sociology, general studies, communication studies, computer studies, economics, languages, government and politics as well as AS levels in business studies, computer studies, accounting languages, media studies with the BTEC National Diploma in business and finance.

Delivery began in September 1991 in two schools in Brent, the Leigh CTC, Lewes Tertiary College, Newman School, Hove, and

Bexhill Sixth Form College. Courses established in the initial stages of the project included a selection of the range of subjects which, it was planned, would eventually be covered. In 1992 these were: business studies (A level); computer studies (AS level); accounting (AS level); and computing (AS level).

## Northern Modular Science Scheme

This scheme originated from work by TVEI officers in the north west. It was also supported by ICI and Unilever and was enthusiastically welcomed by delegates at the national Association for Science Education conference in Birmingham in 1991.

In essence the scheme responded to the challenges facing post-16 science provision by providing:

– clear progression from the National Curriculum to science study, post-16;
– flexible accreditation routes that provide a variety of awards to meet the differing needs of students;
– common accreditation for BTEC awards and A/AS levels;
– a variety of teaching and learning styles which develop students' personal skills;
– balance between student outcomes which stress intellectual rigour and cross-curricular skills identified by National Curriculum Council; and
– a lively and relevant context in which to study and develop the knowledge, understanding and applications of science.

Eleven LEAs agreed to support the scheme and to enable teachers to work together in writing modules with colleagues from higher education and with industrialists.

## North Bradford Commonwealth Board

This A level enhancement scheme was led by Shipley College, Bradford, and was run jointly by the college and five local schools: Beckfoot; Nabwood Grammar; Saint Bede's Grammar; Saint Joseph's College; and Salt Grammar.

It aimed to deliver the BTEC National Diploma in business and finance concurrently with A levels in communication studies, economics or sociology and/or AS levels in computing, European studies or modular mathematics. An extract from publicity material of the scheme is succinct and apposite:

the choice between an academic and a vocational course is not an easy one, especially as both routes can lead to employment or higher education. Now we are able to offer you a new opportunity: 'Don't choose: Do both'.

## Summary and conclusions

Although the four examples given of BTEC-A/AS level combined courses are not exhaustive of those developed during 1990-92, they do constitute all those which were officially supported by BTEC. The first two mentioned are already in operation; the North Bradford scheme began recruiting students in 1992. Crucially, each scheme synthesised what had hitherto been separate academic and vocational learning pathways into a single learning process, broadened the range of opportunity available to post-16 students whilst extending and informing their choices.

The 'Y' model with its process of enabling choice at the bifurcation point (i.e. at the end of the student's first post-16 year) was influential for a number of reasons. It could be extended into a 'roll-on, roll-off' model, where the single learning process could be as long — or as short — a time as was required by the learner. The point at which the learner chose to move from the single learning process could be likened, diagrammatically, to the movement of a tag on a zip fastener! The decision point could be early; alternatively, the single learning process could carry on throughout the two years post-16 — a 'full zipper' model. The North Bradford-Shipley project was of this type — students were offered an opportunity to complete the process at 18 with both BTEC and A level qualifications. Moreover, city technology colleges, particularly Kingshurst, Solihull and Djanogly, Nottingham were interested in exploring these forms of delivery.

These schemes attempted to bridge the academic/vocational divide; they could not, however, constitute the overall solution to improving post-16 provision. There were problems in both design and delivery but they indicate a pattern of development which better meets the needs of the learner — and of the wider economy — than the traditional English practice of adding fresh schemes to those already existing.

The examples of development work given in this case study relate, in part, to the post-16 reform framework outlined by the Institute for Public Policy Research (IPPR, 1990) in which foundation and advanced stages constitute a single process of progression and replace the existing of jungle of qualifications. The IPPR's proposals offer formalised, wholesale solution. The developments outlined in the preceding pages were pragmatic, almost instant solutions to the problems of moving forward within the existing system and were motivated by the need for readily available provision to remedy the inadequate curricula currently offered to so many students. Large numbers of teachers and pupils/students could not afford to wait an indefinate period for improved course structures to emerge.

The introduction of General National Vocational Qualifications (GNVQs), incorporating as they do many of the student-centred, work-related features of BTEC programmes, is to be welcomed. Indeed, BTEC has declared its commitment to their promotion and, where GNVQs correspond to existing BTEC programmes, to the phasing out of the latter in favour of 'BTEC GNVQs'. Nevertheless, the prospective post-16 student remains faced with alternative 'streams' of provision from which to choose – with the attendant dangers of mis-selection. The stated intention of the government and the NCVQ to achieve 'parity of esteem' between vocational programmes and A/AS levels is laudable. However, even where GNVQ combined with A/AS level is suggested as a pathway, students will still be expected to perform mental gymnastics in moving from one style of learning to another. The opportunity to engage in the single learning process advocated in this case study remains elusive.

## Note

1   The views expressed are those of the author and do not necessarily represent official BTEC policy.

Further information about the programmes described in this case study may be obtained from: Max Burgess, BTEC, Central House, Upper Woburn Place, London, WC1H OHN.

## References

Bath (1991) 'Evaluation report on the Wessex project', University of Bath.
CBI (1989) *Towards a Skills Revolution*, Confederation of British Industry, London.
DES (1990) *Statistical Bulletin*, Department of Education and Science, January.
FEU (1979) *A basis for choice*, Further Education Unit.
IPPR (1990) *A British Baccalauréat: ending the division between education and training*, Institute for Public Policy Research.

---

### Case history C
### The International Baccalauréat
#### *Philippa Leggate*

---

The International Baccalauréat (IB) has been described both as an 'international passport to higher education' and merely as a two-year course for students aged between 16 and 19. Yet, the IB aims to provide a balanced education and a suitable qualification for students aiming at higher education in any part of the world. The educational aims of this programme of studies could be encapsulated in a single sentence of Alec Peterson (1987), one of the founding fathers of the IB: 'to develop to their fullest potential the powers of each individual to understand, to modify and to enjoy his or her environment, both inner and outer, in its physical, social, moral, aesthetic and spiritual aspects' (p.33). To turn this vision into a reality, these aims have been translated into the curriculum and examinations which make up the IB programme today. Before considering these in detail, however, it is worth considering how the IB first emerged, for it has a pedigree and maturity which has withstood the test of time.

## Origins, aims and development

The origins of the IB curriculum and the International Baccalauréat Organisation (IBO) may be traced back to the 1960s and the initial efforts of the International School of Geneva, and the International Schools Association (ISA), with some support from UNESCO, to develop an internationally recognised school leaving qualification. A unified international programme of studies was envisaged that would meet the particular needs of those mobile student populations likely to attend international or multi-national schools.

The pioneers of the IB in the mid-1960s were undoubtedly idealists who saw the opportunity to learn from the past and to create an educational environment in post-war Europe where harmony between peoples and nations should be strived towards as a priority. Their concept of international education was based on the premise that if students were exposed to a variety of points of view, were encouraged to think independently and to approach issues with a sense of tolerance and respect for other cultures and traditions, then a more informed and peace-loving population would surely begin to emerge: 'an international education which being really liberal and general, goes well beyond information and includes an appreciation of the art of other cultures and a discussion of the basis of morality in other cultures, is inevitably involved in the development of attitudes

[and] embraces the affective as well as the cognitive domain. Its intention is not simply to help the next generation to know better their enemies or their rivals, but to understand and collaborate better with their fellow human beings across frontiers' (Peterson, 1987, pp.194–95).

In 1963, with such ideals in mind, an International Schools Examination Syndicate (ISES) was established in Geneva to co-ordinate the gradual establishment of an International Baccalauréat curriculum and school leaving examination. This included the formation of international committees to work out the structure of the curriculum and examination as well as the preparation of trial examinations to test the newly established syllabuses.

During the period 1963 to 1967 the project gathered momentum and further support. Schools such as the United Nations International School (UNIS) in New York and the United World College of the Atlantic joined the experiment. Some welcome donations from foundations such as the Twentieth Century Fund and the Ford Foundation were contributed, as was support from certain governments. These developments made it possible, in 1967, to establish officially the IBO.

The experience gained by the IBO over the past 27 years has been both varied and enduring. Individuals, schools and countries have all contributed to a rich tapestry but, throughout, the aims of the organisation have been constant in their objective to provide an internationally recognised pre-university curriculum and entrance examination (the IB Diploma) which will give students access to higher education worldwide.

This has served as a pragmatic goal, but within the structure of the IB curriculum and within the general aims of the IBO, there co-exists a blend of the idealist and the functional.

Thus the aims of the IBO remain:

– to improve and extend international education and so promote international understanding;
– to facilitate student mobility and provide an educational service to the internationally mobile community; and
– to work in collaboration with national educational systems in developing a rigorous, balanced and international curriculum.

During the first 27 years of its existence the IBO has developed significantly. After its official establishment in 1967, it underwent an experimental period with the emphasis on preparation, planning and negotiation, as it sought to establish its identity and gain the initial steps towards recognition.

After some years delineating the structure of the programme, syllabuses, course outlines, teachers' guides and field testing examinations, the first candidates were presented for the full Diploma in 1971. The first three years constituted a trial period during which university entrance was assured to Diploma holders from a restricted number of pilot schools. The project received unanimous recognition by UNESCO's General Conference in 1974 and the end of the trial period was confirmed at the first Intergovernmental Conference at the Hague, Netherlands in 1976.

By 1976 the investigations carried out in the previous two years with schools, governments, universities and other educational experts showed that it was worth establishing the IBO as a permanent institution and in encouraging the involvement of further categories of schools and students in the IB. By 1976 the number of schools offering the IB programme had grown to 55, there were 1,600 candidates entered for the examination, and the IB Diploma had gained recognition in 37 countries. Rapid expansion has followed as clear interest continues to be demonstrated in the programme. By 1992, the IBO looked to serve some 450 schools and colleges in 62 countries around the world where the programme has been adopted. Of these schools and colleges, 28 are in the United Kingdom.

A Board of Chief Examiners, largely independent of the main administrative structure, is ultimately responsible for the setting of question papers and the award of grades. Chief Examiners are usually university teachers distinguished in their own field and of any nationality. A team of over 1,400 assistant examiners worldwide assists the Board of Chief Examiners and the examination administration is handled by the Examinations Office in Cardiff, Wales.

What does the IB programme offer students aged between 16 and 19, why has it continued to grow and how does it seek to meet the needs of young people approaching the twenty-first century?


## The IB Programme


In translating the aims of the organisation into a tangible reality, the IB curriculum seeks to incorporate the best aspects of several, national upper secondary school systems within its design. Emphasis is placed on a programme which ensures rigour and excellence covering the main fields of human experience and academic pursuits. Students are required to follow more subjects than the average British GCE A level student, thereby emphasising the importance of breadth. Yet, IB programmes are studied over a two year period which allows for a greater degree of depth than is provided by American Advanced Placement (AP) subjects, for example. The philosophy of the IB emphasises the international coherence and integrity of the programme as a whole and this coherence is reflected in the overall design and balance of the Diploma programme.

## General objectives of the IB

The programme of studies leading to the examinations for the IB Diploma is a two-year sequence for students. It is designed to be comprehensive, demanding, and yet available to qualified candidates throughout the world. Based on the pattern of no single country, it represents the desire of the founders to provide students of different linguistic, cultural and educational backgrounds with the intellectual, social and critical perspectives necessary for the adult world that lies ahead of them.

The education of the 'whole person' takes on a special significance as we approach the twenty-first century when the explosion of knowledge has made former concepts of general education increasingly difficult to achieve. The young adults of today are faced with a bewildering variety of choices; it is essential, therefore, that their academic training provides them with the values and opportunities that will enable them to choose wisely.

The weight of available information in each discipline is now such that an encyclopedic approach to education is inappropriate. Learning how to learn has become as important as the learning of the disciplines themselves. The consequent challenge to educators arises in the attempt to offer programmes that are broad enough to enhance the awareness of a common humanity, and also specific enough to ensure the acquisition of those skills (both disciplinary and interdisciplinary) that are the essential prerequisites for higher education or employment in a competitive world.

The individuals entrusted over the years with the shaping of the IB have faced this challenge. The framework remains the customary examination, a practical recognition of the fact that for the foreseeable future the achievement of students will continue to be measured by existing standards, and that an international standard must first be expressed in terms that can be understood and accepted by separate national groups. However, within this framework, the concept of flexibility has guided the design of both the curriculum and the assessment procedures.

The basic plan is derived from two principles:

1. the need for a broad general education firmly establishing the basic knowledge necessary for whatever career may be chosen or whatever academic path may be followed in further studies; and
2. the need for a choice among the subjects to be studied so that the students' options may correspond as far as possible both to their particular interests and capacities and to a pattern which ensures a properly balanced education.

The IB programme, with its three subjects at higher level (HL) and three at subsidiary level (SL), requires all participants to engage in the study of languages, sciences, mathematics, and humanities until the completion of their secondary schooling. It is a deliberate compromise between the preference for specialisation in some countries and the emphasis on breadth preferred in others. The intent is that students should indeed learn how to learn, how to analyse, how to reach considered conclusions about man, his languages and literature, his ways in society, and the scientific forces of his environment.

Three further requirements contribute to the unique nature of the Diploma: the compulsory participation in artistic activities and community service (CAS); the extended essay of some 4,000 words which demands independent work under appropriate guidance and gives candidates a first experience of personal research; and a course on the Theory of Knowledge which explores the relationship between the various disciplines, encourages internationalism and ensures that students engage in critical reflection on the knowledge and experience acquired both within and beyond the classroom.

This critical reflection is intended to extend also to the larger issue of international awareness. The various programmes of the curriculum have been created by colleagues from different national systems with the aim of encouraging in all students an appreciation of cultures and attitudes other than their own. In an age of global tension and mistrust, it is the goal of the IB to encourage students to be informed, to be tolerant and to be willing to communicate readily with others. They should be able to do so on a range of topics about which they have already formed considered opinions as a result of having shared a common two-year experience with other young adults around the world.

## Summary of the curriculum and examination

The curriculum consists of six subject groups accompanied by three other central and fundamental programmes.

Group 1      Language A1: (first language) including the study of selections from world literature;

| Group 2 | Language B: (second language), a second Language A1 or, in future, an *ab initio* language; |
|---|---|
| Group 3 | Individuals and Societies: history, geography, economics, philosophy, psychology, social anthropology, business and organisation; |
| Group 4 | Experimental Sciences: biology, chemistry (HL), general chemistry (SL), applied chemistry (SL), physics, environmental systems; |
| Group 5 | Mathematics: mathematics (HL) advanced mathematics (SL), mathematical methods (SL), mathematical studies (SL); |
| Group 6 | One of the following options: |

- art/design, music, Latin, classical Greek, computing studies; or
- a school-based Syllabus approved by the IBO.

Alternatively a candidate may offer instead of a Group 6 subject a third modern language, a second subject from Individuals and Societies, a second subject from Experimental Sciences or advanced mathematics (SL).

In addition, there are currently four pilot programmes: history and culture of the Islamic world; the language B pilot; design technology; and theatre arts.

To be eligible for the award of the Diploma, all candidates must:

- offer one subject from each of the above groups;
- offer at least three, and not more than four, of the six subjects at higher level and the others at subsidiary level; and
- participate in the three central fundamental programmes:
    i.   the submission of an extended essay in one of the extended essay subjects of the IB;
    ii.  the undertaking of a course in the theory of knowledge; and
    iii. engage in activities representing creativity, action and service (CAS) which aim to:
        - provide individual student challenge;
        - provide opportunities for service, bearing in mind that, for IB students, service may not just be to the local community, but could also be service on behalf of the environment or the international community (service to the school community could also be appropriate);
        - complement the academic disciplines of the curriculum and counter-balance the academic self-absorption of the IB student;
        - challenge and extend the individual student by developing a spirit of discovery and self-reliance;

–   encourage the development of the student's individual
    skills and interests.

Candidates may also offer single subjects, for which they will
receive a Certificate.


## Assessment and moderation procedures

Consistent with the general and subject-specific objectives of IB
courses, which focus on the development of cognitive skills and
affective capacities, assessment procedures are designed to emphasise
process rather than content and to achieve a balanced assessment of a
candidate's performance. Therefore, a variety of assessment methods
are used in order to take account of different learning styles and
cultural experience and to ensure that all candidates have the
opportunity to demonstrate their abilities. Conventional external
examination techniques are complemented by internal assessment of
coursework conducted by the teacher who thus contributes to the
overall assessment of each candidate.

1.  **Basic principles**
    –   assessment is led by curriculum and not the other way
        round;
    –   curriculum development leads to assessment development;
    –   assessment methods are based upon the need for 'fitness for
        purpose';
    –   assessment procedures and processes are fully validated;
    –   assessment within the IB is directed and managed by a
        partnership of the Chief Examiners and the IB
        Examinations Office, with external consultant support as
        necessary.

2.  **Assessment of subjects**
    The form of assessment is defined with reference to the specific
    performance criteria for each subject and at each level, and will
    consist of some or all of the following:
    External assessment
    –   written examinations which may include essay and short
        answer questions, document and data-based questions, or
        multiple choice objective tests;

- oral examinations which may be conducted by a visiting examiner as face-to-face encounters or by the teacher according to procedures established by IBO.

Internal assessment

- according to the requirements of the subject assessment may take the form of guided coursework, project work, fieldwork, practical and/or laboratory work. All internal assessment is subject to external moderation by IBO (note: in the case of approved school-based syllabuses, assessment procedures are supervised by moderator appointed by the IBO).

3. **Assessment of additional requirements for the award of the diploma**

The forms of assessment and moderation of the additional requirements for the award of the Diploma are:

- Extended Essay: the essay must be written in one of the subjects of the IB curriculum under the supervision of a qualified teacher at the school. It is externally assessed.
- Theory of Knowledge: based on a programme outline provided by the IBO, the course is designed and implemented by the teacher. It is internally assessed and is subject to external moderation.
- CAS: the CAS programme of activities should be designed and implemented by the school according to the guidelines provided by the IBO. Each school is then responsible for monitoring the individual student's activities as a part of the school's CAS programme. This, in turn, is monitored by the regional offices of the IBO.

The growing number of schools and colleges that offer the IB worldwide no longer represent simply the international or multi-national school that the IB was originally designed to serve, but a mixture of state schools, colleges and private schools. Great variations exist in the location and composition of these schools, but they all share a commitment to the IB philosophy and programme.

The nature of the IB curriculum with its particular combination of balance, breadth, specialisation and coherence provides an attractive but demanding pre-university course which has proved itself to be a good preparation for future higher education. In working towards the continued future development of the IBO, particular emphasis continues to be placed upon curriculum development, the administration of further improvements to assessment provisions and an extended regional structure of support for schools offering the IB programme around the world.

## Note

Further information about the International Baccalauréat may be obtained from:
Philippa Leggate, International Baccalaureate Organisation, Route des Morillons 15,
CH-1218, Grand-Saconnex, Genève, Switzerland.

## References

HMI (1991) *A Survey of the International Baccalauréat*, Department of Education and
    Science.
Peterson A. (1987) *Schools across frontiers*, Open Court.

# EMERGING FRAMEWORKS

---

## Emerging framework A
## Towards a Unified 16+ Curriculum
### *Andrew Morris*

---

## The academic–vocational divide

The question of the separation in England and Wales of students and courses (and sometimes teachers/lecturers and institutions) into two types — academic and vocational — has troubled many educators for a long time. The relatively low esteem accorded to vocational education, the narrowness of A level studies and the physical separation of people between different buildings, sites, departments or courses are all seen to contribute to a lowering of the performance and potential of the post-16 education system. These smouldering issues blazed into prominence with the publication of the report *A British Baccalauréat* (IPPR, 1990) by six educational and economic analysts, and the subsequent publication by leading scientists in the Royal Society of their policy document on post-16 education — *Beyond GCSE* (Royal Society, 1991).

*A British Baccalauréat* took the experiences of practitioners in schools and colleges and set these in the context of a broad economic and social analysis. The report helped to explain the enigma of why the imagination and effort of lecturers, teachers and education managers up and down the country have had such a limited effect on our educational — and economic — performance as a nation. The central problem identified in the report was that, in a fundamentally divided system, effort and resources are easily wasted through low student retention or lack of appropriate progression routes. An effective transformation of educational participation-rates and performance, it was argued, will only be sustained when the very dividedness of the system itself is tackled.

The effects of the separation of theory from practice in education provision, powerfully described in *A British Baccalauréat*, occur in the development of educational policy as well as in the student experience of the curriculum. Examination boards for A level and GCSE subjects are divorced from the validating bodies for vocational courses, whilst the training policy of the Department of Employment is not related to the educational policy of the Department for Education. Furthermore, the institutes of teacher training and educational research centres often operate in splendid isolation from the schools and colleges to whom they might be expected to offer a service.

The lessons of experience can, and to some extent do, lead to improvements in the learning and teaching strategies within specific schools or colleges. However, it becomes apparent after visiting a number of different institutions, that the fundamental problems of the post-16 curriculum are common to all colleges — and to adult education and community education providers, voluntary sector organisations, universities and polytechnics as well as businesses and training organisations. Consequently, efforts to solve problems of quality of provision will have limited effect if restricted to development in individual institutions.

The vision of a synthesis of theory and practice in the learning process lends itself neatly to the question of curriculum reform. In pursuit of the aim of developing a foundation for reform that is more thoroughly thought through than any one institution alone might be able to produce, a collaborative relationship was initiated in 1991 between the Post-16 Centre of the London University Institute of Education and the Islington Education Authority. This enabled the two organisations to explore how they might fruitfully work together. After a number of seminars, working groups and conferences, the collaboration culminated in the secondment of the author (the vice principal of a sixth form college) to the Institute of Education to investigate possible ways in which a local authority might make moves towards the creation of a more unified 16+ curriculum.

## The Unified Curriculum Project

### The 'mission'

The over-arching purpose of the Unified Curriculum Project was simple:

> to explore the ways in which a local education authority and its institutions might take practical steps towards the vision of a unified 16+ curriculum given in *A British Baccalauréat*.

As a first step, the project sought to identify specific barriers which have inhibited change in the past, particularly the problem of rigidity in provision.

### The analysis

Inflexibility in the organisation of the curriculum is partly due to the use of the 'course' and the 'subject' as the unit of delivery. These structures often result in syllabuses which minimise the involvement of the teacher and the learner in the design of the learning programme. They also help determine an educational calendar that begins in September, offers no intermediate entry points or branching points and thereby excludes many groups of intermittent, work-based or returning learners. By the same token, innovation in the curriculum is made difficult in practice, because the curriculum unit is so large. This has grave implications not only for learning in 'leading edge' topics, such as applications software, but also insofar as such rigidity inhibits the economic and cultural responsiveness of the education system as a whole. Entry into the single European market, to take an economic example, implies a spectrum of new learning demands in European languages at different levels and for specific commercial and scientific purposes — demands which are beyond the capacity of the curriculum as currently organised. Similarly, the increasing need for deeper careers counselling and for some direct experience of the workplace for all students suffers from the failure of these activities to be conceptualised as 'courses' or 'subjects'. Clearly, to overcome such inflexibility is to imply a new structure for the way the curriculum is organised and a reshaping of the units into which learning activities are organised.

Because the curriculum in Britain has long been dominated by the pressures of examinations, undue influence over education provision has been exerted by the administrative considerations of examining and validating bodies. However, there are areas of post-16 provision in England and Wales that have escaped the strictures of examining and validating bodies. Radical alternative curricula have managed to emerge in areas well away from the mainstream, particularly in spheres of post-16 provision where traditional qualification structures are blatantly dysfunctional. Furthermore, these developments at the margins have become influential in the mainstream. Access courses for mature students, for example, originated as a means of tapping into the obvious wealth of undeveloped capability present amongst ethnic minorities, working class adults and others who lacked some of the prerequisite skills and knowledge for degree study. The conviction that the system was failing the users rather than the other way round led to the rapid development of entirely original course material, adapted to the special requirements of the learners. A Level qualifications were clearly incapable of providing a useful criterion for entry into higher education for these learners, so the nature of provision and its assessment was rethought in the light of its true function. Initially, the overpowering need to facilitate the progression of this group of students enabled a pact to be drawn up locally between individual institutions in the further and higher education sectors. The criterion of success — both for students and the access courses

— was the effectiveness of student progression from one phase of the education system to another.

This combination of an institutional partnership to ensure opportunity for student progression together with a functional approach to assessment, also characterises the Compact mechanism that brings employers and educators together. In this case, the failure of conventional qualification structures to give an adequate role to employers, or to serve many of their underlying needs, has encouraged education-business partnerships to shape vital new educational developments. Through the forging of systematic education-business links that aim both to motivate learners and to invigorate the image of the workplace in the curiculum, a significant impact has been made both on the transition to work process and on raising the staying-on rate into post-16 education.

In both the Access and Compact examples, what began as local initiatives subsequently grew into national networks. In both cases the strength of the initiatives is their use of institutional, cross-sector partnerships to provide the kind of curriculum thinking that the traditional qualification system tends to suppress.

**The approach**

In trying to move towards a more unified 16+ curriculum, the approach adopted in Islington was to start from the accumulated experience of good practice and innovation within the post-16 institutions of the borough. A large conference, whose participants included lecturers and teachers in secondary, further, higher and community education, from businesses, the Training and Enterprise Council (TEC), the Compact, the Open College Federation and the careers service, generated a remarkable consensus about what the key issues for investigation were to be.

The Unified Curriculum Project needed to synthesise several different strands of experience that seemed to bear on one another. These ran across many of the boundaries that traditionally separate institutions:

- a curriculum was needed that offered the individual learner a choice of learning opportunities from the academic, pre-vocational and vocational traditions;
- encouragement was needed for individual learners to broaden their learning programmes to include a wider range of both 'subjects', skills and processes;
- a deeper, curriculum-based partnership with employers was needed which allowed the full range of students to relate their studies to the world of work;

- a framework for effective collaboration between providers of post-16 education was needed, one that would value both the school-based and FE traditions;
- a more flexible model of curriculum organisation (including intermittent study, part-time study and different combinations of work-based and college-based learning) was needed to enable new groups of potential learners to enter education and to permit continous choice for those already in the system;
- the many 'links' between higher education institutions and post-16 providers needed to be developed into a systematic partnership focusing on student progression; and
- guidance, counselling and more learner participation in the decision-making processes of learning needed to be recognised as central educational activities.

## Partnership

Some of the ideas that lay behind the Access and Compact schemes were effectively combined by the Islington Sixth Form Centre into an all-embracing system for organising student progression — a partnership called the 'Connect' scheme. Central to the scheme was a consortium of higher education institutions within which a variety of modifications to the admissions process were agreed. Similar arrangements were made in establishing a cluster of employers (identified through the Islington Compact) and further education colleges within which progression in education and training could be negotiated for those not entering higher education.

This experience of fruitful but gradual change achieved within the security of a consortium suggested a possible starting point for a more ambitious development — the move towards a more unified 16+ curriculum. If progression agreements could be constructed on a functional rather than a traditional basis, then curriculum reform would not have to rely on the vagaries of the examining and validating bodies which are, after all, independent organisations seeking profitability and market share in a fiercely competitive qualifications market.

## Modularisation

The Islington proposals (Morris, 1991) call for a process of gradual, co-ordinated modularisation across a network of post-16 providers. Thus, curriculum planners can select appropriate modular syllabi offering student choice. By delivering courses in a modular manner, the learning is organised into coherent units with clear and explicitly stated learning outcomes, and assessments are made at the end of modules. Regardless of the rate of progress in the modularisation of traditional courses, a variety of new modules can be introduced that are supplementary to existing, well-established courses of learning and available to diverse groups of students. Such supplementary modules can embody the main attributes of the unified curriculum of the future. For example, some might eschew the academic–vocational division by fusing together theoretical and applied knowledge. Others might challenge the separation of knowledge from skill by emphasising project work that integrates the two. Others, in fields such as management studies, might involve collaboration between an employer and a college or school. Such modules would need to be available to the maximum range of students at times that fit with their principal course of study.

## A credit framework

In order that all modules of learning should play a part in the progression of learners, each need to be accredited on a similar basis, whether derived from a traditional course structure such as an A level or Business and Technology Education Council (BTEC) award or from an alternative source such as an information technology certificate or locally devised study skills package. An open credit framework within which all validated modules of learning would find a place has been proposed by the Further Education Unit in its report *A Basis for Credit?* (FEU, 1992) and preliminary suggestions have been made as to how the issues of levels, credit-rating, and module specification should be managed. Using such a credit framework, where the unit of credit is based on the quantity of learning at a given level, would enable credit to be accumulated by learners through both traditional course-based learning and new, integrated supplementary modules.

## Progression arrangements

The Unified Curriculum Project envisages learners moving through a credit framework from national vocational qualification (NVQ) level 3 modules, (e.g. BTEC courses; access courses; or A levels) into higher education or employment on the basis of having accumulated a given amount of credit. Selectors would then be able to set a general credit level denoting 'eligibility' for employment or degree study, as well as proceeding to a finer-grained definition of how they require the credit to have been accumulated for particular purposes. In such a system, representatives of the progression partners (i.e. higher education selectors and recruitment staff from companies) would help to shape the credit rating and credit accumulation systems.

*Examples*

1.  A YT trainee might enrich her office practice programme with six modules from the young managers' programme earning six credits at level 2 to add to her two GCSE grade Cs. She could use these credits as a foundation for entry onto a BTEC National Diploma in business and finance at a college within the consortium.
2.  A learner, following a one year modular foundation programme in a sixth form might also accumulate credit through the same young managers' modules, in addition to completion of modules in study skills, action planning and information technology totalling 18 credits at level 2, thereby gaining entry to the same BTEC National Diploma course.
3.  A student following a course of two A levels would gain a number credits at level 3 (16 for each if using the proposals in the FEU report *A Basis for Credit?*) upon satisfactory completion. If, in addition, she gained certificates in word processing and successfully completed modules in management systems, career planning, higher education preparation and intermediate French for business, she might have accumulated a further eight credits. A polytechnic or university department within the consortium would have interviewed her because she was on target for the threshold number of credits and offered her a place on a modular humanities and business studies degree course on condition that she accumulated 40 credits and exceeded a certain grade-point average for those credits.
4.  A student might be offered a place in higher education on condition that A levels in chemistry and physics were successfully completed (earning, say, 32 credits at level 3) and that a locally devised module in mathematics for engineers had been completed together with a further five credits of the student's own choosing.
5.  In a hospital biochemistry laboratory, a junior technician may find herself accumulating credit through in-house training, day release and accreditation of her prior experience, enabling her to progress to a BTEC Higher National Diploma in a polytechnic within the consortium.

## Work in progress

In January 1992 a six-month project was launched, funded by The Paul Hamlyn Foundation, to investigate the feasibility of the proposals made in the report *Towards a Unified 16+ Curriculum* (Morris, 1991). By this time interest had spread well beyond the original base for the project in Islington. A team of teachers, lecturers, careers staff, and accreditation specialists was rapidly assembled from Warwickshire, Croydon, Harrow, Hackney, Camden, Newham and Islington to undertake the investigation. A module specification is (mid-1992) currently being developed that will present information to the learner and her/his adviser in agreed categories, as suggested in *A Basis for Credit?* The format will be common for modules delivered in colleges, schools, workplaces, training centres or adult education institutes, whether aimed at 16–19 year olds, adult returners, new employees or experienced workers.

A small group, led by a development officer with experience of the accreditation procedures used by open college networks, is investigating the methodology that will be required to establish the credit-value of a module. This will be refined through debate with tertiary practitioners from a range of colleges, schools, adult education, training and business organisations to establish its consistency. Credit values will then be negotiated in detail with the higher education and employer partners within the consortium to establish the utility of the framework.

Other members of the development team are investigating practical ways in which the modularisation and credit accumulation systems can be gradually introduced and tested within their institutions through pilot schemes. Initially, this might involve progression routes that have been carefully selected, so allowing a 'progression contract' to be negotiated within a college — for example between level 2 courses and the BTEC National Diploma in business and finance.

Other team members are developing modules, either from scratch or through adaptation, that might be offered as supplements to existing courses. These modules include:

–   management education;
–   careers education and action planning;
–   design for all;
–   studio technology;
–   dance;
–   study skills for higher education; and
–   information technology.

A consortium of universities and polytechnics has been established whose representatives are working with the project team to develop procedures for the recognition of credit.

## Future plans

When the feasibility phase of the project is completed in August 1992, a report will be published and plans will be made on the basis of the findings. Subject to continued funding from the Paul Hamlyn Foundation, the project will move into a two-year development phase that will involve piloting some aspects of the work in schools, colleges and elsewhere. The details of this phase remain to be agreed. However it looks likely that work will proceed on:

-   modularising a range of activities including careers education and performing arts activities;
-   establishing an accreditation system in collaboration with a number of accreditation agencies;
-   continuing to test some of the proposals made in the FEU report *A Basis for Credit?*;
-   establishing procedures for the recognition of credit by higher education institutions within the consortium;
-   collaborating with a Training and Enterprise Council on involving youth training schemes within the project;
-   developing an employer consortium; and
-   improving connections with other networks that share similar aims.

The project will probably continue to work with a range of organisations across the country as well in Islington. It is also likely to seek a balance between the provision of some centrally based services and a number of locally-based pilot schemes.

## Networking

Meanwhile, it is becoming ever more apparent to the project team that examples of good practice in many of these areas abound up and down the country.

Enrichment programmes are developing out of practice funded through the Technical and Vocational Education Initiative (TVEI), in HE and in employer Compacts. For example, the Youth Awards Scheme based at Bristol Polytechnic places a huge variety of enrichment activities, such as work experience, after-school clubs, sports and performing arts activities, onto a basis for systematic recording. Similarly, Liverpool University has developed a system of curriculum enrichment for 16–19 year olds that uses companies to provide realistic settings for project work. Compacts between institutions of tertiary and higher education are emerging all over the country. Some are restricted to disadvantaged 16–19 year olds, others are open to all or focus on adults. Credit awarding systems are also developing separately in different sectors. Open college networks have developed a framework using four levels and a sophisticated system of peer-based validation. The Open University has its own system and the Council for National Academic Awards (CNAA) credit accumulation and transfer system (CATS) is gaining ground rapidly in universities as well as colleges of higher education. The NVQ framework may well develop speedily with the introduction of modular, credit-based general national vocational qualifications (GNVQs).

In this rapidly shifting post-16 environment, the goals of unification, flexibility and broadening might be achieved through a harmonisation of these disparate developments. In one sense, the localisation and diversity that characterises British educational development is to be applauded. It means that, locally, teachers, planners, advisers and others can feel empowered to work creatively on behalf of the learners they serve. Diverse efforts in Liverpool, Tower Hamlets, Warwickshire and Newcastle provide much needed enrichment for those learners fortunate enough to be involved. As there are rarely single solutions to educational problems, a diversity of methods and aims is to be expected and encouraged.

However, in other, important respects, the lack of national coherence can be damaging. At the practical level, there is a limit to the number of special arrangements a university can respond to effectively, and to the number of well intentioned initiatives a school or college can sustain. Nationally, our emphasis now should turn from what one locality can achieve for one specified group of learners, to what kind of sub-structures must be evolved to sustain the growth of local initiatives aimed at creating a unified curriculum. Just as the growth process is frustrated by fragmentation, so it thrives on connectivity, nourishment, information flow and replication.

It may be helpful to draw on an analogy from the world of information technology to illustrate how a unified curriculum may develop. Computers have emerged as tools for mass use for the varied purposes of leisure, education and business, out of their earlier life as specialist instruments for restricted, technically literate groups. This has been achieved through a number of critical design revolutions. First, systems for communicating with ordinary members of the public had to be developed, often in the teeth of professional scorn, through the use of innovative approaches to graphics and formatting. Second, various operating systems developed for different groups of users had to be made compatible with one another. At the point at which different operating systems became able to communicate with one another through a single interface, the mass market became possible. Is it not possible that, in the post-16 curriculum, the various concepts of modules and of credit that have developed for different groups of learners could be integrated through the development of an open credit framework? Is it not likely that, as a result, a more unified curriculum might emerge and lead to mass participation in 16–19 education and training?

## Conclusion

Despite the many examples of excellent practice in work-based training and full- and part-time education in schools and colleges, the overall quality and quantity of provision in this country remains inadequate in comparison to those countries with whom we compete for economic survival. Although this may be partly explained by pockets of poor practice within each sector, the overiding cause must be the dividedness of the system itself. In a divided system, one sector thrives through the undervaluing of another. Universities were construed as superior to polytechnics as are A levels to BTEC qualifications; too often the success of learners has been defined in terms of someone else's failure. Such division diverts attention from the underlying questions of institutional capability and national need. It wastes scarce resources and creates barriers to progress. So long as achievement is based upon the learner's ranking in relation to the norm, rather than their capability in relation to agreed criteria, obstacles will remain to prevent the achievement of full potential by all but a small elite of learners.

A flexible curriculum, based on a firm credit framework, open to all forms of attainment, composed of learning modules of varied shapes and sizes can begin to bring together our many post-16 traditions. As the common threads begin to emerge and status differences lose their pre-eminent importance, a unified system of education and training will spread choice to a wider range of learners and will equip our citizens with the skills and knowledge that the twenty-first century will demand.

## Note

Further information about the Unified 16+ Curriculum Project may be obtained from:
Andrew Morris, Islington Federal College, Annette Road, London N7 6EX.

## References

FEU (1992) *A Basis for Credit?*, Further Education Unit.
IPPR (1990) *A British Baccalauréat*, Institute for Public Policy Research.

Morris, A. (1991) *Towards a Unified 16+ Curriculum*, Institute of Education Post-16 Centre, University of London.
Royal Society (1991) *Beyond GCSE*, Royal Society, London.

**Emerging Framework B
Towards a Coherent Post-16
Qualifications Framework: the Role of GNVQs**
*Gilbert Jessup*

## Introduction

Now that the National Curriculum for children in England and Wales
between the ages of five and 16 is largely determined and is being
phased in, the central debate in British education today is on the form
of the post-16 provision. This case study looks at the recent
programmes initiated by the government with particular reference to
the introduction of General National Vocational Qualifications
(GNVQs).

Post-16 education is dominated by the influence of A level
qualifications and preparation for higher education, even though A
levels are only considered to be suitable for about a quarter of the
16-year-old cohort and only a fifth progress to higher education. By
according such status to this minority route the majority of young
people are disadvantaged by comparison. The situation is particularly
unhelpful at a time when there is widespread recognition that we need
to raise the standards achieved across the whole cohort to prepare
young people more effectively for employment in a modern economy.

In line with most industrialised countries, and many emerging
economies in the third world, there is a consensus in the UK that we
need to increase participation in full-time education within the 16–19
age group. More generally it is felt that all young people in the age
group, including those in employment, should pursue some form of
education and training leading to qualifications.

A related government target is to increase the numbers entering
higher education by about 50 per cent over the next ten years,
bringing them up to about a third of the cohort. At the same time there
is no expectation that the numbers gaining A level qualifications will
increase significantly. The intention is to preserve A levels largely
unchanged as the 'gold standard' for 18 year olds and suitable for only
about a quarter of the population. Thus, the expansion in higher
education will come largely via other routes.

### National vocational qualifications

A qualification system to meet the future needs of occupational and
professional training is being created through national vocational
qualifications (NVQs). Work on the development of NVQs started

some six years ago and the framework of qualifications was largely in place, at levels 1 to 4, by the end of 1992. The NVQ framework is being designed to set standards for all occupations and, in time, all professions. This last point needs emphasising because it means that, for the first time in the UK, we shall have a qualifications system which promotes training relevant to all employment functions and not simply the traditional craft and professional areas.

Perhaps of even greater significance is the distinctive form of NVQs. NVQs have been deliberately designed to open access to learning for the maximum number of people. This has been achieved by defining the requirement for an award in a 'statement of competence' which is independent of any course or training programme. NVQs thus allow and encourage people to acquire competence through a variety of modes of learning, formal and informal, full-time or part-time and in a variety of locations. It is thus quite legitimate to learn and practise skills in the workplace as well as in schools, colleges and training workshops. In some occupational areas the workplace is the only place where skills can be realistically practised. Similarly, the knowledge and theory which underpin occupational or professional practice can be acquired through experience, private study or open learning as well as through more formal programmes.

The assessment criteria for NVQs also promote access to qualifications by allowing different kinds of evidence to be presented for assessment, provided it is relevant to the units being assessed. In particular, NVQs encourage assessment in the workplace and in other 'real-life' situations where such opportunities exist. The NVQ model is also ideal for the accreditation of prior learning, which is now flourishing. This flexibility in the assessment regime should not be interpreted as a relaxation of standards. The situation is quite the reverse as real demonstrations of competence, in the present or past, provide more relevant and valid modes of assessment than simulations and contrived tests.

A further feature which promotes access to NVQs is their unit structure. All NVQs are made up of a number of units, based upon occupational functions, which can be separately assessed and certificated. This provides a considerable degree of flexibility in the way in which NVQs can be built up through credit accumulation over time and in different locations. A national system of credit accumulation and transfer is gradually being established based upon the common currency of units. The unit structure also provides scope for rationalisation within the NVQ framework as many of the same functions are common to many occupations.

Another distinctive feature of NVQs, compared to many of the qualifications which NVQs are replacing, is that the requirements for awards as presented in the statements of competence are set by employers and employees within industry and not by the educational establishment. This makes NVQs more directly relevant to employment requirements and provides a sense of ownership by employers as well as a benchmark for them as major providers of training. The NVQ framework is the ideal vehicle to promote the mass uptake in training within employment that will be required to meet the highly ambitious national training targets that are being supported by all the relevant national agencies and government (CBI, 1991). The primary characteristics of NVQs can thus be summarised as access, flexibility and relevance. A detailed description of the NVQ model of qualifications and the concepts and methodology which underlies the development of NVQs is given in Jessup (1991).

## General NVQs

In May 1991, the White Paper *Education and Training in the 21st Century* was published (DES/DE/WO, 1991). In this document the government declared its intention of establishing 'parity of esteem' between academic and vocational education. In particular, the National Council for Vocational Qualifications (NCVQ) was given a remit to extend the NVQ framework to include broad-based vocational qualifications which could be delivered through full-time programmes in schools and colleges. The new qualifications were to be called General National Vocational Qualifications (GNVQs).

The particular target audience for the new qualifications was to be the 16–19 age group although it was envisaged that they would also be relevant to adults and, possibly, to the 14–16 age group. One objective in introducing GNVQs was to encourage a far higher proportion of young people to stay in full-time education beyond the end of compulsory schooling at age 16 than hitherto.

GNVQs will provide a broad-based vocational education. In addition to acquiring the basic skills and an understanding of the underlying principles in a vocational area, all students awarded a GNVQ will have achieved a range of core skills. The combination of vocational attainment plus core skills will provide a foundation from which students can progress either to further and higher education or into employment and training via NVQs. GNVQs have been designed to link the academic and vocational systems. In particular, the GNVQ at level 3 is to be aligned to GCE A levels as well as to NVQs at level 3.

It is the government's intention that GNVQs, together with NVQs, will replace other vocational qualifications and become the mainstream provision for vocational education and training similar to, and aligned with, the framework for academic qualifications of GCSEs, A levels, and first and higher degrees.

From June to September 1991, the NCVQ, working closely with the major vocational awarding bodies, the national education and training agencies and government departments, developed the criteria for the new qualifications and, simultaneously, the specifications for GNVQs in five broad vocational areas.

Both the criteria and specifications were the subject of wide-scale consultation between October and December 1991. The response indicated overwhelming support for the main proposals put forward and much detailed feedback was received that has helped to shape the form of the qualifications (Harrop, 1992). The revised criteria were accepted by Secretary of State for Education subject to changes in some of the detailed proposals for assessment and grading. Immediately following this, the Prime Minister announced on 23 January 1992 that GNVQs were to be introduced from September 1992. Since then there has been intensive work by the NCVQ, the City and Guilds London Institute (CGLI), the Royal Society of Arts (RSA) Examinations Board and the Business and Technology Education Council (BTEC) to produce the qualifications and prepare for their introduction.

The GNVQ consultation document had, as appendices, examples of draft GNVQ specifications. The wide support given to the criteria and structure of the qualifications provided a basis for the continuing development of the specifications. These were subsequently the subject of further extensive consultation among specialists within the vocational areas to which they relate. The specifications now form the basis of the GNVQs introduced in September 1992.

## The characteristics of GNVQs

GNVQs have been designed to incorporate the essential features of NVQs and they may be perceived as an extension of the NVQ model into the education system. The student outcomes in GNVQs are set out in a 'statement of achievement', similar in form to the NVQ 'statement of competence'. All GNVQs will be made up of a number of units which can be assessed and awarded as separate credits towards attainment of the qualifications. The distinction between the two forms of qualification is that GNVQs are not designed to develop occupational competence directly — that is to say that the award of a GNVQ will not provide evidence that students will be able to perform competently in an occupation but, rather, that they have achieved a foundation of skills, knowledge and understanding which underpin a range of occupations.

GNVQs have been designed for delivery in full-time education and assume students have only limited access to the workplace. The outcomes of GNVQs are stated in a way which promotes the development of active modes of learning through projects, assignments, surveys and, where the opportunity exists, experience of real life activities in work or outside. They will allow considerable flexibility in delivery, as GNVQs do not specify the syllabus or learning programme but only the outcomes that need to be achieved. The time taken for a student to gain a GNVQ may vary, recognising individual differences in the speed at which students learn and differences in learning opportunities. It will also be possible for candidates, particularly adults, to pursue GNVQs through studying part-time at a college, experience at work, open learning or private study, or a combination of such methods. GNVQs are designed to offer a genuine alternative to A levels for students who respond better to active and flexible modes of learning and more vocationally relevant topics.

In the first phase GNVQs will be introduced at levels 2 and 3, although it is expected that qualifications at levels 1 and 4 will follow. The levels are comparable to those in the NVQ framework although defined on a somewhat different basis to reflect the different objectives of the qualifications. At the same time, GNVQs have been designed to align with academic qualifications.

## GNVQ at level 3

GNVQs at level 3 will provide access to higher education as well as a foundation for further training and employment. They have been specifically designed to meet a standard comparable to that of A and AS level qualifications. This has been achieved by making each vocational unit comparable in its demands and coverage to one-sixth of an A level qualification or one-third of an AS qualification. This provides a means of comparing achievements in the two systems and offers the potential for credit transfer between GNVQs and modular A/AS qualifications (see Rainbow, this volume), particularly in programmes which are arranged on the basis of six modules per A level or three per AS qualification.

GNVQs at level 3 will be awarded on the achievement of 12 vocational units, the equivalent of two A levels. In addition, candidates will be required to achieve three core skill units at level 3. The features of core skills are described below. The 12 GNVQ vocational units consist of eight mandatory units in a vocational area chosen by the student, plus four optional units chosen from a given list. The mandatory units cover the fundamental skills, principles and processes that are common both to the student's chosen GNVQ as well as to a wide range of related occupations. The optional units both extend the scope of the mandatory units and cover more specialised applications.

Students may be encouraged to gain units beyond the 12 vocational units, to add to and broaden their range of achievement. Some students may wish to gain units in foreign language competences, particularly as these are likely to be required for the new Advanced Diploma referred to below. Others may need to cover certain additional units in mathematics to gain entry to degree programmes in science or engineering. It is intended that the GNVQ provision will be extended to meet such needs through the creation of additional units as these are required. It may also be appropriate for students to take some NVQ units to add to their overall achievement. The flexibility provided by additional units is proving to be a particularly attractive feature of the GNVQ provision in those schools and colleges where they are being introduced. It will be possible for students, if they wish, to combine a GNVQ at level 3 with one A level or one or more AS qualifications, although the GNVQ provision alone will provide a complete and varied curriculum. Figure 5.4 sets out the provision at level 3, based upon the first five GNVQs.

**GNVQ at level 2**

GNVQs at level 2 will follow a similar structure but with six vocational units instead of 12 and with units which are less demanding. It is assumed that level 2 will normally be offered in a one year programme for post-16 students whose achievements at GCSE are limited and who would have difficulty in tackling level 3 at the outset. Level 2 and 3 GNVQs have, however, been designed with some requirements in common to allow for students to make a choice between, or be selected for, one or the other at the age of 16. This will also allow for flexibility later — level 3 students not meeting these requirements will be able to gain credit at level 2, while those doing well at level 2 will be able to gain the full level 3 qualification. Core skills and additional units are features of level 2 GNVQs as they are at level 3. Progression from GNVQ at level 2 could be to a GNVQ at level 3, or to employment and training towards an NVQ at level 2 or 3, depending on the occupational area.

**Assessment of GNVQs**

The assessment regime adopted for GNVQs has been a major issue of debate. The outcome-based model of qualifications chosen for GNVQs relies heavily on assessment methodology to shape the content and modes of learning. This happens in all qualifications, of

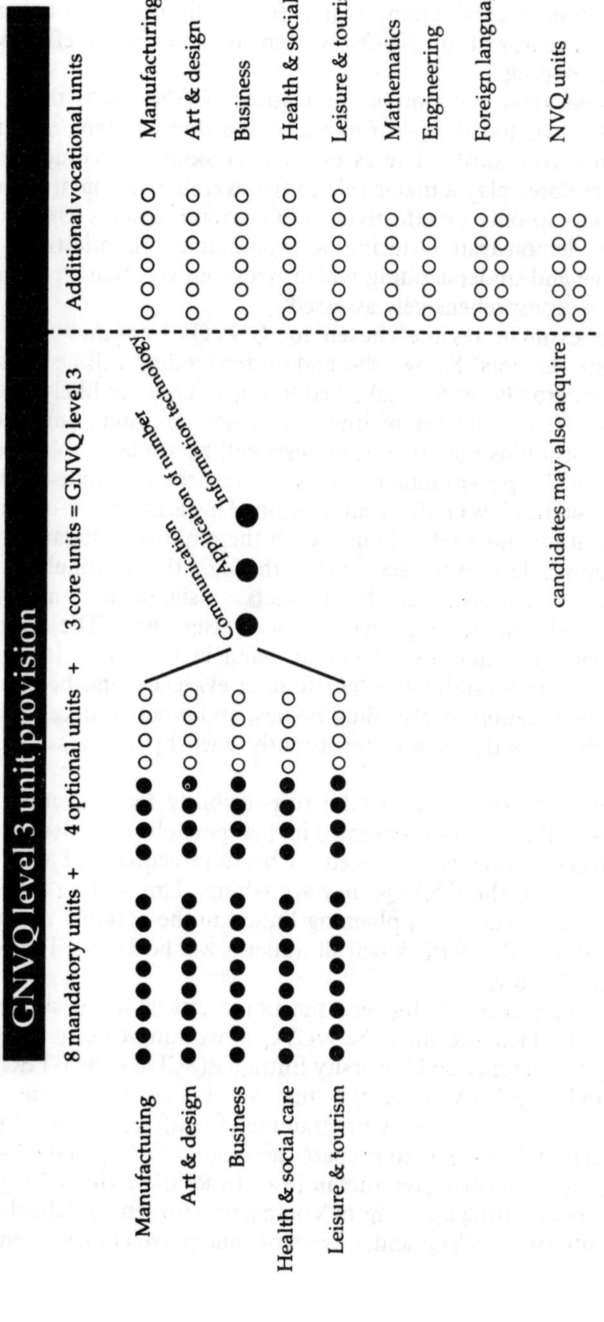
GNVQ level 3 unit provision
8 mandatory units + 4 optional units + 3 core units = GNVQ level 3
Additional vocational units
Manufacturing
Art & design
Business
Health & social care
Leisure & tourism
Communication
Application of number
Information technology
candidates may also acquire
Manufacturing
Art & design
Business
Health & social care
Leisure & tourism
Mathematics
Engineering
Foreign languages
NVQ units

Figure 5.4

course, but is more explicit in GNVQs and NVQs. Rather than assessment being seen as an undesirable necessity which interferes with the desired curriculum, as it is frequently perceived amongst teachers, assessment in NVQs is seen as a means of effectively targeting learning.

As stated above, an important feature of GNVQs is that they promote active forms of learning and the development of skills, particularly core skills. The assessment of skills and competences must, therefore, play a major role in the overall assessment regime. Such skills can only be effectively and comprehensively assessed as they are demonstrated during a programme. In addition, the knowledge and understanding which underpin vocational processes needs to be comprehensively assessed.

The assessment regime chosen for GNVQs combines both the above requirements. Knowledge and understanding will be assessed through externally set tests attached to units. They are likely to take the form of short answer or multiple-choice questions linked to a variety of stimulus materials. The tests will be available to students throughout the programme at times to meet the different needs of students and to allow credit accumulation. The facility for re-testing is also crucial for those who do not reach the required standard at the first attempt. However, assessment through the accumulation of evidence as demonstrated by projects, assignments and other activities will remain the primary form of assessment. The evidence must meet the standards set out in detail in the units. It will be accumulated in a candidate's 'portfolio of evidence' and be open to external verification by awarding bodies, and others if necessary, to ensure that standards are consistently met by centres offering GNVQs.

Students are expected to take responsibility for collecting and maintaining the evidence presented in their portfolio of evidence. As a consequence, students will need to be fully acquainted with the requirements of the GNVQs they are taking. This will be achieved through individual action planning linked to the national record of achievement (NRA) with which all students will be issued. The NRA is described below.

Establishing access to higher education is crucial to the success of GNVQs. To facilitate this, the NCVQ is working closely with the Standing Conference on University Entrance (SCUE), the BTEC, the CGLI and the RSA to ensure that admissions tutors are fully acquainted with GNVQs. A programme of conferences has already started and will continue to prepare the ground for the first GNVQ-based applications to universities in 1994. In addition, the NCVQ is in the process of setting up forms of 'compacts' between the schools and colleges offering GNVQs and universities and polytechnics, to ensure that all students who gain a GNVQ at level 3 and wish to go on to higher education are interviewed by universities. In so doing, the NCVQ hopes to ensure that their applications are all seriously considered.

## Core skills

Another significant new feature in post-16 education in England and Wales is the introduction of units which promote the development of core skills and their assessment and certification. The origins of the current programme lie in the proposals of Kenneth Baker when Secretary of State for Education (DES, 1989) and followed by John McGregor who succeeded him, that a common set of core skills should be developed in all post-16 education and training programmes, both because of their inherent value for progression into employment or higher education and as a means of aligning the different forms of provision. Also highly influential in these developments was the report of the Confederation of British Industries *Towards a Skills Revolution* (CBI, 1989), which included similar recommendations.

In education and training, core skills are naturally developed and used. But because they are embedded in a subject or occupation they will tend not to be identified as such and their potential for transfer and application to other contexts may be lost or limited. There is much evidence to suggest this is so. If, however, the core skills are recognised as such by learners their potential ability to use the skills elsewhere is increased. This implies that students would benefit from the opportunity to analyse and label the core skills they are acquiring.

The treatment of core skills within the current initiative goes considerably further than identification. The requirements set in the core skill units are such that the development of the core skills in enhanced. The range over which demonstrations are required, or their applications can be inferred, will often stretch learners by requiring application beyond that which would necessarily be required in the immediate pursuit of their occupation or subject.

The initial work on core skills development followed a ministerial remit and was carried out by the National Curriculum Council (NCC) and the NCVQ, and published in separate but complementary reports in April 1990 (NCC, 1990 and NCVQ, 1990). The six core skills identified were:

- problem solving;
- communication;
- numeracy (now described by the NCVQ as 'application of number');

- personal skills
- information technology; and
- competence in modern foreign languages.


This work was then taken forward in a joint initiative by the NCVQ, the School Examinations and Assessment Council (SEAC), the NCC and the Further Education Unit (FEU) in which a framework of core skills and methods for their assessment was agreed. Building upon this, the NCVQ has formulated the core skill statements as units like other units in the NVQ/GNVQ system. The units were subjected to intensive consultation and piloting in a variety of programmes during 1991/92 (Oates, 1992).

The features of this development that distinguish it from many initiatives in the 1980s and earlier are that the core skills have been:

- expressed in a manner that makes possible their assessment and certification;
- expressed at five levels, loosely related to the five levels of the NVQ framework, to facilitate and recognise progression in core skill achievement;
- specified to align with the National Curriculum, A levels and NVQs, as far as this is possible; and
- expressed independently of any qualification and form of education and training provision so that they can be built into any academic or vocational programme or qualification.


The core skill units in communication, application of number and information technology were introduced into GNVQs in September 1992. The foreign language units were also offered within the GNVQ provision during 1992/93 as additional units. The units in problem solving and personal skills are being further piloted and refined prior to their probable introduction, in September 1993. Development work continues with all the core skills to provide further guidance on assessment and their effective use in different contexts.

Now that the first core skill units have been accredited within the NVQ system they will be generally available for adoption within other programmes and qualifications. The five level framework makes the core skills relevant to a wide range of provision from National Curriculum level 4 to degree-level study, and their incorporation in the Advanced Diploma (see below) ensures that they will be widely used. Moreover, discussions are already taking place with the Open University to explore how they might be incorporated into its foundation programmes and other higher education courses.

## The Advanced Diploma

A further initiative announced by the Government in the White Paper *Education and Training in the 21st Century* (DES/DE/WO, 1991), and restated in a speech by the Prime Minister on 23 January 1992, is the introduction of the Advanced Diploma. Its objective is to set a target or standard for education and training at 18+ which will enhance the status of vocational education. A further objective is to promote a greater degree of breadth in the post-16 curriculum. The proposals announced in January 1992 indicated that the Advanced Diploma would be awarded to those who achieve: one A level + two AS qualifications (or two As + one AS or three As); or a GNVQ level 3; or NVQ level 3 plus a specified level of attainment in English, mathematics and a modern foreign language. The latter level is a matter of debate but is likely to be pitched at National Curriculum level 7 or GCSE grade C. It has also been indicated that the equivalent level of attainment in the core skill units described above (level 3) in communication, application of number and foreign languages would be accepted as an alternative to GCSE.

The proposal for an Advanced Diploma is a clear signal that the vocational route should have parity of esteem with the academic, fixing the alignment between A levels and NVQs/GNVQs at level 3. Further, it formally recognises the core skill credits and their alignment with the National Curriculum/GCSE. Assuming that the Advanced Diploma achieves recognition and credibility as a means of progression to employment and higher education, it will also encourage young people to aim at a broader level of attainment than is currently achieved through A levels and NVQs alone. It is interesting to note that GNVQs at level 3 already meet the requirements of the Advanced Diploma, with the exception of foreign languages which will be offered initially through additional units. It is expected that in future years modern foreign language attainments will be incorporated as a requirement of GNVQs to align them with the Advanced Diploma.

## National Record of Achievement

Also relevant to the emerging post-16 strategy in England and Wales is the future development of the national record of achievement (NRA). The NRA was launched early in 1991 by the Secretary of State for Employment and reinforced the requirement already established through the Technical and Vocational Education Initiative (TVEI) that all pupils leaving full time education should be

provided with a written record of achievement. Initially, the NRA was made freely available to all who wished to use it but was targeted mainly at the 16 year old cohort. In April 1992, NCVQ took over the distribution of the NRA and its future development.

The NCVQ is funded to make the NRA available free of charge to school students, in quantities based upon the numbers in their last year pre-16, although we would hope to encourage its adoption from the age of 14 or earlier. It will also be available free of charge to all trainees entering the Youth Training and Employment Training programmes, and promoted for sale to other target groups in further and higher education and employment. The plan is to encourage its adoption as the universally recognised record of achievement spanning different forms of education and training.

Within the NRA system the concepts of individual action planning and the continuous recording of achievement will be promoted, as will the curriculum models that these processes assume. The NRA will encourage recording of evidence and achievements within formal qualification systems such as the National Curriculum and NVQs, as well as the less formal achievements which have tended to be associated with records of achievement in schools. There is no intention that the various approaches to recording which have been enthusiastically and successfully developed in schools through the 1980s should be discontinued. There is no need for standardisation when the primary function of such recording is formative. But when students wish to summarise their achievements for employers or others outside their institution, the adoption of widely accepted conventions is desirable to achieve clarity of communication. The development and recording of core skills, which has always had an important role in the record of achievement movement, will become more systematic and rigorous with the adoption of the new core skill units in GNVQs.

The NRA has an important role to play, and a symbolic significance, in bringing together achievements at different ages and across different forms of education and training provision.

## Coherent framework

It will be apparent from the foregoing discussion of post-16 initiatives that the government's strategy is to enhance the status of vocational education and training in the UK. The implications of this move are profound, not only in preparing young people more effectively for employment — a matter of major concern in the UK currently — but also in its effect on the national education system as a whole.

The introduction of GNVQs will have major implications for post-16 education. GNVQs could well become the means of encouraging mass participation in full-time education for the 16–19 age group if A/AS levels are unchanged and remain the preserve of the academic minority. Nevertheless, if GNVQs do become established within the post-16 curriculum over the next few years and the potential benefits of its outcome-unit-based provision are realised, it is difficult to imagine that A levels will remain unchanged in the latter part of the decade. GNVQs offer an evolutionary way forward, in which the A level standard can be maintained while a parallel form of provision is tried and established.

Not only are the barriers between academic and vocational qualifications likely to be gradually eroded, but so are the artificial barriers which divide pre-16 education, post-16 education and training, and higher education. NVQs do not recognise such distinctions, nor will GNVQs after their initial introduction. The movement towards outcome-based qualifications leads inevitably away from tightly defined, institution-based provision, thus opening access to learning to a far larger proportion of the population than hitherto.

The intention behind the recent initiatives is that the UK should adopt a coherent national framework of qualifications embracing all forms of education and training achievement such as that indicated in Figure 5.2. A version of this figure appeared in *Education and Training for the 21st Century*.

There are, however, limitations to the coherence that can be achieved given the different curriculum structures and assessment regimes which currently exist in the UK system. We shall not be able to achieve a fully integrated system until all forms of learning provision are formulated in a similar manner, namely through the specification of outcomes. Not only would this provide a coherent system and raise the status of vocational education and training, but many other benefits would accrue.

It would greatly improve access and flexibility to learning programmes. It would expand the range of learning opportunities available and provide scope for individually tailored provision to suit the needs and circumstances of different people. It would result in a more cost-effective system of education and training, focused upon the real development opportunities sought by individuals and society. Perhaps most importantly, it would encourage people to take responsibility for their own learning, both initially and on a continuing basis throughout their careers.

**Figure 5.5:** A National framework for education and training

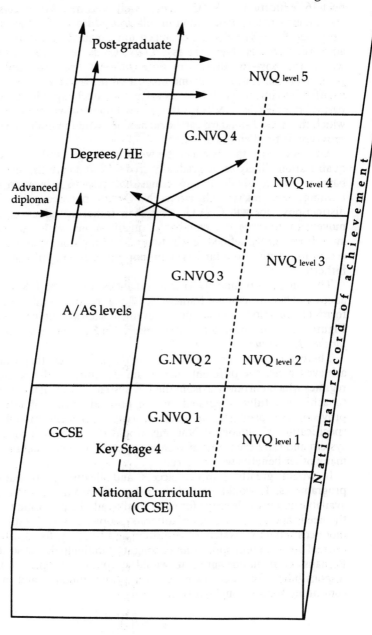

# References

CBI (1989) *Towards a Skills Revolution*, Confederation of British Industry, London.

CBI (1991) *World Class Targets*, Confederation of British Industry, London.

DES (1989) *Further Education, a new Strategy*, speech by Kenneth Baker, Department of Education and Science.

DES/DE/WO (1991) *Education and Training for the 21st Century*, Volume 1, Department of Education and Science/Department of Employment/Welsh Office, HMSO.

Harrop, J. (1992) *Response to the Consultation on General National Vocational Qualifications*, NCVQ Report No.15, National Council for Vocational Qualifications, London.

Jessup, G. (1990) *Common Learning Outcomes: Core Skills in A/AS Levels and NVQs*, Report No.6, National Council for Vocational Qualifications, London.

Jessup, G. (1991) *Outcomes: NVQs and the Emerging Model of Education and Training*, Falmer Press, London.

NCC (1990) *Core Skills 16–19*, National Curriculum Council, York.

NCVQ (1990) *Common Learning Outcomes: Core Skills in A/AS Levels and NVQs*, National Council for Vocational Qualifications, London.

Oates, T. (1992) *Developing and Piloting the NCVQ Core Skills Units*, Report No.16, National Council for Vocational Qualifications, London.

# 6 Analysis: the reform of qualifications within a divided system

## Ken Spours

### The dual track and the role of external frameworks

The aim of this chapter is to explore how, in England and Wales, the process of reforming qualifications for the 16–19 age group has been undertaken within a divided system. First, this means analysing the government's strategy of creating an explicit 'dual track' system of academic and vocational qualifications 16–19, including changes in GCSE and A levels and the emergence of general national vocational qualifications (GNVQs) within the vocational track. Second, we need to acknowledge and analyse local and national attempts to tackle divisions within the system of qualifications initiated by examining and validating bodies, 16–19 providers and HE institutions. Included in this analysis is an evaluation of the significance of the case histories and qualification frameworks described in Chapter 5 as contributions to further development of 16–19 provision.

How can we understand the changes currently taking place in 16–19 qualifications and their significance? At the outset it is important to appreciate the nature of the government's own strategy signalled by the White Paper *Education and Training for the 21st Century* (DES/DE/WO, 1991). Here the intention is to establish more formally the existing dual track system of academic and vocational qualifications. The strategy consists of three basic elements: first, the retrenchment of the academic track by restricting the amount of course-work in GCSE and A levels; second, the construction of a

broad vocational track consisting of GNVQs and NVQs which, at level 3, offer access to higher education; third, though less evident so far, is the development of external and over-arching diplomas to confer 'parity of esteem' between the separate tracks.

These changes represent a new phase in post-16 qualifications. They are attempts to reform our already deeply fragmented system of qualifications, to modernise it, but at the same time to keep it formally divided. They are also part of a new government emphasis on early specialisation both at 11 and at 14, highlighted in the most recent schools White Paper *Choice and Diversity* (DFE, 1992a).

But this is not the complete picture. Despite the increase in centralisation of education policy-making and functions, the English and Welsh system of education and training has, over the last decade or so, offered room for local innovation. Specifically, the operation of market-oriented examining and validating bodies and increased institutional autonomy has made local diversity more rather than less likely. We find, for example, a range of initiatives in the qualifications field which, in varying degree, set out to challenge the perpetuation of a narrow, divided and inflexible system. But given the capacity of the English system to absorb change by simply adding initiatives and thereby increasing complexity and confusion, it is important to evaluate the relative impact of these initiatives. To what extent do they contribute towards a less divided and more unified system or do they, on the contrary, function as an integral part of a reformed dual system?

An evaluation of the impact of such reforms can be aided if a set of distinct categories is identified:

- changes to the structure and content of *mainstream qualifications* (A levels and NVQs) which do not challenge the logic of the dual track system, e.g. AS levels; coursework assessment;
- changes *external* to mainstream qualifications but which co-exist with the divided dual track system, e.g. the over-arching Ordinary and Advanced Diplomas; the qualifications framework developed by the National Council for Vocational Qualifications (NCVQ); the International Baccalauréat; and the recording of achievement process;
- local pilot schemes which change *internal* arrangements within and between mainstream qualifications and which can be seen to challenge the logic of a divided qualifications system, e.g. case histories from Chapter 5 such as the Wessex Modular A Level Project and the A level/BTEC National Diploma 'Y' model.

Not all of the initiatives described in Chapter 5 fall neatly into these categories, however. GNVQs and the Unified Curriculum Project (including its credit accumulation and transfer arrangements), for example, straddle the boundaries between the second and third categories. Nevertheless, the distinction between reform internal to existing qualifications and the development of external qualification frameworks is helpful when analysing current reform and prompts four fundamental questions.

1.  What effect will changes in the academic track have upon the qualifications system as a whole?
2.  To what extent does the development of GNVQs represent a form of rationalisation and enhancement of the vocational track?
3.  To what extent is the development of external qualification frameworks such as over-arching diplomas, a feature of a divided system or a challenge to it?
4.  What is the significance of pilot schemes which have promoted or suggested structural change *within* and between qualifications — in particular the use of strategies of modularisation and credit accumulation and transfer?

The remainder of the chapter attempts to address these questions by focusing on four aspects of 16–19 reform: the academic track; the vocational track; external frameworks; and movements towards a unified system. It is concluded with an overall analysis of the current state (1992) of the qualifications system in England and Wales.

## Reform of the dual track system: changes in academic qualifications

Academic qualifications have always dominated the post-16 scene in England and Wales and continue to do so. But there have been significant twists and turns of policy in recent years. Until 1989/90 it looked as if, despite the rejection of the Higginson Report (HMSO, 1988) there would continue a slow but marked change in A level syllabuses with the prospect of more modular development, increased components of coursework, the introduction of criterion-referenced assessment and an expanded role for 'core skills'. But this process of diversification of the academic track came to an abrupt end with the publication of *Education and Training for the 21st Century* (DES/DE/WO, 1991).

Academic qualifications at 16 and 18 appear now to have 'frozen over' with many of the previous changes having been pushed into reverse. This retrenchment of the academic track suggests three future developments: first, the negative impact of limited coursework on student motivation, future pass rates, patterns of participation and curriculum development; second, a narrowing of the concept of core skills as the focus for reform moves from A levels to the overarching Diplomas and GNVQs; and third, the limited impact of AS levels upon the existing system and their fragile position within a reformed dual track system.

## GCSE, A levels and the issue of coursework

The situation facing the Conservative Government in 1990 was that of a mismatch between GCSE, with its extensive coursework components, and A levels with their emphasis on terminal examinations. This tension has been resolved in favour of keeping current A level methods of assessment and spreading these to GCSE through the decision to restrict the amount of coursework undertaken at this level.

In the area of core skills, on the other hand, the government has had to confront a stark choice. As the School Examinations and Assessment Council (SEAC) and NCVQ could not agree on how to integrate core skills into both A levels and occupationally-focused NVQs, the Conservatives either had to create more common ground between A levels and NVQs or abandon the exercise. The latter course was chosen and there commenced (with the advice of right-wing think tanks) a new phase of government policy to restrict the expansion of the academic track and, instead, to broaden the vocational track.

The policy to restrict coursework to 20/30 per cent in the case of most academic subjects examined at 16 and 18 is the determining feature of the current stage of government policy on qualifications and will have dramatic effects on the whole of post-16 education and training. It is a policy of retrenchment in three fundamental respects.

- First, it is turning back the clock to an emphasis on assessment by terminal examination regardless of a broad professional consensus that increased coursework components have helped to improve levels of motivation, resulted in greater levels of student application and increased levels of performance, particularly for those at the margins of the academic track.
- Second, the policy of setting papers of different levels of difficulty in English, maths and a foreign language in GCSE, is a reinforcement of the 'early selection' function of our qualifications system and will predetermine the level of pupils' attainment. Furthermore, it could negatively interact with the syndrome of teachers' low expectation of pupils, prevalent in inner city areas. This emphasis on early selection is entirely

consistent with the more recent emphasis on specialisation highlighted in the 1992 schools White Paper *Choice and Diversity*.
–   Finally, it is retrenchment in terms of the pattern of post-16 participation. The most significant effect of the proposed measures is that participation in the academic track post-16 (that is, participation with a prospect of attaining two A-C grade A levels) will probably not spread beyond the first quartile (the top 25 per cent) of the cohort. It could fall below 20 per cent if restrictions in coursework have the anticipated negative effect on participation. At present about 22 per cent of the cohort achieve two or more good A levels (a rise from 13 per cent in 1979) (Hughes, 1991). However about 30 per cent of those entering A level courses end up with nothing at all. More students than ever want to take A levels but the government is caught between wanting to use high failure rates to preserve standards and having to deal with the problem this causes — most notably the negative effect on student motivation and, therefore, on sustained participation to 18. For these reasons, A levels can now be regarded as having reached their saturation point and those who cannot cope should be advised to take up vocational qualifications.

This latter tension in policy is given little publicity; instead the official government stance on assessment — with its emphasis on terminal examination — is that coursework, which is locally validated, leads to difference in the measurement of levels of attainment. Whilst there is some evidence of problems of rigour in relation to assessing coursework in A and AS levels, (SEAC, 1992, pp. 10–12) it is a matter of debate as to how serious the problem is and whether there is an optimum trade-off between rigour and increased student motivation and performance. There has been little discussion about the degree to which increased moderation could improve rigour in assessment based predominantly upon coursework. Since the 1991 post-16 White Paper there has been some flexibility in favour of increased assessment through coursework in business studies and technology due to their practical nature. The danger here is that success in these subjects may be dubbed as second-rate achievement in the academic track — particularly when students seek access to the more prestigious universities.

However, the issue of coursework goes much deeper than this and reflects an exclusive attitude towards student potential and achievement. The *Times Educational Supplement*, reflecting upon a speech by Sir Christopher Ball, put this point succinctly:

. . . the British have persistently underestimated the human potential to learn. The worthy plodder, so the received wisdom goes, will never make the grade. The gifted layabout (if he pulls his finger out for a minute or two) probably will. (TES, 1992a)

Coursework tends to reward the plodder. But it also makes life more interesting and challenging for the gifted. More significantly for the system however, higher performance due to coursework tends to reduce the exclusive nature of an academic award and it is precisely this form of selection which has been historically dominant in English qualifications. This point is illustrated very clearly in the case-history by Bob Rainbow (Chapter 5), who reflects on the ambivalence of examination boards at the increased number of high grades achieved by students in the Wessex Modular A level Project due to coursework in option modules.

The immediate effect of the government's 20/30 per cent coursework limit, in the case of most subjects, is to increase the possibility of failure for those around the margins of the cohort taking GCSE and A levels. As the Wessex Project shows, most students appear able to perform to a higher level through coursework than in examinations. Coursework tends to offer opportunities for pass grades to those who may have struggled with a high examination component in a subject. The reasons for increased performance through coursework are complex but it is arguable that two factors stand out. Sheer hard work in coursework can lead to higher grades whereas success at terminal examinations is based more upon the demonstration of particular range of skills (e.g. being able to write and marshal facts quickly). Second, locally-validated work is less prone to norm-referencing. That is, there is not the same pressure from examination boards upon external examiners to ensure that the proportion of students gaining certain grades should be broadly the same from year to year. Instead, coursework has to have criteria and if students demonstrate the criteria they achieve the grade.

But this argument for coursework is rejected by education ministers. The attitude of the government to the academic track and the role of coursework is not based primarily upon technical questions about assessment, but is a reflection of ideological and political considerations. These continue to equate education qualifications with the selection of an elite and talk of maintaining standards rather than improving them. This approach is reflected in the August ritual of debating A level standards in the educational press when the national results are published.[1] If more students are passing examinations, the argument goes, then surely standards are falling.

Given current post-16 policies, recent rises in post-16 staying-on rates present a dilemma. More students are wanting to take A levels —

a reflection of their increased educational aspirations. Parents realise that these examinations are still the passport to success, even though the risk of failure is daunting. In fact, some appear positively attracted by failure rates arguing that something scarce must be worth having. But here lies a critical contradiction. The government evokes the importance of parental choice yet many parents' perceptions (and those of many employers) directly undermine the aim of a publicly recognised and enhanced vocational track. To achieve its aims of more highly regarded vocational qualifications, the government needs to challenge public perceptions of the relative value of academic and vocational study yet it undermines this possibility by communicating mixed messages. Its approach of pushing those unable to cope with the academic track into an 'enhanced vocational stream' is reinforcing the message that the vocational is second best. It should, therefore, some as no surprise if many parents and students continue to risk failure in their search for three good A levels and the 70 per cent chance of acceptance in the long-established universities that such qualifications bring.

**The narrowing of the post-16 'core'**

The Conservative Government has been a very reluctant convert to the argument for breadth of study in post-16 education having, until recently, put its trust in narrow forms of specialisation, whether these be single-subject A levels or occupationally-focused NVQs. Its flirtation with the curriculum development of core skills was a feature of DES/ED collaboration during the period 1988 to 1990 and was seen, in a rather minimalist way, as a means of bridging the academic/voational divide whilst, at the same time, providing what industry says it wants from post-16 education.[2]

The developments for promoting core studies in post-16 education announced in *Education and Training for the 21st Century*, see a narrowing of what should constitute the 'core' as policy focuses on a broader vocational track and on overarching diplomas. Two elements survive.

–   There will be a core which focuses upon maths, English and a modern language. These subjects may be accredited on the basis of previous attainment of GCSEs or National Curriculum study (at, say, National Curriculum level 7 or above). They may also be tested externally as part of the award of the overarching Ordinary Diploma for those who have not achieved a sufficiently high level of attainment within the National Curriculum.
–   A broader concept of core skills will be an integral part of GNVQs, as they are currently in the case of BTEC awards. In this

context, however, they can no longer be seen as the government's attempt to bridge the academic/vocational divide. This task, it is hoped, will be achieved by the award of the Advanced Diploma which straddles the two tracks.

The effect of this development within post-16 studies is a double reduction. First, it reduces a diverse concept of 'core' outlined by the National Curriculum Council in a consultative document of 1990 (NCC, 1990) to three essential subject areas. Second, it reduces the proportion of the cohort to be affected by requirements for breadth of attainment. Not all students will have to broaden their study post-16 since most of those in the academic track will have already attained the required levels in maths, English and a modern language during pre-16 study. In this way, the core studies issue further underlines the government's curriculum policy. It is prepared to broaden the curriculum requirements slightly for those outside the top quartile in the vocational track, but the curriculum of the 'elite' remains unchanged. The government's concern — understandably given its position over A level examinations — is that A level subjects should not be 'distorted' by the inclusion of core skills.

From the perspective of a more unified and integrated approach to post-16 education and training, the proposals fall well short of what is required. Those arguing for a unified post-16 qualifications system (such as Morris in Chapter 5) have defined its core in multi-dimensional terms: a greater core content of study; the promotion of core awareness in such areas as scientific, technological, economic and industrial understanding; the integration of core skills into qualifications; and the promotion of core learning and assessment processes as part of a unified qualifications structure (Young, 1991, 1992).

### The role of AS levels: breadth of learning or just more A level points?

Charting the current progress of AS levels provides another interesting commentary on the effect of more additions to the post-16 system. In 1991 the government rejected the idea that AS should be an intermediate examination despite lobbying from the independent schools' Headmasters' Conference (Brookes, 1991). Instead it opted for an examination covering half the breadth of an A level but studied to the same depth and with the same intellectual demands as A levels. The official aim of AS levels is to allow for greater breadth of study in the academic track and the government has openly supported a 2A+ 2AS combination (DFE, 1992b). But the system has not developed in this direction and AS development has been much slower than officials hoped. In 1990 there was one AS level entry for every fourteen at A level (Nash, 1991).

The Universities' Central Council for Admissions (UCCA) statistics for 1990 would seem to confirm that AS levels suffer from low credibility due to the continued dominance of A levels in university selection. AS studies appear to be being used to supplement an A level diet, not so much in order to add breadth but in order to show students' capacity to work beyond the three A level work-load. Meanwhile, competition is increasing to gain entry to the established universities. To have a majority chance (60 per cent plus) of being accepted, a student needs at least three A levels or better still, between three and four. This appears to be the most significant use of AS attainment. With one extra AS on top of three A levels UCCA reports that students increase their chances of acceptance into higher education from 60 to 72 per cent.

The rising pattern of higher education (HE) participation is likely to produce a paradoxical effect. The most prestigious universities will demand more A level points in response to rising demand. The new universities, on the other hand, under pressure to increase student recruitment, will be more inclined to accept AS levels as well as low thresholds of entry points across both levels of examination. In this way AS has a future in a divided HE system but not as an equal to A levels.

### Retrenchment of the academic track and the problems of internal change in qualifications

The retrenchment of the academic track will have far-reaching effects on wider post-16 curriculum reform strategies. As explained in Chapter 4, the period from 1985 to 1990 witnessed noticeable experimentation with the academic track marked by the development of GCSE, the impact of Technical and Vocational Education Initiative (TVEI) curriculum development projects, a growth of modular A levels and a slow but marked increase in the coursework component of many A levels. Two of the case histories in Chapter 5 — the Wessex Project on Modular A levels (Rainbow) and the linking of Business and Technology Education Council (BTEC) awards and A/AS levels (Burgess) — can be characterised as imaginative attempts to alter further the internal nature of qualifications by modularising and promoting common learning processes between the two tracks.

The 'freezing' of the traditional academic track through a reduction in coursework and an increased emphasis on external testing endangers this kind of reform strategy. The promotion of modular developments and creation of common ground between academic and vocational qualifications is highly dependent upon flexible forms of assessment, carried out locally and validated nationally. These experiments may survive because of continued demand for modular developments both locally and by some examination boards but, for the time being, it is difficult to see how they can progress further in current conditions. Nevertheless, they are significant innovations and remain as signposts for the future direction of reform when political conditions change. The Wessex Project, in particular, with its widespread success in pilot form, shows how the academic track can be amended to produce higher results, improve motivation, broaden choice and build effective bridges with the vocational track. With the closing down of reform opportunities in the academic track, however, the focus of attention has switched to the prospects for reform of vocational qualifications.

## The vocational track: breadth and flexibility?

The reform and broadening of the vocational track in post-16 education and training is the substantive proposal in the qualifications section of *Education and Training for the 21st Century*. It is also represents a classic policy U-turn. Since 1986 the government has been determined to reform vocational qualifications through the work of NCVQ and the development of narrow, occupationally-focused NVQs. In the quest for broader vocational qualifications this policy is being reversed through a new emphasis on GNVQs in 16–19 education and training.

In comparison with its European counterparts, the English system of vocational qualifications has been characterised by low levels of participation and the absence of clear ladders of progression (Smithers and Robinson, 1991). Earlier attempts at vocationalism such as TVEI did not result in support for the development of a distinct vocational route. Instead, in its extension phase, TVEI has emphasised a broad vocational entitlement for all students. In contrast, the prime government aim of post-16 policy is now to move from the current estimate of 25 per cent to a situation in which 40 per cent of the cohort attain NVQ Level 3 through the vocational track.[3] It is against this aim of nearly doubling the level of achievement at NVQ level 3 that we can judge both the significance and success of the construction of an alternative vocational track and the potential role of GNVQs in this process.

### General NVQs: alternative track or coherent framework?

GNVQs are designed to appeal to students in full-time education and training by focusing them on a broad vocational education. Because of this and their emphasis on broad skills, it is hoped that GNVQs will have equal standing with academic qualifications and will provide a more clearly defined vocational route, not only into higher skilled jobs, but also into HE. The analysis by Gilbert Jessup in Chapter 5 states clearly how a broad-based vocational education can utilise the NVQ framework to provide an alternative ladder of progression to HE.

The concept of GNVQs will receive substantial professional support because, to a large extent, they are based upon tried and tested practices in the awards of the BTEC. But there has been criticism of the narrow pilot base for GNVQs of 90 institutions, the relative secrecy of GNVQ development and a lack of real consultation over their introduction. GNVQs may win support as a concept but their design and implementation may draw less unanimity.

The criteria for judging GNVQs should not be based upon how closely they resemble past awards but upon how far they can meet the targets of the future — in particular the government's aim of enhancing the vocational route. Can GNVQs achieve parity of esteem with academic qualifications and double the number of vocational students attaining level 3? Here, once again, we come to the nub of the issue: the relationship of vocational awards to A levels and the academic track. There appear to be three basic strands of opinion as to the potential of GNVQs. The government clearly sees them as defining a separate but highly regarded post-16 route. Others involved in their development such as Gilbert Jessup (this volume) see GNVQs as an 'evolutionary path' in which the barriers and divisions will be gradually eroded. A third position, argued here, is that the real barrier to any of these developments are A levels, the retention of which will ensure that history repeats itself with vocational awards falling under the shadow of academic qualifications. At present it appears that the development of GNVQs is being dictated by traditional A level provision and the opportunities for reciprocal development are being ignored. This is reflected in the proposal for a substantial examined element of GNVQs.[4] A further problem for GNVQs is that the plans to reduce A level coursework also reduce the potential for reciprocity between the award systems. Less coursework means less modularity and less modularity means less flexibility to mix study. This, in turn, will affect the aim of running common A level-GNVQ units such as those pioneered in 'Y model' schemes described by Max Burgess in Chapter 5.

Further tensions between the academic and vocational are reflected in the complex combination of assessment requirements for GNVQs which, as Gilbert Jessup explains, have been the subject of major debate. Running through the development of GNVQs has been the aim of achieving parity of esteem with the academic track whilst, at the same time, upholding the competence-based approach of NVQs. The result is a compromise based on the external testing of knowledge and understanding combined with a pass/fail assessment of students' core skills demonstrated through the GNVQ units. Despite this, the assessment debate has given rise to some innovations: the external test will be multiple choice and be available for students when they feel ready; and the use of the national record of achievement (NRA) to report GNVQs is a definite advance for the records of achievement movement. However, the overall assessment package still looks too messy and complex for easy recognition or for acceptance by HE tutors.

The degree to which GNVQs can be judged to be part of a coherent framework is the degree to which they can interrelate with A levels. The design of GNVQs at level 3 provides only a limited interface with A levels. Each GNVQ unit is equivalent to one sixth of an A level qualification and the requirement of twelve units for the award of a GNVQ leaves some room for students to undertake either additional GNVQ units or an A/AS level. But this is an *external* interface between the academic and vocational, based upon a very limited addition of academic study to a student's vocational programme; A levels on the other hand, have been deliberately altered so as *not* to articulate with vocational awards. So it is a one-way street down which the vocational chases the academic. It remains to be seen the extent to which institutions will attempt to provide flexibility of study and blur the boundaries between the tracks. In turn, such developments determine the extent to which GNVQs can help break down the academic/vocational divide or become imprisoned by it.

## GNVQs, at 'Foundation' level: a low-level alternative to GCSE?

If the effect of GNVQs on the whole system is open to debate, their effect on existing vocational qualifications is not. The GNVQ framework will have far-reaching effects on 14–16 vocational qualifications and at 16-plus. At GNVQ level 1, the most well-known certification is the City and Guilds London Institute (CGLI) Foundation Award which, in anticipation of the emerging GNVQ framework, has been transformed into the Diploma of Vocational Education: Foundation Level. This is seen by the CGLI as the first step in a vocational ladder of certification which, in theory, can take students to post-graduate level study.

The foundation level is distinctly pre-vocational in nature and inherits many of the pedagogic features of the joint BTEC/CGLI Foundation Programme and the Certificate of Pre-Vocational Education (CPVE). The major changes, however, are to be found in the assessment of outcomes. The previous programmes were undifferentiated, whereas the new diploma is graded with merits and distinctions aimed at encouraging progression to the next national level. A merit grade at foundation level is designed to be equated to one GCSE pass whilst a distinction is supposed to be equivalent to two GCSEs. Two GCSE passes (or a merit pass plus three GCSEs) allows access to the national stage of the CGLI Diploma or to the BTEC National Diploma. The foundation level diploma appears, therefore, to carry little credit relative to that of GCSE subjects and may be aimed at 'topping up' the grade profile of those who will struggle to find sufficient GCSEs to enter a national level programme. Furthermore, FE tutors are notoriously fickle about entry requirements to national level (most currently require four GCSEs A-C or merit/distinction at BTEC First Diploma) and the requirements tutors place on students are heavily influenced by the supply of places in relation to the demand for them.

Apart from its new (and problematic) potential for progression, the central issue surrounding the new foundation level award is the role it will play in relation to key stage 4 of the National Curriculum and GCSE. The CGLI insists the foundation level diploma is appropriate for the entire ability range of students in education years 10 and 11. The basic question is, therefore, whether it will become part of a reinforcing dual track system from 14+ or part of a more balanced curriculum for all.

The Diploma of Vocational Education (currently being piloted in 200 centres which previously offered the BTEC/CGLI Foundation Programme) tends to have two different models of implementation. One is the integration of the foundation level programme for all pupils through personal and social education programmes (double period), other subjects (e.g. English) and a module on media. The main positive effect of this model is its diversification of students' learning styles. In this sense it is seen as emulating the best features of its predecessors — the joint Foundation Programme and CPVE. The second model (less favoured by CGLI) is to offer the diploma as an option timetabled in areas such as technology, for pupils not taking those subjects to GCSE level. In some cases it will be targeted at pupils — for instance those with special needs — who might take a complete foundation programme timetable. This pattern of development confirms suspicions that differentiation between pupils will be focused on assessment rather than on content. Within key stage 4 there is still a substantial common curriculum around subjects such as maths, English, science, technology, humanities, languages and PE (art is optional). Pupil uptake for either the foundation programme or the GCSE appears, therefore, to be based less upon the amount of vocational or academic content of an individual's learning programme and more upon whether pupils are deemed able to take certain subjects as GCSEs.

In view of the proposed reduction in GCSE coursework, the pressures for an 'alternative' approach will be irresistible to teachers who do not want to increase the sense of failure amongst students. Meanwhile, in schools where the vast majority are capable of achieving in GCSE (e.g. in middle-class areas) there may be progressive experiments to offer a timetable which encourages more flexible learning and which accredits areas of the curriculum which are not currently certificated.

An added twist is that the CGLI is ready to respond to GCSE coursework restrictions by permitting submission of case-studies for external assessment and, if need be, external tests so that the foundation level programme can satisfy the requirements of the overarching Ordinary Diploma announced in the post-16 White Paper (DES/DE/WO, 1991). The BTEC is also planning to submit vocational course proposals for contribution to the Ordinary Diploma with a possible 30 per cent examined component.[5] The problem with the Ordinary Diploma proposals is that they are either focused too narrowly upon the attainment of four GCSE subjects or pitched at too high a level such as national Curriculum Level 7 in maths and English.[6] The only way the foundation level can really work in this context is either to develop an external testing element (and thus risk compromising the case-study approach) or to press on with pupil differentiation. This, however, would contradict the last decade of practice in this type of award and, in the context of a pre-vocational programme, is unlikely to gain much acceptance with FE admissions tutors.

The Diploma of Vocational Education: Foundation Level has the hall-marks of a framework trying to find a role in an increasingly hostile climate dominated by GCSE. The latest announcement (1992) by NCVQ on GNVQ level 1 arrangements confirms fears as to the low-level nature of 14–16 vocational qualifications. It is reported that GNVQ level 1 will cover the bottom four of the ten National Curriculum attainment levels (TES, 1992b). Despite attempts by CGLI to develop a more integrated role for the diploma, it may be overwhelmed by the forces around it. Its very presence may ensure that pupil access to GCSE becomes more selective; the low-level design of GNVQ 1 is an impediment to the diploma achieving parity of esteem with GCSE and many teachers are looking for alternative courses for those unable to cope with the academic track as it is now being re-defined within GCSE course regulations. There will be notable innovative examples of how to use GNVQ 1 as an 'entitlement' for all students but, in true English style, the risk is that, in most cases, pupil access to GCSE or to the foundation diploma will be made on a 'sheep and goats' basis.

## GNVQ level 2: the end of narrow vocationalism 16–19?

The development of GNVQs marks the beginning of the end of the role of occupationally-focused NVQs as a significant qualification in full-time 16–19 education and training. The 1991 White Paper represents a reversal of the strategy that has prevailed since the mid-1980s — that of the narrowing of the vocational track through work-based learning. Mark Jackson (1992) has offered one explanation for this change:

> . . . [a] declared aim of the reforms is to raise the status of vocational qualifications and give them parity of esteem with academic awards. It was never very clear how this could be achieved by gutting occupational qualifications of much of their educational content, and the latest twist in the government's reform strategy suggests that it no longer takes the idea seriously as far as under-19s are concerned.

As Jackson and others have pointed out, a change of heart by the government as to the importance of work-based learning is not the reason why NVQs have encountered difficulty in becoming established in full-time education and training. Rather, the changes heralded by GNVQs are an acknowledgement of the difficulty of delivering NVQs in schools and the admission that they did not constitute a sufficient basis for an alternative vocational track. The problem is best illustrated by NVQ developments in the BTEC First Diploma in business and finance (the BTEC's most popular vocational award). In a well-publicised critique, Watson and Wolfe (1991) stated that the BTEC First Diploma had an unmanageable loading of work-based competences and had neglected the role of knowledge and broader skills. This critique was accepted by John Hillier, Chief Executive of the NCVQ, when he replied (1991):

> it is true that the NVQ requirements are demanding and it is not surprising that schools may experience difficulty, but NVQ was not designed for schools. To cover the requirement of most NVQs a period of work experience is required, if not full-time employment in a job. This is one reason why the Government announced the introduction of general NVQs . . .[7]

Other practitioners have criticised the narrow content of the BTEC First Diploma and its mismatch with the type of learning required for progression to national level study. This problem is particularly acute in inner cities where more students are staying on in education after the age of 16. Such students often need to strengthen their general numeracy, communication, problem-solving and study skills.

Consequently, and in anticipation of the arrival of GNVQ level 2, the BTEC has now advised institutions offering its First Diploma that it is to be modified in 1992 (BTEC, 1992b). The new Diploma will be based upon specifications dating from 1986. These offer modular balance and breadth insofar as they require students to undertake core modules, common skills and option modules (or level 2 NVQ units). When it comes to assessment, however, the new diploma will follow its predecessor by describing student attainment in outcome terms. Many FE colleges and schools will breathe a sigh of relief at the reversion to the old, pre-NCVQ, curriculum design.

Not only have GNVQs pushed vocationally specific NVQs to the margins of 16–19 education, they have also brought an end to the era of post-16 pre-vocational certification. CPVE is to be phased out in September 1993 and replaced by the Diploma of Vocational Education: Intermediate Level. Like the Diploma at Foundation Level, this award inherits many of the pedagogic innovations of CPVE albeit with major differences in assessment where there are differentiated and graded outcomes.[8]

These developments suggest that GNVQs are beginning to bring some sort of order to the post-16 vocational field at NVQ level 2. Both occupationally-focused and undifferentiated pre-vocational awards are being replaced by a broader and more differentiated assessment framework. This is an advance and could help to establish a firm rung on the vocational ladder. However, the whole enterprise could still be endangered by the main vocational examining and validating bodies competing with each other to market their versions of GNVQs to institutions. Each of the boards has its own pedagogical tradition and, despite the GNVQ kitemark, their courses are being marketed under different titles, with different rules. It is a situation in which a dysfunctional proliferation of certification for the system as a whole is rapidly emerging. How far will GNVQs rationalise and give clarity to a qualifications scene which is rapidly getting out of hand?

## GNVQ 3 and the BTEC National Diploma

The BTEC National Diploma and its future is worthy of specific comment. For many it has been the jewel in the crown of FE vocational awards and its progress, particularly in relation to access to HE, is critical to the whole GNVQ enterprise. As a broad vocational award, the 'BTEC national' has been a rallying point for resistance to narrow NVQs and it is well known that, in recent years, relations between the BTEC and the NCVQ have, at times, been very tense, even though constructive agreements have now been forged.

From the general statements that have so far been published (1992), GNVQ level 3 methodology would seem to support past practice in BTEC national awards and an accommodation between the two seems likely. The BTEC, however, has been wary of its best known course being hijacked by the NCVQ and 'narrowed'. Accordingly, the BTEC (1992a) continues to promote a 'quality agenda' through its staff development programme and to advance the argument that BTEC courses can have their own measures of quality regardless of their relationship with other awarding bodies, including academic examination boards and the NCVQ. The emphasis is on the development of quality processes by local BTEC teams with a focus upon common skills, guidance and counselling, accreditation of prior learning, review and evaluation (an agenda which has much in common with post-16 areas of development in TVEI).

This survey of the direction in which various awards are developing within the vocational track confirms the 'dual track' analysis outlined at the start of Chapter 4. The vocational developments are at their weakest and most contradictory for the 14–16 age group where GNVQ 1 is meant to co-exist within the National Curriculum and GCSE examinations. The proposals look at their strongest at NVQ levels 2 and 3 at which point it is assumed that students have already divided themselves into academic and vocational groups at the age of 16 and where the non-academic student may benefit from a broad vocational education with clear progression possibilities. Nevertheless, there is precious little evidence of any real signs of parity of esteem between academic and vocational. The main government strategy in this regard is to rely upon external frameworks to unify the two tracks and it is to this development that we now turn.

## External frameworks — a peculiarly English solution?

A new feature of the current phase of qualifications development in England and Wales is the use of external frameworks as an addition to mainstream qualifications. The overarching Ordinary and Advanced Diplomas and the national record of achievement (NRA) are examples of two kinds of frameworks which are meant, respectively, to confer parity of esteem and to provide a common format for reporting a disparate range of achievements.

These initiatives can be regarded as external frameworks because they offer an alternative to changing the internal nature of qualifications. For example, the over-arching diplomas are seen as necessary because the government does not wish to encourage common curriculum features such as substantial in-course assessment or modularisation between the dual tracks. The NRA contains a section on qualifications and credits in which GNVQ progress can be recorded (but which is not intended as a reporting framework for the academic track). The two types of frameworks discussed in this section have different origins and functions but they share a common characteristic. They are examples of a peculiarly English solution which attempts to reform the system by adding more layers and increasing complexity, rather than by overhauling its component parts.

## Ordinary and Advanced Diplomas — conferring parity of esteem between vocational and academic?

The proposal to develop over-arching Ordinary and Advanced Diplomas, announced in the post-16 White Paper (DES/DE/WO, 1991), is a recognition on the part of the government that the academic/vocational divide has to be addressed. Both the Ordinary and Advanced Diplomas are due to be introduced in 1994 when GCSE is, for the first time, to be assessed against key stage 4 of the National Curriculum. They also coincide with the first award of GNVQs. But how much recognition will the diplomas gain and, as a consequence, how effective will they be in raising the status of vocational qualifications?

The *Ordinary Diploma* has marginally greater credibility than its advanced equivalent because it is trying to recognise combined academic and vocational study through the award of GCSE (a broader framework than specialised A level study). The main features of the Ordinary Diploma are attainment via GCSEs (four GCSEs including maths and English) or NVQ/GNVQ level 2 (also including equivalent — National Curriculum level 7 — attainment in maths and English) and it is intended to be a 'stepping stone' to the Advanced Diploma.

However, the Ordinary Diploma has structural difficulties in its design. The demand for four GCSEs would seem to offer too little incentive for those successful at academic learning and is certainly not an encouragement to breadth of study. On the other hand, subject-based attainment at National Curriculum level 7 looks very ambitious for the majority of pupils who will be following vocational courses, even though it may be slightly easier to achieve the core of maths and English within a vocational course rather than via GCSE. This being the case, the Ordinary Diploma may be aimed at encouraging young people to choose vocational alternatives to GCSE both pre- and post-16.[9]

In terms of pupil incentive, however, a strict insistence on National Curriculum level 7 could be the worst of both worlds if it fails to appeal to the academic student and, at the same time, depresses progression possibilities within the vocational track, particularly for inner city students. Moreover, the level 7 requirement may serve to cast doubt on the diploma as a credible summative statement for employment and diminish its effectiveness as a means of progression to the next level of study. Some employers may benefit from knowing that vocational applicants who hold the Ordinary Diploma have the equivalent of a GCSE C grade at English or maths, but for many students, such academic requirements are unnecessarily ambitious and not sufficiently 'work-related' for entry to a level 3 course such as the BTEC National Diploma.

The *Advanced Diploma* is an attempt to create parity of esteem between the two post-16 tracks whilst retaining the 'gold standard' of A levels. This tension makes the proposals seem weak and contradictory and there are four broad arguments which support this assertion.

–   Restriction of the coursework component of GCSEs and A levels — aimed at preventing a mass expansion of the academic track — undermines parity of esteem between the tracks at each stage. It is implausible to claim that academic and vocational qualifications are equal when the vocational track is being constructed for those identified as 'academic failures' at the age of 14.

–   Ordinary and Advanced Diplomas attempt to encourage a mix of study by introducing common 'kitemarking' of different qualifications but they do not provide *a compatibility of design and comparability of fundamental elements* between the academic and vocational necessary to realise these aims. This is because there is little of real 'added-value' within the diplomas; they are likely to be judged by the qualifications within them rather than by virtue of what they represent in themselves.

–   The proposed equivalence of a GNVQ and NVQ at level 3 to three A levels at any grade suggests that vocational achievement at whatever grade is not worth more than an E grade at A level.

–   The equivalence, through the Advanced Diploma, of three A levels and a GNVQ, is unlikely to provide students or teachers with an incentive to mix academic and vocational study. Either GNVQs are to be a full-blown (700–900 hour) vocational award like the BTEC National Diploma or a GNVQ will have to be offered in combination with one A or two AS levels. This would appear to be a much more labour-intensive route to an Advanced Diploma than the attainment of three A levels at any grade.

These arguments suggest that the Advanced Diploma is unlikely to be highly rated by those who can obtain three A levels. So to whom is the Diploma meant to appeal? Within the context of rising staying-on rates at 16+ it is clearly targeted at the second quartile of the cohort as measured by conventional 'ability', and is designed as an incentive for these students to embark on the vocational track as the surest means of obtaining a respectable qualification.

Neither the Ordinary Diploma or the Advanced Diploma deploys achievement-led incentives; both are preoccupied with comparability through kitemarking rather than the encouragement of high student performance as a result of curriculum change. As designed, they make no requirements that courses have:

- modular flexibility;
- substantial in-course assessment;
- emphases on core processes; or
- more than one matriculation level for the next stage.

The creation of an over-arching framework will, in effect, introduce a little more breadth into the post-14 system by requiring minimum attainment in the areas of maths and English (and possibly in a modern language at some future date). But this will be achieved in such a way as to leave students in the academic track largely untouched. The demands for breadth are really only being made of students in the second quartile of ability — those who, it may be anticipated, will form the main clientele for GNVQs. As such, a kind of second chance is being offered for this group to attain some kind of parity of achievement with the academic minority in the cohort.

## Movement towards a unified approach: opportunity and constraint

The last decade or so has shown that the English system of education and training always provides room for local development. The effect of this, however, is to add initiatives, layer upon layer, to existing arrangements. Previous sections of this chapter have illustrated how these developments can be part and parcel of a divided system, providing room for 'molecular change' without disturbing the basic structure of the qualifications system as a whole. But this dynamic also provides space for initiatives to make more assertive challenges.

All of the initiatives described in Chapter 5 are critical of the narrowness and divisiveness of the qualifications system in England and Wales. But they represent different types of strategy. The International Baccalaureate reflects efforts to broaden post-16 education by offering an internationally recognised alternative to A levels. It has had a limited impact in England and Wales and is an addition to the system.

The Wessex Project, the 'Y model' innovations to bridge BTEC awards and A/AS levels, the Unified Curriculum Project and GNVQs represent a greater challenge to the existing system. They take as their starting point criticism of the academic/vocational divide itself and, in so doing, evoke the vision of a unified post-16 system outlined by the Institute for Public Policy Research (IPPR, 1990). They seek not only to create greater breadth and flexibility of learning but to break down the divisions which perpetuate the dual tracks. This they do in different ways. The Wessex Project starts with *internal* modularisation of A levels and, from this foundation, creates the possibility of reaching out to BTEC provision. The 'Y-model', using modular A levels, has the aim of creating a unifying learning process which can 'zip' A levels and BTEC awards together.

The Unified Curriculum Project is different again. It seeks to promote a broader and more unified curriculum through Compact arrangements with HE institutions. In effect it wants to subvert A levels by challenging their predominant right to act as selectors for HE. The project's strategy is based on a calculation that many HE institutions are seeking to promote increased access via a future-looking and imaginative curriculum. In addition to being a curriculum reform project, however, the Unified Curriculum Project also offers a local and external curriculum framework for promoting changes in an incremental way. As a first step, the Compact arrangement challenges the selection function of the A level examination rather than the internal structure of the award itself.

Despite their diverse strategies, the reference to a credit framework in each of these three initiatives is a common challenge which could strike at the heart of the current qualifications system. An FE credit accumulation and transfer (CAT) framework would seek to break down different types of qualification into units of credit (e.g. 16 credits per A level) (FEU, 1992). As Andrew Morris points out in Chapter 5, these kinds of calculations of credit can be used as part of a local HE Compact agreement — universities can demand a broader range of credits (at 30 hours per credit) than that provided solely by A levels, as a means of diversifying access to HE courses. But more fundamentally, credits are a means of conferring real parity of esteem between the tracks. To agree a 'common credit' you have to agree the relative worth of each of the currencies which make up the credit. This is why the CAT arrangements have been dubbed an educational 'Ecu'.

The calculation of a common credit depends, however, on having strong currencies in the vocational track as well as the academic. This means that movement towards a unified system will depend upon the strengthening of vocational education. In this sense Gilbert Jessup is right when he argues that a well-established outcome and unit-based system in the form of GNVQs will pose a challenge to traditional A levels in the longer term. But the English system has always found ways of confounding optimists.

## Conclusions — a dual track system overwhelmed by confusion

This is a time of maximum uncertainty and confusion in post-16 education and training. We are still waiting to see the initial impact of GNVQs; the viability of the Ordinary and Advanced Diplomas seems unclear; examining and validating bodies are marketing different products; and post-16 institutions are becoming locked in competition. Post-16 education and training appears to be in unprecedented confusion.

There is a danger that any positive changes will be swamped by the very complexity of existing arrangements. This unsatisfactory situation stems, in the main, from the government's refusal to reform A levels and its insistence that market competition will resolve long-standing problems. In addition, the foregoing analysis suggests that there are too many different initiatives and institutions pulling in opposite directions. Our recent and dominant experience has been of complex stratification between different types of certification rather than a straightforward academic/vocational alternative. This is the outcome of an increasingly diverse range of qualifications and competing delivery agencies trying to react to a highly differentiated cohort of students. The impulses for increased complexity and division are not so much found in deliberate attempts to create three or more tiers of provision (academic, broad vocational and specific vocational) but in the ways in which market forces respond to new types of demand set against long-standing patterns of stratification in student attainment. If the reforms are to work, they need maximum transparency and simplicity so as to be understood by students, employers and professionals.

This state of affairs appears to be a repetition — on an increasing scale — of the mistakes of the early 1980s, when additions, such as pre-vocational awards, were made to the post-14 system in response to rapid increases in youth unemployment. Developments in the early 1990s can be seen as 'divisive or differentiated expansion' and a response to the incremental improvements in student performance which are taking place in most areas of the compulsory education system and in the expanding post-16 sector.[10] But it is an inherently divisive response through two clearly differentiated tracks rather than the creation of more common patterns of study.

Despite the confusions, however, vocational education for the 16–19+ age group will be numerically strengthened as a result of the proposed reforms. GNVQs are far more attractive and deliverable than narrow NVQs and increased post-16 participation rates will build on this momentum. Furthermore, a more carefully constructed ladder of progression in the vocational track will ensure that a greater number of students can progress to qualifications at level 3. Consequently, more students with vocational qualifications will progress to HE. But at the same time, as has been argued throughout this chapter, progress towards recognition of the vocational will be undermined by the continuing academic elitism enshrined in A levels and by market competition between institutions. So we will make some progress but it will not be enough.

First, the changes announced in *Education and Training for the 21st Century* will not achieve the quantitative targets that have been set because of the inhibiting effect of A levels. A levels will continue to deliver what — in common political parlance — is known as a 'double whammy': students will still want to take the examinations and will continue to fail in droves. At the same time A levels will continue to devalue their weaker and less prestigious vocational rivals.

Second, the way in which market forces appear to reinforce division means that any analysis of qualifications has to take account of the context in which they are implemented. Institutional arrangements have an enormous influence (see Huddleston, this volume). In an intensely competitive climate, in which examining and validating bodies are marketing courses and institutions are in competition for students whilst attempting to drive down unit costs, a philosophy of 'something for everyone' will prevail, no matter how divisive this is in the longer term. This tendency, which adversely affects progression and sustained participation, will only be resisted if institutions make student progression to successive levels of attainment a priority. This logic of progression involves a commitment to institutional collaboration to ensure a range of progression routes is available to students. Institutions can also reduce division by encouraging the development of common learning and support processes for all students regardless of their course of study. This is one of the prime aims of post-16 TVEI practice and the development of institution-wide approaches to the recording of student achievement, guidance, core skills, and diversity in styles of learning.

The negative relationships of a divided qualifications system, fragmented and competing institutions and low-level demands from a weakened labour market, threaten to keep us trapped in a low-achievement, low-skill system. The challenge facing those in post-16 education and training in the coming years is two-fold. The first is to work creatively with the initiatives and frameworks at our disposal to reduce division and increase coherence and progression. The practitioner in England and Wales has had plenty of practice of 'innovating in chaos' and has become very adept at it. The second challenge is more profound and difficult. It is to forge and develop a more unified concept of qualifications, curricula and institutional provision so that these goals come to dominate post-16 policy and overcome the current frustrations of political postponement.

# Notes

1   A recent episode was an accusation by Vivian Anthony (an A level chief examiner in economics) in the *Times Educational Supplement* (TES) 20 September 1991, that examination boards have increased the number of A level awards to make them more attractive to schools. This claim was vigorously refuted by one examination board which proudly declared that the award of A-Cs had actually dropped by 0.8 that year (see letter from K. Schoenenberger, Secretary of the Oxford and Cambridge Examinations Board, *TES*, 4 October, 1991).

2   The CBI Report *Towards a Skills Revolution* (1989) argued for the further development of core skills in the post-16 curriculum as did the MSC/TA/TEED throughout the 1980s.

3   The CBI has a target of 50 per cent of the age group attaining NVQ level 3 by the Year 2000, see CBI, 1991, *World Class Targets*, Summer.

4   A further example is the winning suggestion of 'Vocational A levels' in a competition to find the best name for GNVQs: 'Readers chase GNVQ out of a fog', *TES*, 6 March 1992.

5   Diane Billam (Director, Product Development, BTEC) quoted in the *TES*, 31 May 1991.

6   These points are made by the Further Education Unit in its 'Draft Response to the Government's Consultative Document' November 1991.

7   Letter from John Hillier to *TES*, 20 September, 1991, p. 24.

8   This attempt by the CGLI to create a second rung on its vocational ladder with a more rigorous version of CPVE has caused concern insofar as it neglects students with special education needs. To ameliorate this problem CGLI recommends (1991) that providing institutions make recourse to students' records of achievement, which document credit accumulation within the Diploma, or to profiles of achievement which allow institutions to set up their own banks of profile statements. The emergence of GNVQ 1 may resolve this problem but there is still a lack of clarity about the role of Foundation Level at 16+. Taken in the context of increasingly cost-conscious FE colleges, many tutors feel that students with significant learning needs are being abandoned. CGLI, 1991, 'Diploma of Vocational Education Phase 2 — Further Information', City and Guilds London Institute, November.

9   This point is made by the FEU, see above, note 6.

10  Recent increases in post-14 performance are commented upon in the annual report of the HM Senior Chief Inspector of Schools *Education in England 1990/91*, (DES, 1992).

# References

Brookes, C. (1991) 'Change is not as good as a test', *Times Educational Supplement (TES)*, 21 June.
BTEC (1992a) *Staff Development for You*, Business and Technical Education Council, London, January.
BTEC (1992b) 'BTEC First and National Qualifications in Business and Finance and Public Administration, NVQ and General NVQs', Circular 92/04, February.
DFE (1992a) *Choice and diversity: a new framework for schools*, Department of Education, HMSO.
DFE (1992b) Kenneth Clark, Secretary of State, speech to employers, Oxford, 3 January.
DES/DE/WO (1991) *Education and Training for the 21st Century*, Department of Education and Science, Department of Employment, Welsh Office, HMSO.
FEU (1992) *A basis for Credit?*, Further Education Unit, February.
HMSO (1988) *Advancing A levels* (The Higginson Report), HMSO.
Hughes, C. (1991) 'More pupils studying for A levels', *The Independent*, 21 June.
IPPR (1990) *A British Baccalauréat: ending the division between education and training*, Institute of Public Policy Research, London.
Jackson, M. (1992) 'Just the Job?', *Vocational Education and Training*, January.
Nash, I. (1991) 'Science A-level entry falls for the 10th year', *TES*, 16 August.
NCC (1990) *Core Skills 16–19*, National Curriculum Council, York.
SEAC (1992) *A and AS Examinations 1990: General Scrutiny Report*, School Examinations and Assessment Council, London, February.
Smithers, A. and Robinson, P. (1991) *Beyond Compulsory Education*, Council for Industry and Higher Education, London, December.
*TES* (1992a) 'Can the ladder replace the sudden drop?', 31 January.
*TES* (1992b) 'Low-level course to fill gap in GCSE', 17 July.
Watson, J. and Wolfe, A. (1991) 'Return to sender' *TES*, 6 September.
Young, M. (1991) 'The post-16 core: issues and possibilities' in Annette Hayton (ed.) *The Post-16 Core: Issues and Possibilities*, Post-16 Education Centre, Insitute of Education, University of London, Report No.6, May.
Young, M. (1992) 'General vocational qualifications and over-arching diplomas: can they work?' Post-16 Education Centre *Newsletter*, Issue No.5, January.

# PART III
# INSTITUTIONS AND
# MARKETS

# 7  Delivering the new 16–19 curriculum in FE colleges

## Prue Huddleston

### Introduction

Previous chapters have focused on the range of new courses and qualifications for 16–19 year olds which have proliferated during the last few years. This chapter aims to examine the ability of the further education (FE) sector to deliver the new qualifications. It will analyse how the changes outlined in the 1991 White Paper: *Education and Training for the 21st Century* (DES, DE, Welsh Office) will affect FE colleges in terms of their structure, organisation, funding and capacity to achieve the National Education and Training Targets.

Since the 1988 Education Reform Act the scale and pace of change in the 400 or so maintained FE colleges in England and Wales has been considerable, accelerating as the colleges prepared for independent status in 1993. It would be impossible to deal adequately in a single chapter with the effects of such changes, many of which have still to work their way through the system; instead, this chapter attempts to focus on the effects of some of these changes on the delivery of programmes within colleges up to mid-1992.

The evidence is drawn from eight colleges, most of them within the Midlands region. Two case studies are included which are based on detailed observations and interviews with staff in a tertiary college in outer London (for the purposes of this study called Lake College) and an FE college in the West Midlands (Manningham College). 'Further education colleges are not standard, bureaucratically defined institutions but rather, each is a product of its own history' (Hall,

1990 p.7) and there is no reason to believe that the institutions represented here are any different. Some of them have been the focus of attention as part of the Further Education Unit's recent project, *Flexible Colleges*; others not so. Colleges have not been selected on the basis of exemplars of best practice; rather, they represent a range of responses to changes which are currently underway in the FE sector.

Further education has traditionally served a multiplicity of clients/customers, though as Müller and Funnell (1991) point out, it is not always clear who these customers are. Is it the company or agency who is paying course fees or the students who are involved in the learning process? In some cases both may be the customer but not always, and further education colleges have to market themselves as multi-product, multi-service organisations. Maintaining the balance between public service provision and the generation of private business has been a delicate operation, causing concern among certain lecturers about the apparent conflict of roles. 'The blossoming in colleges of posts responsible for Public Relations, Marketing, and so on, is not just a response to financial pressures from outside', according to the *NATFHE Journal* (Martin, 1991), 'but is a symptom of the lack of direction brought by failure to make teaching and its values a priority to the college'.

Against this background, the following sections will examine four of the main external pressures currently facing those responsible for FE delivery: expanding student numbers; funding; Training and Enterprise Councils (TECs) and National Vocational Qualifications (NVQs).

## Student numbers and franchising

When the eight colleges in this sample were visited during Spring term 1992, all were filled to capacity, most noticeably with increased numbers of full-time students in areas such as business studies. Many colleges had waiting lists for their programmes and in one college there had been some student action as a result of overcrowding. Those colleges offering advanced (A) level courses had also seen large increases in student numbers. In 1991, the Further Education Unit (FEU) reported that over 40 per cent of A level courses were taken in FE colleges.

In addition, there were some franchising arrangements with local schools where schools were unable to support particular A level subjects — for example, business studies or economics. The development of Business and Technology Education Council (BTEC) programmes in schools had led, in some cases, to similar arrangements with school pupils being taught on college premises for part of their timetable. In one case college staff were delivering a BTEC Care course on school premises. It remains to be seen if this trend will continue when schools become more familiar with BTEC courses. Schools, however, must address a number of resourcing and staff development issues if they are to deliver a wide range of BTEC courses. BTECs necessitate different teaching styles, are concerned with whole programmes not discrete subjects, and require staff to have had relevant experience in business or industry. Few schools, for example, are equipped to offer engineering; so far the most popular BTEC choices for schools have been the First and National Diplomas in Business and Finance.

It also remains to be seen how relationships between schools and newly independent FE colleges will be sustained after 1993, when some schools remain under LEA control while others have grant-maintained status. Those schools wishing to maintain viable sixth forms may be unwilling to enter into arrangements with their local colleges for fear of losing students. A marketing director from one of the eight colleges in this sample reported that he was not allowed to promote college courses in some schools with sixth forms. In other schools, he was allowed access, but on the condition that he promote only those courses which the schools did not offer.

Franchising is one way in which schools and colleges can cooperate to offer a broader range of programmes to students, but there are cost and organisational implications. Would it be cheaper for schools to offer BTEC programmes themselves or to pay colleges to do it for them? Where do students fit into all this? What sort of coherent view can they form about the provision offered and about their entitlement to it? Some of these issues have already been raised in the FEU document *Towards a Framework for Curriculum Entitlement* (1989). In addition, the opportunity has been taken to explore them in greater depth at a college in this study.

A group of A level school students were taking three A Level courses — one at college, the others at school. The college lecturer involved appeared unaware of what subjects the students were studying at school and said that he 'tried to avoid going to parents' evenings', although he had been invited by the school. The pupils moved between buildings, some of them 'getting lost' in the process. They had to wear school uniform when in the college and seemed to have no contact with anything that was going on in the rest of the building. There was little time for tutorial support since students usually had to move off quickly at the end of class to get back to school.

At the other end of the franchise spectrum, two colleges had franchising arrangements with universities. One was a 'two plus two' degree programme, namely two years in the FE college followed by two years in the university. Manningham College had three degree programmes franchised from two different higher education institutions with teaching taking place almost entirely on college premises. In other colleges, lecturers were delivering programmes on company premises, a Saturday college was being operated for those who could not attend courses during the week and a series of 'access centres' — outreach initiatives aimed at linking local schools and community organisations with the college — were being resourced. The rationale for this latter activity is that the 'access centre', with its local delivery, should provide 'eventual admittance to the college's total curriculum by acting as the first stage in such a transition' (Franklin, 1992).

## Funding

The detailed proposals of the new Further Education Funding Council (FEFC) for funding the sector have yet (1992) to be delineated. An extension of the model for funding based on inputs, i.e. student enrolments, however, could stifle innovation in a climate of change where new styles of access, delivery and accreditation will be crucial to many colleges' survival. The move now underway within the FEFC to develop an outcome-related model of funding could encourage colleges to consider alternative modes of access and provision.

While waiting for the FEFC to make transitional funding available in October 1992, some colleges were experiencing serious financial pressures. Not only had they experienced cuts in their budgets from LEAs reluctant to fund institutions that will be outside their control, but they were also facing significant costs in preparing for independence in April 1993 (Tysome, 1992). In this sense, colleges have been doubly disadvantaged by cuts in funding at a time when student numbers are increasing. Furthermore, there is a disincentive for colleges to expand beyond their full-time equivalent (FTE) targets for even if the funding targets are exceeded, the unit of resource remains the same. An inspection of staff student ratios (SSR) for the past five years in one of the colleges visited revealed a rise from 10.44:1 to 13.10:1 overall, and from 11.15:1 to 16.26:1 in the Business Studies Department. There is no reason to assume that this is exceptional.

Cuts in full-time staff due to budget shortfalls have led to increased group sizes or the cancellation of certain programmes. At the time of writing, one Midlands college is proposing to increase some adult part-time fees by 500 per cent in order to avoid staff redundancies. Wirral Metropolitan College, perhaps the largest in Europe with 30,000 students and a national reputation for its pioneering work in access and flexible delivery, is currently faced with the possibility of making 400 part-time staff redundant as a result of financial cut-backs

(Nash, 1992b). The findings of the FEFC working party to consider the new funding arrangements are unlikely to impact on the college system until 1994. Meanwhile, TECs are charged with the responsibility of driving forward the new system in order to meet National Education and Training Targets which include the aim that by 1996, 50 per cent of the workforce will be aiming for NVQs or units towards them.

If colleges are to deliver the new vocational qualifications and to play their part in the effort to achieve the National Education and Training Targets, there are potentially huge financial implications which have yet to be addressed.

According to a report in the *Times Educational Supplement* (Nash, 1992a) 'colleges cannot hope to benefit from the NVQs without a "revolution" in the way the entire institution and all its courses are organised and managed'. Lack of resources has also had an impact on the structure and appearance of some colleges, causing delays in essential repair work to buildings often already in very bad condition (Maclure, 1991). The changes in delivery presaged by modular curricula, more open access and flexible learning may also require substantial alteration to college facilities. Developing open learning materials, for example, can be prohibitively expensive. Added to this is the uncertainty of how many customers will 'turn up on the day'. This has led to the need to maintain reserves of part-time staff on whose services the college may or may not call. These are the sorts of issues currently facing the 'new breed' of financial directors, resources directors, personnel directors and marketing managers whose posts were appearing in the classified advertisements prior to colleges' incorporation in 1993.

It has to be recognised that colleges also receive funding from other sources such as the European Social Fund, direct government grants, and private businesses for whom colleges provide bespoke training programmes. It may well be that in terms of delivery 'he who pays the piper calls the tune', as less lucrative forms of provision suffer at the expense of profitable courses. In 1989 a note of concern was sounded by Gleeson about the quality of accommodation and staffing for Youth Training (YT) and special needs students in some colleges. This is echoed by the current study where in some cases temporary accommodation on the car park was being used to house special needs groups and access courses. In stark contrast, rooms in the main buildings had been the subject of refurbishment for management programmes. Some colleges have designated special parts of their buildings as conference centres, while a college in south Wales has secured funding to renovate a substantial old property as a residential management training centre. It was pointed out that this was not for the 'normal' clientele of the college.

Whilst FE colleges are thus responding to the numerous exhortations to become responsive to the market (FEU, June 1985; Theodossin, 1989), it is still not clear what effects this will have on access and the quality of provision. Colleges are having to make strategic and organisational decisions about what their portfolio of programmes will look like and how these will affect delivery. As a result, the market place may lead them away from the achievement of the National Education and Training Targets for lifetime learning, which will depend very significantly on the acquisition of skills at NVQ levels II and III, rather than the higher level managerial and professional competences.

## Training and Enterprise Councils

If the Training and Enterprise Councils (TECs) are to assist in the achievement of the National Education and Training Targets they will need to co-operate with the FE college sector — the major provider of vocational education and training in England and Wales.

Through the Work-Related Further Education (WRFE), YT and Employment Training (ET) budgets the influence of the TECs on the provision of programmes in FE colleges could be considerable. However, relationships with TECs, across the range of colleges represented in this sample were extremely variable. The reasons for this were diverse and there was insufficient time to explore such variations in detail. However, there are a number of emergent issues which are worth noting.

First, where there has been significant growth in full-time college provision, local TECs have been less important because their role is primarily to promote and fund part-time training, not to fund full-time courses. Likewise, where colleges have decided to concentrate their efforts on HE franchising, A levels and BTECs, those on YT programmes for whom TECs have a responsibility have suffered. These trainees are required to be in training which leads to the acquisition of NVQs yet warning signals to TECs have already been sounded by some colleges (Nash, 1992c) which have threatened to withdraw from NVQ training.

Second, TECs are charged with the responsibility of matching the provision of training to the needs of the local labour market yet, in many cases, colleges feel that their expertise and successful record in this endeavour is not being utilised by the TECs. Colleges also have significant experience in the provision of vocational education and training both for the 16–19 age group and for adults, with 3.5 million students in 1987/88 (DES, 1988). Some TECs appear to be aware of this; others not.

Third, whether or not relationships with TECs are sustained and improved will depend to a significant extent upon the new funding arrangements introduced by the FEFC. Colleges have to make their own way in an increasingly competitive market and they will need to attract funding from a variety of sources. If TECs become less significant as fund holders — for example, if the WRFE budget passes to the FEFC or if colleges remain funded on the basis of input measures — TECs will lose most of their financial leverage with the FE sector.

## National Vocational Qualifications

Another area which is having a significant impact on delivery of the 16–19 curriculum in colleges is the introduction of NVQs. The pace of change has continued to increase since Haffenden and Brown (1989) considered the implications of the introduction of the NVQ system for the key FE areas of curriculum, staff and institutional development. The present study identifies three particular aspects of NVQ development which are challenging traditional modes of FE college course delivery: the modularisation of curricula; the work-based requirements of NVQs; and the staff development issues raised by NVQ delivery.

The modularisation of curricula is essential to the delivery of NVQs as they are unit-based and defined in terms of outcomes rather than in terms of programmes of study or the length of time taken to achieve specified outcomes. Some colleges had been working towards modular curricula before the introduction of NVQs, but the absence of a system of credit accumulation and transfer impeded any real progress. In general, students enrolled on a programme in September and followed it through to July; this applied equally to full-time and part-time day release students.

The FEU has recently published a discussion paper: *A Basis for Credit*? (February 1992) which outlines the issues involved in attempting to develop a common credit accumulation and transfer system across all post-16 provision (see Spours, Chapter 6). Clearly, the implications for college organisation of such a system would be enormous. Meanwhile, the colleges in this study were attempting to come to terms with the introduction of NVQs and modularisation of curricula on a departmental basis. Pockets of innovation appeared to exist in some parts of the colleges, but were isolated due to poor communication within the institutions. However, it is recognised that some colleges have made significant progress in this area and *Flexible Colleges* (FEU, 1991) provides some examples of good practice. By expressing programmes in terms of competences which are common to a variety of courses or qualifications it is possible for students to undertake shared practical activities whilst preparing for different qualifications. This is fairly common in catering and in secretarial training. The case study of Lake College (see below) illustrates how such a scheme may be implemented although such provision remains the exception rather than the rule. The FEU study concludes that, thus far, 'few colleges, if any, have succeeded in modularising/ unitising more than a small part of their provision' (p. 42).

A second challenge for colleges is the requirement of NVQs that learning and assessment take place, as far as possible, in the workplace. When such opportunities are not available realistic simulated working environments have to be provided. This has created difficulties for some colleges both in obtaining sufficient numbers of work experience places for full-time students and in providing realistic simulated opportunities within the college itself. A head of section in one college reported that 150 hours of lecturers' time had been spent on accrediting 30 work places suitable to assess student competence.

Even those students who are employed and attend college on a part-time basis may be unable to experience all the work-based activities necessary to achieve some of the units for a full NVQ. During a recent discussion with students at a 'workshop' in a college where the lecturer was engaged in verifying workbased competences, one student remarked that he 'never had to photocopy at work'. The lecturer proceeded to introduce the student to a photocopier, explain its operation and test the student's competence accordingly. At Lake College, literally hours of staff time had been spent 'watching students photocopy'.

Some colleges have used their own facilities to provide workbased learning experience and assessment in areas such as hairdressing salons and restaurants. At Manningham College the foyer resembles a shopping mall complete with 'Fresh Baked Bread Shop' and 'Travel Bureau'. It is difficult for all colleges to provide such opportunities. Some colleges simply do not have the resources either within the institution or in the surrounding area, particularly in regions hard hit by recession (Nash, 1992c).

In addition to the difficulties of finding sufficient places is the issue of the staff development implications of NVQ delivery. Lecturers have to be accredited by the relevant NVQ Lead Body to undertake work-place assessment and internal verification and this may smack of undue interference by employers, leading experienced college staff to feel that they are being de-professionalised. There are also resource implications for the accreditation of staff as work-place assessors. One possibility being investigated by a college was to pay independent assessors to undertake the work-based assessment of its students. Haffenden and Brown reported in 1989 that of all the changes created by the introduction of NVQs it was the issues surrounding new forms of assessment which were causing the greatest concern in colleges. Certainly, the whole process of assessment and verification of competence can be extremely time-consuming. During the course of this study the author attended workshops where evidence from work-place experience was being assessed in order to record competence in student log books. Some students reported that they found the process 'boring' and that there was a duplication of effort in 'endlessly writing up the same things'. Other students, however, felt that completing the log book helped them to focus on what they had learned and gave them confidence in their own competences, one student commenting 'this is good because we do all this stuff [filing] all the time at work'. Overall, there was a sense in which these students felt that some staff — both in college and at work — were more rigorous than others in considering the evidence and from observation within this sample of colleges it was clear that some staff left all the verification to the end of term rather than collecting it on a continuous basis. Equally, some work-based assessors preferred to 'sign off' a list of competences on a single day rather than record achievement as it occurred.

Clearly, the accreditation of staff as work-place assessors is one staff development issue. There are other staff development implications set in train by the implementation of NVQs. Teaching and learning styles are likely to be different — lecturers being required to facilitate learning rather than hand out information. Consequently, they may have to adopt a more passive, yet supportive, role in the learning process and staff may be asked to develop specialised learning materials, as well as take on new responsibilities for guidance and counselling to help students make sense of the new qualifications. One way of bringing staff up to date on current work-place practice is through industrial placement. In this way college lecturers may also develop closer relationships with those who are responsible for their students' on-the-job training and work-place assessment.

## Coherence in the 16–19 college curriculum

As Burgess (Chapter 5) suggests, where A level courses run in schools or colleges which also have BTEC provision a possible way toward greater curriculum coherence might be to combine the elements common to both programmes and make them available to all students as units. This would go some way to bridging the academic and vocational divide, allow for credit transfer and make for a more economic use of resources. There is, however, a significant gap between theory and practice. One of the colleges visited in this study had an A level economics course running in its general education department and a range of vocational programmes delivering economics within the business studies department. There was virtually no communication between the two, and even when staff shortages appeared in one department, additional personnel were not sought from the other.

A curriculum audit of the whole college can identify where there are units common to different courses or programmes. Successful delivery of common units requires careful joint planning and prescribed formulae for calculating interdepartmental payments. The establishment of strong departmental empires, however, mitigates against this and the question arises: 'To which department are student numbers accredited'? Where funding is based on full-time equivalent numbers, how is the type of short 'top-up' training required to achieve a full NVQ competence to be costed and to whom is it payable? Introducing modular curricula thus requires not only flexible delivery but also sophisticated management information systems.

The following two case studies — based upon the observations and interviews which took place during the spring term 1992 — provide some insights into the ways in which colleges are responding to the changes outlined in the previous sections of this chapter.

---

## Case Study 1 — Lake College: the modularisation of secretarial training

---

**Rationale**

Lake College is an expanding tertiary college in the outer London area. In 1989, it combined with two other tertiary colleges in its borough to develop a modular programme for secretarial training which would allow for flexible delivery based on NVQ accreditation and be attractive to a wide client group of both adults and young people.

The accreditation of secretarial skills has traditionally been covered by a wide range of qualifications and awarding bodies. There are also specialist secretarial qualifications such as those for legal and medical secretaries. The focus of the project at Lake College was to develop a competence-based, modular secretarial curriculum so that units could be taken by individuals or groups in order to build towards NVQ accreditation at levels I, II and III. The units could be built into individual student action plans irrespective of the programme which students were following and the achievement of units was not time-dependent. The project also considered the implementation of a system for accrediting prior achievement (APA). Units could be taken at any of the three colleges and a credit accumulation and transfer system was incorporated into the final scheme.

## Development

Funding for the two year project was made available by the Department of Employment so that staff in the colleges could be released from teaching to undertake development work. All staff in the section were involved in the project at some time, as were other members of the college. This was found to be an effective way of disseminating the outcomes more widely to encourage other sections of the college to consider modularising their curricula.

Staff development was seen as central to the success of the project, with guidance and counselling skills identified as particular areas requiring improvement. Staff also needed help in drafting learning materials, a time-consuming and costly process. New systems had to be designed in order to record competences and to take account of APA. There was a need to develop closer relationships with employers who would have responsibility for work-place assessment.

## Outcomes

Enrolments almost doubled during the life of the project, although further expansion was curtailed by lack of resources and by the delays in some of the awarding bodies incorporating competence-based assessment. Learning resource packs were developed for NVQ levels I, II and III as were the assignments and assessments to support these units. Staff became proficient in drafting materials and it was possible to transfer these skills to other areas.

The timetable was rescheduled in blocks of time to facilitate flexible starts and to allow those students on a full-time programme to gain all the units within a reasonable period. A guidance service was introduced to help students select appropriate routes through the units and to provide APA. This was supported by a paper recording system although the need for a computerised system was recognised.

## Conclusion

Within the space of two years this project was successful in modularising secretarial training within and across three tertiary colleges. This would not have been possible, however, without the extra resources made available to release staff to plan and develop the scheme. Not all colleges will be in such a fortunate position. The Project also raised some unresolved issues, many of which were organisational; for example, how to charge for initial diagnostic assessment and guidance, how to resource workplace assessment and how to integrate this modular approach across the entire college.

---

### Case study 2 — Manningham College: a tutor placement to investigate the implications of NVQ for the practical training and assessment of nursery nursing students.

---

### Rationale

Manningham College is a large city college with a national reputation for excellence in some areas of provision. It offers a wide range of programmes: short courses for industry, day-release 'craft' courses, higher national diploma (HND) and degree programmes. It has always had an unusually large number of full-time students for an FE college.

The college recruits about 200 nursery nursing students each year. During their two year programme all students have to spend about 40 per cent of their time in nursery establishments. At any point there could be a need for the college to provide some 400 work experience placements.

A health tutor undertook a week's placement in a nursery school in order to investigate the implications of the introduction of NVQs for curriculum change, assessment and APA. The intention was to view the training from a practical perspective by working alongside students in training. The placement was also aimed at judging the readiness of nursery staff to act as work-place assessors.

### Development

The placement was arranged by the Teacher Placement Service and supply cover funding was provided by the tutor's local education authority. The tutor interviewed staff and students in the workplace and observed student assessments. She also worked alongside students in the classroom. The whole exercise was viewed as staff development in preparation for the introduction of NVQs into the college's provision for the care sector.

### Outcomes

The placement revealed that the staff at the nursery school, who in the future will be responsible for assessing students in the work-place, appeared unaware of the implications of NVQs. The results of the questionnaire distributed by the tutor to nursery staff revealed that work-place supervisors had little understanding of how their own competences might be assessed or how they might assess the competences of students in training. The existing procedures for reporting on students' progress whilst on work experience were found to be inadequate for NVQ accreditation as they tended to be too subjective, comparing one student's progress with another. Some staff were unwilling to fail students, whilst admitting that they would not wish to employ them. Sometimes students were reported as satisfactory and then went on to fail the course.

It was recognised that by providing more detailed guidance for work-place supervision on competence assessment these problems could be avoided. Guidelines and a check-list have now been produced by the college which will prepare the way for the introduction of the NVQ competences.

With the introduction of NVQs into the care sector much of the students' experience and assessment will be on employers' premises. Regular meetings between work-place supervisors and college staff have now been established in order to facilitate joint curriculum planning, to prepare assignments and to plan work-place experience and assessment. It is recognised that work-place supervisors have an important contribution to make to the training of students and, therefore, should have a more central role in curriculum planning.

## Conclusion

This case study reveals that there may still be some way to go before competence-led assessment in the workplace becomes a reality. Developing such a system is time-consuming and costly. The nursery school in this study asked the tutor if there would be payment for undertaking such a role. The volume of administration required for assessment may mean that some schools/nurseries will simply take smaller numbers of college students, making it even more difficult for the college to find 400 placements a year.

There are also staff development implications for those who are now required to assess competences in the work-place. How they are to be trained and at what cost, is a question still unanswered. Nevertheless, the introduction of the 'new style' courses at Manningham from September 1992 suggests that answers will need to be found.

## Conclusion

Every college is different, serving a variety of students and specific local social and economic needs. Nevertheless, colleges are responding to a common set of institutional, funding and curriculum pressures. The customer/client profile is also changing, as colleges seek to find their particular market niche. All these factors are likely to have a significant impact on the type and quality of provision offered by colleges and on the ways in which such provision is delivered. Hall (1990) suggests that colleges have coped well with the 'hostilities' and 'indifference' which they met during the 1980s and that they are now 'leaner, more flexible and more responsive to the needs of the communities which they serve' (p. 139). Of the colleges visited in this survey, some appeared poised for further expansion while others, including the college which had perhaps been the most enterprising, faced financial difficulties. In spite of all the changes currently facing the sector, staff were still very much concerned with 'getting on with the job'. Student numbers were buoyant and there were indications that this situation would be repeated the next academic year. Modularisation of curicula had taken place in some areas, notably in catering, hairdressing, and business and finance, although in most cases this was still within a framework of academic years rather than on a flexible, 'roll-on, roll-off' basis.

The major pre-occupation of staff was the constant changes to which they were being subjected, both internal and external. Hours of work could be expended designing new programmes, modularising curricula and preparing for the implementation of NVQs only to have all undone by the arrival of another set of externally imposed changes. Those carrying the burden of the teaching load, many of whom were part-time, felt themselves at a distance from the key management decision-makers, a situation illustrated in the case of a marketing manager who had successfully attracted new business without assessing the capacity of the college to deliver it.

All the colleges were also concerned about the lack of resources available to implement the changes necessary to deliver the type of education and training envisaged by the government reforms. This chapter has focused on some of these changes, pointed to ways in which the FE sector is responding and concludes by suggesting that the system is flexible enough to adapt to future requirements providing that sufficient development time and dissemination of best practice are made available.

## Acknowledgements

I should like to thank the staff in the colleges in this study who contributed so much to the findings reported here. I am particularly indebted to the vice-principal and staff in the business studies department at Lake College and to the nursery nursing tutor at Manningham College.

## References

DES, (1988) *Education Statistics for the United Kingdom: 1989 Edition*, London, HMSO.

DES, DE, Welsh Office (1991) *Education and Training for the 21st Century* (CMND 1536), London, HMSO.

Franklin, L. (1992) 'Quality and Equality: The Case of East Birmingham College', *Journal of Further and Higher Education*, Vol. 16, No.1, Spring 1992.

Further Education Unit (1985) *Marketing Further Education*, London, FEU.

Further Education Unit (1989) *Towards a Framework for Curriculum Entitlement*, London, FEU.

Further Education Unit (1991) *Flexible Colleges: Access to Learning and Qualifications in Further Education*, London, FEU.

*Further Education Unit (1992) A Basis for credit? Developing a Post-16 Credit Accumulation and Transfer Framework: A Paper for Discussion*, London, FEU.

Gleeson, D. (1989) *The Paradox of Training: making Progress Out of Chaos*, Milton Keynes, Open University Press.

Haffenden, I. and Brown, A. (1989) 'Towards the Implementation of Competence Based Curricula in Colleges of FE', Burke, J. (Ed) *Competency Based Education and Training*, Lewes, Falmer Press.

Hall, V. (1990) *Maintained Further Education in the United Kingdom*, Blagdon, Further Education Staff College.

Maclure, S. (1991) *Missing Links: The Challenge to further Education*, London, Policy Studies Institute.

Martin, A. (1991) 'Want a Career in Education? Then Don't Teach', *National Association of Teachers in Further and Higher Education Journal*, No.4, Autumn 1991.

Müller, D. and Funnell, P, (1991) *Delivering Quality in Vocational Education*, London, Kogan Page.

Nash, I. (1992a) 'Revolution in the Suburbs', *Times Educational Supplement*, 12 June.

Nash, I. (1992b) 'Colleges Doubt Scope for Growth', *Times Educational Supplement*, 19 June.

Nash, I. (1992c) 'Colleges Threaten to Ditch Training', *Times Educational Supplement*, 22 May.

Theodossin, E. (1989) *Marketing the College*, Blagdon, Further Education Staff College.

Tysome, T. (1992) 'Merseyside College Fights for Survival', *Times Higher Education Supplement*, 12 June.

# 8 LEAs and TECs in partnership: the case of education– business partnership in Clwyd

## Keith Evans

The last decade and a half has seen the evolution of education–business partnerships as an important national priority; as experience has been gained, the principle that successful partnerships are founded in trust and derive their strengths from local relationships has been more fully appreciated, and the need for a continuing drive for quality in partnerships more widely recognised.

Recently, this process has received a new thrust from central government in a number of policy directives first outlined in the White Paper *Education and Training for the 21st Century* (DE/DES/WO, 1991) and subsequently given statutory form in the Further and Higher Education Act 1992. Building upon the local partnerships developed between industry and education in recent years, the government now wishes to consolidate further such developments in education and training through additional responsibilities vested in Training and Enterprise Councils (TECs).

The current roles of TECs in education include managerial responsibility for:

- TVEI plans and annual reviews;
- compacts;
- education–business partnerships;

- work-related further education;
- high technology national training;
- youth training and credit pilots.

In addition, TECs now have 'extra responsibilities for working with the Careers Service, with FE colleges and with the Colleges Funding Council' and the government has encouraged LEAs 'to join voluntarily with a TEC partner in overseeing the operation of the careers service in its area'. To bring about these aims legislation has been enacted which is designed 'to open up other options, including direct TEC management of the Careers Service' and to 'enable LEAs to contract it out to the private sector through competitive tendering if they wish' (DE/DES/WO, 1991, paras 7–8–9).

In this chapter the development of a formal education-business partnership (EBP) and of a Careers Service Partnership between the two North Wales TECs and the Clwyd Local Education Authority (LEA) is described against a background of sustained local education–industry collaboration in the 1980s. Proposals developed in the county in 1992 for an education and training charter are presented in the last section of the chapter.

## Partnership background: TVEI, its extension and post-16 policy in Clwyd

The Technical and Vocational Education Initiative (TVEI) has had a profound influence in Clwyd and is now accepted locally as the beginning of vocational education reform, focusing on concepts of entitlement, promoting developments in teaching and learning styles, and bringing about structural changes in course delivery and accreditation. Thus foundations have been laid for current structural and curriculum reform, particularly in the post-16 phase of provision.

The significance of TVEI as an instrument of educational change in Clwyd is demonstrated by the following examples of innovation in education provision introduced since the initiative was launched in 1983:

- increased student autonomy;
- increased institutional autonomy;
- a 'total quality' approach to management stressing planning linked to resources and cost effectiveness in education;
- encouragement for flexible learning;
- encouragement for accreditation of prior learning;
- increased modular course development in schools and FE;

- design of National Curriculum accreditation to provide possible future credits on post-16 vocational courses;
- a sharper focus on records of achievement and individual action plans leading to personal training plans;
- a sharper focus in education on industry and the world of work;
- enhanced careers education and guidance as a central means to bring about empowerment of the individual and effective progression;
- a sharper focus on the concept of an entitlement curriculum 5–16;
- a stronger focus on a lifelong, post-16 entitlement to full-time education, part-time education and training, or employment with training.

Within the LEA a number of important initiatives have been taken to enhance post-16 provision. One of the most fundamental has been the setting up of three consortia, each based on a College of further Education (FE) and its associated 11–18 schools. As a result, teachers and lecturers in these consortia have seen themselves as belonging to a 'family' of institutions committed to the common objective of offering a comprehensive range of post-16 courses and programmes. These consortia have been given additional strength by the arrangement of joint inservice training programmes, often under the aegis of TVEI and its extension; by the work of education-industry fora which are, in some ways, consortia-based microcosms of EBPs and in which educators, teachers, and industrialists have met together on a regular basis to discuss matters of common concern. Each of the fora has an industrialist as chairman and an educator/trainer as secretary, or vice versa.

A particular feature of post-16 development in Clwyd with its characteristics of rurality and sparse population, has been the setting up of the Vale of Clwyd Link. The Link is an association between a large college of further education (FE) at the northern end of the Vale, a diversified college of agriculture at the southern end of the Vale, and three 11–18 schools, one of which is a Welsh-medium school, set in market towns within the Vale. The problems of providing coherent academic and vocational programmes at the post-16 level are substantial when the medium of learning is English; when the bilingual dimension of the rural heartland of Clwyd is added, the problems and the resource implications are multiplied. The Vale of Clwyd Link, however, demonstrates vision and a genuine commitment by all the partners to ensure that all the young people of this rural hinterland shall have access to the widest possible range of education and training resources.

The most important post-16 policy, which by now would have been coming to fruition with the publication of a series of 'Section 12' notices setting up three tertiary colleges, has been frustrated by the removal of the FE colleges from LEA control. Interestingly enough, however, the vigorous debate on tertiary re-organisation which spanned a period of some five or six years has led to broad acceptance of the tertiary ideal. The implementation of that ideal is now possible only on a voluntary basis, and through a lengthier and more complex process.

At the same time as these developments were occurring, the LEA has achieved a measure of success in increasing the participation rate in post-16 education. Since 1989, the number of students continuing in post-16 studies grew from 48 per cent in 1989; to 52.4% per cent in 1990; and to 60 per cent in 1991. This occurred despite a fall of 2 per cent in the student population in 1991. This remarkable increase from 48 to 60 per cent within three years represents a steady growth, and cannot be attributed solely to the current recession. The positive experiences of students at school up to the age of 16 are undoubtedly influencing the decision they make about whether to remain in full-time education and training.

These important initiatives are key components in an educational model (Figure 8.1) into which TECs and EBPs have been incorporated within the Clwyd authority and elsewhere. The Clwyd model starts with values and aims, highlighting the concepts of equal value, opportunity and access. It goes on to list the major policy thrusts of the last decade and the innovative delivery systems and teaching/learning styles which this new educational culture has engendered. In addition it highlights the crucial importance of quality management, with its emphasis on performance indicators, and lists new forms of accreditation which have been designed to reflect specific aspects of the learning process. The emphasis here is on formative evaluation or 'military strategy' as opposed to summative evaluation or 'military history'. The model has at its heart the key concept of student progression.

## The aims and objectives of TECs and the rationale for TEC/LEA collaboration

The fundamental aim of every TEC is to foster economic growth and contribute to the regeneration of the community which it serves. TECs' special focus is on strengthening the national skills base and assisting local enterprise to expand and compete effectively. Both the TECs in North Wales aim to create a dynamic environment for economic growth and the encouragement of an enterprise culture. Among their stated objectives are a number which recognise the need

**Figure 8.1:** Education and training post-16

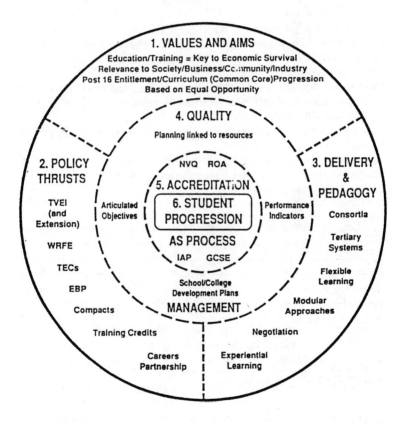

for collaboration with the education service if they are to be achieved. These include an intention to:

–   present a cohesive plan for education and training in the local area, through partnerships between employers and education and training providers;
–   strengthen the development of vocational education and training;
–   understand what has, and is, being done by LEAs in the field of education and to build on this;
–   help ensure that young people acquire the skills needed in the local economy;
–   develop a relationship with the LEA in order to match the aspirations of students with the needs of the community as closely as possible and facilitate the transition from education to employment;
–   understand the bilingual policies of LEAs and to encourage the continuation of such policies which develop bilingual competence to meet the needs of industry;
–   network into and improve existing links between employment, schooling and training;
–   strengthen the role of careers education and guidance;
–   integrate TVEI, further education and higher education into the planning process.

These objectives are particularly important in the county of Clwyd because of a steady decline in the number of jobs requiring merely strength and manual labour, and the increasing application of technology demanding greater diagnostic skills and judgment of employees. The accompanying growth in service-based occupations means that personability, reliability and social skills in the workplace are growing in importance. Such trends are increasing the opportunities for people with high level qualifications and the availability of skilled labour is exerting an increasingly powerful influence on regional economic growth, especially in the deregulated trading environment of Europe, post-1992.

Much of the attention of TECs, including those in North Wales, will be focused on short-term programmes designed to meet immediate skill shortages, assist small business growth and facilitate the re-entry of those in full-time training or unemployment back into the labour market. The development of a high skill economy will depend upon increasing the supply of qualified technicians, technologists, scientists and managers. If the labour and education 'markets' are to work in harmony in support of economic regeneration, collaboration between TECs and LEAs in the formulation of objectives and in developing strategies for their achievement will be essential.

Education and industry in Clwyd, as elsewhere, are not separate worlds but two complementary sectors that have a high degree of interdependence, each having its own purposes and functions. Yet the education system does not exist solely to provide skilled manpower for industry; it has other purposes which relate to the development of individuals and to the transmission of knowledge and culture from one generation to another. Furthermore, it has an important role in influencing the values, attitudes, interests, skills, knowledge and the career choices of young people. Industry contributes to that process by the creation of employment and training opportunities, by its influence on the curriculum, by its support for teachers and for teaching, by the expertise and advice it makes available to those who manage the education service and who work in it, and by the demands it generates for particular kinds of qualified labour. These are among the factors which have led to the establishment of the Clwyd EBP.

## The Clwyd education-business partnership

### Constitution

The County of Clwyd in North East Wales is covered by two Training and Enterprise Councils, the east of the county (four District Council areas) being covered by the North and East Wales TEC, known locally as 'Training and Enterprise', the other two District Council areas being covered by the North and West Wales TEC, known locally as 'Targed' (a TEC which also covers the whole of the County of Gwynedd). The partners in the Clwyd education business partnership are, therefore, Training and Enterprise, Targed and the Clwyd LEA with the funding of the EBP reflecting the relative size of the partners' involvement. The partnership is to be based upon five operating principles outlined by the Secretary of State for Employment (Michael Howard) in a departmental press release of November 1991, i.e:

- a common vision and purpose to give strategic cohesion to the enterprise over the long term;
- clear objectives which are stretching but realistic;
- agreed roles and responsibilities which define the obligations of each partner;
- a system by which these partners are held accountable for their results;

–   a degree of trust which allows the partners to consult and
    communicate freely with each other.

Clearly the imminent effect of setting up parallel funding councils
for further and higher education and the possibility of further re-
organisation of local government will lead to a review of the actual
participants in the partnership, but for the time being the two TECs
and the LEA remain the founding partners.

The participants believe that successful partnerships can mobilise
the resources of the community more effectively, designing education
and training strategies suited to local circumstances; they can share
responsibility for workforce development, presenting a positive
image and a united front to the world at large; they can model for the
future, stressing the close interdependence of the partners and
ensuring that they can 'see the whole picture' before coming to any
conclusions or decisions.

Creating successful partnerships is never easy; it requires honest
self-appraisal and clarification of values by all the partners. But the
prize — a powerful new dynamic born of mutual trust — is clearly
worthy of the effort involved. In order to address the first four of the
Secretary of State's operating principles, the Clwyd EBP will be
considering the mission, objectives, roles and accountabilities
outlined in the following sections as a 'starter' for discussion.

### 'Mission'

The Clwyd Education Business Partnership commits its partners to
promote mutual understanding and active collaboration between
employers and the education service with a view to improving
employment and education opportunities for young people, enabling
them to become part of a skilled, well qualified and committed work
force and also to ensure that the education service and training
providers become more responsive to the needs of business (see
Figure 8.2). To this end it will keep national training targets firmly in
focus and ensure that they are pursued within the context of shared
values, shared aims and priorities specific to their area.

### Objectives

In common with other education–business partnerships, the
objectives of Clwyd EBP include:

–   increasing the rate of participation in formal education and
    training post-16;
–   generating a highly skilled work force;

**Figure 8.2**

## THE BUILDING BLOCKS IN THE CLWYD EDUCATION – BUSINESS PARTNERSHIP

-   ensuring that all available talents, including those of people with special needs, are given opportunities to flourish.

The Department of Employment's *Partnership Handbook* (1991) provides a valuable list of measurable objectives and these will be considered by the Clwyd EBP (set up in the summer of 1992) as a starting point in identifying local targets. Figure 8.3 summarises this agenda.

---

**Figure 8.3**: Clwyd EBP — specific objectives

**Objectives for schools**:

-   to achieve a 10 per cent increase in the number of students staying on into full-time education over the next two years;
-   to ensure that school-leavers have their Records of Achievement matched by Individual Action Plans within three years;
-   to ensure that 10 per cent of teachers in primary schools have spent a period of time on an industrial placement over the next twelve months.

**Objectives for colleges**:

-   to secure a 5 per cent increase in the numbers of employer sponsorships for students in the next year;
-   to negotiate quality work experience placements for all students within their own Individual Action Plans within three years;
-   to arrange short business secondments for all full-time lecturers over the next two years.

**Objectives for employers**:

-   to provide 20 work placements for student teachers during the next twelve months;
-   to release ten company staff to shadow teachers in school in the next year;
-   to promote practice interviews (probably preceding work experience) in the next year.

**Objectives for TECs**:

-   to develop a board-level strategy for education-business partnerships within the next six months;

---

> – to compile and publish a directory of 200 small employers
>   prepared to support partnership activities, over the next 12
>   months.
>
> **Objectives for parents:**
>
> – to increase by 5 per cent per year for the next five years the
>   number of parents providing voluntary support and
>   mentoring in the school.
>
> **Objectives for the Careers Service Partnership:**
>
> – to supply the EBP with updated information on the local
>   labour market every three months;
> – to ensure through existing mechanisms that every student is
>   tracked throughout education, training and early
>   employment.

## Roles and responsibilities

The originating partners of the Clwyd EBP are keenly aware of the
danger of confusion stemming from the 'alphabet soup' of acronyms
which have proliferated in recent years to describe changes in
education and training arrangements. It is particularly important to
avoid any charges of bureaucratisation of the partnership, and the
partnership model which is to be followed in Clwyd will consist of a
small team operation with links into the other teams already active in
such enterprises as Compact and TVEI extension. The relationship of
the EBP team to all the other 'players in the game' will be similar to
that of the CBI to its members, i.e. a voluntary federation united by
common aims and objectives, identifying common priorities which
transcend individual concerns, projecting an image of the federation
in high profile and ensuring that its voice is heard — and heeded — by
policy formers and decision makers.
    The central EBP team will, on a regular basis two or three times a
year, report to, and take guidance from, a representative body or
'standing conference' comprising delegates from all the interested
groups. The EBP is an organisation which 'holds the ring', and can
therefore take a synoptic view of an arena in which there are already
many highly active and successful participants (see Figure 8.2, above).

**Accountabilities**

The lines of accountability within the EBP must lead to the principal partners. In the case of Clwyd these will be the Boards of the two participating TECs and the Education Committee of the LEA. As the EBP develops it is anticipated that an ever widening range of partners, including universities, individual companies, development agencies and community organisations will be embraced by the EBP, but the day-to-day accountabilities of the core team will need to be kept within a tight focus to ensure efficient working. The broad accountabilities to all the participants will be discharged at the regular standing conference at which the whole partnership scene will be kept under review.

The situation in Clwyd may be atypical in that many education business partnerships of various kinds were well in place before the EBP was formed. It is *not*, therefore, the role of the EBP to deliver specific programmes. It is vital that the EBP should maintain its over-arching, all embracing-nature so that it can serve both as a tangible reality and as a symbol of the interdependence of the two cultures of education and business. As this interdependence is illuminated by a shared vision, collaborative working will cease to be a matter for self-congratulation, and will become a natural way of life. Only when we have reached this stage of development will we be able to offer young people an education and training provision which genuinely reflects the totality of our culture in all its aspects.

# The North Wales Careers Service Partnership

The transition from school to work is a critical interface between education and industry, and essential to the development of a high skill economy; the development and management of this transition, the quality of education and training, its accessibility and its attractiveness are clearly too important to be left to chance. As a consequence, new management arrangements for the provision of careers guidance were announced in *Education and Training for the 21st Century* and a new partnership is emerging in North Wales to seize the opportunities being created.

In North Wales the operating areas of the two TECs are not coterminous with the LEA county boundaries; Targed's area consists of the County of Gwynedd and West Clwyd while Training and Enterprise covers the remainder of Clwyd. In order to avoid problems stemming from this boundary complication the Careers Service Partnership in North Wales embraces both TECs and both LEA

Careers Services, thus improving coherence in a way that would have been impossible through two separate Partnerships.

The Partnership's vision is to build upon the foundation of the valuable work currently undertaken by the LEA's careers services to provide a high quality, professional, client-centred service suitably resourced and extending to all age groups. To achieve this it needs: to be well informed, with the latest labour market information being readily available; to be accessible to the whole community; to take account of the long-term future as well as shorter term needs; to reflect the needs of the local economy whilst maintaining a wider national and international perspective of opportunities in education, employment and training; and to reflect the cultural and linguistic heritage of the communities it serves.

It is envisaged that the creation of this partnership will be a major step towards mobilising all relevant resources in North Wales towards a coherent and comprehensive advice and guidance service for all those in, entering or preparing for working life.

**The Partnership's aims are identified as:**

–    raising the quality and improving the accessibility of careers guidance, counselling, assessment and information for all age groups;
–    enhancing the quality of labour market intelligence and its use;
–    improving participation in the guidance process of all 'key players', in particular by involving employers;
–    establishing an influencing rôle in the provision of training opportunities through a variety of methods of delivery;
–    minimising the effects of vested interests in the provision of opportunities and of guidance;
–    promoting a culture of continuous progression of learning and training to higher levels of attainment;
–    promoting equality of opportunity to maximise human resource development in the region;
–    embracing developments in assessment (e.g. accreditation of prior learning and occupational testing) and promoting such innovations to a wider audience.

It is anticipated that substantial benefits will be obtained from the Careers Service Partnership, and that it will be well placed to ensure continuation of its services, whatever the outcome of any local government reorganisation might be. The partnership is also designed to minimise any difficulties that might arise from boundary issues, e.g. the delivery of a service to young people who may live in one partnership area, be educated in another, and trained in a third. It will ensure parity of provision across the region as well as providing economies of scale, cross fertilisation of ideas and coordination of effort, resources and expertise. As far as individual young people are concerned the partnership will offer a freely available service with improved accessibility, common standards and continuity of provision based upon the case-work principle and up-to-date labour market intelligence and economic information.

The TECs have welcomed an involvement in the strategic planning of the Careers Service. The LEAs see the partnership as offering several opportunities: to introduce more work related elements into the curriculum; to provide access to additional sources of funding and expertise, especially via Training Credits; to enhance careers information including improved access to labour market intelligence; and to achieve a measure of coherence in vocational education and training. The Careers Service should benefit from a higher profile, and from improved marketing, management, and strategic planning.

Whilst in some respects the partnership is a golden opportunity for the Careers Service to secure that recognition which, within the 'academic' context of British education, it has not previously achieved, one of the effects of the Education Reform Act 1988 and of the proposals outlined in the Department for Education schools White Paper *Choice and Diversity* (DFE, 1992) may be to reduce the impartiality of the service as schools and colleges compete for students and for funding geared to student numbers.

## An education and training charter for Clwyd

A pressing task of local educators and businessmen alike is to understand and appreciate the stark realities of the 'patchwork quilt' of post-16 provision legislated for in the Further and Higher Education Act 1992 and proposed in *Choice and Diversity*, and to join together in a search for coherence in provision based on common ground, free from the mindless shibboleths of educational 'gold standards'. Such a search is a matter of urgency if a 'new deal' for 16–18 year olds is to be constructed as:

> the scandal is that about half the young people of this country leave education without any qualification . . . The country is in danger of producing Nobel laureates at one end and unskilled labourers at the other (and in the nature of things many more of the latter than the former). Germany is in exactly the opposite position [as] almost everybody has a qualification . . . To be exact, in 1989 nine per cent of all boys and six per cent of all girls

left formal education without a qualification, and even this is
regarded as shameful by many [in Germany]. An educational
offensive in Britain has to be a skill offensive and has to aim at
qualifications for everyone. (Dahrendorf, 1992).

A constructive starting point for bringing education and training
provision together into one coherent strategy based on shared vision
and values, with all partners working towards a common agenda of
clear and targeted activities could be the adoption, by common
consent, of an education and training charter.

Such a charter has been drafted in Clwyd. It builds upon the work
being undertaken by the EBP and the Careers Service Partnership and
enshrines a commitment to:

– ensure that TECs and LEAs can work in partnership, based on
   trust and a high level of mutual credibility;
– develop educational expertise within the TECs, and a better
   understanding of business within the education service;
– substantially increase participation rates in education and
   training;
– facilitate access, progression and the attainment of higher levels
   of qualification;
– enable greater participation by non-traditional groups, ethnic
   minorities, and those with special needs;
– encourage an increase in the take up of open and flexible learning;
– achieve a genuine understanding throughout society of the merits
   of vocational and academic qualifications, including
   demonstrating their complementarity within modular course
   structures;
– make life-long learning available to all, based on employment
   with continuing education and training;
– provide a quality all-age guidance service;
– seek quality through measurable outcomes and performance
   criteria;
– implement plans to achieve increased attainment in line with
   national foundation and lifetime training targets and keep
   progress towards their achievement under review.

A framework of principles for an education and training charter
should acknowledge the reasonable expectations and mutual
responsibilities of the stakeholders. The extent to which we can
reconcile and harmonise these claims and obligations with genuine
empathy will determine the extent to which the rhetoric of
partnership can be translated into practice. To be meaningful, such
local charters must reflect the legitimate expectations of all the

participants, and not merely those of so-called 'consumers'. This has been the guiding principle behind the development of the Clwyd charter (see Figure 8.4) which puts in place medium-term objectives for three key groups of stakeholders: employers; students/trainees; and teachers. Through this initiative Clwyd is tackling the problem of institutional fragmentation in the provision of post-16 education and training.

**Figure 8.4:** The Clwyd charter — expectations of the stakeholders

*Employers*, whose interests will be brought into sharp focus within the TEC, can legitimately expect that trainees or students:

- will have pursued a National Curriculum up to Key Stages 3/4;
- will be literate, numerate, have acquired some knowledge of IT, and will be adequately prepared for entry to further or higher education;
- will have been given adequate personal, educational and vocational guidance;
- will have substantial Records of Achievement as a basis for Individual Action Plans;
- will have been socialised into the virtues, attractions and rewards of work;
- will have been treated as individuals and prepared for life in the 'work community' through work experience;
- will have some moral sense and will have been offered health education, personal and social education and political education;
- will have learned some of the skills of team-work in the context of problem solving
- will understand the realities of the local and national economy;
- will have had opportunities for community involvement, and for a wide range of sporting and cultural activities.

*Students/Trainees* may legitimately expect of their employers that:

- their previous school careers and their Records of Achievement will be properly valued and carefully discussed;
- they will have a proper induction into employment and a clear understanding of their employer's mission;

–  they will have detailed discussion with their employer of
   their FE and training requirements, stressing progression
   routes and leading to the preparation of individual action
   plans;
–  there will be proper concern for their health and safety;
–  they will be treated with dignity and respect, reflecting
   those mission statements which describe staff as 'the most
   precious resource';
–  they will be encouraged to join supportive 'peer group'
   networks;
–  they will be encouraged to take part in extramural,
   community-based and charitable activities.

Reflecting these employer and student/trainee expectancies
*teachers* (and by extension their employers, the LEAs) will be
expected:

–  to give proper attention to core skills, e.g. numeracy,
   literacy, oral fluency, information technology;
–  to understand clearly the economic significance of their task
   and to eschew the tunnel vision of over-academicism;
–  to retain their commitment to a value system involving
   equity, openness, understanding and a student-centred
   culture;
–  to stress individualism, autonomy, self-reliance, enterprise
   and team-building;
–  to offer impartial guidance, especially at the end of
   compulsory schooling;
–  to ensure that the school's boundaries are permeable to
   community influences as well as to parental pressures;
–  to provide a wide range of extramural, sporting, cultural
   and community activities;
–  to pursue the ideal of the teacher as a reflective professional,
   concerned with curriculum and management innovation,
   but at the same time seeking enhanced relevance for
   schooling as business and education move ever more closely
   together in the pursuit of common objectives.

In turn teachers themselves may reasonably expect:

–  that a society which seeks a worthwhile education must be
   prepared to will the *means* as well as the *ends*;
–  that their professional training, experience and
   commitment will be properly valued;

> – that they may have opportunities to contribute to the development of aims, policies and partnership activities which will permeate the boundaries between education and business.
>
> Source: Clwyd, 1992

## References

Clwyd (1992) 'An Education and Training Charter', Clwyd Education Department, Mold, March.

Dahrendorf R. (1992) 'Education for a European Britain', *Royal Society of Arts Journal* Vol.CXL, No.5426, February 1992, pp.168–78.

DE/DES/WO (1991) *Education and Training for the 21st Century*, Employment Department, Department of Education and Science, London, HMSO.

DFE (1992) *Choice and Diversity*, Department for Education, London, HMSO.

# 9   Training credits: the pilot doomed to succeed

## Lorna Unwin

### Introduction

By 1996, every 16 or 17 year old leaving full-time education in England, Wales and Scotland will be entitled to receive a training credit to pay for part-time vocational education and training (VET). First announced in March 1990 by the then Secretary of State for Employment, Michael Howard, training credits were to be initially piloted by ten Training and Enterprise Councils (TECs) and one Local Enterprise Company (LEC). As Howard stated in 1990:

> There has been widespread interest in individual training credits as a means of motivating young people to participate more effectively in the training market . . . The approach is, however, untested. I have therefore decided that there should be pilot schemes at local level. (ED, 1990)

Nevertheless whilst the original pilots were still being evaluated, the 1991 White Paper *Education and Training for the 21st Century* revealed that the scheme was to be extended to a further seven TECs and two LECs in 1993 and would have national coverage by 1996. Known colloquially as the pilot 'doomed to succeed', training credits represent yet another intervention by the Conservative Government to transform post-16 VET. Like previous initiatives, and most notably the Youth Training Scheme (YTS), training credits have been launched as the answer to this country's youth training problems.

Much of the material for this chapter was gained through an evaluation of the first year of South and East Cheshire TEC's pilot.

Each of the eleven original pilots underwent similar local evaluations, all commissioned by the Employment Department (ED) and completed by January 1992. In addition, Her Majesty's Inspectorate, the Careers Service Inspectorate and the ED's Training Standards Inspectorate carried out their own evaluations of each first round pilot. Despite this considerable amount of evaluation, however, it was not until Summer 1992 that the ED published a summary report of the findings, some ten months after second round pilots had begun developing their operational models.

The chapter begins by examining the Government's approach to credits and draws on the experience of the implementation models adopted by the original pilots. It then turns to the operational issues faced by pilots using illustrations from South and East Cheshire TEC in particular to show how credits were working at local level by mid-1992. A significant difference between training credits and previous youth training initiatives is the extent to which local groupings other than the young people themselves have been involved at both the planning and operational stages of the pilot. The way in which those groupings — school teachers, careers officers, employers, college staff and training providers — have responded to credits is explored in this chapter, along with the reactions of the young people themselves. In so doing, questions are raised in relation to VET funding, employer recruitment policies, the provision of careers education and guidance, and the extent of the TECs' influence and acceptance within their local communities. The chapter concludes by considering the long-term viability of training credits given the increasing numbers of young people staying in full-time education after 16 and the continuing impact of economic recession on the availability of jobs for school leavers.

## Background to credits: VET in the marketplace

> I've been given this Prospects card to buy a course at college but first I've got to find an employer who will let me use the card. There aren't many jobs round here so I'll be lucky to find anything decent. What happens when I get to the interview and the employer says I've got the job but doesn't mention anything about going to college? The woman from the TEC said we were supposed to tell the employer that we had the right to go to college and this card would pay for the cost. What if he says he's not interested in any card and I can take the job or leave it?
>
> (16 year old school leaver, Crewe 1992)

In 1989, the Confederation of British Industry (CBI) called for the introduction of individual education and training credits as a key step develop personal and social skills and an understanding of the workplace to make young people more attractive to employers. The rationale of credits comes at the problem from a different angle, however. It suggests that by giving young people purchasing power, not only will this motivate them to seek jobs with training but it will also encourage employers to create such jobs.

The government responded within eight months to the CBI's suggestion and in March 1990 announced that it would set up 11 pilot credit schemes to operate from April 1991. The CBI's call for credits to purchase post-16 education as well as training was rejected, however, lest it revive the controversy surrounding the early Thatcher administration's enthusiasm for education vouchers. Credits were now to pay for vocational training to a minimum of NVQ level 2, undertaken by young people who had left full-time education to be either directly employed or to join a YT programme. TECs and LECs were invited to bid for pilot status and out of the 32 which submitted proposals, 17 were given development funding of up to £10,000 to prepare detailed bids. In August, 1990, the ED announced that the 11 successful pilots were: Birmingham, Bradford, Devon and Cornwall, Grampian, Hertfordshire, Kent, North East Wales, Northumberland, South and East Cheshire, SOLOTEC in South London and Suffolk.

In its prospectus to TECs and LECs, the ED stated that the main purpose of training credits 'is to expand and improve the training of young people', and that credits had the potential to:

- strengthen the motivation of the individual to train, and to higher standards;
- help to establish an efficient market in training;
- make training which is relevant to employers' needs an accpeted part of normal working life (ED, 1990).

The prospectus went on to stress that:

It will be a requirement for all pilots that they increase participation in training; raise the level of skills attained; and generate more jobs with training for young people. They will also have to ensure appropriate arrangements for careers advice, working wherever appropriate through the Careers Service and careers teachers. Whether through the credits arrangements or otherwise, all TECs running pilot schemes will have to ensure that, in their area, they meet the Government's Guarantee of a training place up to the age of 18 for all young people who have left full-time education and are unable to find a job. (ED, 1990)

The prospectus acknowledged that TECs and LECs might also have their own additional objectives in operating a credits pilot '. . . such as raising general awareness of training for young people in their area, tackling key skill needs, or increasing training in small companies'.

Despite the enormity of the task facing the first round pilots, they had about six months to develop their systems and procedures in order to be ready to issue credits from April 1991.

## Models of delivery

The basic credits idea is a simple one which presupposes the following context: school leavers find employment, which could be on the basis of trainee status, and use the credit to purchase a training course leading to a minimum NVQ level 2 from a provider of their choice; the enhanced vocational guidance they received before leaving school coupled with their developed negotiation and decision-making skills will have enabled each young person to persuade their employer to release them for training; in return, the TEC/LEC or the training provider supplies the young person with regular statements showing how the credit is being spent having been encouraged to treat young people as valued customers; if the young person and/or their employer is unhappy with the service, they can transfer the credit to a different provider or use their purchasing power as a weapon to force providers to improve; the concurrent expansion of a unit-based qualifications system is intended to facilitate the transfer of students' credits between providers.

In reality, of course, credits were launched into a very different context. Pilots have, therefore, had to tackle several interrelated deficiencies in terms of VET provision when developing their own models of credit delivery. Indeed, by working in partnership with local education authorities (LEAs), colleges, schools and the Careers Service, credits pilots have given a higher profile to the need for improvement across the VET infrastructure. Provision of vocational guidance has, for example, been considerably strengthened in pilot areas with credit funding being used to appoint extra careers officers whose role involves preparing Individual Action Plans for all Year 11 pupils. As a consequence, careers officers have spent more time in schools helping careers teachers to promote the need for careers education, often the poorest relation when it comes to curriculum priorities. Teachers in South and East Cheshire reported that credits had 'put careers education on the curriculum map' and had made both them and their pupils address the concept of post-16 entitlement to training and further education in a fresh way. At the same time, teachers and careers officers were wary of the fact that credits could become yet another short-term measure to boost youth training. They questioned how far employers were being encouraged to play their part in the initiative and were concerned that employers had, for some time, showed signs of 'initiative fatigue'.

Eight of the original pilots decided to make credits available to all school leavers — including those with special needs — seeking work in any occupational sectors, whilst two pilots (Birmingham and Kent) restricted the scheme to certain sectors in which there were skill shortages. Grampian LEC placed no restriction on occupational sector but required any credit holder to be properly employed before they could use the credit. First round evaluation showed that the selective model of delivery was prone to considerable difficulties. Two further ways in which pilots differ concern the age range within which a credit is valid and whether or not to include young people who live outside the TEC area but who enter that area for employment. Subsequently, due to low take-up, some pilots have extended their eligibility criteria. Hertfordshire TEC, for example, has opened its scheme to 18–24 year olds employed in the county, whilst Kent includes 18–20 year olds who are in a job which previously did not offer them the chance to gain a qualification. All first-round pilots have made special provision to try and meet their YT guarantee of a training place for any unemployed school leaver. Such arrangements include allowing the credit to pay for full-time courses at further education colleges and for full-time training programmes with private providers who 'mind' the young people until they find places with employers. The numbers of young people using their credits under these special arrangements could be considerable in areas where youth unemployment is rising. As such numbers are counted in the overall totals for the take-up of credits, the true take-up figure, which should reflect the number of young people using their credit in employment, is distorted.

The packaging of the credit varies among the pilots with the majority opting for some sort of 'credit card' format. Four pilots opted for a local brand name (South and East Cheshire — *Prospects*; NE Wales — *Career Link*; Grampian — *SkillSeekers*; SOLOTEC — *Training Accounts*) — in order to create both a fresh image for credits and one that was distinctly different from previous government-led youth training schemes. In South and East Cheshire TEC, for example, early market research revealed that young people were very wary of any scheme using the term 'credit' as they associated this with potential debt. The TEC was also concerned about the poor image of YT in its area and decided to launch credits under the new title *Prospects*. The term YT has been replaced by Traineeship for placements with employers and Careership for placements which have employed status with the TEC's intention being to place the majority of young people on Careerships. Evaluation findings from this TEC's pilot subsequently bore out the TEC's concern for nomenclature for they showed that young people not only distrust the word 'credit', but associate the term 'training' with low-skilled, manual jobs and see it as having no relevance to anyone staying in full-time education after 16. Comments to this effect from young people included:

'I am doing 'A' levels; I do not intend to do any training.'
'I am not going into a career that needs training' (nursing, radiography, teaching).
'I am going to college to do business studies and I'm not sure I'll need training for the sort of job I'm going to do.'
'I am going into a job where training isn't important — where you learn from experience, not training' (Care sector).

It is ironic to discover that the main achievement of some sixteen or so years of government-led youth training schemes has apparently been to embed a negative view of 'training' in the minds of young people.

Finding a suitable name for credits schemes becomes more problematic as new regions become involved. The ED appears to want TECs and LECs to use the universal branding 'Training Credits' to avoid confusion as the initiative grows. There is, however, a much more fundamental issue than language at stake. Evaluation findings from South and East Cheshire showed that the vast majority of young people, regardless of their post-16 destination, welcomed the idea of an individual credit for which they would be personally responsible. Those who had decided to stay in full-time education felt they should be able to use the credit just as much as those who were leaving to seek work. They may have distanced themselves from 'training' but they clearly wanted to have more control over their post-16 futures and saw their *Prospects* card as the key to this. Nevertheless, if credits are only available for young people who leave full-time education at a time when the majority are choosing to stay at school or college, they are likely to become tainted in the same way as previous youth training initiatives. South and East Cheshire, in an attempt to maintain the interest of young people who stayed in full-time education and avoid such negative connotations, have introduced individual *Prospects* awards so that young people on full-time courses can use these to pay for experiences such as for field trips, university taster programmes and special projects for A level.

The way in which a young person acquires their training credit varies across the pilots. In South and East Cheshire, the Careers Service is responsible for distributing *Prospects* cards and information packs to young people before they complete Year 11 of schooling.

This distribution forms part of an extensive marketing campaign in which TEC staff and careers officers give presentations, including the use of video, to pupils, teachers, parents and college staff. Young people are also given a registration form which they are asked to complete once they have made a definite decision about their post-16 destination. If they are seeking work, they are asked to wait until they have found a job, be it Traineeship or Careership, before completing their form which they return to the TEC. On receipt of the form, the TEC sends the young person a cheque for £15 which can be spent in any way the young person chooses. Given that there are just under 4,000 eligible school leavers in the TEC area, the decision to hand over £15 per person was criticised by many teachers who felt the money could have been used by schools. The TEC's registration system, however, is central to the operation of its credits model for it provides the TEC with a means of tracking every eligible school leaver in South and East Cheshire recorded on its registration database. Cheshire Careers Service and the LEA have both praised the registration system for providing destination data more quickly than the existing Careers Service system. It has also, for the first time, provided the LEA with details of the type of courses young people are taking in colleges outside the LEA boundary.

Those young people who return cards showing they have taken jobs without training are visited by a TEC training advisor who attempts to persuade the employer to activate the credit by allowing the young person to attend a course offered by a college or a private provider. Similarly, young people who remain unemployed are sent details of vacancies and Traineeships. In the first year of its pilot, the registration system enabled the TEC to convert many jobs into Careerships and, therefore, to become one of the few TECs to reach its target for credits take-up.

## Recycling resources to fund credits

Training credits funding is made up from the following three sources:

- planned provision for YT in each TEC or LEC;
- a proportion of the Revenue Support Grant (RSG) allocation for part-time VET currently controlled by local education authorities and previously given direct to colleges;
- a further £12m (in 1990/91) from existing Government expenditure plans to be spent on enhanced careers guidance and to be used as top-up to deliver higher levels of training.

In addition, the first round pilots received £4.8 million in development money. The bulk of the available funding, therefore, was to be recycled from existing YT programmes. Procuring and managing the RSG element, though much smaller than the YT budget, has proved to be highly problematic both at the initial planning stage and subsequently when young people began cashing their credits. Clearly, the TECs and LEC had to work in partnership with their LEAs, whose colleges were to act as training providers. For some of the larger pilots, this meant making arrangements with more than one LEA as TEC/LEC boundaries do not equate to LEA boundaries. In all pilots, it also meant ensuring that financial provision was made to ensure some credits could be cashed at colleges outside the TEC/LEC boundary but to whom young people and employers had traditionally gone for reasons of quality and/or choice. The second round pilots will have the added complication of making new arrangements with the Further Education Funding Council for transfer of whatever equates to the RSG element in the new independent world of further education institutions.

In attempting to create effective and workable financial structures within which credits can be delivered, TEC/LEC managers, their local authority partners and, indeed, ED civil servants, have found themselves at the mercy of the arcane and obscurely complicated world of VET funding. A myriad of locally agreed pricing arrangements has developed over the years between colleges, private training providers and employers. The RSG funding is supposed to cover further education costs for all 16–18 year olds, apart from those on YT, thus in theory making it possible for any employer to send a young person for day-release classes at no cost. In practice, most employers have always paid towards that training, usually in the form of a locally agreed subsidy of around 70 pence per student hour or through their association with an industrial training board. Colleges have been cushioned by the automatic annual payment of RSG monies and work-related further education funding, amounting to some 5 per cent of a college's overall budget, direct from the ED. In addition, since the late 1970s, colleges have either run their own YT schemes or serviced others and received payment for this on the basis of a minimum number of students in any one group. This mixture of funding arrangements has meant that the true cost of supporting a student in the further education sector has never been decisively calculated and colleges have been able to transfer money from one pot to another in order to subsidise courses which fell below projected numbers or which required extra support. The credits concept challenges the group-based approach to costings and, importantly, presupposes that every course is clearly costed in order that an appropriate value can be assigned to each credit, taking into account, for example, that an engineering course costs far more than one in business administration. As such, assigning a meaningful value to the credit has proved to be impossible as the true costs of training vary so much according to occupational area and chosen qualification. South and East Cheshire's *Prospects* card states that it is worth a minimum of £750 whilst Northumberland's and SOLOTEC's cards have face values of £1500. Such values are misleading as they relate to training costs only and do not reflect items such as travel and equipment expenses and employer contributions to trainees' weekly allowances.

The RSG figures themselves have also caused problems for credits pilots. The Department for Education (DFE) calculates the RSG from the annual Further Education Statistical Return (FESR) it receives from the LEAs. This meant that TECs and LEAs based their credits take-up figures on DFE statistics which would be two years out of date by the time the pilots began operating. Crucially, for the original pilots, those statistics reflected a pre-recessionary situation in which part-time numbers were quite buoyant. As the recession started to bite, TECs and LEAs realised that colleges were likely to lose out on the RSG transfer as part-time numbers fell. In order to protect colleges' income, some pilots developed special procedures for ensuring the RSG was paid back, procedures which look set to continue as part-time numbers fail to reach their pre-recession levels. The most notable procedure in this regard has been arrangements which allow colleges to receive credits as payment for new full-time courses supposedly set up specially for unemployed school leavers. Private training providers have, quite naturally, been complaining that such procedures are a direct contradiction of the credits' objective to create a customer-led training market and that they simply maintain the *status quo* in further education.

## Private VET providers and credits

As they prepare for independent status in 1993, colleges are likely to reappraise their participation in government-led initiatives. Some have never been happy servicing youth training schemes and may decide that they prefer to recruit students from the cosier and more profitable markets of adult business studies courses, full-time 16–18 A level programmes and franchising arrangments to deliver degree courses in conjunction with local higher education institutions. Some, however, may find they are under political pressure to join credits pilots as TEC board members may also be college governors and/or influential local employers.

Involvement with a credits pilot should, in theory, make many demands on colleges. It presumes, for example, that they are able to identify the exact source of funding for every student they enrol. In a typical college with several thousand students on the books and classes containing students funded by a variety of sources, such identification can take several months after initial enrolment. Many young people, for example, arrive at college unsure as to whether they are on YT or directly employed. Under credits, young people should be arriving at college with an action plan ready to negotiate entry to an appropriate course and have access to tutors and student support staff who fully understand and appreciate that they are now dealing with a customer. In the first round pilots, young people found their purchasing power to be illusory. Their credit card was simply regarded as yet another form of funding to be noted on the appropriate form. The following comments reflect the views of many young people in South and East Cheshire:

> 'I keep my card in my pocket in case anyone wants to see it and in case I can use it but so far it's stayed in its plastic wallet. I still think it's a good idea but I'm not sure the college knows what to do with it.'
> 'All the college did when we enrolled was use the card to get our number. I thought we'd use the card once a week and have to plan how we spent the money.'[1]

To the same extent, credits have offered little incentive to the private training provider to become more customer-orientated. Contracting arrangements between the host TEC/LEC and providers vary across the pilots with a few, including South and East Cheshire, having dismantled the existing Managing Agent structure in order to deal directly with employers recruiting school leavers. In these cases, private providers operate like colleges in that they provide the off-the-job training. In contrast, private providers are vital when it comes to meeting the YT guarantee as they can house young people until placements are found with employers. Payment of the output related funding (ORF) — a requirement of all ED training credit contracts and a sum which can represent as much as 25 per cent of the credit value — also varies according to how much is paid to the young people on achievement of their NVQ and how much to their employer or training provider. A major anomaly in terms of the ORF, however, is that it does not categorise the gaining of a job as a positive outcome so that those agencies which place young people as trainees with employers are not penalised financially if they do not make efforts to convert Traineeships into real jobs.

## Employers: active players or passive recipients?

That a major attitudinal change on the part of employers is needed when it comes to releasing employees for training has been

well documented elsewhere (see Finegold and Soskice, 1988;
Steedman and Wagner 1989). Evidence from the first round pilots
shows that Training Credits have not only had little impact on that
attitudinal change, but that the understanding and awareness of
employers of credits themselves was very disappointing. It has already
been noted that credits were launched during a severe economic
recession when many employers, including the largest, had frozen
recruitment of young people. For some time, the ED has been
relaxing the administrative burden placed on employers by the early
youth training schemes and credits pilots have sought to keep the new
initiative as simple as possible for employers to understand.

There is evidence to suggest that where employers have understood
the rationale of credits, they have welcomed the initiative, particularly
with regard to its insistence on young people achieving qualifications.
There are two major problems, however, related to the link between
credits and NVQs, the qualifications to which the government and
TECs are commited. Firstly, understanding and awareness of NVQs
is very limited among employers of all sizes and in all sectors.
Secondly, when employers do have experience of NVQs they often
criticise their applicability to local labour market need and the
slowness with which they are being introduced. Employers also still
harbour deep-seated prejudices about the basic and social skill
abilities of school leavers.

In South and East Cheshire, which has a fairly strong labour market
even in recession, employers who wish to participate in credits have to
become members of both the TEC and its Business Education
Partnership which manages the credits pilot. Here, young people are
recruited to Traineeships or Careerships under TEC contract but paid
a wage directly by the employer and only employers who take young
people with special needs are given extra support towards the trainee's
weekly allowance. SOLOTEC, on the other hand, has had to
reintroduce a system of paying the weekly allowance to encourage
employers to recruit young people during the recession, whilst in
Kent small employers (less than 25 employees) now receive a
supplement of £100 per quarter, per employed trainee. It seems
highly likely that some of the 1993 pilots, for example Merseyside,
will also have to offer a substantial allowance to employers and create
their own work placements. Under such arrangements, credits
funding simply becomes YT funding under a new name.

All first round pilots reported that they were having to put far more
time and resources into marketing credits to employers than had been
envisaged and that special funding arrangements would definitely
continue for the forseeable future as there were no signs of an
improvement in their local economies. Ironically, however, at their
annual national conference in July 1992, TECs were told by Gillian

Shepherd, Employment Secretary, that public spending on youth training was unlikely to rise and could be cut (*The Guardian*, July 3rd, 1992). This news came despite the fact that TECs had been telling the government for some time that, due to funding cuts, they were finding it increasingly difficult to meet their youth training guarantee of a place for every 16–18 year old who could not find employment. The TECs' problems were supported by a report from the leading youth charities which showed that nationally there were too few places available in 1992 to enable TECs to deliver the youth training guarantee (Youthaid, 1992). A further problem for medium and large sized employers who deal with more than one TEC or LEC is that they are faced with varying administrative procedures which means employing someone specifically to deal with the paperwork. Meanwhile, the very employers upon whom the success of credits depends and who sit on the boards of TECs are becoming more vociferous in their dealings with Government and some, notably in London, are delaying signing their annual contracts in an attempt to secure better funding.

## Young person as consumer

A small employer in the 25–50 employee band in South and East Cheshire encapsulated the burden placed on the credit-carrying young person:

> School leavers need to present themselves to employers properly and be prepared to explain that they now come with a package of benefits — *Prospects*, Action Plan, Record of Achievement and so on. We employers need school leavers to help us understand these new initiatives.

The lack of coherence and co-ordination concerning a range of school-based initiatives adds to the confusion young people feel about processes and products which are, in theory, supposed to be for their benefit. In many schools, careers education, which often does not begin until Year 10, has to be squeezed into an already small timetable slot for personal and social education. At the same time as they are preparing for their GCSEs, pupils are taking time out for work experience, to complete progress charts for their record of achievement, to attend guidance interviews with careers officers and to make an Action Plan. In schools where there are still sixth forms, pupils may be coming under increasing pressure to stay on regardless of whether they are traditional A level candidates as schools compete for the declining pool of 16 year olds. The number of schools offering Business and Technology Council (BTEC) First Certificate courses and the willingness of others to pilot general national vocational qualifications (GNVQs) as alternatives to A levels is testimony to their need to increase their post-16 numbers. At the same time, in areas where a tertiary system operates, schools may work in conjunction with colleges to increase staying-on rates as they are now themselves in the marketplace for pupils.

Training credits sit awkwardly alongside the government's drive to increase staying-on rates for they are the mechanism via which young people who do not want to pursue an academic route post-16 can combine workplace learning and vocational education. This mixture was, of course, the basis of apprenticeships and was continued in the better youth training schemes. The mixed-model of post-16 VET has, however, been severely damaged by the poor performance of many youth training schemes which failed to convert placements into real jobs or to provide young people with nationally recognised qualifications. In addition, the introduction of a competence-based model for vocational qualifications, the very reform which was supposed to inject real quality into workplace learning, has also been heavily criticised for the narrowness of its approach, the complexity of its assessment procedures and the disparity between the lower and higher level qualifications (see Steedman and Wagner, 1989; Raggatt, 1991; Unwin 1990).

Nevertheless, the following case studies from South and East Cheshire illustrate how appropriate the mixed-model can be when enlightened employers offer work-based training and access to meaningful qualifications:

Ian was persuaded to stay at school by his parents and teachers even though the school did not offer information technology, his main interest, in the 6th Form. He began two A level courses — geography and French — and was trying to improve his GCSE grades in science and human biology. After six months, Ian decided academic study was not for him and, using his training credit (*Prospects*), took up a Traineeship with a local building society. He is now (1992) attending his local further education college one day a week studying for his BTEC National in computing technology. He said: 'I'd kept the *Prospects* card in my wallet all the time I was in the 6th Form. I knew all along school wasn't right for me but my parents wanted me to get a good qualification. The card made me realise I had a say in my future and I'm now getting what I wanted in the first place.'

Susan has always wanted to be a primary school teacher but by the middle of Year 11 felt that she had had enough of school. During her guidance interview, she discussed with her careers officer the possibility of leaving school to start work in a company which would allow her to study for qualifications which give her access to higher education at a later stage. In her school's eyes, Susan was an automatic A level candidate and teachers were, naturally, concerned that she might never make the switch from employment to higher education. An offer of a Careership with a large manufacturing company persuaded Susan to leave school and she is now combining work in the marketing department with study for a BTEC National Diploma in Business and Finance. She is also taking French A level at her local college in the evening. Susan said: 'I still want to teach eventually but working has made me more confident and I love the atmosphere. The *Prospects* card was like a passport to a different future for me.'

In the light of current levels of youth unemployment, Ian and Susan are doubly privileged, first in that they found employment and, second, in that they were academically gifted enough to have succeeded in full-time education. Both, however, challenge the growing consensus that full-time education should be the norm post-16.

The next case study demonstrates the reality of staying on at college for many young people, who may come out after one or two years with a level 1 or 2 qualification but who will not, necessarily, have gained enough credits to progress to a level 3:

Gary enjoyed school but his predicted GCSE grades were very low. During his two week work experience in Year 10, Gary discovered an interest in catering and decided he would like to work in hotels. Gary's school does not have a sixth form so pupils transfer to the local tertiary college. When it came to deciding which route to take, Gary found that most of his closest friends were going to college to do general courses which did not require GCSE passes. He was offered the chance of a Traineeship with a local restaurant but decided to follow his friends to college where he is taking a food-related Diploma in Vocational Education. Gary said: 'the Traineeship was only going to pay me £29 a week but I can get £20 working three nights in the fish and chip shop where I live. All my mates were going to college and I wanted to stay with them. My dad said it was better to stay-on.'

For young people like Gary, full-time education is replacing a locally available youth training scheme as the new post-16 rite of passage.

Young people in South and East Cheshire interviewed after they had left school said that much of their careers education and vocational guidance had been wasted either because they were too concerned with GCSE work or because they found it difficult to project themselves beyond the school leaving date. Now that they had left, they felt ready to listen and think through the options available. Those in work said that they were better able to understand the relevance of the credit but that neither their employer nor their college tutor regarded it as a mechanism for facilitating individual career progression.

The Careers Service only has a statutory duty to provide vocational guidance to eligible school leavers, though in some areas a limited service is available to Year 12 pupils and full-time college students. In the light of the increased numbers of young people staying in full-time education, many of whom will leave to seek work rather than enter higher education, there is an urgent need for independent vocational and educational guidance to be available to all young people up to the age of 18. To be worthwhile, Records of Achievement and Individual Action Plans must become meaningful products which support young people as they progress to the next stage of education and training and be used to inform those professionals whose job it is to create education and training plans for each young person. Young people also need the opportunity to develop the skills which will enable them to participate fully in the guidance process and then act on their decisions. At the same time, employers have to be aware of the benefits to them of allowing their employees to activate the credit.

Although all TECs and LECs operating training credits have to conform to ED guidelines, they have been given considerable freedom to design local models of delivery, a freedom which has continued for the second round of pilots. This diversity of process and practice has led to a complex web of local funding arrangements and eligibility criteria. For the young person, now supposedly newly empowered to purchase the training of his or her choice, that empowerment and choice will differ significantly from one county to the next. Employers, too, will find that they are wooed in different ways according to their TEC or LEC area, whilst the providers of training, whether they be private agencies or colleges of further education, will be paid at different rates and be expected to meet varying requirements for each credits scheme with which they are involved. Such diversity poses problems in trying to evaluate training credits in the context of national policy objectives and in attempting to make meaningful comparisons between the different pilots. Moreover, there is a danger that the detailed reality of credits delivery could be hidden from the public scrutiny applied to, say, YTS which, though delivered locally, was prescribed by a nationally designed operating framework.

**Just another initiative? The future for credits**

Responding to the fact that fewer than half of the 27,000 training
credits offered to young people who left school in 1991 had been taken
up by November of that year, Michael Howard referred to the
increase in staying-on rates. At the same time, the TECs and LEC
involved were blaming the recession. Undoubtedly, the training
credits initiative could not have been launched at a worse time, as
employers of all sizes and in all sectors stopped recruiting young
people. To what extent the concurrent rise in staying-on rates is a
consequence of the recession is difficult to measure but it is certain
that many young people will only remain in full-time education for
one year. An important credibility test for training credits will be to
see how many of those 17 year olds take up their entitlement.

Both factors — the recession, the effects of which will haunt
training credits pilots for some time to come, and increased staying-on
rates — present TECs and LECs with practical problems. In terms of
their impact on national training policy, they each represent a
paradox. If the main purpose of training credits is, in the words of the
government, 'to expand and improve the training of young people',
how can this be achieved, recession or boom, if credits are reliant on
employers recruiting young people to jobs with training? At the same
time, the government appears to be succeeding in encouraging
schools and tertiary colleges to retain as many students beyond the age
of 16 as possible, thus promoting the status of full-time student over
that of part-time trainee.

New initiatives are useful in that they often expose weaknesses in
the current system. Despite all the problems with NVQs, for
example, the shift to a competence-based approach to qualifications is
exposing the cosy world in which awarding bodies annually rubber-
stamped college provision, the reliance on written tests for assessment
purposes regardless of the need to assess practical skills, and the
disparity between educationally derived curricula and the working
practices in modern industry and commerce. Similarily, and perhaps
ironically for the government, Training Credits are serving to expose
even further the weaknesses of this country's VET infrastructure.

For young people in South and East Cheshire, the training credit
has made them, their parents and teachers, aware of their entitlement
to receive vocational education and training after the age of sixteen. A
credit represents, quite simply, the key to unlock that entitlement
even though, in practice, the credit currently unlocks a choice of
events some of which are empowering for the young person whilst
others, often according to local labour market conditions and the
TEC's credit model, offer no choice of education and training route.

Credits have been launched into a hostile economic environment in which youth unemployment is rising and the funding of educational institutions is becoming increasingly dependent on the numbers of full-time students they retain. Moreover, empowered young people pose a big problem to educational institutions. They demand course combinations which upset the smooth operation of the timetable and if an astute employer is involved, colleges may increasingly face demands for flexibility in terms of the start and finish dates of courses.

Yet whilst upsetting the educational apple cart would seem to fit quite happily with the Conservative Government's and the ED's agenda during the 1980s and early 1990s, other circumstances are combining to make the use of credits far from easy. Specifically, unless training credits are upgraded to become the key which unlocks a young person's entitlement to both further education and vocational training regardless of full or part-time status, then they will be by-passed by the majority of eligible school leavers in the 1990s. Those in the minority who choose to leave full-time education to seek work may find that the credit merely buys them a re-vamped youth training place. This polarisation of youth reflects the seemingly different and conflicting policy agendas of the Employment Department and the Department for Education (DFE). On the one hand, the ED is attempting, via a funding mechanism which routes funds through individuals rather than providers, to increase the numbers of young people entering jobs with training and, hence, the numbers of part-time students in further education. On the other hand, the DFE continues to route funds through institutions and to promote full-time 16–18 year old provision over part-time. The grand design of the CBI referred to at the start of this chapter and the ED's claims that credits would 'expand and improve the training of young people' appear to be a long way from being realised.

## Notes

1   These and other comments by those involved in training credits in south and east Cheshire form a part of my local, unpublished evaluation of the initiative for the TEC.

## References

CBI Task Force (1989) *Towards a Skills Revolution*, London, Confederation of British Industry.
ED (1991) *Education and Training for the 21st Century*, HMSO.
ED (1990) *Training Credits Prospectus for TECs and LECs*, Employment Department, Sheffield.
Finegold, D. and Soskice, D. (1988) 'The Failure of Training in Britian: Analysis and Prescription', *Oxford Review of Economic Policy*, Vol.4, No.3.

Raggatt, P. (1991) 'Quality Assurance and NVQs', Raggatt, P. and Unwin, L. (eds) *Change and Intervention: Vocational Education and Training*, Falmer Press, London.

Steedman, H. and Wagner, K. (1989) 'Productivity, machinery and skills: clothing manufacture in Britian and Germany', *National Institute Economic Review*, May 1989.

Stronach, I. (1989) 'Education, vocationalism and economic recovery: the case against witchcraft', *British Journal of Education and Work*, Vol. 2, No.1. pp.5–31.

*The Guardian*, 'Crisis-hit training councils face new cuts, minister says', July 3rd 1992.

Unwin, L. (1990a) 'The Competence Race: We Are All Qualified Now', Corbett, J. *Uneasy Transitions: Disaffection in post-compulsory education and training*, Falmer Press, London.

Unwin, L. (1990b) 'Staff Development, Competence and NVQ', *Journal of Further and Higher Education*, Volume 14, No.2.

Youthaid and the Children's Society, (1992) *A Broken Promise — the Failure of Youth Training Policy*, London, Youthaid.

LIBRARY
HANDSWORTH COLLEGE
SOHO ROAD
BIRMINGHAM
B21 9DP

# 10 Towards a world-class system

## John Woolhouse

The discussion throughout this book demonstrates the complexity of the factors involved in the design and operation of the post-compulsory phase of education. The system by which the transition from general education to professional training, qualification and status is achieved, is made up of a series of 'subsystems' which present 16 to 19 year olds with the problem of making decisions about a bewildering variety of routes, destinations and rewards.

The inherent difficulty of making informed education and occupational choices in a modern society is compounded by the unpredictable behaviour of labour markets, particularly local labour markets, and by the uncertainties of individuals, and of many employers, about the benefits to be derived from long-term investment in education and training. To function effectively, post-compulsory education and training systems need to bring order, coherence, stability and intelligibility to an increasingly volatile scene.

The issue is further complicated by the effects of technological, social and demographic change. The businesses that exist now, and the jobs that are available, are not necessarily those that will be needed in 10 or 20 years' time. A balance, therefore, needs to be struck between short term skill requirements and the attainment of educational standards on which longer term strategies for a high-skill economy depend.

International comparisons of education and training systems demonstrate the variety of strategies pursued by different nations, each in its own distinctive cultural, social and economic context. There is no single, right solution; there are many options and combinations that may be pursued. The most important lesson for England and Wales is not that someone else has 'the solution', but that the creation of a 'learning society' will only be achieved by pursuing a set of coherent, interlocking and mutually supportive strategies involving all of the stakeholders in a coherent, intelligible and rewarding system.

At the heart of the matter are complex and difficult judgments on the balance between: long- and short-term interests; breadth and specialisation; voluntary and compulsory participation of learners and of providers; competition and collaboration; and the distribution of costs to individuals, employers and the state.

The performance of education and training systems, like any other system, must be judged on outputs and on net efficiency. Will the system now under construction generate a flow of well-educated and highly qualified people in sufficient numbers to enable the UK to reconstruct its economy, to achieve a highskill equilibrium, and to promote that degree of social justice and equality of opportunity that is a prerequisite of a healthy and vigorous society?

Much is at stake; measures now in hand are a long overdue attempt to recover from 40 years of neglect and confusion in post-compulsory education and training. Many would argue that our failure either to understand, or to act effectively to maintain the nation's competitive advantage in skills and in education dates from the middle of the previous century. The economic and social imperatives for reform are powerful and long-standing. Whilst no useful purpose is served by cavilling at serious attempts to rebuild the system, it is essential that deficiencies in the design and operation of any system are identified and corrected; it is in this context that 'eternal vigilance' is necessary.

The White Papers *Employment for the 1990s* (Employment Department, 1988); *Education and Training for the 21st Century* (Department of Education and Science and Employment Department, 1991); *Higher Education: A New Framework* (Department of Education and Science and Employment Department, 1991); and *Choice and Diversity* (Department for Education, 1992) set out the government's view. 'Over the last decade, there has been a revolution in Britain's Education and Training' says the Prime Minister's foreword to *Education and Training for the 21st Century*. 'The government,' he continues, 'are now launching a new wave of reforms which will give Britain's young people an even better start in life. With the introduction of a new Advanced Diploma, we will *end* the artificial divide between academic and vocational qualifications . . . we will be giving new freedoms to those responsible for our further education colleges and our sixth form colleges.' 'The education and training system,' it is claimed, 'has improved substantially over the last decade.' Seven specific improvements are cited:

– increases in participation rates and in standards of achievement;

- higher levels of qualification;
- a stronger education base;
- better initial training;
- a revolution in learning;
- an open market in education and training;
- employer involvement secured through TECs (*ibid*. Chapter 2).

The strategic guidance offered to Training and Enterprise Councils (TECs) by the Secretary of State for Employment is couched in similar terms. The 1990s is 'the skills decade' in which a partnership between government, business, individuals and the broader community will enable Britain to acquire 'the skills that are required to meet and beat the standards of the best in the word' (ED; 1991).

The theme is taken up by the Confederation of British Industry (CBI, 1992). The setting of 'world-class targets' for 'foundation learning' and for 'lifetime learning' reinforces the message of an earlier CBI statement that 'a quantum leap is needed in Britain's education and training performance. To maintain Britain's position in an increasingly competitive world, nothing short of a skills revolution is required' (CBI, 1989).

Of the many questions that merit further debate, four are central to the theme of this book and form the focus of this concluding chapter:

1. Have sound foundations been laid for a coherent and intelligible framework of courses and qualifications for the 16 to 19 age group?
2. Will the 'open market' in education and training operate, in practice, as the government intends that it should, and are the incentives now available sufficiently powerful to influence the decisions of individuals, firms, and educational institutions in the desired directions?
3. Can a voluntary system, led by TECs, supported by a network of Industry Training Organisations, and reinforced by local Education Business Partnerships and Compacts, generate the capacity needed to meet the quantitative and qualitative standards of a 'world-class' system?
4. How effective will the system be in creating the 'strategic reserve' of qualified scientists, technologists and technicians needed to sustain a high-skill economy?

## Qualifications

Have the foundations been well and truly laid for 'a fully integrated system of education and training . . . which allows steady progression from school through to further and higher education, and to training in work,' (DES/DE, 1991: 1–4) or is the design of the system seriously flawed? Do the arrangements in their present form constitute a fully-integrated system or, as Spours suggests in Chapter 6 of this volume, 'a dual track system overwhelmed by confusion'?

The main criticisms of current government policy are now well rehearsed. Writing in 1989, Smithers and Robinson observed that:

> what we have now are arrangements that can be accused of elitism and fragmentation, with a proliferation of courses, assessment methods and qualifications which are confusing to employers and higher education alike. It is as if pieces from several different jigsaw puzzles, which are themselves incomplete, had been thrown up in the air together . . . We need to ask ourselves whether we want an advanced (A) level system which caters for a small minority or a common assessment system, embracing both the academic and the vocational, within which individuals can be assessed at different levels, and from which everyone emerges with certification of his or her achievements (p.35).

*The Economist* (1990) points out that, although the 1988 Education Act introduced some major reforms, 'Conservative policy has been much less radical in practice than in theory . . . The government', says *The Economist*, 'has been slower to offer a solution to Britain's worst educational problem: the number who abandon formal education at the earliest opportunity . . . Policy-making has been frantic but confused . . . the politics of education in the 1980s could largely be written in terms of the rise of free market solutions to social problems.' Finegold (Chapter 2, above) concurs, arguing that 'while the White Paper adopts the rhetoric of 'a fully-integrated education and training system . . . it offers no substantive measures for bridging the academic-vocational divide.'

Maclure (1991) observes that 'the failure to integrate "academic" and "vocational" education is the classic weakness at the heart of English education . . . a great deal will depend on when and how the government decides to grapple with A levels, which will sooner or later have to be reformed.' Phillips (1991) develops the argument further: 'in the absence of a single examination framework for the entire 16 to 19 age group, a binary system at 16-plus will continue to perpetuate artificial and out-dated distinctions between the pure and applied, the academic and the practical, and the abstract and the empirical.'

Whilst combinations of A and AS levels, or other units of complementary study, do provide scope for some students in some institutions to pursue a wider curriculum (see case studies in Chapter

5), the retention of A levels clearly remains a contentious issue. In the view of many commentators, their continuation is a major obstacle to the development of an integrated system.

However, a number of analysts have identified positive aspects of recent reforms. The Chief Executive of the Business and Technology Education Council (BTEC) believes that, for the first time, 'parity of esteem with vocational education is within our grasp' (Sellars, 1991). Education in England and Wales, he suggests, could provide three parallel routes, each maintaining 'the integrity of its own objectives': an academic route with a wider curriculum; a vocational route providing preparation for broad career areas such as business or engineering; and job-specific skills courses. Modular structures within the national vocational qualifications (NVQ) framework would enable students to combine elements from different routes or to move from one route to another during their working lives.

Jessop argues (Chapter 5, above) that 'for the first time in the UK we shall have qualifications and a system to promote training relevant to all employment functions' and that 'GNVQs offer a revolutionary way forward, maintaining the A-level standard whilst other forms of provision are tried and established. Not only will the barriers between academic and vocational qualifications gradually be eroded', but also those which divide pre-16 and post-16 education and training. The movement towards outcome-based qualifications will 'open access to learning to a far larger proportion of the population'.'

Spours (Chapter 6, above) recognises that general national vocational qualifications (GNVQs) are a significant advance and could provide the basis for a broader framework, not only for post-16 qualifications, but for 14 to 16 qualifications. 'GNVQs are more attractive and deliverable than narrow NVQs and increased post-16 participation rates will build on this momentum . . . a more carefully constructed vocational track will ensure that a greater number of students can progress to qualifications at level 3 . . . and to higher education.'

Despite these more optimistic assessments, there are grounds for questioning the coherence of the system, in its present form. Raffe, comparing the English and Scottish systems, takes the view that England and Wales still lack a unified model of education and training. The Scottish National Certificate has a modular framework which 'permits flexibility of delivery, a diversity of providers and progression within coherent curriculum structures'. He adds that the relatively open and flexible system of post-compulsory education in Scotland is a critical factor in raising participation rates, and in moving progressively towards the integration of academic and vocational studies. The Scottish system allows more young people to keep their options open and to have access to higher status academic courses. Raffe goes on to argue that 'occupational NVQs or SVQs based on industry-defined standards are a good basis for the training of adults, including the training of young adults entering the labour force after a broad-based vocational education; but they are not an adequate alternative to general education for 16 to 18 year olds' (see Chapter 3).

In an 'agenda for change' Raffe proposes, *inter alia*, two measures for developing a more coherent system:

-   'a more unified system of courses, possibly modular, to erode the academic-vocational divide and enable students to keep options open longer';
-   'reform of courses and credits to make it easier for students to move between full and part-time careers or to pursue the same qualifications via either or both routes' (Raffe, 1992a).

The thrust of government policy now appears to be directed towards the establishment of a two-track (or three-track system if the vocational track is subdivided into NVQs and GNVQs) in which it is intended that some 40 per cent of the age cohort should attain NVQ level 3 through the vocational track. The academic track continues to be based on A level or A and AS level combinations. As a consequence, participation in the academic track is unlikely to extend beyond the first quartile of the cohort, and could even fall to below 20 per cent. In short, A levels may now be reaching saturation point, and vocational qualifications must therefore provide the main avenue for achieving higher participation rates.

One of the distinctive characteristics of this emergent system is its retention of a peculiarly English model of early specialisation. The concept of 'breadth and balance' which is accepted as a basic principle for the design of the 5 to 16 curriculum, ceases to apply with remarkable abruptness at the age of 16. Whilst a degree of specialisation is inevitable at some stage in the transition from general to professional or higher education, the English system is notable both for the degree of specialisation *and* for the age at which such specialisation occurs. The issue is not simply that some routes within the system are specialised, but that *all* routes are specialised, including courses followed by the nation's most able pupils. Whether the pursuit of so narrow a course of study for so large a proportion of the nation's most intellectually gifted pupils is desirable, is debatable.

A second characteristic of the new system is a direct consequence of the first — the 'parting of the ways' at 16 (or at 14 if vocational courses in schools grow at the rate anticipated). Specialisation at an early age forces choice at an early age. In a changing world, the consequences of such choices are increasingly difficult to foresee and in the context of the 21st century, it may be in the best interests of the individual and of the community that options, for example between arts and science, are kept open beyond the age of 16. Consequently, accelerating rates of change, not only in the structure of industries and occupations, but in the advance of knowledge, and in epistemology constitute a powerful case for broader inter-disciplinary studies for able 16 to 19 year olds.

Supporters of the traditional system in England and Wales take a more 'pragmatic' view. The main threads of the argument are that 'for many years A levels have successfully prepared hundreds of thousands of pupils for a higher education system with one of the lowest drop-out rates in the world. They should not be abandoned lightly' (Marks, 1992). 'Apart from Sweden, no other Western European country,' it is said, 'combines vocational and academic subjects in one system. In France, post-16 students either follow a traditional academic baccalauréat course at a lycée or go to a lycée professionelle (the vocational qualification). In Germany, the division occurs even earlier. Yet vocational courses enjoy great prestige in both countries and seem to benefit from their free-standing status . . . The real problem is not A levels, but the lack of an acceptable vocational alternative' (Pilkington, 1991).

The challenge, as Spours has stated it in this volume, is 'to work creatively within the initiatives and frameworks at our disposal, to reduce division and increase internal coherence and progression' and to forge and develop 'a more unified concept of qualifications, curricula and institutional provision so that these goals come to dominate post-16 policy and overcome the current frustrations of political postponement.'

## The open market

One of the central strands of current government policy is the creation of 'an open market in education and training' (DES/DE, 1991: Vol. 1, p.12). As a result of this, the government has identified a number of ways in which the system has benefited. 'Decision-taking has been delegated to the local level, making schools and colleges more accountable to those who use them' and has 'for the first time given leadership of training to top business people and other key local people'. Through the part-funding of work-related further education and other initiatives 'further education is now much more responsive to individual and employer needs' and 'is serving the customer better by offering more flexibility in the method of delivery . . . Employers are more committed to raising skill levels than ever before. Young people are better motivated to develop their capabilities for work . . . Business needs have been brought to the fore in schools and colleges' (*ibid*. paras. 2.15, 16, 12).

These assertions have some substance, in the sense that significant changes in the allocation of responsibilities through the establishment of Training and Enterprise Councils and new funding councils are already in hand. However an 'open market' in post-compulsory education and in training is not as radical a change as the wording of the White Paper implies. Young people completing the years of compulsory education have always been free, in principle, to seek education, training or employment. Employers have always been free to offer employment with training, and training combined or alternating with further education. Most colleges have had a considerable measure of freedom to respond to 'market needs', and many have done so with considerable success over many years. The issue is not that a form of 'market' did not exist, but that it did not succeed either in attracting the majority of school leavers, or in generating the flow of highly trained people needed to create and sustain a successful economy.

Among the operational reasons for the failure of the market to deliver greater post-compulsory participation, three stand out. Too few of Britain's companies are producing and selling high value-added world-class products; the demand for well-educated and trained employees is relatively weak; and even where demand exists, aggregate investment in training by UK employers is at too low a level either to provide an efficient system of manpower resourcing, or to create 'learning opportunities' for the large numbers of young people in Britain who elect to leave full-time education at a relatively early age (Finegold and Soskice, 1988).

Using the 'rational actor model', Finegold (1991) offers an alternative to cultural explanations for under-achievement in the UK by arguing that a nation or a region can break out of a low-skill equilibrium by making appropriate changes in the structures of education and training systems, and in the incentives which determine the actions of the three sets of 'players' or investors in education and training — individuals, managers of firms and policy makers. Those changes must ensure that it is in the interests of each of the players to make decisions that will move the system towards a high-skill equilibrium. For the majority of the 16 to 19 age group, this set of decisions involves not only choices about career paths, but a willingness to forego short-term income in the expectation of enhanced income, status and personal satisfaction at some future date. For young people in poorer families, the sacrifice of immediate earnings, or at least of the prospects of earnings, may not be a realistic option.

The underlying assumptions of this argument are that incentives for young people to seek education and training, for employers to offer quality training, and for 'providers' in the education system must be sufficiently attractive to bring about significant increases in the scale and quality of provision. There are, however, grounds for questioning whether policies now in hand are sufficiently powerful to pull the UK out of the low-skill equilibrium in which it has for too long been trapped.

## Incentives for young people

The principal way in which current policy attempts to increase the incentives available to young people is the training credit. The efficiency of training credits as an incentive depends on the availability of high quality training places, yet the combined effect of recession and of manpower reductions may lead to a mismatch between supply and demand. This problem is borne out by recent reports of local difficulties in fulfilling Youth Training guarantees, by research showing that, in the year to April 1992, only 38 per cent of trainees had gained qualifications, and by statistics on the numbers of young people who are not in employment or full-time education. In January 1992, 103,000 16 and 17 year olds, about one in six of those not in full-time education, were reported to be out of work. The great majority were not in receipt of any state benefit.

Training credits may, when extended to all school leavers, provide an additional incentive, but their potential should not be overestimated. A House of Lords Committee warned, in July 1990, that whilst 'it would be possible to extend the training-credits approach to provide a mechanism for guaranteeing universal access to training for young people . . . such an approach would not go far enough as it would still be possible for employers and employees to agree not to exercise the entitlement provided by the credit . . . The Committee consider that a variety of incentives (tax allowances, maintenance and travelling allowances) may be necessary in addition to training credits, which they support' (HL, 1990).

There are other important factors which may limit the effectiveness of credits. First, if credits are available only for employer-based training, with or without part-time study, students pursuing courses of full-time education may by-pass the credit scheme. Second, credits do not provide income support, and will not therefore remove existing disincentives to accept low income training where opportunities for relatively high wage employment continue to be available. Third, credits may only have a marginal effect on individual decisions if progression to qualified status is perceived as being unduly difficult and complex, or if pay differentials for such highly qualified work are too narrow.

Local variations in credit schemes make it extremely difficult to assess their effectiveness. As Unwin points out (Chapter 9, above) TECs and LECs have considerable freedom, in the pilot schemes, to design their own models; 'diversity of process and practice has led to a complex web of local funding arrangements and eligibility criteria. For the young person . . . empowerment and choice will differ significantly' from one area to another. Employers will be approached in different ways; providers of training will be subject to different requirements and will be paid at different rates. Two TECs in the pilot scheme have restricted credits to sectors with immediate skill shortages, whilst others have placed no restrictions on occupations or sectors. The extent to which colleges will participate is equally difficult to assess. The cost and complexity of the procedures involved may prove a deterrent to colleges and to private training providers, whilst constraints on funding and, in some areas, shortages of places are compromising the Government's Youth Training (YT) 'guarantee'. For the training 'consumer' — the young person — there is the danger that many will be confused about the options open to them, or that they will come under pressure to stay on in school, whether or not it is in their best interests to do so.

In addition to such local disparity, training credits will, in Unwin's view 'sit awkwardly alongside the government's drive to increase staying on rates' and will constitute a deliberate distortion of the market, and of individual freedom of choice, if they are restricted to work-based training or, worse still, to occupations in which there are immediate skill shortages. It is difficult, she concludes, to conceive of a more short-sighted and self-defeating strategy if the purpose is to raise standards of attainment.

Credits are designed to enable young people to purchase training; income support, apart from limited and variable LEA grants for students in full-time education, is not available to 16 or 17 year olds without a paid job or a Youth Training (YT) place. Despite this, there is some evidence that selective maintenance grants for 16 to 18 year olds in financial need could be one of the keys to raising participation rates. As Smithers and Robinson (1989) point out 'few 16 to 18 year olds in full-time education receive a maintenance grant [and] it is anomalous that there should be this gap between 16, when compulsory schooling ends, and 18 before financial support becomes available. Some financial support, if only in the form of loans, could persuade more students to remain in education'. Furthermore, many TECs are reported to be sympathetic to the need to restore income support for 16 to 17 year olds, at a time when the labour market situation appears to be deteriorating. At least one London borough has abolished all such awards. A survey by the Association of County Councils in 1992 showed that one in three counties are cutting back on discretionary awards. 'The analysis of our survey', the Association said, 'shows that the discretionary award system is clearly in a mess' (Nash, 1992a).

Some of Britain's biggest companies share this view and are sponsoring their own initiatives, for example BP's £3 million 'Aiming for a College Education' initiative; others are providing bursaries for students going on to sixth forms or to further education. City Challenge funds may also provide some help for young people in run-down urban areas, but neither of these sources is an adequate substitute for a fair and consistent national scheme of selective income support.

The government's reluctance to commit resources to a 'downward extension' of the income support available to students in higher education is understandable in public expenditure terms, but in a country with low participation rates and significant poverty levels, a system which fails to provide income support at so critical a phase in the education of young people is not consistent with the attainment of national targets. It is also debatable whether calculations of net cost take proper account of reductions in the total costs of unemployment that would flow from increased participation in full-time education by young people and adults.

### Limitations of market models

There are theoretical as well as operational reasons for being cautious about the application of inappropriate or simplistic 'market' models to education and for questioning whether an 'open market', in the form proposed in *Education and Training for the 21st Century* is an effective means of achieving the transition from a low-skill to a high-skill economy.

A number of commentators have pointed to the dangers inherent in concentrating power within managerial control structures geared towards short-term cost minimisation, and to the damaging long-term effects of 'number-driven' rather than 'issue-driven' management. 'The management of public sector organisations is part of, and subject to, the political process in ways in which the private businesses are not . . . Strategic choices about such issues as levels of service and product mix, will not be the result of market forces, but will instead express 'values determined through the political process' (Stewart and Ransom, 1988). Moreover, it is pointed out that, in practice, 'firms recognise that the total, unregulated competition of the theoretical marketplace creates levels of complexity and instability which make management impossible'; they will therefore act collectively to try to limit uncertainty (Keep, 1992).

The college sector, with its 624 autonomous institutions and two million students, of whom only 40 per cent are under the age of 19 is, of course, far from being an unregulated market, but the problem of resolving the tensions that exist between the short-term pressures and longer-term strategic goals in the 'education industry' may prove to be just as intractable as they have proved to be in other sectors of the British economy.

In a recent article entitled 'Market fails to deliver the goods', Raffe challenges the market concept: 'market or employer-led provision, as it has developed in Britain, has failed to meet, and is probably incapable of meeting, the needs of 16 to 18 year olds. Provision needs to give more regard to their wider educational needs, their future educational progression, and the skill needs of a much broader range of occupations' (Raffe, 1992b).

## Problems of implementation

In support of the theoretical reservations which have been expressed about current policy reforms, is evidence to suggest that numerous problems are arising in implementing the new arrangements. Some are undoubtedly 'teething troubles' which can be resolved by relatively minor modifications in policy or procedure. Others may prove to be more fundamental, and may be giving an early warning of serious 'design faults' in the system.

There are, for example, widespread reports of problems being experienced in implementing NVQs and GNVQs. Recent press statements suggest that some colleges may shun NVQs in favour of existing National and Higher National Diplomas or of GNVQs. NVQs are said to be expensive and the demands of some industry lead bodies to be unrealistic, and bureaucratic (Nash, 1992b). In May 1992 the *Times Educational Supplement* (TES) reported that 20 per cent of the schools and colleges which were planning to offer GNVQs were pulling out on the grounds that ill-constructed pilot schemes were launched in a rush against impossible deadlines (Dean, 1992). Similar problems have been reported on the introduction of BTEC First Diplomas in business and finance, which are said to be 'bedevilled by complacency and confusion' (TES, 1992). Nevertheless, the registration of 16,000 students in 1991–92 is an encouraging sign.

Teething troubles abound not only in education, but in industry, for companies appear to be showing little interest in NVQs. The TES headline of 7 June 1991 — 'Firms unexcited by revolution' — may overstate the position, but a warning note is sounded in an HMI report on business administration courses which observes 'that the level of NVQ awareness among some employers and in the community is low' (Dean, 1991).

A more fundamental issue is raised both by Finegold and Spours in this volume. In Chapter 2, Finegold argues not only that the effect of a changing economic climate is problematic for training credits, but that 'the outcome which drives the whole system — NVQs — is not, at least at present, up to the task. The industry lead bodies responsible for drawing up these new qualifications have been given the near impossible task of reconciling the existing low skill requirements of British employers with the education and training needs of 16 to 19 year olds.' Spours voices the same concern in Chapter 4: 'NVQs have many features of a low-skill approach to qualifications — their narrow occupational focus' and 'concentration on the segmentation of tasks.'

At this stage, the evidence about how NVQs are being implemented is not conclusive. An Institute of Manpower Studies (IMS) report on the introduction of NVQs in the construction industry notes that more than 140 employers' organisations are setting standards, but that their work is poorly co-ordinated. This may reflect 'the current narrowness [of] employer-led training' and leads the IMS document to conclude that 'NVQs will require some significant changes if they are to meet the challenges of the 1990s' (Callender, 1992). The picture is not all gloom, however. Unwin (1992), in a case study of NVQs in the man-made fibre industry, cites a company 'so convinced of the value of NVQs, that the company is introducing them to the USA'.

## 'A new college sector'

There are inherent disadvantages in both college-based and in employer-based systems of education and training. The British system is a mixed system, the advantage, or potential advantage, of which is that a strong and adequately resourced college 'sector' can act as a counterbalance to the instabilities and uncertainties of employer-led training provision.

In any economy which is seeking to *raise* its skill levels rather than to maintain an existing level, an employer-led system, unless enriched by a substantial flow of qualified young people whose access to education and training is independent of short-term labour market demand, will tend to be caught in the very trap from which it seeks to escape. Furthermore, as skill requirements rise in industry and commerce, longer periods of specialised professional education and training, and of general education, become necessary.

The role of self-governing schools and colleges in stimulating the supply of qualified young people is therefore crucial, but the potential of the further education system may not be fully realised under the arrangements proposed. First, there is the question of capacity, and of the capital investment and recurrent costs of an expanded system. In a survey of Midlands colleges, Huddleston (Chapter 7, above) found that all the colleges surveyed in the spring of 1992 were filled to capacity and that many had waiting lists. Meanwhile, the budgets of some colleges had been cut, with corresponding reductions in capacity and the cancellation of programmes. Second, there are problems related to the cost of innovation, in particular that of the introduction of NVQs and GNVQs. Some colleges have threatened to withdraw from NVQ training, a decision which, if implemented, would have serious consequences for YT. Third, there is a question mark over the way in which the incentives operating on colleges will affect both the mix of courses which are 'profitable' and the balance of full and part-time provision. The current funding model — based on student enrolments or 'inputs' — could, if retained, 'stifle innovation in a climate of change where new styles of access, delivery and accreditation are crucial'. On the other hand, should the funding mechanism move to an exclusively 'output-related' model, colleges may be driven to gear their provision toward fast learners to the particular disadvantage of those with learning difficulties. A fourth effect of market-driven policies may be to draw colleges away from national education and training targets towards more profitable fee-earning activities. In this instance, market competition would have the unintended consequence, Spours concludes in Chapter 4 of this volume, of pressurising individual institutions to 'reproduce their different and divisive traditions'.

As Spours points out, however, institutional competition, is not confined to schools and colleges but involves the main examining and validating bodies. Whilst qualifications will operate within the five level NVQ framework, the diverse array of providing institutions and qualifications compares unfavourably with the single vocational qualification awarded by a single validating body in Scotland, and may perpetuate confusion and duplication in a further education system in which it is alleged that 4,000 different qualifications can be pursued (Tysome, 1991).

To counteract this situation, the Further Education Unit (FEU) discussion paper *A Basis for Credit?* (1992) sets out ten criteria which a post-16 credit accumulation and transfer framework would need to satisfy. This system, the FEU suggests, would extend the model of broad equivalence used in *Education and Training for the 21st Century*. Some of the FEU's proposals are to be tried out in the next phase of the Unified 16+ Curriculum Project described by Morris in Chapter 5 (above).

The consequences of under-investment which apply in high-tech industrial and commercial markets, apply equally to the creation of a 'world-class' education and training system. In this context, a further set of managerial and logistical questions for the college sector is raised by the Chief Education Officer of Lancashire. 'The proposed changes', he believes, 'will raise a host of organisational issues. How will the Technical and Vocational Education Initiative (TVEI) consortia of schools and colleges continue to operate? What about other arrangements for curriculum continuity, in-service training, inspection and advice?' (Collier, 1991). Reductions in capacity and staff redundancies in colleges and in some local education authorities, combined with the reduction or abolition of discretionary maintenance awards, are not the most encouraging signals; *Education and Training for the 21st Century* promises that 'a new system of funding for the colleges will reward expansion' with funding councils 'responsible for a new funding regime designed to recruit additional students and to reduce unit costs' (DES/DE, 1991; summary of paras 9 and 9.5). The fulfilment of that pledge — by no means assured by present policies — is an important prerequisite for building a world-class system.

## TECs and the voluntary system

Training and Enterprise Councils (TECs) (Local Enterprise Companies (LECs) in Scotland) have a big role to play within a 'national, sectoral and local' framework, in achieving a 'skills revolution' in Britain. A critical question is whether TECs are equipped with the tools necessary to transform the existing training system. At present TECs have no 'structural' support in the form of legislation or incentives for employers to train and, even more importantly, they have to rely on the voluntary support of those firms in their areas who are willing to work with them. Whatever the medium or long-term effects on their individual businesses, there are no 'penalties' for employers who fail to carry their share of collective responsibility for training, and few 'external' incentives for those who do.

The case for achieving national education and training targets by voluntary means is set out in *Education and Training for the 21st Century* in the following terms:

– Compulsion on employers is unnecessary.
– Compulsion on young people is unnecessary.
– Other major industrial countries achieve high levels of skill without compulsion.
– Employers in Britain are raising their investment in skills without being forced to do so.
– The effects of compulsion would be damaging because:

— young people would be forced to follow routes they had not chosen;
— employers would be burdened with bureaucratic requirements;
— small firms would be particularly hampered;
— there would be far fewer jobs for young people.

(para. 6.12)

The logic of this argument is not entirely convincing. It is not immediately obvious why some of the world's most successful manufacturing nations which use the German model of vocational education and training are able to operate a highly regulated system *without* stifling their economies through excessive bureaucracy; to offer significantly better opportunities to young people; and to achieve higher levels of participation and qualifications.

Earlier in this chapter, it was suggested that the supply-demand equation to which this argument is directed is extremely complex. The proposition is that voluntary arrangements, reinforced by credits and by local collaboration between education and employers, will achieve a balance between demand and supply in any given area; and that the outputs of qualified people, aggregated to national levels, will match 'occupational' and 'industry sector' demand and so provide the manpower resources needed to create a high skill economy. The equation is further complicated by the need, not only to match supply to current quantitative and qualitative requirements, but to achieve standards of education and training that will lay the foundations for subsequent economic development in a context of advances in technology and of rising, and possibly 'polarising', skill requirements (Prais, 1989).

It is an open question as to how robust the proposed system will prove to be in times of recession, in the context of worldwide changes in the distribution of industry, and of volatile and unpredictable labour markets. In particular, the government's confidence in the capacity of the UK industrial system to raise its level of investment in skills at a sufficiently rapid rate to sustain or achieve competitive advantage is not borne out by the track record of a significant proportion of British firms. Decades of sustained under-investment by British firms might, in the opinion of some observers, reflect an acute condition which urgently requires the application of powerful incentives and, perhaps, of statutory provision.

The contrast between past performance and expectation is striking. The achievement of national targets for qualification attainment depends on an employer-led system with the capacity to provide high quality training for a large proportion of the 16 to 19 age group. If one of the effects of the retention of A levels is, as Spours and others suggest, that participation in the 'academic' track will be confined to a single quartile of the age group, employer-based training, including YT, will for the remainder of this decade need the capacity for 40 per cent or more of an age group which will increase from 613,000 in 1993/4 to 701,000 in 2000/1. However regional variations are significant and, in some areas, capacity equivalent to 50 per cent or even 60 per cent of the age group may be needed (ED, 1992: figs. 1.3 and 1.4).

Given the capacity and quality requirements implicit in the realisation of the current national training targets, the challenge for TECs and LECs is formidable and the viability of a voluntary system open to question. The consequences of a voluntary system are that young people under the age of 19 have no obligation to pursue their education beyond the age of 16, nor an entitlement to release from employment for part-time education and training. Moreover, employers are under no obligation either to provide training, or to collaborate with TECs and LECs in such provision, nor to be affiliated to any form of employer organisation with the power and responsibility to set and monitor standards. It is perhaps the last of these omissions which is the most serious cause for concern. To place so much reliance on a system in which the mechanisms for achieving 'total quality' are so weak may not be consistent with the specification of a world-class system, nor does it give TECs sufficient leverage to cope with local circumstances in which there is a significant mismatch between the numbers of young people aspiring to full-time further education and the availability of places.

In 1990 this specific point was addressed by the House of Lords Committee on the European Community. Its report stated that 'given the scale of the gap between the United Kingdom and its main industrial competitors, and given the long history of failure which has marked the voluntary approach to training in this country, the Committee considers that some form of statutory underpinning is needed to act as a catalyst for change. The Committee concluded that legislation should be introduced which would ensure that all 16–18 year olds are provided with education or training' (HL, 1990). Other prominent figures have adopted a similar position and their stance serves to cast further doubt on the 'voluntarist' nature of current policy. Sir John Cassels has referred to the recommendation of CBI's Vocational Education and Training Task Force that 'any under-18 employment not involving structured education and training leading to recognised qualifications should be eliminated'. From this he concludes that: 'it is unfortunately certain that this (voluntary) approach will not be successful in eliminating jobs for 16 to 18 year olds which provide little or no training'. He goes on to say, 'however far we develop the concept of educational and training markets, and for all the vigour and enterprise with which that might infuse education and training in this country, it is still necessary to regulate the market to a minimum degree . . .' (Cassels, 1990). Similarly Sir Bryan Nicholson, who took a leading role in the development of the concept of 'careership' which marks the CBI Task Force recommendations, was reported as saying, in July 1992, that the government should give industry 'a two-year deadline to get its act together over training 16 to 19 year olds. If business fails to act, then it would become unlawful to employ a young person without offering training' (Clement, 1992).

**Education-business partnerships**

One of the most promising developments in recent years is the growth of community-based education-business partnerships, compacts, and higher education compacts. The UK is the first country in the world, apart from the rather different collaborative arrangements which are a characteristic of the 'dual system' of training in the Germanic countries, to establish a nationwide network of publicly supported education-business partnerships. Many of these have been inspired by the creative energy of local communities and local institutions and realised through a combination of TVEI, education-business partnerships, compacts, access schemes and careers partnerships. The process of establishing effective TEC or LEC partnerships, and the problems encountered in bringing together not only different institutions and initiatives but different cultures in business, in education and in public administration within a common strategic framework is one example of comparable, voluntary developments taking place across the country.

The Clwyd 'Education and Training Charter' (see Evans, Chapter 8) which seeks to reflect and make explicit the legitimate expectations of all the contributors to such partnership arrangements — employers, students and educators — within a context of national education and training targets, was designed as a constructive starting point for providers of education, training and guidance to work together in one coherent strategy, based on shared vision and values. Advocates of this type of local collaborative action from both the business and education sectors who share Evans' view that government policies for post-16 education and training are a 'patchwork quilt' of overlapping and sometimes conflicting initiatives, believe that the best hope of achieving some measure of coherence is through the combined efforts of the business and education communities at local level.

Despite their promise, however, education-business partnerships and compacts may prove to be more fragile than they currently appear. As TVEI 'extension' contracts come to end between 1992 and

1996, and as the 'pump-priming' phase of public funding for partnerships and compacts is completed during the same period, it may in practice prove difficult for partnerships to sustain a sufficient level of effort to accomplish the purposes for which they were established. Moreover, if existing LEA support in money, manpower and expertise is significantly reduced as a result of current government policies, some of the 'building blocks' of the partnership movement in the UK will be removed; their future will then depend on employers to provide the necessary resources. At local level the availability of substantially increased and sustained employer investment remains problematic.

## High level skills

The fourth question posed at the beginning of this chapter was that of the effectiveness of proposed reforms to the education and training system in generating the 'strategic reserve' of qualified scientists and technologists needed to create a high skill economy.

The problems of generating a sufficient flow of highly qualified professionals, and of creating an environment in which their skill and creativity can flourish go beyond the scope of this book. Nevertheless, one of the criteria against which the reform of 16 to 19 education and training must be judged is its capacity for increasing the flow of young people seeking and achieving those standards of professional competence needed in modern economies, not only in commerce and industry, but in research and development, in public services including education and health, and in public administration.

Porter's survey of the economies of ten nations leads him to the conclusion that 'the training of a significant proportion of the outstanding students in a nation in science and technology seems to provide the greatest benefit to an upgrading economy'. As a consequence, technical universities and vocational colleges are 'respected alternatives to universities' in a number of countries. Their role is crucially important; an economy cannot upgrade rapidly unless the majority of students who do not enter university 'gain the skills required for continued personal development as well as the specialised skills needed in industry'.

Among the characteristics of a sound educational policy identified in Porter's study, are high educational standards combined with open access, pre-admissions programmes, and generous financial support to students from all economic backgrounds. Teaching must be 'a prestigious and valued profession' and there should be close connections between educational institutions and employers: 'many of the most successful industries we studied in every nation had established strong ties with universities and technical schools' (Porter, 1990).

## The need for a 'strategic reserve' of qualified manpower

The rate of change in markets, technology and products is now so rapid in many industries that it outstrips the response rate of educational systems, particularly in relation to the high standards of general education which are a prerequisite of professional competence and adaptability. For this reason, nations or industries seeking to upgrade their skill levels have to have access to 'reserves' of well-educated and qualified people whose 'foundation learning' will be started, and often completed, long before any accurate predictions can be made about the precise nature of their roles in the economy, and the choices that they will be able to exercise as new industries and economic opportunities emerge.

The capacity of educational systems to generate this 'strategic reserve' of educated, 'scientifically-' or 'technologically-literate' people is a dynamic force for longer term economic regeneration. Furthermore, the arguments for breadth and for cross-disciplinary or multi-disciplinary studies become more persuasive as the task of predicting future opportunities and future work roles becomes more difficult.

The need for indicative planning of the broad dimensions of a strategic reserve is reflected in recent British attempts to set national education and training targets. These attempts are a constructive first step, but the process needs to be taken much further, and expressed on a broader conceptual basis than NVQs. In building up a 'strategic reserve', the flow of highly qualified *technicians* is likely to be as important, and in some respects even more important than the flow of 'graduates'. A number of studies, and particularly those conducted by the National Institute for Economic and Social Research over a decade or more, have highlighted the difference in technician-level skills between Britain, France and Germany, and the divergence in the flow rates achieved by different systems. A mass of evidence suggests that the problem of low attainment appears to be endemic in Britain. Moreover, shortages of technicians have persisted over decades, if not over a century or more. In a collection of essays published in 1966 under the title *The Training of Youth in Industry* the importance of this issue was identified: 'in industry, in the armed forces, and in many of the professions it is becoming increasingly clear that the supply of highly trained technicians may prove to be the most critical manpower problem of the next decade' (Woolhouse and Haxby 1966). Almost 30 years later, the problem is still unresolved.

The scale and quality of technician education is important for three reasons. It is important as a means of meeting current demand; it is important because, in the 'internal' labour markets of firms it provides a key part of the 'strategic reserve' of people whose skills can relatively rapidly be upgraded; and it is important as a part of the national 'strategic reserve' because a proportion of those who achieve technician-level qualifications are thereby encouraged and enabled to progress directly, or later in life, to graduate or equivalent professional qualifications.

Many of the most challenging questions about the capacity of our 16 to 19 system stem from these considerations. The view that NVQs are too narrow a definition of ability is widely held. 'Measured against the national goal of creating a competent, adaptable and flexible workforce [the system of vocational qualifications] has an inherent weakness: the standards of competence, as currently defined, are too occupationally specific. They provide no basis on which workers could transfer the competences that they develop to different occupational sectors as industries decline and new ones develop' (Raggatt, 1991). What is surprising, is that it took so long for these limitations to be recognised. In this context Richardson raises an important issue by asking 'how far did the ideological commitment to employer control over the definition of standards impede the realisation of an effective vocational education and training system?' (see Chapter 1).

## Conclusion

In the opening chapter of this book, the process of reform of 16 to 19 education and training from 1987 to 1991 is divided into four phases in which momentum, slow and hesitant in the first phase, builds up to a fourth phase in which the 'reform floodgates' were opened. The policy that emerged is characterised as a form of 'homogeneous differentiation' in which separate academic and vocational tracks remain, but are bridged by 'umbrella' qualifications in the form of a new system of Ordinary and Advanced Diplomas.

These reforms, in combination with the 1988 Education Act, the Further and Higher Education Act 1992 and the proposals put forward in the schools White Paper *Choice and Diversity*, constitute a shift of power in three directions; responsibility for the structure and content of the curriculum is centralised; existing LEA structures are broken down by the creation of self-governing and centrally funded institutions; and a range of measures is taken to increase the influence and responsibility of employers for education and training, including measures which are profoundly important for the 16 to 19 age group.

The debate on the strengths and weaknesses of these policies, and of the merits of specific measures now in hand, is likely to continue for many years to come. The vigour of the debate reflects deep concern about the means of achieving the economic and social regeneration of individual communities, and of the nation as a whole. Consequently, the central issue is not about the need for reform, but whether the proposed system will achieve outcomes that match both our own 'national' criteria, and the standards of education and training in the world's leading industrial nations.

Two powerful warnings about how to achieve this aim are given by Finegold in Chapter 2 of this volume. The first is the danger that pre-occupation with 'supply side' problems may obscure the reality that deficiencies in education and training systems can only be remedied by changes in both sides of the supply-demand equation; educational reform is only one dimension of the problem. The second warning is that it may be a mistake to overstate the 'cultural' factors in the relative economic decline of Britain and, as a result, to underestimate the power of new structures and new incentives to generate change.

The argument in this chapter is that the incentives so far put in place are unlikely to secure the policy objectives they are designed to promote. Nevertheless, now that the process of reform has begun, it is important that this weakness and other fundamental problems in the design of the system are identified and that opportunities to improve policy are taken. In addition, as the White Paper *Education and Training for the 21st Century* (DES/DE, 1991: para 2.16) rightly emphasises, it is important to build on the experience and achievements of other initiatives. In particular, the rich harvest of TVEI developments in 16 to 18 education is not yet fully exploited.

As the debate continues, some of the questions raised in this book will need to be examined more fully, and careful consideration given to the need for modification and adjustment of policy reforms. 'Total quality' will only be achieved if old ideologies are replaced by rational analysis, and by a commitment to continuing improvement.

In particular, the following issues emerge from this study and are among those which merit such further consideration:

1.  Rightly or wrongly, the opportunity to create a unified system of academic and vocational education has not, at this stage, been taken. Advocates believe that we already have the technology to develop a unified system, better adapted to the educational needs of a new age, and to promoting high levels of participation and attainment. They ask, in effect, why we are using 'piston engine technology' in the age of the jet. Specifically, the place of A levels in a modern age is under challenge: are they a 'gold standard', or a

red flag in front of the educational motor car? Defendants of A levels point to successful 'early selection' systems such as that of Germany but, as yet, have failed to identify a convincing strategy for raising the esteem of vocational study at home to the levels enjoyed on the continent.

2.  A more open market, together with self-governing status for colleges is already stimulating enterprise and innovation in many educational institutions. There are, however, dangers in applying simplistic market models to education; many of the world's most effective education and training systems are highly regulated and have developed sophisticated ways of developing and meeting longer-term strategic objectives for increasing skill levels, informed by a clearer vision of the economic policies needed to maintain national competitive advantage.

3.  In the present system, incentives for individuals and for employers are relatively weak. Given the acute nature of Britain's education and training problems, and the urgent need to provide the skill base for economic regeneration, the rejection of statutory measures to regulate the youth labour market, together with the absence of any convincing measures to secure the quality and quantity of provision in an employer-led system may not induce the rate of change needed to match advances in competitor nations.

4.  TECs and LECs have great potential in mobilising the energy and the resources of local communities, but are constrained by the difficulties of trying to tackle tomorrow's problems with yesterday's tools. The strategic role of TECs and LECs is a crucial element of current arrangements but their funding and their systems were designed mainly for tactical and operational purposes; these constraints, combined with the absence of powerful incentives or any form of statutory underpinning for training provision, leaves them with a formidable challenge.

5.  Education–business partnerships and compacts, building on TVEI and other initiatives, are beginning to make a valuable contribution to 16 to 19 education and training. The best TECs and LEAs are demonstrating their ability to build a degree of local policy coherence despite the confusion and the contradictions which sometimes afflict national policies and initiatives. The funding base of such partnerships is fragile, and their future uncertain without the active support of a large cross-section of the business community.

6.  A critical outcome of the reforms undertaken must be an increasing flow of highly qualified scientists, technologists and technicians. The decline in the number of A level students obtaining qualifications in science is disturbing, and more

powerful and better targeted supply and demand side measures may well prove necessary.

7.  The flow of information on educational and career opportunities for young people, careers guidance, tutoring or 'mentoring', progression and access arrangements, and in particular arrangements designed to encourage and facilitate entry to courses in science and technology, must be significantly improved in every community. The system of maintenance grants for 16–19 year olds is chaotic, inadequate, and inconsistent with the principle of enabling all young people, irrespective of parental income, to fulfil their potential.

8.  'Teaching must be a prestigious and valued profession.' The principles and practice of 'Investors in People' are as important to the performance of the 'education industry' as they are to the performance of other 'high-tech' industries.

9.  Rhetoric is no substitute for capital investment. The role of colleges of further education, including tertiary colleges, in creating a high-skill economy is crucial. In France, and in other countries, it is the colleges rather than work-based training facilities, which are seen as the power-houses of educational advance for this age group.

The process of reform has undoubtedly begun; as yet however, it is tentative and incomplete. The case for further reform comes not from any one section of society, but from a remarkable cross-section of institutions and associations within and outside the education service. This consensus indicates that, contrary to the government's view (DFE, 1992: para. 1.20), the process of education and training reform is far from accomplished. On the contrary, there is a large body of informed opinion, including the contributors to this book, whose perception is that there is still much to be done in England and Wales to build the foundations of a world-class system of education and training.

# References

Callender, C. (1992) 'Will NVQs work? Evidence from the construction industry', Institute of Manpower Studies Report no.228.

Cassells, J. (1990) *Britain's Real Skill Shortage*, Policy Studies Institute, London.

CBI (1989) *Towards a Skills Revolution*, London, Confederation of British Industry.

CBI (1992) *World Class Targets: A joint initiative to achieve Britain's skills revolution*, London, Confederation of British Industry.

Clement, B. (1992) 'Revolution? What Revolution?, *The Independent*, 13 July.

Collier, A. (1991) 'A sense of loss', *Times Educational Supplement*, 19 April.

Dean, C. (1991) 'Firms unexcited by revolution', *Times Educational Supplement*, 7 June.

Dean, C. (1992) 'Colleges withdraw from vocational pilot', *Times Educational Supplement*, 26 June.

DES/DE (1991) *Education and Training for the 21st Century*, 1991, Cm.1536 Department of Education and Science/Employment Department, London HMSO.

DFE (1992) *Choice and Diversity; A New Framework for Schools*, Cm.2021, Department for Education/Welsh Office, London, HMSO.

*Economist* (1990) 'The non-politics of education', 10 March.

ED (1992) *Labour Market Quarterly Report*, February, London, Employment Department.

ED (1991) *A Strategy for Skills; Guidance from the Secretary of State for Employment on Training, Vocational Education and Enterprise*, London, Employment Department.

FEU (1992) *A basis for credit: developing a post-16 credit accummulation and transfer framework*, London, Further Education Unit.

Finegold, D. and Soskice, D. (1988) 'The failure of British training: Analysis and prescription', *Oxford Review of Economic Policy* 4, 3.

Finegold, D. (1991) 'Institutional incentives and skill creation: Preconditions for a high-skill equilibrium', Ryan, P. (ed.) *International Comparions of Vocational Education and Training for Intermediate Skills*, London, Falmer Press.

HL (1990) *Vocational Training and Retraining* [House of Lords select committee on the European communities, 21st report] London, HMSO.

HMI (1991), *Business Administration Courses leading to National Vocational Qualifications in Further Educaiton Colleges*, London, DES Publications.

Keep, E. (1992) 'Schools in the marketplace', *British Journal of Education and Work*, Vol 5 no 2.

Maclure, S. (1991) 'Let's dump the dunce cap', *The Times*, 15 April.

Marks, J. (1992) 'No advance on pure gold', *Times Educational Supplement*, 18 September.

Nash, I. and Prestage, M. (1992) 'Promise to train all learners not kept, *Times Educational Supplement*, 5 June.

Nash, I. (1992a) 'No second chance for the grantless', *Times Educational Supplement*, 2 October.

Nash, I. (1992b) 'Spanners in the works', *Times Educational Supplement*, 22 May.

Phillips, G. (1991) 'Too spoilt for choice', *Times Educational Supplement*, 10 May.

Pilkington, P. (1991) 'Education must discover its true sense of vocation', *Times Educational Supplement*, 10 June

Porter, M. (1990) *The Competitive Advantage of Nations*, Macmillan.

Prais, S.J. (1989) 'Qualified manpower in engineering: Britain and other industrially advanced countries', *National Institute Economic Review*, No.127.

Raffe, D. (1992b) 'Market fails to deliver the goods', *Times Educational Supplement*, 29 May.

Raffe, D. (1992a) *Participation of 16–18 year olds in education and training*, Briefing No.3, London, National Commission on Education.

Raggatt, P. (1991) 'Quality assurance and NVQs', Raggatt, P. and Unwin, L. (eds.), *Change and Intervention: Vocational Education and Training*, Brighton, Falmer Press.

Ranson, S. (1984) 'Towards a tertiary tripartism: new codes, of social control and the 17+' in Broadfoot, P. (ed.), *Selection, Certification and Control: Social Issues in Educational Assessment*, Lewes, Falmer Press.

Sellars, J. (1991) 'Coming in from the cold', *Times Educational Supplement*, 24 May.

Smithers, A. and Robinson, P. (1989) *Increasing Participation in Higher Education*, London, BP Educational Service.

Ranson, S and Stewart, J. (1989) 'Citizenship and government the challenge for management of the public domain', Political Studies, 37, 1, pp 5–24.

*Times Educational Supplement* (1992) 'Competence confusion' 27 March.

Tysome, T. (1991) 'A facelift fraught with pain', *Times Educational Supplement*, 19 April.

Unwin, L. (1992) 'NVQs and the man-made fibre industry', Raggatt, P. and Unwin, L. (eds) *Change and Intervention*, London, Falmer Press.

Woolhouse, J.G. and Haxby, P. (1966) 'The training of technicians,' Nesbitt-Hawes, R. (ed), *The Training of Youth in Industry*, Oxford, Pergamon Press.

# Index